THE PSYCHOLOGY
OF LEARNING AND MOTIVATION

Advances in Research and Theory

EDITED BY KENNETH W. SPENCE
AND JANET TAYLOR SPENCE

UNIVERSITY OF TEXAS, AUSTIN, TEXAS

Volume 1

1967

ACADEMIC PRESS   New York San Francisco London
A Subsidiary of Harcourt Brace Jovanovich, Publishers

ACADEMIC PRESS, INC.
111 Fifth Avenue, New York, New York 10003

United Kingdom Edition published by
ACADEMIC PRESS, INC. (LONDON) LTD.
24/28 Oval Road, London NW1

LIBRARY OF CONGRESS CATALOG CARD NUMBER: 66–30104

PRINTED IN THE UNITED STATES OF AMERICA

LIST OF CONTRIBUTORS

Abram Amsel, University of Toronto, Toronto, Canada

Gordon Bower, Stanford University, Stanford, California

E. J. Capaldi, University of Texas, Austin, Texas

Harry Fowler, University of Pittsburgh, Pittsburgh, Pennsylvania

George Mandler, University of California, San Diego, La Jolla, California

PREFACE

During a period of several decades in this century, there appeared a series of theoretical accounts of the process of learning and the variables affecting behavior in the learning situation, most notably those of Thorndike and Guthrie, and, somewhat later, those of Tolman, Skinner, and Hull. Although these behavior theories were to a large extent built around a limited number of relatively simple learning situations, often involving animal subjects, their intent was clearly to provide a set of empirical propositions and theoretical concepts that would be found to be applicable to a broad range of behavioral phenomena.

These behavior theories have had a crucial impact on subsequent developments in the field and have stimulated much of the research that has been conducted in the area. Inevitably, gaps and inadequacies have been found in these theories, even with respect to the simple kinds of learning and motivational phenomena on which they were based. It has seemed important to investigate new phenomena, including more complex cognitive functions in human subjects; new concepts have been devised and old ones modified or discarded. Yet despite the ever-increasing volume of research, often programmatic in nature, few attempts to revise or expand any of these theories in their entirety have been made and no new comprehensive theories—with the possible exception of some of the mathematical models—have been devised to rival the old. We appear to be in a period of intensive data collection and, theoretically, of the development of "miniature systems" based on relatively limited types of experimental phenomena.

Reflecting this state of affairs, *The Psychology of Learning and Motivation* intends to provide experimental psychologists who are actively engaged in research on some specialized topic within the fields of learning and motivation with a vehicle for presenting a systematic integration of the relevant research data—particularly those from their own research programs—on either a purely empirical level or oriented around the evaluation or development of some theory. This serial publication is thus expected to provide a source for papers of a more specialized and original character than review articles now appearing in annual form and of greater flexibility with respect to length and format than is currently found in psychological journals.

For purposes of these volumes, learning research is broadly conceived, varying from studies of classical and instrumental or operant conditioning in human and animal subjects to investigations of complex learning, memorial processes, and problem-solving activities. Similarly, motivational research is intended to include the study of acquired and complex forms as well as simple, primary ones. Contributions to this serial publication are by invitation.

Preparation of this, the first volume of *The Psychology of Learning and Motivation*, had proceeded to the stage of receipt of final page proof, and manuscripts for the second volume were being received at the time of the death of the senior editor, Kenneth W. Spence. Unfortunately, his plans for preparation of the Preface to this volume could not be brought to fruition.

JANET TAYLOR SPENCE

March, 1967

CONTENTS

PARTIAL REINFORCEMENT EFFECTS ON VIGOR AND PERSISTENCE

Abram Amsel

A SEQUENTIAL HYPOTHESIS OF INSTRUMENTAL LEARNING

E. J. Capaldi

SATIATION AND CURIOSITY

Harry Fowler

PARTIAL REINFORCEMENT

EFFECTS ON VIGOR AND PERSISTENCE:

Advances in Frustration Theory Derived

from a Variety of Within-Subjects Experiments[1]

Abram Amsel

UNIVERSITY OF TORONTO

TORONTO, CANADA

[1] The research reported here and the preparation of this chapter were supported by grant GB-3772 from the National Science Foundation and by grant APT-72 from the National Research Council of Canada. I am indebted to many of my students and associates in research who are responsible for the experiments to which I have referred; and particularly to Dr. Michael Rashotte for a very helpful critical reading of the manuscript.

1

I. Introduction

This chapter examines phenomena of partial reinforcement (PRF) in discriminative and nondiscriminative situations, with particular emphasis on experiments conducted according to within-subjects (within-S) procedures.

My aim is to bring together a number of experiments conducted in our laboratory over the past two or three years and to show how an integration of the results from these experiments leads to some further understanding of intensity and persistence phenomena in complex behavior sequences. For the most part, intensity will mean speed of an instrumental running response during acquisition, and persistence will mean resistance to extinction and to discrimination.

The chapter is written in five sections. Section I introduces the problem by (a) identifying that aspect of the larger study of intermittent reinforcement with which we will be concerned, (b) outlining the characteristics of a theory of frustrative nonreward from which the experiments derive, and (c) presenting a viewpoint, derived from such a theory, that instrumental behavior can be understood in terms of three behavioral dimensions: intensity (vigor); direction (choice, preference); and persistence. Section II provides a simple classificatory scheme for within-S experiments; Sections III and IV describe, respectively, within-S acquisition and within-S extinction results from a number of experiments and contain suggestions for theoretical treatments of within-S vigor and persistence phenomena. Section V is a brief summary of our findings in these experiments and of the theoretical consideration these findings provoke.

A. Some Approaches to the Study of Partial Reinforcement Effects

The phenomena that fall under the heading of partial reinforcement effects (PRE) have been among the most examined and most interpreted in psychology for the last twenty years. Although this is not the place to review in detail the great variety of findings and interpretations that might be included in this area, an *outline* of such a review is nevertheless apt, in order to delimit the portion of the larger study of partial reinforcement that will concern us here.

A response is said to be partially or intermittently reinforced if it is rewarded according to some probability less than one, and according to any of a variety of patterns. Although references to reinforcement on schedules of less than 100% can be found in Pavlov (1927) and Skinner (1938), the major early systematic attack on the problem was by L. G.

Humphreys who, in the late 1930's and early 1940's, published a variety of experiments in which he compared partial with continuous reinforcement. Studying many different responses, including eyelid conditioning (1939a), verbal expectancy or guessing (1939b), galvanic skin response (GSR) conditioning (1940), and the acquisition of bar pressing in a Skinner box (1943), he came to the conclusion, as did a later review of the literature (W. O. Jenkins & Stanley, 1950), that partial reinforcement, as compared with continuous, resulted in greater resistance to extinction, and that partial reinforcement acquisition was either only slightly inferior to or equal to acquisition under continuous reinforcement conditions.

Since that time, major lines of research on partial or intermittent reinforcement have been developing in four kinds of experimental situation: (a) classical conditioning; (b) discrete-trial instrumental learning, using such devices as simple runways; (c) the free-responding (or free operant) lever box of the Skinnerians; and (d) the verbal expectancy (guessing) situation pursued mainly by developers of mathematical models. (Apparently each of the lines of investigation pursued by Humphreys has become a specialized area in its own right.) The first two of these situations and the last typically involve discrete and separate trials, more or less spaced. The third type of situation owes its origin to some early observations of Skinner (1938) on intermittent reinforcement and is the one for which the Skinnerian classification of reinforcement schedules was developed (Ferster & Skinner, 1957). When we speak of fixed-interval and variable-interval schedules (or of fixed-ratio and variable-ratio schedules) of reinforcement, it seems clear that we are involved with the concept of response chaining and feedback, the stimulation arising from the nth response being part of the stimulus pattern affecting the $n + 1$th response; the reinforcement of the nth response also affecting the $n - 1$th response and others even more remote in the chain when the organism effects a burst of responses for a terminal reinforcement. It also seems clear that our phenomena are not coextensive with those studied by Skinner and his associates. The Skinnerian situation, involving free responding, differs from the discrete-trial runway situation in a variety of ways; perhaps the most important difference is in the separation of trials, that is, in the integrity of the individual-trial experience. In our work we are at some pains, as will be evident from some of our design considerations, to achieve discreteness of trials. Although we may not always be entirely successful in this, the type of thinking we pursue is most effective in those situations in which the carried-over traces or aftereffects from one trial are not a part of the stimulus complex for the next trial.

While the Skinnerian work on schedules has been tremendously important for its own sake, providing sensitive techniques for the analysis of behavior, and while it had its origin in the theory of the reflex reserve (Skinner, 1938), it has generated no appreciable amount of theory. By far the greater amount of theory has emerged from the work on discrete-trial partial reinforcement, a development of the experiments of Humphreys. As I indicated, these early experiments involved classical as well as instrumental conditioning, and it has become increasingly clear that different explanatory schemes may be required to understand partial reinforcement effects in these two kinds of experiment. Until the present time, most of the theoretical emphasis has been on the discrete-trial instrumental experiment, and three classes of explanations have been offered. (1) There are a variety of cognitive-expectancy explanations of the PRE. Some have simply stressed a "common sense" approach (see earlier references to Humphreys); others have developed more formal hypotheses. Among the latter are (a) the discrimination hypothesis advanced by several investigators but often attributed mainly to Bitterman and his co-workers (e.g., Bitterman, Fedderson, & Tyler, 1953; Elam, Tyler, & Bitterman, 1954; Tyler, Wortz, & Bitterman, 1953); and (b) the cognitive dissonance interpretation of Lawrence and Festinger (1962), which attributes the PRE to increased attractiveness resulting from deterrence and effort. (2) Contiguity–interference interpretations of the PRE (Estes, 1959; Weinstock, 1954; Weinstock, 1958) have emphasized counterconditioning during PR acquisition as the factor that reduces the effect of nonreinforcement in extinction. (3) The neo-Hullian (conditioning-expectancy) interpretations of the phenomenon (Amsel, 1958; Amsel, 1962; Kendler, Pliskoff, D'Amato, & Katz, 1957; Logan, 1960; Spence, 1960), stress the role of hypothetical classically conditioned responses and their assumed motivational and associative effects as the mechanisms determining the various partial reinforcement phenomena.

In this chapter, all of our experiments will involve—and our discussions will all concern—discrete-trial instrumental learning with moderate to wide spacing of trials. We will not be dealing with schedules of reinforcement in the free-responding sense, nor with the somewhat comparable procedure of employing training conditions involving very short intertrial intervals in runways. For these conditions, but perhaps only for these, Capaldi's modification of the Hull-Sheffield hypothesis (Capaldi, 1966) provides an adequate alternative explanation of partial reinforcement effects. Nor will our treatment be general enough to include partial reinforcement in classical conditioning; as a matter of fact, the explanatory mechanisms for PRF effects in instrumental behavior advanced in this chapter are themselves hypothetical classically conditioned responses, and therefore could not readily be used to explain classical conditioning.

No attempt will be made to provide in detail the cognitive expectancy, dissonance, or contiguity–interference explanations for the experimental results to be presented. Although such explanations may now seem possible for some of our results, it is difficult to see how such theories would have led to these particular experiments or predicted these results.

In the latter part of the chapter some experiments, mainly from our own laboratory and derived from stimulus–response frustration theory, will be described, and an attempt will be made to integrate these studies as a basis for further extensions of the theory. Before proceeding to the experiments, however, we will review the theoretical background.

B. CHARACTERISTICS OF FRUSTRATION THEORY

Some time ago (Amsel, 1951), I advanced the point of view that the major weakness in Hull's inhibition theory was its inability to account for phenomena that depended on goal events. The proposal at that time was to modify the two-factor inhibition theory (I_R and sI_R) so as to recognize frustrative events resulting from nonreward as a third aspect of inhibition. I regarded this simply as a return to an earlier, more workable, position (Spence, 1936).

Shortly thereafter it became clear (to me, at least) that in order to develop the notion of frustrative inhibition, it would be necessary, first, to demonstrate that nonreward following an extended period of reward had certain active properties—properties not assigned to nonreinforcement in Hull's theory of inhibition. It also seemed to me that frustrative inhibition, having the characteristics of an anticipatory response and serving as a mediator between the external stimulus and the instrumental response, must be a learned or secondary form of the more basic unlearned frustration. The result was (a) a series of experiments, beginning with a study by Amsel and Roussel (1952), investigating the effects of nonreward on the vigor of immediately subsequent responses in an apparatus that was essentially two runways in series, and (b) a study of the mechanism of anticipatory frustration, which led eventually to an interest in phenomena of noncontinuous reinforcement and to the proposal of a more or less formal theory of frustrative nonreward (Amsel, 1958).

In this section I want to review the basic features of that theory, both as to form and content, and to suggest some areas of thinking about behavior in which such an approach seems to be useful. In this I

will be going over ground recently covered (Amsel & Ward, 1965), but it
is appropriate and advantageous to present this material here as background for the experiments and discussion that follow.

1. *The Form of the Theory*

Our conceptual analysis is neobehavioristic theory in the Hull-Spence
tradition, a form of theorizing that combines elements of Pavlovian and
Thorndikian conditioning. Termed *conditioning model theory* (Lachman,
1960), this kind of approach emphasizes the role of classically conditioned (implicit) responses in instrumental learning and, as did many of
Hull's earlier theoretical papers, attributes to such hypothetical classically conditioned responses the capacity to provide feedback stimulation and incentive motivation and to serve as major mediational mechanisms. Spence's use of such a theoretical approach is well known (e.g.,
Spence, 1956; Spence, 1958; Spence, 1960). The following paragraphs
and Fig. 1 and 2, taken from Amsel and Ward (1965), provide an introduction to this kind of theory.

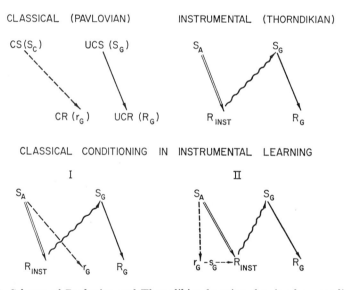

Fig. 1. Schema of Pavlovian and Thorndikian learning showing how conditioning
processes are assumed to be involved in instrumental learning (after Spence, 1956,
p. 60). In this figure and in Fig. 2, dashed lines represent classically conditioned,
learned connections; double lines represent strengthened instrumental connections;
solid lines represent unlearned connections; and wiggly lines represent a contingency
relationship between the instrumental response and the appearance of the goal
stimulus in instrumental learning. From Amsel and Ward (1965).

A schematic representation of [the relationship between classical and instrumental conditioning in this form of theory] is presented in Figure 1. The top portion of the figure shows, separately, classical (Pavlovian) and instrumental (Thorndikian) conditioning. Interchangeable symbols have been provided for the stimuli and responses of classical conditioning: the conditioned response is also designated r_G, the unconditioned stimulus, S_G, the unconditioned response, R_G, and so on. Clearly, the schema or paradigm for Pavlovian conditioning applies to the conditioning of r_G(the anticipatory goal response). The bottom part of this schema shows how classical conditioning is involved in instrumental learning, and provides the essence of the classical conditioning model of instrumental behavior with which we will be concerned. Represented are two stages. In *I,* the classical-conditioned response (r_G) is formed as part of the instrumental sequence; and in *II,* the classical-conditioned response once formed moves forward in time and, through its feedback stimulation (s_G), becomes part of the mechanism for the evocation of the instrumental response.

The relationships shown in Figure 1 are based upon a general conception of goal events (R_G). In an earlier article (Amsel, 1958), it was proposed that goal events were of three kinds: rewards (R_R), punishments (R_P), and frustrations (R_F). To these three, following Mowrer (1960), a fourth kind, relief, might be included. Such a classification of goal events would set relief and punishment into the same relationship as reward and frustration. We will deal only with the latter two members of such a four-fold classification; that is to say, with reward-frustration factors in learning. However, as Martin (1963) has shown, the kind of reasoning contained here and in earlier treatments of reward and frustration can also be applied to an analysis of punishment and relief.

Figure 2 represents our assumptions as to the manner in which reward and frustrative nonreward are involved in simple instrumental learning. It shows, schematically, the (classical) conditioning of anticipatory reward (r_R) and antici- patory frustration (r_F) in instrumental behavior. Rewarded trials occasion the development of r_R (anticipatory reward) which moves forward in the temporal se- quence to become part of the mechanism affecting the instrumental response. When r_R and its feedback stimulation, s_R, affect the instrumental response, the behavior can be said to involve incentive motivation. The right-hand side of Figure 2 indicates that when reward-incentive motivation is operating, and the goal is a nonrewarding

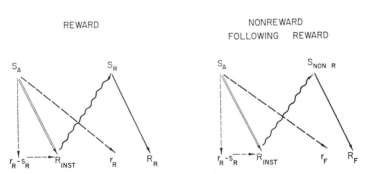

FIG. 2. Schematic representation of the conditioning of anticipatory reward (r_R) and the involvement of r_R and nonreward ($S_{non\ R}$) in the conditioning of anticipa- tory frustration (r_F). From Amsel and Ward (1965).

($S_{non\ R}$) rather than a rewarding event, primary frustration (R_F) results. Frustration is then defined as nonreward in the presence of r_R. Anticipatory reward and nonreward are both necessary, but not sufficient, conditions for frustration. Since R_F operates as an unconditioned response to $S_{non\ R}$, nonrewards will occasion the conditioning of r_F (right-hand side of Figure 2 to the cues of S_A. This conditioned response of anticipatory frustration moves forward in time or backward along the instrumental sequence to affect the instrumental response, presumably in a manner antagonistic to that in which r_R affects the instrumental response [p. 2].

2. *Four-Stage Hypothesis of Partial Reinforcement and Discrimination Learning*

The foregoing develops the concept of anticipatory (secondary) frustration. The interaction of such a postulated mechanism with other forms of implicit conditioning in partial reinforcement and discrimination learning has been outlined in several published accounts (Amsel, 1958; Amsel, 1962; Amsel & Ward, 1965; Spence, 1960, Ch. 6) and a version of this set of hypotheses represented as stages of acquisition training is presented as Fig. 3.

A theory such as Fig. 3 represents divides partial reward acquisition (and discrimination learning) into four stages, each involving processes quite different from the others, especially in regard to the operation of

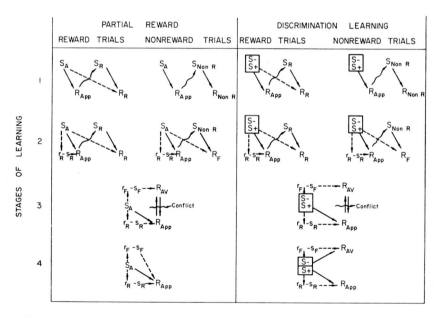

Fig. 3. Diagramed sequence of hypotheses relating frustrative nonreward to stages of partial reward and discrimination learning. From Amsel and Ward (1965).

the conditioned anticipatory response mechanism depicted in Fig. 2. Through the use of a double (tandem) runway apparatus (Amsel & Roussel, 1952) it has been possible to separate and measure two responses, each reflecting a property of frustration. The *frustrated response* and changes in speed indicating anticipatory (secondary) frustration (r_F) are measured in Alley 1, while the *frustration-motivated response*, measured in Alley 2, is indicative of the magnitude of primary frustration (R_F) that develops in Goal 1. Increase in vigor of responding in Alley 2 following nonreward in Goal 1 has been termed the *frustration effect* (FE) and is an indicant of the strength of the primary (immediate) frustrative reaction to nonreward. Although the theory outlined in Fig. 3 depends on this primary frustrative reaction as a UCR to nonreward at the end of a behavior chain, it is still mainly concerned with the conditioned form of the frustration reaction (r_F) and with the manner in which this hypothetical conditioned response and its feedback stimulation (s_F) come to affect behavior in partial reward learning and in discrimination learning.

The action of a mechanism such as r_F–s_F represents what is often termed *mediation*. Hypothetical implicit events that act as mediators of overt behavior presumably do so because they are under the control of identifiable external stimulus events; in turn, they exercise control over identifiable behavioral events. It can fairly be said that a stimulus-response theorist is one who *conceptualizes* such internal mediating events as reponses and response-produced stimuli; a cognitive theorist is one who prefers *not* to conceptualize hypothetical internal events as stimuli and responses; for him, the mediators take other conceptual forms. A stimulus–response theorist who is also a conditioning-model theorist is likely to want to treat such *hypothetical* responses as if they were derived exclusively from classical (Pavlovian) arrangements between manipulable stimulus (CS and UCS) events.

The sequence of four hypotheses schematized in Fig. 3 differentiates four stages of practice in partially rewarded acquisition and in discrimination learning. The theory describes the process of formation of internal classically conditioned responses and the manner in which these responses, through their associated stimuli, come to exercise control over observable behavioral events.

The following paragraphs are excerpts from the discussion of Fig. 3 in Amsel and Ward (1965).

In Stage 1 of partial-reward training (Figure 3), reward trials operate to effect the conditioning of r_R; nonreward trials cannot effect any significant amount of frustration until r_R develops in strength. In Stage 2, when r_R is already strong and is a factor in the evocation of the instrumental response, the occurrence of non-reward results in primary frustration (R_F). During this second stage there is also the beginning of a buildup of r_F, conditioned on the basis of primary frustration (R_F) as the UCR. In Stage 3, r_F counteracts r_R, anticipatory frustration producing avoidance and anticipatory reward producing approach, and the result is conflict. Finally, in Stage 4 of partial-reward acquisition, which is reached if partial-reward acquisition is carried on long enough, the anticipatory frustration-produced cues (s_F) come to evoke approach as well as avoidance. This conditioning of cues (s_F) signalling nonreward to continued approach is the very important mechanism that we meet with in these experiments. It is a mechanism of persistence; the kind of persistence that shows up as greater resistance to extinction following partial- than following continuous-reward acquisition.

The predictions that can be made depend entirely on what response the feedback stimuli (s_F) from r_F evoke. At the level of Stage 3 they are assumed to evoke avoidance responses, and should hasten extinction. At Stage 4 they evoke the criterion approach response, or responses compatible with the criterion response, and should retard extinction. Anticipatory frustration-produced stimuli can therefore provide the mechanism for persistence, or for rapid abandonment of responses, depending on prior experience.

In more general terms this analysis says that extinction in instrumental learning is partly, at least, a frustration phenomenon, and that the tendency to continue responding in the face of negative indications is acquired under partial reinforcement conditions when cues from anticipatory frustration become connected to continued approach. In terms of such a conceptualization, the PRE does not have to mean that partially reinforced subjects fail to discriminate acquisition from extinction; it may reflect learning to approach rather than to avoid in the presence of cues signalling nonreward.

There are, in addition to these rather general considerations, some specific experimental implications of the analysis. For example, (a) at Stage 3 of partial-reward acquisition (the "conflict" stage), behavior should be more variable than it was at Stage 2 or will be in Stage 4; and (b) if PR acquisition does not reach Stage 4, there should be no PR extinction effect. That is to say, if training is discontinued when PR acquisition behavior is still variable, then PR acquisition should be followed by decreased rather than by increased resistance to extinction. Both of these deductions have been supported by earlier experimental results (Amsel, 1958) . . . [p. 4].

And later in the discussion:

In discrimination learning, Stages 1 to 3 are conceptualized as being virtually identical to those of partial-reward training. The schema of Figure 3 suggests that it is only at the fourth stage that discrimination learning involves mechanisms that are different from those in partial-reward acquisition. We are considering here discrimination learning of a certain kind, to be sure: discrimination learning with single and successive presentation of stimuli. This is not to say that with simultaneous presentation of two or more discriminanda these mechanisms would not operate; but they would be much more difficult to untangle. At the beginning of a discrimination procedure involving separate and successive presentation of S+ and S−, the two discriminanda are not differentiated. Consequently, as far as response evocation is concerned, they are the same stimulus. They operate in the same manner as S_A on the partial-reward side until Stage 4, when one begins to evoke anticipatory frustration, the other, anticipatory reward.

In short, the difference between the two situations depicted in Figure 3 is that, unlike discrimination learning, the partial-reward situation affords no basis for differential responding to stimuli. In PR acquisition, the same response is sometimes rewarded and sometimes not in the presence of the same general pattern of stimulation. In discrimination learning, a response originally nondifferential in the presence of two physically different stimuli ultimately becomes differential in relation to the two stimuli, on the basis of differential reward and nonreward to S+ and S—. The suggestion has been that in discrimination learning of this sort one of the factors involved is differential evocation by S— and S+ of r_F and r_R, and that since these processes also affect PR acquisition, implications of some importance follow, although few of these have yet been reported. For example, the analysis implies that the frustrative reaction to nonreward, as indicated by the FE in Runway 2 of a double runway, should diminish or even disappear once a discrimination is formed on the basis of differential stimuli in Runway 1. The reasoning here is that discrimination implies the evocation of r_R by S+ and of r_F by S— as a terminal state of affairs. However, by definition, frustration must be preceded by r_R (anticipatory reward is a necessary antecedent to R_F and the FE); therefore, when the discrimination has been learned and S— evokes r_F rather than r_R, the frustrative reaction to nonreward should be attenuated [p. 6].

C. THREE DIMENSIONS OF BEHAVIOR

The theory I have outlined and its implications for behavior in situations involving reward intermittency would seem to require measurement in three behavioral dimensions—direction, intensity, and persistence. The distinction between direction and intensity of behavior is an old one in psychological theorizing, and recent versions of this distinction have appeared most often in connection with discussions of motivation (e.g., Berlyne, 1960; J. S. Brown, 1961; Hebb, 1955; Hull, 1943; Hull, 1952; Spence, 1956). The usual statement has been that the motivational state seems to have at least two functions: (a) steering or guiding, and (b) energizing or arousing; or, to put it another way, that motivational systems seem to be characterized by two outstanding attributes: (a) each provides stimulation (e.g., Hull's S_D) characteristic of that particular need, and (b) all contribute to the generalized drive (Hull's D) of the organism. These same two attributes of a motivational state would presumably be discernible (or, more properly, inferable) whether the state was of a primary or a secondary nature.

According to such a view, the frustration response (R_F) would, in J. S. Brown's (1961) terms, be a "primary source of drive" and have its effect on subsequent behavior (the FE) through a contribution to the generalized drive strength (e.g., Amsel & Roussel, 1952; Wagner, 1959); it would also be regarded as providing characteristic stimulus cues for the formation of associative connections between the frustrated state and a variety of possible alternative responses (e.g., Amsel & Prouty, 1959; Amsel & Ward, 1954). Anticipatory frustration (r_F), like anticipatory reward (r_R) an implicit response to external stimulation, would also be regarded as contributing to the energizing and directive or steering functions of behavior, in this case as a secondary or learned source of drive.

In terms of the Hull-Spence type of theorizing, the learned or secondary form of the frustration reaction (r_F) contributes to incentive motivation, a generalized drive-like state designated K (rather than D), while the drive stimulus function from this secondary source of drive is taken over by the feedback stimulation (s_F) from this implicit response. It should therefore be clear, as I tried to point out some time ago (Amsel, 1958), that the introduction of a concept of frustration is entirely compatible with the distinction between primary and secondary motivation and with the further distinction between the drive and cue function of motivational states whether primary or secondary. The introduction of a primary frustration condition really required no changes in the older Hullian (1943) thinking about motivation; it was only the introduction of the concept of secondary (anticipatory) frustration that required any modification of approach.

In 1943, Hull's theory of simple behavior took as the four main dependent variables response frequency, response amplitude, response latency, and resistance to extinction. These were regarded by Hull as four alternative and more or less equivalent ways of assessing the excitatory potential at any moment, although the function relating E to each of these four dependent variables was not the same in each case. By controlling appropriate variables in an experiment, it would be possible, according to the early version of Hull's theory, to use any of the four dependent variables as an indicant of excitatory potential reflecting habit (H) or drive strength (D) or, speaking loosely, as reflecting the directive or intensive attributes of behavior. It has become clear, however, that the four classes of dependent variables selected by Hull as alternative indices of the excitatory potential are not equivalent in the sense he intended. The first indication of this arose out of the treatment of partial reinforcement by Humphreys (to which I have already referred), who was quite explicit about the fact that the finding of greater resistance to extinction following partial reinforcement was not consistent with Hull's view that H was an increasing function of number of reinforcements (N). Of course, an alternative view is that, whereas H is a direct function of N, resistance to extinction is not an indicant of habit strength but of persistence, and that responses high in H may still be subject to rapid extinction because they are low in persistence.[2] In his *Behavior Theory and Conditioning,* Spence (1956, p. 91) tacitly acknowledges the correctness of this view when, in a diagram representing his own version of a theoretical model for conditioning curves, he omits resistance to extinction as an empirical response measure of the excitatory potential, although he had referred to this measure, R_N, two pages before in relation to earlier Hullian statements. In a recent discussion of neo-Hullian behaviorism (Amsel, 1965, p. 194) I commented on the possibility of separate theoretical treatments of the Hullian dependent variables in the following terms.

The trend . . . is toward fragmentation of the Hullian system into separate theoretical treatments—and perhaps very different ones—of the various response attributes. One move in this direction is already well under way in the Yale laboratory, where Logan (1956; 1960) has put to use Hull's (1952) distinction between macromolar and micromolar approaches to the treatment of the dependent variable, particularly for vigor or amplitude measures of response strength. The macromolar treatment assumes that quantitatively different behaviors are different strengths of the same response, whereas the micromolar treatment assumes that different speeds, latencies, and amplitudes (vigors) of behavior (for instance, running) are different responses. Within the framework of the micromolar-macromolar distinction, Logan has developed the interesting distinction between correlated and noncorrelated reinforcement, which shows great promise as a theoretical strategy for handling changes in response magnitude as a function of changes in magnitude and delay of reward. And, certainly, the resistance to extinction measure, one of four dependent variables in Hull's early theorizing, has been handled by neo-Hullians in a manner which amounts to a separate conditioning model (Amsel, 1958; Amsel, 1962; Spence, 1960).

I have been suggesting that, regardless of the particular theoretical treatment that is likely to prove most successful for such dependent variables as response latency, response frequency, and response amplitude, there is a possibly great advantage in describing behavior in terms of direction, intensity, and persistence and in developing explanatory schemes to account for these attributes of behavior. The impetus has come from partial reinforcement experiments where, in the same experiment, running speed differences between the partially reinforced (PRF) and continuously reinforced (CRF) groups show up in both acquisition and extinction—but the direction of these differences is not constant over different segments of a runway during acquisition, nor constant in even the same segment of the runway from early to later

[2] A mathematical treatment of considerations similar to these as they operate in overlearning-reversal and overlearning-extinction situations has been provided by Theios and his associates (Theios & Blosser, 1965; Theios & Brelsford, 1964).

acquisition, nor constant or consistent from acquisition to extinction. The result is that although response amplitude (speed) is a *reliable* indicant of behavior in all segments, at all stages, and from acquisition to extinction, it cannot be regarded as representing in a consistent manner the strength of a single underlying habit or excitatory tendency. We are led, therefore, to regard differences in response speed *in partial reinforcement acquisition* as representing a dimension of behavior that might be called intensity or vigor, reflecting an underlying motivational or "excitement" level, and to regard differences in response speed *in extinction,* the PRE, as reflecting a persistence dimension of behavior—a primarily associative mechanism determined, according to the present view, by the conditioning of anticipatory frustration (s_F) to responding.

While direction, intensity, and persistence do not themselves describe with any precision dependent variables employed in our research or in any other, they do represent, conceptually, behavioral characteristics that are identifiable and separable, and some of our recent efforts have been directed at trying to understand better the relationships that hold among them. This will be made clearer in the following pages.

I will, in the next section, discuss the characteristics of within-S experimental analyses of reward–nonreward effects, and will subsequently present a number of experiments from our laboratory which have in common that they are all, in one sense or another, within-S designs; that they involve variations on the study of PRF acquisition effects, PRF extinction effects, and discrimination learning; and that they involve the conceptualization of anticipatory frustration, within a conditioning-model theory, as the mediator of intensity (excitement), persistence, and, to a lesser extent in these experiments, directional effects.

II. The Within-Subjects Experimental Analysis

Earlier (Amsel, 1958, p. 108), I pointed to an overlap that exists between partial reinforcement and successive discrimination procedures.

Partial reinforcement and discrimination learning procedures are highly similar; in fact, they are almost indical if we compare partial-reinforcement training to the early stages of discrimination training with separate (successive) rather than joint (simultaneous) presentation of stimuli. In both, at the outset, S is rewarded on some occasions and not on others for the same instrumental response. The difference is that, in partial-reinforcement experiments, E is training S to make the same response on every trial, whereas in discrimination learning different stimulation is involved when S is rewarded and not rewarded and S comes ultimately to respond (or not respond) selectively; but only, as a rule, after S has learned to respond nonselectively on the basis of partial reinforcement.

This earlier conception of the overlap between PRF and discrimination procedures compared S_1-S_2+ discrimination training to $S_1\pm$ PRF training. Here the reward and nonreward of discrimination were to different stimuli whereas in PRF they were to the same stimulus and the similarity was seen to exist in those stages of discrimination training that preceded differential responding to $S+$ and $S-$.

A. WITHIN-SUBJECTS DESIGN AS A FORM OF SUCCESSIVE DISCRIMINATION

We have recently begun to study experimentally the similarity of processes in PRF and discrimination learning from a different point of view based on the recognition that the successive discrimination procedure is the extreme case of the within-S PRF experiment. To put it the other way around, if instead of rewarding the response to S_1 on 0% and response to S_2 on 100% of the trials, you reward to S_1 on, say, 50% of the trials ($S_1\pm$) and to S_2 on 100% (S_2+), you have devised a within-S PRF experiment. [This is like saying that in the free-responding (operant) situation discriminative (Sd and SΔ) conditioning is an extreme form of multiple schedule.]

A digression to clarify a matter of terminology seems worthwhile at this point. The trouble I would like to anticipate is this: When we get into an examination of within-S acquisition data, we will find instances in which S is obviously responding more vigorously to $S_1\pm$ than to S_2+ in some portion of the response chain. Clearly S must discriminate S_1 from S_2 in order to respond differentially to them, whether this differential responding suggests that S_1 is aversive relative to S_2 or (as in this case) not. We also have some evidence (as there was in some of the early continuity versus discontinuity experiments as well) that following a short period of S_1-S_2+ training, too brief to provide any suggestion of acquisition differences in responding to S_1 and S_2, extinction differences can be shown between responding to S_1 and S_2. The point is that S may not always show, through differential *acquisition* behavior, that he is making "perceptually" different responses to S_1- and S_2+, and when he does make visibly different responses to S_1- and S_2+ or to $S_1\pm S_2+$, these responses may or may not suggest that S_1 "signifies" something aversive to the subject relative to S_2.

It is for reasons such as these that I prefer to use the term *differential reward training* for the S_1-S_2+ case instead of *successive discrimination* or *go–no-go discrimination*. Variations of the S_1 reward along a percentage or magnitude dimension relative to a constant S_2 will be termed *differential percentage* and *differential magnitude training*, respectively. This will leave us free later to distinguish between differential responding and discrimination and to handle the case in which Ss

may show discrimination by responding *more* vigorously to stimuli related to the *lower* percentage or *lower* magnitude of reward in within-S experiments. We will also find it possible to handle the $S_1 — \to r_F$ and $S_2+ \to r_G$ relationships as mechanisms supporting the onset of differential responding because of goal "signification," leaving open the questions whether S_1 and S_2 are discriminated on earlier trials and what effects such discriminations may produce.

In short, we have been working with procedures in which different percentages (and amounts) of reward, not only 0% versus 100% as in the usual discrimination experiment, are manipulated within subjects, these manipulations occurring in some cases within the same phase of the experiment, as in Pavlovian differentiation, and sometimes in separate phases, as in acquisition and extinction. It will be useful to clarify this distinction between same-phase and separate-phase procedures. In the next section, I will describe characteristics of such experiments and provide an example of each type.

B. SAME PHASE AND SEPARATE PHASE

It may be useful to make an explicit distinction between the words *phase* and *stage* as they are used here. We have already used the word stage, here as elsewhere, to connote the sequential development of processes during learning. For example, our four-stage hypothesis of partial reinforcement acquisition effects states that the development of r_R in Stage 1 is necessary to the occurrence of primary frustration (R_F) in Stage 2, which is, in turn, necessary to the conditioning of r_F and its evocation in Stage 3, and so on.

Phase, on the other hand, represents some relatively large segment in the course of the experiment itself. For example, we separate in our descriptions the "acquisition" from the "extinction" phase in learning experiments, or the "pretest" from the "test" phase. In some learning experiments there are, of course, more than two phases: continuous $\to$ partial $\to$ extinction (Amsel & Surridge, 1964), and partial $\to$ continuous $\to$ extinction (Theios, 1962) are two examples of three-phase procedures, and experiments could be cited that involve four and more phases (for example, successive reacquisition–extinction or successive discrimination-reversal studies). In our usage, a phase represents a relatively large block of trials in a learning experiment during which some reinforcement treatment (partial reward, continuous reward, continuous nonreward) is consistently applied.

While changes in experimental phase seem always to be followed by some alteration in processes within the organism, changes representing successive stages in a developing process do not require, and can occur in the absence of, changes in phase of an experiment. Our hypothesis of four stages developing during PRF acquisition is, in fact, meaningful only in relation to a single (unchanging) experimental phase.

The distinction between separate-phase and same-phase within-S experiments is clear in terms of discrete-trial differential reward training. In *same-phase* procedures the S+ and S— trials are intermixed in a single trial-time block and differential responding emerges within that block. In *separate-phase* procedures all of the S+ trials (or S— trials) are conducted together in one trial-time block (Phase 1), all of the S— (or S+) trials are conducted in another separate block (Phase 2), and a test for differential responding is made in a third block (Phase 3). When same-phase PRF experiments are conducted in a within-S manner, S is always partially rewarded for a response made to S_1 and always continuously rewarded for that same response to S_2 within the same block of trials. This is followed by extinction in relation to either one or both stimuli. In separate-phase within-S procedures S is exposed to PRF (or CRF) in Phase 1 in response to S_1, and to CRF or PRF in Phase 2 in response to S_2, followed by extinction tests in Phase 3 to one or both stimuli.

The theory outlined in Section I, B has led to a number of experiments whose purpose has been to manipulate PRF and CRF training within Ss in such a way as to test the role of the hypothesized mechanism of persistence, $s_F \rightarrow$ approach. All of these experiments have been concerned with the transfer of persistence effects across stimuli within Ss, but rather different strategies have been adopted from one study to another. In the next section we will examine in some detail (a) an experiment by Ross (1964), which is an example of a separate-phase manipulation, within Ss, of partial and continuous reward effects, and (b) the recent experiment (Amsel, MacKinnon, Rashotte, & Surridge, 1964) that has been our point of departure for a series of same-phase experiments.

C. A SEPARATE-PHASE PROCEDURE: THE ROSS EXPERIMENT

A summary of the conditions of the experiment is presented as Fig. 4. The experiment was in three phases: (1) preliminary learning; (2) the acquisition of a running response; and (3) extinction of the running response. In the preliminary learning phase Ross used a short black wide box (A); the Ss were hungry, and depending on their group assignment they made one of three responses in the box. Two of the six groups, running partial (RP) and running continuous (RC), ran over the short segment to get food; two other groups (JP and JC) jumped across a gap to get food; and the final two groups (CP and CC) climbed to get food.

Some preliminary experimentation had made it possible to select running, jumping, and climbing tasks that were about equal in difficulty (the animals learned them at about the same rate and performed them about equally well at the end). For the second and third phases of the experiment, the experimental conditions were changed for all Ss: their motivation was changed from hunger to thirst, and they ran in a long white narrow runway (B), with high wire-mesh walls. Phase 2 was acquisition of running in the long white runway under CRF, and Phase 3 was extinction. The experimental question was: What is the effect of Phase 1 acquisition on Phase 3 extinction? The answer was reasoned

DESIGN OF ROSS EXPERIMENT

PHASES OF EXPERIMENT	(1) PRELIMINARY LEARNING	(2) ACQUISITION RUNNING RESPONSE	(3) EXTINCTION RUNNING RESPONSE
APPARATUS	(A) SHORT BLACK WIDE BOX	(B) LONG WHITE NARROW RUNWAY	(B)
MOTIVATION	HUNGER	THIRST	THIRST
EXPERIMENTAL CONDITIONS	RUNNING CONTINUOUS (RC) PARTIAL (RP) JUMPING CONTINUOUS (JC) PARTIAL (JP) CLIMBING CONTINUOUS (CC) PARTIAL (CP)	RUNNING CONTINUOUS REWARD	RUNNING CONTINUOUS NONREWARD

FIG. 4. Outline of the Ross (1964) experiment.

as follows: Whatever S learns to do in the black apparatus should transfer to and, to some extent, affect what he does in the white runway. More specifically, whatever the animal has learned *under partial reward* in apparatus (A) should transfer to what he does *in extinction* in apparatus (B). For example, if under PRF conditions in (A) anticipatory frustration has been conditioned to running, S's persistence should take the form of running to cues from anticipatory frustration; if under PRF conditions in (A) s_F has been conditioned to jumping, S has learned to persist in jumping; and if climbing has been the partially rewarded response in (A), S has learned to persist in climbing. When the response that was continuously rewarded in Phase 2 in the white alley is extinguished in Phase 3 and s_F becomes a part of the stimulus complex, the course of extinction should be affected by S's earlier history in relation to s_F. Ross argued that neither running nor jumping in (A) should be incompatible with running in (B), so that any transfer of persistence in the RP or JP group to extinction should result in a mediated PRE. Any tendency to climb, however, would be incompatible with running. In extinction of the running response in (B), which has never been partially reinforced, anticipatory frustration (s_F) should evoke whatever was learned in relation to it in the first phase of the experiment. That is to say, whatever the animal learned in his earlier training as a means of responding to s_F in a partial reinforcement situation should become part of his performance in an extinction situation later on.

On the basis of this reasoning Ross predicted that transfer of the persistence effect from Phase 1 to Phase 3 would yield a PRE of the conventional sort for the running and jumping groups, but that transfer of the persistence effect from climbing in (A) in Phase 1 acquisition to running in (B) in extinction would result in a reverse PRE: the CP *S*s should extinguish more quickly than the CC *S*s. Of course, going from *black* and *hunger* in Phase 1 to *white* and *thirst* in Phases 2 and 3 was meant to effect such changes, exteroceptively and motivationally, that the basis for transfer from Phase 1 to Phase 3 would have to be cues from anticipatory frustration that operate across motivational conditions and are not specific to particular appetitive states.

The results of the extinction phase are shown in Fig. 5 for the running measure—starting and goal are not different. The three continuous curves are together in the middle and are not significantly different. The dashed-line curves for RP and JP show, in comparison with the RC and JC curves, the usual PRE: these groups are even faster on the first extinction point than at the end of acquisition, undoubtedly because performance at the termination of acquisition was still improving. The comparison of CP with CC shows the *reverse* of the usual PRE. Of great interest, also, is that the animals in the partial climbing group climbed during extinction, not at the outset of extinction, but after several extinction trials, presumably when nonreward produced anticipatory frustration. Parenthetically, I regard the Ross study as an excellent experimental analog of regression: reversion to an earlier mode of behavior in the face of anticipated frustration, that mode of behavior being determined by what the organism learned to do earlier in a partial reinforcement situation when it was frustrated.

To summarize, Ross's experiment, like earlier work (H. M. Jenkins, 1961; Theios, 1962), demonstrates that the partial reinforcement effect can be transferred over a block of continuous reinforcements. It also demonstrates, however, that persistence acquired in one situation can be transferred to a different situation involving a different response under different motivational conditions, and that this transferred persistence can produce either a *positive* or a *negative* partial reinforcement effect in the new situation. If the external cues and motivational stimulation have been changed and a different overt response is involved, what is left to provide the mechanism for the transfer of this positive or negative partial reinforcement effect? The only remaining factor common to the original learning under partial reinforcement conditions, on the one hand, and the final extinction of the running response, on the other, is the stimulation (s_F) arising from the conditioned (anticipatory) frustration response (r_F). This develops in the original learning of partial reward groups and is present at some stage of extinction for all groups. The appearance of s_F in extinction elicits whatever responses

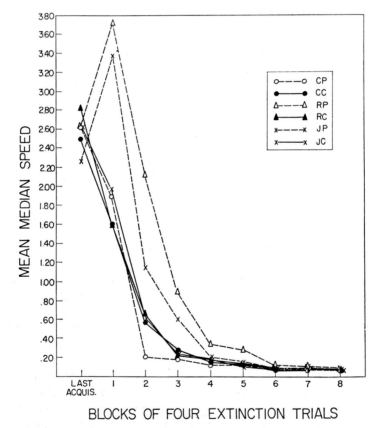

Fig. 5. Data from the Ross (1964) experiment showing performance at last acquisition block and over all extinction trials. Data are plotted here in speeds; times were plotted in the original report.

were previously evoked by this stimulus: running, jumping, or climbing. Ross (and others who observed parts of the extinction phase of this experiment) reported that as extinction proceeded climbing was actually observed in the long high white runway on 33 occasions in partial-climbing subjects who had learned to climb to anticipated frustration. Two instances of climbing were observed in all of the other five groups of subjects in extinction. There was no climbing during Phase 2. In more general terms this experiment points up a very important consideration: although frustrative nonreward may indeed provide the mechanism for persistence, this persistence may transfer to other situations and responses in such a way as to result in apparent fixation or in apparent rapid abandonment of responses in the face of nonreward. The critical factor is the kind of response to which the mediating anticipatory frustration stimulus has become attached.

Similar considerations relating to the transfer of persistence effects from one situation to another are involved in experiments in which the PRF and CRF effects within Ss are manipulated during the same phase of the experiment. The various same-phase within-S experiments that constitute the bulk of the remainder of this chapter are introduced in the next section.

D. SAME-PHASE WITHIN-SUBJECTS EXPERIMENTS

1. *Nature of Such Experiments*

As mentioned earlier, this type of experiment involves some version of the method of differential conditioning or, as we call it, *differential reward training*. As we conducted it, the experiment involved two stimuli; S was exposed to both of these stimuli and their consequences during the same trial-time block. The stimuli were presented as discrete events at relatively uniform intertrial intervals, according to some random or quasi-random pattern. In such studies, the consequences of response to S_1 need not be *absolutely* negative (never reinforced); they may be only relatively negative (that is, the response to S_1 may be sometimes reinforced and sometimes not, or may be reinforced, but to a lesser degree than is the response to S_2). Experiments of the first kind would involve partial reward of the response to S_1 (while response to S_2 is continuously rewarded); we have designated such conditions $S_1 \pm S_2+$ or $S_1 \pm S_2 \ddagger$, depending on whether reinforcements or trials are equated. Most of the experiments we have performed are of this sort. The experiment by Amsel *et al.* (1964) that served as a pilot experiment for this series was followed by a number of experiments (Amsel, Rashotte, & MacKinnon, 1966; Rashotte, 1966) directed at clarifying and expanding the initial findings. In these experiments, percentages of reward to the two stimuli are $S_1 50$ $S_2 100$, with either number of trials or number of rewards equated to the two stimuli. Another experiment (Henderson, 1966) varies the percentage of reward of response to S_1 between 0% and 100%, holding reward to S_2 constant at 100%. (In this experiment by Henderson and in one referred to later by MacKinnon, the stimulus associated with the lesser, and variable, percentage or magnitude of reward was designated S_2. For present purposes we will maintain consistency by designating it S_1.)

A second form of the same-phase within-S experiment involves differential *magnitude* of reward training to S_1 and S_2. In this type of experiment (see also Goldstein & Spence, 1963) response to S_1 is rewarded with the smaller of magnitudes and response to S_2 with the larger. A version of such an experiment conducted in our laboratory (MacKinnon, 1965) holds the magnitude of reward in relation to S_2 large and constant and varies the magnitude of reward to S_1 over several values from zero to the S_2 value.

All these experiments have one characteristic in common: they vary, within Ss, some attribute of the reward, one value of the reward (for example, "continuous" or "large") being related to one stimulus (S_2), another value ("partial" or "small") to the other stimulus S_1. In such cases, experiments evaluating the effects of partial versus continuous, or large versus small, rewards are conducted within the single S rather than between two Ss or two groups of Ss. Again, the experience of the Ss with these stimuli and their consequences is not separated in blocks of time but occurs within the same phase of the experiment.

Investigations of differential reward percentage and magnitude effects within Ss have also been conducted in choice situations (e.g., Spear & Pavlik, 1966). Although these studies provide extremely important results, we prefer at present to restrict our discussion to the simpler nonchoice situation with which we have been working. Hopefully these two lines of research can be tied together later.

2. The Amsel, MacKinnon, Rashotte, and Surridge Experiment

In order to grasp the implications of the experiment by Amsel *et al.* we should return and have a look at between-S experiments. Workers in this area have recently been led to change their thinking about these experiments, particularly about the manner in which partial, as compared with continuous, reward affects performance during the *acquisition* of a discrete-trial instrumental response (Spence, 1960, Ch. 6). The early experiments of Humphreys and others had suggested that partial reward acquisition yielded either inferior or similar levels of per-

formance to continuous reward acquisition. However, a study by Weinstock (1958) and a series of experiments conducted at Iowa (Goodrich,
1959; Haggard, 1959; Wagner, 1961) studying partial and continuous
reward performance over much longer acquisition periods than had
been done before, provided a consistent picture of results remarkably
different from the earlier ones.

   a. Background: The Goodrich Experiment. Figure 6 presents data
from the Goodrich experiment, showing the typical performance pattern

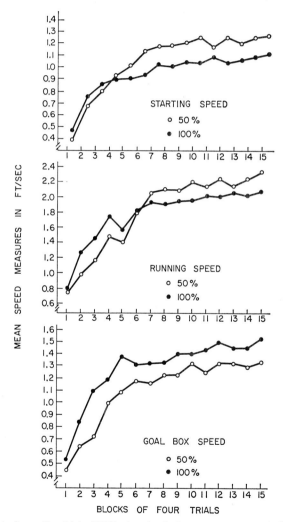

FIG. 6. Data from Goodrich (1959) showing between-groups comparisons of partial
versus continuous reward acquisition for three segments of the response chain.

as it develops in three segments of the response chain in a runway. In this experiment, as in the earlier ones, the continuous and partial treatments were administered to separate groups of *S*s. The response measures taken in the early segments of the runway, that is, starting and running speeds, show the continuously rewarded group running faster initially but slower by the end of training. In the goal measure, the continuously rewarded group was running significantly faster than the partial group at all stages of training. This pattern, which was found in the Haggard and Wagner experiments too, has been reported by others and has been discussed in detail by Spence (1960).

b. Results. The experiment under consideration (Amsel *et al.*, 1964) shows a pattern of findings from a within-*S* design somewhat similar to the Goodrich between-*S* result. Twenty-two rats were run three trials a day in the straight alley for 108 days (324 trials). During this training each *S* was partially rewarded for running when the alley was black (B±) and was continuously rewarded when the alley was white (W+). We reported starting, running, and goal times over the entire acquisition phase; these have been converted to speeds in Fig. 7 to be consistent with Goodrich and the data presented in the remainder of this chapter.

The resemblance of our finding to that reported by Goodrich and the others is that, in the starting and running measures, more vigorous performance to the stimulus associated with partial reward develops after a number of trials and continues until training is discontinued, whereas goal speed shows the reverse: the greater vigor of approach is to the continuous stimulus. There are, however, some interesting differences between our within-*S* data and the earlier between-*S* findings: (a) the more vigorous performance to the stimulus associated with partial reward in start and running measures does not seem to be preceded by a period of faster running to the continuous stimulus, as is the case in the comparable between-*S* data; and (b) the more vigorous performance to the continuous stimulus in the goal measure does not occur from the very outset of training—there is even a suggestion in these data of a reverse of this goal effect very early in training. In a series of experiments following this original one, we decided to examine not only acquisition phenomena such as these but also extinction phenomena from such within-*S* experiments. The remainder of this chapter reports a number of experiments, most of which have been or will be published separately in more detail. Our task here is to try to integrate some of these separate findings.

In several instances, within-*S* acquisition and extinction effects were studied in the same experiments. However, considerations of acquisition and extinction findings have taken us in somewhat different directions, theoretically and experimentally. It will therefore be less confining, for our present purposes, to consider acquisition and extinction effects separately in Sections III and IV, respectively.

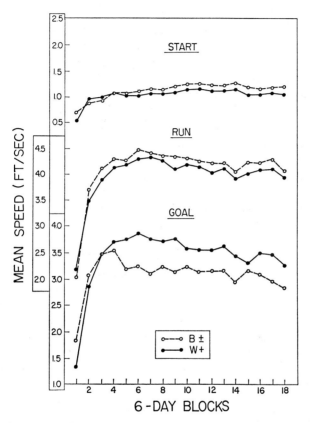

FIG. 7. Performance in three runway segments in a within-S experiment with reinforcements equated. After Amsel *et al.* (1964).

III. Within-Subjects Acquisition Effects

The phenomena uncovered by Amsel *et al.* (1964) suggested similarities between within-S and between-S PRF acquisition effects. In a recent monograph (Amsel *et al.*, 1966) we have made some rather detailed comparisons of the between-S versus within-S sort. I will not discuss these here, but will restrict my attention to an examination of a variety of within-S experiments suggested by the original study.

In this section on within-S acquisition effects I want to bring together aspects of four experiments that will be published elsewhere in more detail, each of which is in a sense a follow-up of the original within-S experiment. The first two experiments are included in the Amsel, Rashotte, and MacKinnon monograph and are (a) a replication of the original within-S study with color controls, and (b) a study of within-S acquisition effects when trials rather than reinforcements are equated across stimuli. The other two experiments, also run under conditions of equated trials, examine (c) acquisition effects as a function of variation of percentage of reinforcement to one stimulus as a between-groups parameter, and (d) within-S acquisition effects when magnitude rather than percentage of reward to one stimulus is varied as a between-groups parameter.

A. REPLICATION OF THE AMSEL, MACKINNON, RASHOTTE, AND SURRIDGE EXPERIMENT WITH COLOR CONTROLS

The apparatus and general procedure used in each of these experiments were virtually identical. The apparatus consisted of a pair of runways, one white and the other black, each of which could be aligned with a common entry box–start box unit painted gray. Response time measures could be taken over either three 1-ft segments (starting, running, and goal) or, by extending the alley, over five 1-ft segments, involving three intermediate running measures as well as the starting and goal measures. The measurements were taken with photocell circuitry and silent Hunter Klockounters.

In this five-segment runway experiment, 20 Ss were run, 10 to B$\pm$W+ and 10 to W$\pm$B+. Thus, rewards between the two stimuli rather than trials were equated. There were three trials a day, two to the partial and one to the continuous stimulus. The minimal intertrial interval was 15 minutes. The experiment involved 270 acquisition trials run over 90 days followed by 36 extinction trials.

The results are shown here separately for the color groups as Fig. 8. The acquisition data for the group in which response to black is partially reinforced (B$\pm$) replicate and extend the previously published data. It is obvious that Ss show differential performance to the two stimuli, and that this differentiation takes two forms. Performance to the partially rewarded stimulus is *more* vigorous than to the continuous in all the measures early in training and remains so in the starting and first running measures. In the other running measures and the goal measure this difference disappears progressively and systematically, working forward in time from the goal measure, where a clear reversal becomes apparent. These data tend to support an interpretation of increasing

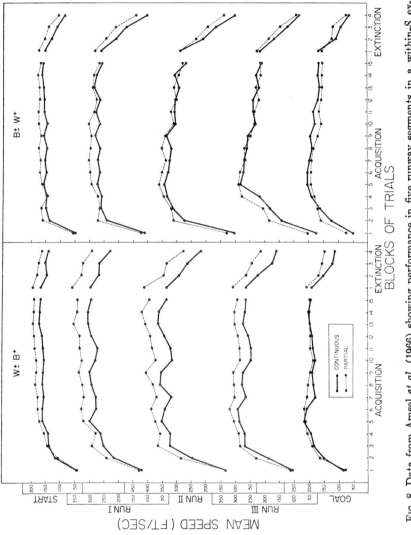

Fig. 8. Data from Amsel et al. (1966) showing performance in five runway segments in a within-S experiment with reinforcements equated under two color-reinforcement conditions.

aversiveness to the partial stimulus as the goal is approached, the aversiveness becoming attached to cues earlier and earlier in the runway after extended training.

In the right-hand panel are the acquisition data from the group where white is the partial stimulus. At first glance, they do not seem to show the same terminal effects: the differences in performance to the two stimuli are absolutely greater in the W±B+ case than in the B±W+ case, and these increased differences seem to be due largely to faster running to the partial stimulus. It appears that Ss run faster to the partial stimulus when it is white than when it is black, and there seems to be little if any between-group difference in running between white and black when these stimuli are associated with continuous reward. This suggestion of a Color × Reinforcement interaction as the factor responsible for the group differences is borne out in statistical analysis. We have found this color factor to be important in our experiments where black and white are the discriminanda, and we seem to be dealing with some kind of stimulus intensity effect characteristic of within-S designs where adaptation level and contrast effects are important (Grice & Hunter, 1964).

Regardless of which panel we look at, there seems to be a progressive change in the level of the partial curve in relation to the continuous curve from the same Ss. The suggestion is that the early segments are reflecting some kind of increased excitation to $S_1\pm$, whereas in the later segments an inhibitory effect to this stimulus seems to be emerging. Where white is the partial stimulus, the excitation seems to hold on longer; where black is the partial stimulus, the inhibitory effect seems to start at about the position of the second running measure, and the curves for both B± and W+ decline together over the last two thirds of the acquisition period.

The extinction data for each measure are presented to the right of the acquisition curves. Extinction effects are treated in detail in the next section, but I might just point out here that it seems possible to account for extinction differences in terms of acquisition differences, and that there appears to be no difference in slope between the extinction curves to $S_1\pm$ and S_2+. Statistical analyses of these data (see Amsel et al., 1966) provided no basis for supposing that we are dealing here with a genuine within-subjects PRE.

We have taken the 20 Ss whose averaged data comprise Fig. 8 and have looked at the performance of each S separately for both acquisition and extinction. An examination of these data suggests that there are three types of Ss in the group. One of each type is shown in Fig. 9. The first type, represented by the data of S_1 in the left-hand panel,

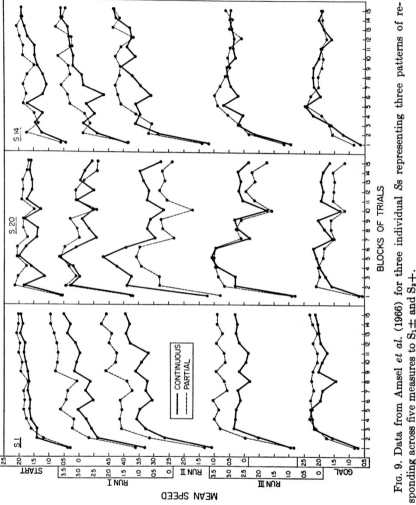

FIG. 9. Data from Amsel et al. (1966) for three individual Ss representing three patterns of responding across five measures to $S_1\pm$ and S_2+.

runs faster to the partial stimulus than to the continuous over-all five measures, although there is a suggestion that the curves are converging in the goal region. The data characteristic of the second type, represented by S_{20} in the middle panel, reflect faster running to the partial stimulus in the start measure but a reversal in the later measures. This pattern suggests a greater inhibitive effect to $S_1\pm$ as compared to the case of S_1, where increased excitatory effects of this stimulus seem to predominate. The pattern represented in the right-hand panel (S_{14}) was also characteristic of about one-third of the animals. It shows faster running to the $S_1\pm$ in the start and running measures and a tendency toward slower running to $S_1\pm$ in the goal region. This type of S most closely resembles the between-S findings (Goodrich, 1959) and the within-S findings of Amsel *et al.* (1964). These three Ss reveal that the major part of the individual S variation in performance is attributable to what the S does to the partially rewarded stimulus. The difference between Ss in their level of response to $S_1\pm$ is far greater than their difference in level of response to S_2+. Not only the group data, but even the individual S data, seem to reflect a progressive systematic change in the level of the $S_1\pm$ curve in relation to the S_2+ curve from the start to the goal segment.

B. ACQUISITION EFFECTS WITH TRIALS EQUATED

The experiment reported in Section III, A held rewards equal across stimuli within Ss. Most of our subsequent experiments equated trials rather than rewards. In one such experiment 10 Ss were run under $S_1\pm S_2+$ conditions, 5 under each of the two possible color arrangements in the black and white alleys. Procedures are identical to those already described, but the apparatus here was a shortened version with only three measurement divisions, a starting, a running, and a goal segment, each measured over 1 ft of alley. Figure 10 shows the running and goal speeds recorded in this experiment. The starting measures showed no substantial difference of any kind. The effect evident in most of the running segments of the earlier experiment can be seen here, too, in the running segment: faster running to the partial stimulus than to the continuous stimulus after the first few blocks of trials. The other acquisition item of note is that in the goal measure there is a clear difference between the curves over the first few blocks of trials also in the direction of faster running to the partial stimulus, following which the speeds to the two stimuli seem equal over the remainder of the acquisition. This early superiority in speed to $S_1\pm$ over S_2+ in the goal measure has been a characteristic of most of the experiments we have performed; we will come back to it in a moment. Note here again

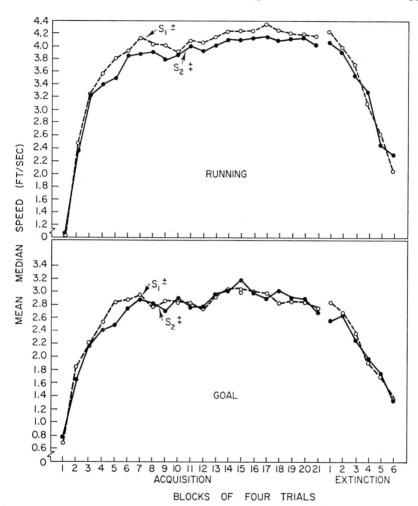

FIG. 10. Running and goal data from a within-S partial reinforcement experiment in which trials rather than reinforcements were equated to S_1 and S_2.

that extinction following within-S PRF acquisition seems to produce no PRE. If anything, the extinction data suggest a reverse PRE in that the slopes to the partial stimulus are somewhat steeper than those to the continuous stimulus, particularly in the running measure, where the partial group starts higher. Statistical analysis, however, reveals no significant difference in extinction.

Returning now to acquisition effects, an experiment was conducted in our laboratory some time ago to permit a closer look at the finding, mentioned earlier, that response to $S_1\pm$ early in acquisition in the goal measure seems faster than response to $S_2\frac{+}{+}$. To test this finding under theoretically "clean" conditions we ran a group of 10 Ss in an experiment essentially the same as that just described except that these Ss were run under one-trial-a-day conditions. Figure 11 shows the results of this experiment for the early acquisition trials of the goal measure. It is very clear from these data that the result is identical to that obtained under four-trials-a-day conditions: even at one trial a day, the Ss run faster to the partial stimulus in the goal region early in training than they do to the continuous stimulus, this difference

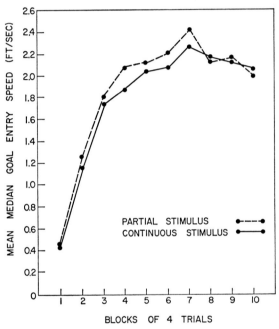

FIG. 11. Data from a one-trial-a-day experiment showing goal entry performance early in training to the partial ($S_1\pm$) and continuous ($S_2\frac{+}{+}$) stimulus.

disappearing by about 30–40 trials of training. We will look at this effect again in connection with data from three other experiments, one by Henderson (1966) and one by MacKinnon (1965), to be discussed in the next two sections, and one by Galbraith that will be treated toward the end of the chapter.

C. VARYING PERCENTAGE OF REWARD TO S_1

As part of an experiment to examine a variety of within-S acquisition effects, Henderson ran five groups of Ss under the conditions shown across the top of Fig. 12. In this experiment, there were five within-S

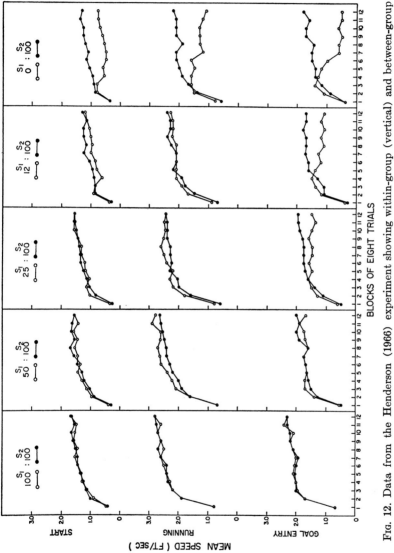

FIG. 12. Data from the Henderson (1966) experiment showing within-group (vertical) and between-group (horizontal) comparisons of performance when percentage of reward to S_1 is varied over groups and to S_2 is held constant at 100%.

groups that differed with respect to the percentage of reward associated with one of the stimuli (S_1), whereas response to the other stimulus (S_2) was continuously reinforced in all groups. Only three measures were taken, a starting, a running, and a goal measure. Hence the 50 : 100 condition of the Henderson experiment is identical in every respect to the first experiment reported in the preceding section. Of course no difference would be expected between the two curves of the 100 : 100 group, and the 0 : 100 group is a straight differential reward training condition. For our purposes, then, the new groups of particular interest in this experiment would be 25 : 100 and 12 : 100, particularly as they compare with the other groups. It should be pointed out that in this experiment the differential color effects were not very substantial, and that it was therefore possible to combine the curves for the color conditions.

The data from Henderson's experiment seem to show clear systematic effects with respect to both between-group comparisons and within-group comparisons. The vertical comparisons show, first of all, that the 50 : 100 condition replicates almost exactly the earlier within-S result: the start measure shows little separation of the S_1 and S_2 curves; the Ss' speed to the partial stimulus is greater than to the continuous stimulus in the run segment; there is an indication of early superiority of performance in the goal measure to the partial as compared with the continuous stimulus; and the terminal speeds in the goal measure at the end of training show only slight if any superiority to the continuous stimulus. The vertical comparison for group 25 : 100 shows approximately the same effects in the start and run measures as in the 50 : 100 group, but in the goal measure of the 25 : 100 group there is a clear indication of reversal of speeds, Ss in this group running faster in the goal to the continuous stimulus, except for very early in training, where the early faster running to the partial stimulus is *again* shown. The vertical comparison for the 12 : 100 group reflects the beginning of aversive responding to S_1 in all measures, although this is still clear and unmistakable only in the goal measure. It is, however, evident that the faster running to S_1 characteristic of the 50 : 100 and 25 : 100 groups is seen only very early in training in the run measure. There is again an indication in the goal measure that the speed to the stimulus reinforced 12% of the time is greater than that to the stimulus reinforced 100% of the time early in training. The 0 : 100 group, of course, shows the typical pattern of differential responding in all measures, but even here there is a suggestion that running to the negative stimulus is faster than running to the positive stimulus in the goal region early in training.

When comparisons are made horizontally in Fig. 12 (that is, across rather than within groups), the systematic nature of the changes prevails. In the start measure, where no group shows evidence of paradoxical faster running to the partial than to the continuous stimulus, differential responding of the usual sort appears in the 12 : 100 group for the first time. In the running measure, where there is a clear indication of faster running to the partial stimulus in groups 50 : 100 and 25 : 100, evidence of differentiation based on S_1 aversiveness does not appear until we get to the 0 : 100 group. In the goal entry measure, apart from the early effect—faster running to the partial stimulus than to the continuous stimulus early in training—there is simply increasing evidence of differential responding and of S_1 aversiveness as we go from the left-hand to the right-hand side of the figure.

In this kind of differential percentage training, there does seem to be a clear indication that aversiveness of lower percentage reward shows up most clearly in the goal measure. This seems true not only in the 0 : 100 and 12 : 100 groups but also in the 25 : 100 group. As a matter of fact, in the 25 : 100 group the aversive effect to S_1 shows up only in the goal measure.

D. VARYING MAGNITUDE OF REWARD TO S_1

The acquisition phase of an experiment by MacKinnon (1965) was very much like the comparable phase of the Henderson experiment except that magnitude, rather than percentage, of reward to S_1 was varied as the between-groups parameter in five groups. The designations of these groups are provided across the top of Fig. 13, which also shows the results of this phase of the MacKinnon experiment. The apparatus was the same as that used in the Henderson experiment and in other experiments in this series, and three response measures were taken. For some reason, not entirely clear, the absolute speeds of running achieved by Ss in the MacKinnon experiment were higher than those in the Henderson experiment. It is possible to make this statement because the 0 : 500 condition and the 500 : 500 condition of the MacKinnon experiment are exactly comparable to the 0 : 100 and 100 : 100 conditions of the Henderson experiment, respectively, the differences between these conditions being only in the designations of the groups (milligrams of reward in the former, percentage of reward in the latter). On every trial of the Henderson experiment that was rewarded, S found a 500-mg pellet, but S did not find a reward on every trial except in the 100 : 100 group. On every trial of the MacKinnon experiment S was rewarded (except in the 0 : 500 group), but the magnitude of reward was varied within Ss and between groups.

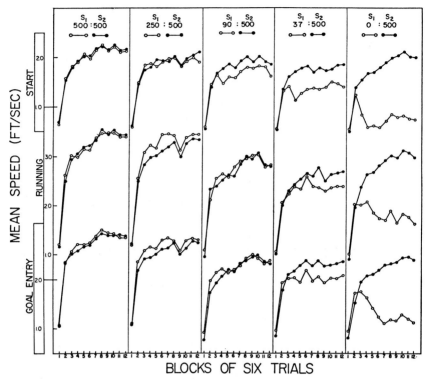

BLOCKS OF SIX TRIALS

Fɪɢ. 13. Data from the MacKinnon (1965) experiment showing within-group (vertical) and between-group (horizontal) comparisons of performance when magnitude of reward to S_1 is varied over groups and to S_2 is held constant and high.

Figure 13 shows performance to both stimuli for the five groups of MacKinnon's experiment over the entire course of training. Mean starting, running, and goal speeds in feet per second are shown, successively, from the top to the bottom of the graph within each panel. As in Fig. 12, horizontal comparison shows the development of the discrimination across groups, while vertical comparison shows the development from start to goal measure within groups. The start measure shows an uncomplicated picture: there is simply a gradual development of the separation of S_1 and S_2 curves as an inverse function of the magnitude of S_1. Even in the 250 : 500 group there is a slight suggestion of separation of the curves with faster running to S_2 in the start measure (supported by a significant Days × Magnitude interaction), and this separation increases as the magnitude of reward to S_1 decreases. This simple inverse relationship between the apparent aversiveness of S_1 and the magnitude of S_1 is not shown in either the running or goal measure. The latter two measures show a surprisingly similar result (unlike the case for differential percentage training). In both measures the 250 : 500 group shows paradoxical higher speeds to the lesser magnitude of reward stimulus; the 90 : 500 group shows approximately equal performance to the two stimuli (apart from a suggestion of faster running to the small reward stimulus in the goal measure early in training); the 37 : 500 group shows the beginning of differential responding, suggesting aversiveness of the lesser magnitude stimulus; and the 0 : 500 group shows the usual full-blown differentiation effect.

E. DISCUSSION OF ACQUISITION EFFECTS

The experiments on within-S acquisition discussed in this section are representative of a larger number of experiments dealing with these factors conducted in our laboratory. These experiments were chosen to be presented here because they point up two characteristics of our data that are worth attention: (1) within-S intensity (vigor) effects; and (2) an interesting difference between differential percentage and differential magnitude results in within-S experiments.

1. *Within-S Vigor Effects in Acquisition*

The four experiments presented in this section, and several others of this sort that we have completed, yield certain paradoxical effects that are open to interpretation in terms of the kind of frustration theory that was outlined earlier. These within-S acquisition effects showing, for example, that Ss run faster in some segments to the stimulus that signals the lesser percentage of reward have now been seen in a number of experiments and must be regarded as genuine effects of this kind of procedure. The finding that under some conditions lesser *magnitude* of reward produces faster running within Ss is less well substantiated, the evidence for such a generalization coming mainly from the single experiment by MacKinnon that I have reported. (MacKinnon has, however, recently indicated (1966), that this result has been replicated.) It is somewhat safer, then, to discuss the paradoxical vigor effects in differential percentage training experiments than in differential magnitude experiments and I will proceed in this cautious manner.

There are really two questions to be considered here: Why, in within-S PRF training, does the partial stimulus, compared to the continuous, elicit greater intensity of response in the goal region early in training and lesser intensity in the goal region later in training? (In between-S experiments, the typical finding in the goal measure is

greater intensity of responding in the continuous group from the beginning of training.) The second question is: Why, in differential percentage within-S experiments (and also apparently under some differential magnitude conditions), do Ss seem to perform more vigorously in
the middle running measure, almost throughout the entire course of
training, to the stimulus signaling less frequent reward? [The pattern
in between-S experiments is again somewhat different, the running
measure showing either a crossing over from early CRF superiority
to later PRF superiority of performance (Goodrich, 1959; Wagner,
1961) or CRF superiority throughout (Amsel *et al.*, 1966).]

The suggestion has been made (Amsel, 1964) that it is the relationship of the strength of r_F to the strength of r_R early and late
in training that produces these effects. The guiding idea is presented
in the left-hand box of Fig. 14. When anticipatory responses are weak

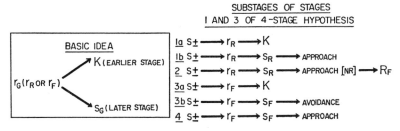

FIG. 14. Schema showing proposed substages of Stages 1 and 3 of the four-stage
hypothesis of frustrative effects in partial reinforcement acquisition. These substages
are derived from the basic idea of earlier and later stages of r_R and r_F effects shown
in the box at the left.

they serve only as sources of generalized drive (in this case K) and
such internal responses must grow and become substantially stronger
before they also give rise to characteristic stimuli that can control the
direction of behavior. To the right of the box in Fig. 14 is a series of
statements in which an abbreviated form of the four-stage hypothesis
for the development of frustrative effects during partial reinforcement
is extended to include two substages of Stage 1 and Stage 3. The sub-
stage 1a statement says that in the early conditioning of r_R there is
only a nondirective and nonspecific contribution of r_R to K, and that
specific response-produced cues (s_R) are not yet operating; the sub-
stage 3a statement says that after nonreward (NR) produces primary
frustration (R_F) and the process of conditioning frustration to runway
cues has begun, there is a stage in which r_F also contributes only
nondirectively, a stage before 3b, in which s_F is present to direct antici-

patory frustrative responses to avoidance or competing reactions. The implications of such a position for effective thresholds of K effects, and of s_R or s_F effects, are shown in Fig. 15. It shows that in any situation involving partial reward training r_R starts to build from the first rewarded trial and reaches its K threshold and its s_R threshold before r_F starts to grow and reaches the same two successive thresholds. The hypothetical situation depicted in Fig. 15 involves a number of stages of learning; for example, for several trials between trials 10 and 20, the strength of r_F is such that it is above the K threshold but not yet above the s_F threshold. According to our present thinking, it is at this stage that r_F would provide facilitation for any response it accom-

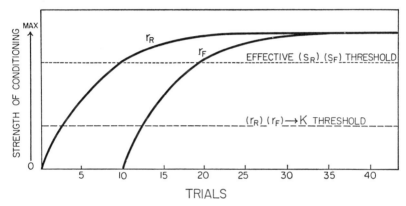

Fig. 15. A development of the notion presented in the box of Fig. 14 showing hypothetical curves of r_R and r_F conditioning and their relation to thresholds of K and of s_R and s_F effectiveness.

panied. Early in training, because of its steep generalization gradient, r_F might be strong enough to potentiate responses to S_1 only in the goal region. Later in training, when r_F becomes strong enough in the goal region to be superthreshold for s_F and to produce conflicting approach and avoidance tendencies to S_1 (the stimulus signaling lesser percentage of reward), r_F might be strong enough to be superthreshold for K in the running or even the start segment, but not strong enough to be superthreshold for s_F in these earlier segments. Hence some suggestion of faster running to $S_1\pm$ than to S_2^+ might begin to appear in the running and start measures. A schema relating strength of r_R and r_F early and late in training to the three kinds of measure taken in our runway is shown in Fig. 16. The assumption here is that the gradient of generalization of r_F is steeper than that of r_R from the goal to the run to the start measure, an assumption we have made before

(Amsel, 1962) on the basis of the theory and experiments of N. E. Miller and his associates (Miller, 1959).

This assumption of differential steepness of the r_R and r_F gradients also helps to explain why the weak r_F does not also facilitate response to S_2 on the early trials in the goal region, and why performance to S_1 and S_2 are close together in strength on the first ten or so trials of within-S training. The flat gradient of r_R, and of approach tendencies generally, can be used to explain the equality of S_1 and S_2 performance on the first few trials of within-S training; and the steep gradient of r_F accounts for the failure of the facilitating effect to transfer from $S_1\pm$ to $S_2\underset{+}{\pm}$ on the next few trials.

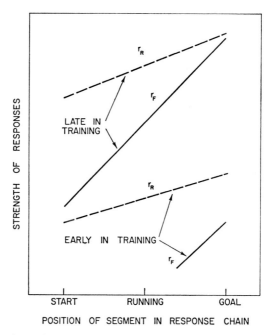

FIG. 16. Hypothesized relationships of gradients of r_R and r_F early and late in training as an explanation of within-S response vigor effects in acquisition.

Although I have not introduced a detailed discussion of between-S acquisition effects into this chapter, between-S groups that were run for comparison with our within-S conditions [see Fig. 18; Amsel *et al.* (1966)] have, almost without exception, shown PRF performance lower than CRF performance throughout training in the goal and in other measures as well. There is certainly *never* any suggestion of the early facilitation of response to PRF in the between-S studies, ours or others, that we have shown to hold in the within-S case. This is not an unexpected difference between these kinds of procedures in view of the mechanisms proposed to account for the phenomena. In the between-S case, there is, of course, no basis for generalization from one subject or one group to another, as there is from S_1 to S_2 and S_2 to S_1 in the within-S case. Consequently, we would expect the CRF curves always to be higher than the comparable PRF curves at the outset. Any early facilitating effect in the goal region of weak r_F in the PRF condition of a between-S experiment would only reduce the difference between the level of the two curves but could not be expected to overcome this CRF–PRF difference in the usual experiment, where trials are equated between groups and CRF involves twice as many reinforcements as PRF. In the between-S experiment, by the time both groups have had enough reinforcements to be responding at similar asymptotic levels in the goal, strong s_F (and $s_F \rightarrow$ avoidance) is a factor to permanently depress performance in the PRF group. The eventual crossover often found in earlier parts of the response chain in between-S experiments is a finding consistent with the view that r_F, generalized from the goal region and consequently weak, will contribute to faster running in PRF than in CRF groups at a stage where they would otherwise be performing at about equal levels.

The theoretical notions just presented are of course *ad hoc*. They seem intuitively reasonable statements of what the mechanisms determining the paradoxical effects that we find in our within-S acquisition experiments might be. It is always possible, of course, that these paradoxical effects are the result of something entirely different. They may reflect, simply, sequential effects in our experiments. It is the case, for example, particularly in straight S_1+S_2- discrimination learning experiments with successive presentation of stimuli that, regardless of how the trials are arranged, a nonreward is more likely to follow a reward than another nonreward, and a reward is more likely to follow a nonreward. It could be the case that early in training, in particular, a factor such as this could produce the apparent early faster running to the negative stimulus that we see even in the 0 : 100 group of the Henderson experiment and have seen many times in other similar experiments, an effect also evident in free-responding discrimination experiments (Bloomfield, 1966). We would be talking here simply about a successive acquisition–extinction effect during early trials of straight discrimination learning. This kind of factor is less likely to operate in any straightforward manner in the usual differential percentage reward experiment, and even less likely to account for paradoxical greater vigor to $S_1 \pm$ that persists throughout the course of training, over many trials, in the running measure of several of our experiments, at a stage where the goal measure is often showing the reverse effect. Nevertheless, this kind of possibility has to be checked out and we are proceeding to do so.

2. Differential Percentage and Differential Magnitude Training Experiments: A Comparison of Results

There are indications, from a comparison of the results of the Henderson and MacKinnon experiments, that the pattern of acquisition effects over segments of a fractionated alley is different depending on whether percentage or magnitude of reward is varied within subjects. Such indications seem to emerge most clearly from a comparison of the 25 : 100 group from the Henderson experiment (Fig. 12) with the 90 : 500 group from the MacKinnon experiment (Fig. 13). In this group of the Henderson experiment the S gets a 500-mg pellet reward 25% of the time to S_1 and 100% of the time to S_2, whereas in the MacKinnon group the S gets a 90-mg reward on every trial to S_1 and a 500-mg reward on every trial to S_2. A comparison of Figs. 12 and 13 for these two groups in particular shows that differential performance of the kind that would reflect an aversive reaction to S_1 relative to S_2 appears only in the goal measure in the percentage experiment and only in the start measure in the magnitude experiment. These are the only two groups, one from each experiment, where it can clearly be said that such differential responding shows up *only in one measure*. In the MacKinnon 37 : 500 group, where there is differentiation in all three measures, differential responding appears earliest in the start measure. In the 0 : 100 group of the Henderson experiment and in the exactly equivalent 0 : 500 group of the MacKinnon experiment, differentiation also seems to be evident first in the start measure. What the latter two groups have in common with any group run under differential magnitude conditions is that reward to S_1 is always the same and reward to S_2 is always the same, and it appears that under such conditions differentiation is first evident in the start measure of an alley. This suggestion from the MacKinnon experiment is supported by some similar data from an experiment by Peckham and Amsel (1967) on differential reward training: here, too, there is an indication that differential responding to stimuli signaling a larger and a smaller amount of reward is first evident in the start measure of the three-segment alley.

All the foregoing suggests an interpretation along the lines that the factor of conflict or "uncertainty" is operating differentially in these two kinds of experiment, and that Ss are less in conflict or less uncertain in the magnitude case than in the percentage case. In the case of reduced magnitude, differential performance shows up at the start, as soon as the S sees the stimulus, since it signals either the lesser or the greater reward immediately. Once the S starts to run, he is simply under the control of different strengths of r_R based on different reward magnitudes and, in extreme cases (for example, 37 : 500), he continues to run more slowly to S_1 throughout. When the stimulus signaling lesser reward at the start does not control the behavior aversively to produce a differential responding effect in the start measure (the 250 : 500 condition), the relative aversiveness of S_1 may build up as the S approaches the goal, but r_F being mild may produce only nonspecific "excitement" and give rise to the paradoxical *faster* running to S_1 (signaling a 250-mg reward) than to S_2 (signaling a 500-mg reward).

In the case of differential percentage training, the lower percentage stimulus (S_1) signals nothing with certainty and the S remains in conflict to this stimulus over all segments of the alley. When the r_F in the conflict is weak (only superthreshold for K but not for s_F), as it is at the start and run positions throughout training and at the goal early in training, only mild additional excitement is generated and the S runs faster to the stimulus signaling low percentage than to that signaling high percentage reward. Later, as r_F grows stronger and provides aversive (s_F) cues, particularly in the 0 : 100, 12 : 100, and 25 : 100 groups, (a) the early facilitation of responding to $S_1\pm$ at the goal is reversed into an aversive reaction, and (b) there is movement of this aversive effect to points earlier in the instrumental sequence, the distance of this forward movement being an inverse function of the percentage reward of response to S_1.

The reader will recognize that the argument developed in this section is sheer conjecture based on a very small amount of data. It does, however, seem intuitively reasonable to suppose that differential magnitude training and differential percentage training within Ss would proceed on somewhat different bases, and that they might in fact be shown to involve the kinds of processes and follow the kinds of courses that have been proposed.

IV. Within-Subjects Extinction Effects

The preceding section was devoted to a discussion of acquisition effects; however, there was some indication in Figs. 8 and 10 of what the extinction data looked like in our early within-S experiments. Figure 8 showed results from an experiment of the $S_1\pm S_2+$ variety in which reinforcements were equated. Following this kind of acquisition training, extinction was carried out to both stimuli, and the picture presented in extinction was that the relative positions of the curves were much the same as they had been in acquisition, that there was no sharp drop in level of performance to S_2+ at the beginning of extinction, as would be expected following CRF training, and that there was no suggestion of the kind of slope difference that would reflect a PRE. The data in Fig. 10 are from an experiment in which within-S extinction followed acquisition training in which trials, rather than reinforcements, were equated $(S_1 \pm S_2 +)$. Here the picture was even clearer: the extinction curves to the two acquisition stimuli were almost completely overlapping and there was, again, no suggestion of differential extinction performance to $S_1 \pm$ as compared with $S_2 +$.

Results of this sort have been characteristic of several of our experiments (Amsel et al., 1966), and we have spent a lot of time recently trying to understand the absence of differential responding in within-S extinction and designing experiments in which a PRE-like effect might be produced under within-S conditions. Some of our recent work in this area is outlined in the remainder of this section. It should be noted that studies of within-S extinction effects have also been going on, independently, in other laboratories (R. T. Brown & Logan, 1965; Pavlik & Carlton, 1965; Pavlik, Carlton, & Hughes, 1965a; Pavlik, Carlton, & Manto, 1965b). We will refer to these studies again.

A. Two Extinction Procedures after Within-Subjects Acquisition

As we have now pointed out in a couple of places (Amsel, 1964; Amsel et al., 1966), a within-S partial reinforcement experiment can be conducted in two ways with respect to extinction procedures. One way is that represented by the experiments already described in the previous section: within-S extinction following within-S acquisition. In this kind of experiment, all Ss acquire the running response to both stimuli—each is partially reinforced for responding to S_1 and continuously reinforced for responding to S_2—and the response is then extinguished to both stimuli. In such a design, it is possible to look for transfer of persistence effects from S_1 to S_2 in extinction. The second method of conducting extinction trials in within-S experiments could be termed between-S extinction following within-S acquisition. Here again the Ss learn the same response to both $S_1 \pm$ and $S_2 +$, but extinction for any one S is to one stimulus only, either to S_1 or to S_2. Such a design has two advantages: first, it provides an opportunity for looking at extinction to one stimulus only, uncontaminated by possible interacting effects from responding to the other stimulus; second, the between-S extinction procedure is a particularly useful one for comparing extinction effects following within-S acquisition with extinction effects following between-S acquisition so that the comparison will reflect mainly different acquisition effects on extinction. An experiment of this sort, reported first at the meetings of the Psychonomic Society (Amsel, 1964) is outlined in the section that follows. This experiment has been very clear in suggesting that failure to obtain a difference in extinction responding to S_1 and S_2 characteristic of the PRE following $S_1 \pm S_2 +$ acquisition in fact means that there is generalization of the PRE from S_1 to S_2. R. T. Brown and Logan (1965) have recently reported a similar result and have referred to the phenomenon as a generalized partial reinforcement effect (GPRE). We will have occasion to consider whether this is an effect of primary or of secondary (mediated) stimulus generalization.

Figure 17 is a schema we have used to clarify the distinction between

ACQUISITION		EXTINCTION	
		BETWEEN $\underline{S}$	WITHIN $\underline{S}$
USUAL BETWEEN $\underline{S}$	STIM$_1$± (P)	STIM$_1$⁻	
	STIM$_1$‡ (C)	STIM$_1$⁻	
WITHIN $\underline{S}$ (PC)	STIM$_1$± (P)	STIM$_1$⁻ OR STIM$_2$⁻	STIM$_1$⁻ AND STIM$_2$⁻
	STIM$_2$‡ (C)		
BETWEEN $\underline{S}$ (PP)	STIM$_1$± (P)	STIM$_1$⁻ OR STĪM$_2$⁻	STIM$_1$⁻ AND STĪM$_2$⁻
	STIM$_2$± (P)		
(CC)	STIM$_1$‡ (C)	STIM$_1$⁻ OR STĪM$_2$⁻	STIM$_1$⁻ AND STĪM$_2$⁻
	STIM$_2$‡ (C)		

FIG. 17. Schema showing between-S and within-S experimental conditions for partial reinforcement experiments. Note that extinction after between-S acquisition must be between S, but extinction following within-S acquisition may be either between S or within S. After Amsel et al. (1966).

the within-S and between-S procedures discussed in this section. The portion of the figure under the horizontal double lines, but not including the right-hand (within-S) column, is an outline of the experiment to be described next.

B. Between-S Extinction Following Between-S and Within-S Acquisition

In this experiment (Amsel, 1964; Amsel et al., 1966), 40 male albino rats were assigned to three experimental groups and were run four trials a day in the single black and white alleys of the apparatus already described. The three groups were designated PC, PP, and CC. The first letter designates reward condition to S_1 and the second to S_2. Therefore, group PC could also be designated $S_1 \pm S_2 +$ (see Fig. 17). Group PC was partially rewarded for running to black and continuously rewarded for running to white, or vice versa, and there were 10 Ss in each of the color controls for this group. On any one experimental day, each S ran two trials to the partially rewarded stimulus (PC$\pm$) and two trials to the stimulus associated with continuous reward (PC$+$). Each of the groups in the between-S acquisition portion of this experiment was made up of 10 Ss. All Ss in group PP were run under 50% reward conditions to *both* the black and white stimuli, whereas the Ss in group CC were continuously rewarded for running in *both* stimulus alleys. Following acquisition, half the Ss in each group were extinguished in the presence of *one* of the two stimuli, and the other half were extinguished in the presence of the other. With group PC split in this manner, half the Ss formed a group extinguished to the stimulus associated with continuous reward in acquisition, the other half to the stimulus associated with partial reward. These separate extinction groups are, in this respect at least, equivalent to the two extinction groups, one continuous and one partial, defined by the between-S acquisition conditions of the experiment. The CC and PP groups were also extinguished to only one stimulus (they had seen two in acquisition) but unlike the case of the PC animals, this stimulus and the other from acquisition had *both* been associated with partial reward (group PP) or with continuous reward (group CC).

Figure 18 shows some of the data from this experiment that are relevant to our present discussion of extinction effects. I will not dwell on the acquisition findings here since they have been detailed elsewhere. It is obvious, however, that the initial superiority of the CP$\pm$ over the CP$+$ group in acquisition confirms the findings of experiments reported in an earlier section of this chapter. This graph also points out the similarities and differences between within-S and between-S acquisition for the goal measure to which we alluded in Section III, E, 1 when we discussed acquisition effects: one difference is, of course, in the initial effect; another is that there is, in the within-S condition, a crossover in the goal measure and, consequently, an indication that the terminal difference in the within-S comparison (PC$\pm$ versus PC$+$) is in the same direction as for the between-S comparison (PP versus CC).

The most interesting comparisons for purposes of this section are in the extinction phase. Extinction in the CC group develops very rapidly, showing the very sharp drop from terminal acquisition to the first ex-

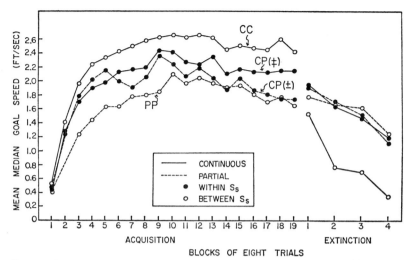

Fɪɢ. 18. Between-S extinction comparisons of the PRE following within-S and between-S acquisition (see Fig. 17).

tinction point that is characteristic of extinction following continuous reinforcement; extinction for all three other groups is different from CC extinction and virtually identical across groups: in no case in these three extinction groups is there a substantial drop in performance from the last acquisition point to the first extinction point, and in every case extinction is extremely gradual and is incomplete at the end of the experiment. This extinction finding is not characteristic of the goal speed measure alone, but of the other measures also. It has also been substantially replicated in an experiment conducted under within-S extinction procedures (Amsel *et al.*, 1966). Along with the R. T. Brown and Logan (1965) experiment, these findings lead us to be fairly confident that when the within-S experiment is run under conditions of equated trials in acquisition and under conditions of 50% reinforcement to S_1 and 100% reinforcement to S_2, there is (a) no difference in extinction between the two curves, whether extinction is carried out between S or within S, and (b) a clear suggestion that the absence of extinction differences is in fact symptomatic of a generalized PRE resulting from some kind of generalization of persistence from $S_1\pm$ to $S_2\ddagger$.

When we came to think about this result a little further, it seemed to us that it was quite reasonable given (a) that the situation in which we were conducting our experiments represented a fairly minimal amount of differential external stimulus control in the within-S condition, and (b) that the rationale guiding the Ross experiment, a separate-phase experiment described in Section II, C, could also be applied to the kind of same-phase experiment I have just described. In the Ross experiment, to take a single group and use it as an example, Ss were trained under partial reward conditions, in Phase 1, to run in a short black alley under hunger motivation. In Phase 2 of the experiment they were trained under continuous reward conditions to run in a very different-looking long white alley under thirst conditions. They were then extinguished in a third phase in the alley of Phase 2. These animals acted in extinction as though they had been partially reinforced in the long white alley of Phases 2 and 3, although they had never encountered partial reinforcement in this alley or under thirst conditions. In the experiment under present consideration, a same-phase experiment, Ss were partially rewarded when hungry in a white alley, and continuously rewarded when hungry in a black alley. Half these Ss were then extinguished in the black alley and half in the white, and all behaved as though they had been partially rewarded in the presence of both stimuli. In the light of the Ross experiment, the present one can be taken as suggesting that there is rather an absence of strong external stimulus control in the extinction phase. To put it another way, the data can be taken to mean that there is a transfer of learned persistence ($s_F \rightarrow$ approach), perhaps through a mechanism of mediated (secondary) stimulus generalization, from $S_1\pm$ to $S_2\overset{+}{-}$ in subsequent extinction. Of course, this kind of transfer cannot occur in the between-S experiment since different organisms are continuously and partially rewarded in the acquisition phase.

However, another possible explanation for the generalized PRE cannot be overlooked—primary stimulus generalization. Such a mechanism could account for the evocation of r_F by $S_2\overset{+}{-}$ in acquisition and subsequent connection of s_F to approach in the presence of S_2 cues. Apart from the Ross experiment, which purposely set out to minimize the possibility of primary stimulus generalization and to put the burden for eliciting a generalized PRE on mediational mechanisms, the major argument against primary generalization as the explanatory factor comes from the acquisition effects, showing that S_1 and S_2 seem to be operating as separate systems. On the other hand, the experiment of Henderson and another to be presented by Galbraith, both of which manipulate percentage reward to S_1 as a between-groups factor in $S_1\pm S_2\overset{+}{-}$ experiments, definitely point to generalization from S_1 to S_2 of inhibitory effects at low percentages of S_1 reward. That is, asymptotic S_2 speeds between groups are directly proportional to percentage reward to S_1 in these studies, and a comparable result holds for reward magnitude in MacKinnon's experiment.

Of course, it is entirely possible that both generalization mechanisms are operating in the within-S experiment, whereas neither can operate under between-S conditions. Figure 19 describes schematically the between-S PRE explanation and the alternative, though not incompatible, mechanisms for the GPRE under within-S conditions. The diagram shows that the between-S and the first within-S cases are identical in acquisition but different in extinction. It is also possible, however, as the bottom panels of Fig. 19 show, that some or all of the generalization in the within-S case takes place not in extinction but in acquisition. At the moment, we feel that the combined weight of the Ross experiment, the kind of experiment described in this section, and some of the experiments that follow favors an interpretation that stresses mediated generalization in extinction rather than primary stimulus generaliza-

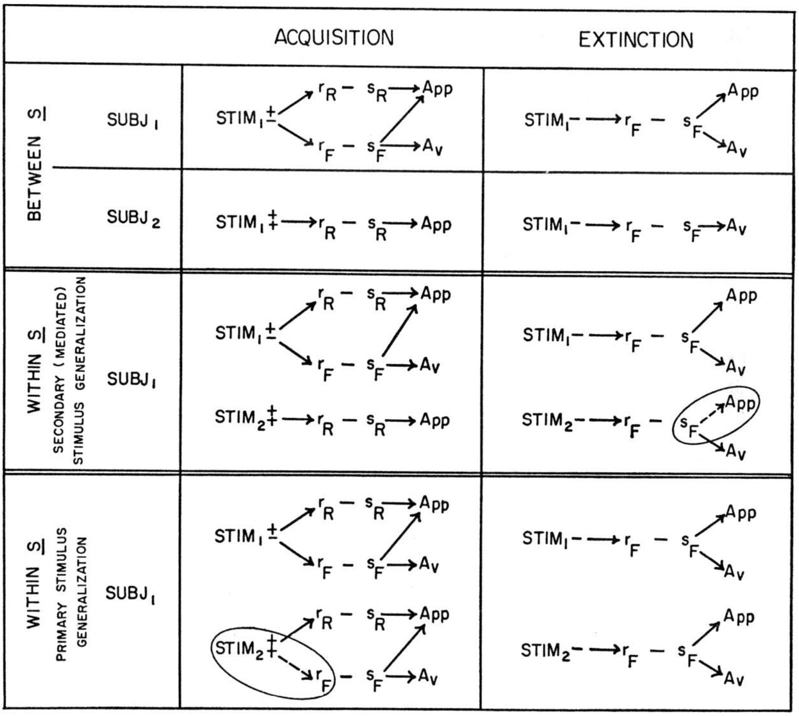

FIG. 19. Schema of explanation of between-S PRE, and the alternative, though not incompatible, explanations of the GPRE in within-S experiments. The two mechanisms circled in the figure represent these explanations of the GPRE. In the middle right-hand panel $s_F \to$ App is shown to operate when response to Stim$_2$— is extinguished and elicits r_F. In the lower left-hand panel Stim$_2 {+ \atop +} \dashrightarrow r_F$ represents the generalization of anticipatory frustration in acquisition.

tion in acquisition as the major determinant of the GPRE. It bears repeating, however, that it is possible, and perhaps even likely, for both factors to operate and thus to provide an even more complicated picture, so that our emphasis on the mediational mechanisms in the remainder of this chapter may represent a somewhat unbalanced point of view.

C. CAN A WITHIN-SUBJECTS PRE BE DEMONSTRATED?

Assume (1) that the experiment just described and others employing runways and discrete-trial training, from our laboratory and elsewhere (R. T. Brown & Logan, 1965; Pavlik et al., 1965a), are convincing in their failure to demonstrate PRE-like differences in extinction performance to $S_1\pm$ and $S_2{}^{+3}_+$; (2) that the generalization of the PRE this suggests is due to powerful stimulus control exercised by s_F in extinction; and (3) that the external stimuli in this kind of experiment, which differ only with respect to brightness and control acquisition effects, are not very powerful in extinction. We are, then, left with the questions: Can a within-S PRE be demonstrated under any circumstances and, if so, what are these circumstances? Attempts to answer these questions can take a variety of experimental forms. One possible approach is to conduct the within-S PRF experiment in much the same manner as described earlier, but to try to make the black and white stimuli more powerful controllers of differential behavior through pretraining procedures that might increase their distinctiveness as stimuli. Another line of attack would be to carry out within-S extinction following within-S acquisition, where the acquisition phase involved different percentages of reward to S_1, as in the Henderson experiment. The reasoning here would be that just because percentages of reward to S_1 and S_2 of 50 and 100, respectively, did not yield differential extinction effects does not mean such effects would not follow within-S acquisition under other (lower) percentages to S_1. Still other possible procedures would involve variation on the response side. For example, it might be possible to produce a within-S PRE if Ss were partially rewarded for running to a black stimulus and were continuously rewarded for climbing to a white stimulus. The aim in each case would be to demonstrate differential extinction rates to $S_1\pm$ and $S_2{}^+_+$ because of some additional

---

[3] There are other experiments in the literature (Pavlik & Carlton, 1965; Pavlik et al., 1965b) that have studied within-S extinction effects in the lever box, using a multiple schedule counterpart of our black and white stimuli. These experiments have demonstrated "reversed" or "conventional" PREs depending on specific scheduling procedures. Although I do want to mention these interesting experiments, I will not attempt to compare them with those of this section or to extend the present analysis to cover these probably quite different cases.

"beefing up" of external stimulus control in the experimental situation, thus reducing the relative effect on extinction of the mediated transfer of persistence from S_1 to S_2. These are, then, somewhat indirect procedures for establishing the importance of mediational effects.

There is another, more direct way of providing support of the hypothesis that s_F acts as a powerful mediator of persistence effects. The rationale in this case is a little different; it involves conducting a within-S type of acquisition procedure in which the subject learns a particular distinctive *pattern* of persistence-responding to S_1 but not to S_2 during an acquisition phase, and is then extinguished to both stimuli in a second phase. What one hopes to find in this kind of experiment is a *pattern* of responding emerging to S_2 in extinction that was characteristic of responding to S_1 in acquisition.

We have been conducting these kinds of experiments recently but it is still too early to say whether they support the mediation explanation or the primary stimulus generalization explanation, or both. The data I will present here should be regarded as preliminary; fuller treatments will be offered later in experimental journals, where full disclosure of details of procedure and data analysis allow a more critical appraisal by the reader.

1. *Attempts to Counteract the Generalized PRE and Produce a Within-S PRE*

Evidence from the Ross experiment and from a number of our within-S partial reinforcement experiments has pointed to anticipatory frustration as the source of powerful internal stimuli which, in within-S PRF experiments, mediate persistence effects to S_2 through the mechanism of secondary stimulus generalization. The difficulty with such a hypothesis is that it explains what is essentially a negative result: a failure to find a within-S partial reinforcement extinction effect. One way to provide additional support for the hypothesis would be to conduct experiments in which the negative result could be converted into a positive one by reducing the degree of control of mediating stimuli relative to external stimuli. To put it another way, this kind of approach is designed to strengthen external stimulus control to the point where one stimulus complex $(S_1 + s_F)$ elicits strong approach tendencies in extinction, whereas the other $(S_2 + s_F)$ elicits weaker approach tendencies or, perhaps, only avoidance. The experiments that follow can be thought of in this way.

  a. Predifferentiation Followed by Within-S PRF Acquisition and Extinction. In one of the first procedures we tried, the plan was to enhance the distinctiveness and control of the black and white alley stimuli in the first phase of an experiment by S_1—S_2+ differentiation training, then to conduct our usual within-S experiment (partial reward to S_1 and continuous reward to S_2) in Phase 2, followed by extinction to both stimuli in Phase 3. We reasoned that if the first phase of such an experiment made the stimuli more discriminable, these stimuli might then be less susceptible to generalization effects in the second phase and more effective in producing a differential extinction effect in the third phase.

The version of this experiment we have completed and analyzed so far involves only 10 Ss. (A recently completed experiment, containing the conditions presented here, replicated the findings to be reported in every detail.) Figure 20 shows the essential design and the results. The experiment was conducted in the same apparatus and, aside from the original phase of discrimination training, under the same general conditions of procedure as our others. It was run in a five-segment alley, so that there are three intervening running measures between the start measure and the goal measure instead of one. As in most of our experiments, we used a large-sized food reward, 500 mg.

As Fig. 20 indicates, we ran the experiment under two conditions, 5 Ss in each. In the condition represented in the left-hand panels, the stimulus that was positive in Phase 1 remained positive in the within-S PRF phase (Phase 2), while the stimulus that was negative in Phase 1 became the partial stimulus in Phase 2. In the condition represented by the right-hand panels, the stimulus that had been positive in Phase 1 became partial and the stimulus that had been negative became positive in Phase 2. In both cases extinction was to both stimuli for each S.

The results shown in Fig. 20 are fairly clear-cut, but the interpretation is something else. It should first of all be pointed out that the drop in performance in every measure at the ninth within-S PRF block of trials resulted from a factor beyond our control—a change of experimenter for a 3-day period. However, this does not seem to affect the data systematically. The condition depicted in the left-hand panels seems to produce results in accord with our expectation: the period of predifferentiation (discrimination) training preceding the within-S PRF phase did seem to produce, in at least the three middle running measures, some indication of a within-S PRE. This was statistically significant in our analysis of these data. It is important to note, however, that this is not the usual between-S PRE pattern, in which there is a very sharp drop in the CRF curve at the first block of extinction trials. Here the S_1 and S_2 curves seem to hang together for the first two extinction blocks before the S_2 curve begins to decline at a faster

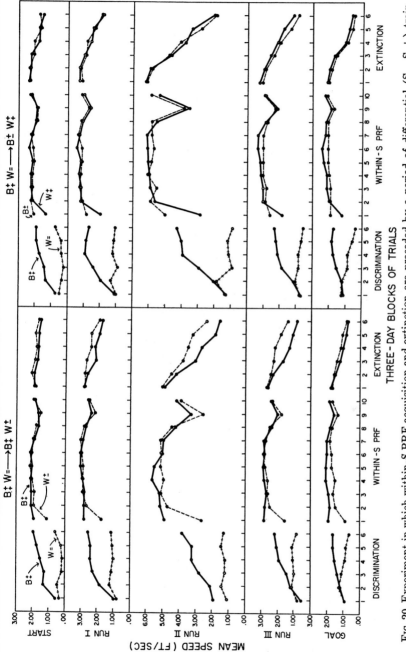

FIG. 20. Experiment in which within-S PRF acquisition and extinction are preceded by a period of differential (S_1-S_2+) training. The graph shows the findings of the three phases of the experiment over the five response segments of the alley.

rate than the S_1 curve. We will see this kind of within-S extinction effect again later.

The same extinction pattern is not discernible in the condition represented by the right-hand panels, and we are faced again with questions that amount to alternative explanations: Does the continuous stimulus have to remain continuous and the negative become partial $(B^+_+W^-_- \rightarrow B^+_+W\pm)$ in order for the "priming" effect on the within-S PRE to be demonstrable? Or is it simply that, over the first two phases of the experiment preceding the extinction phase, the left-hand condition is one of over-all CRF to one stimulus and small-percentage reinforcement to the other, whereas the right-hand condition represents PRF to both stimuli? If the special set of conditions represented by the first question is required, then other Ss run to these same over-all percentages of reward to B and W, but not in the $B^+_+W^-_- \rightarrow B^+_+W\pm$ sequence, should not show the within-S PRE. We are replicating this experiment with the necessary additional groups to find out if this is the case.

b. Within-S Extinction after Varying Percentages of Reward to S_1. In Section III, C we examined an experiment by Henderson in which each group represented a within-S experiment of the $S_1 \pm S_2^+_+$ type and percentage of reward to S_1 was varied as a between-groups parameter. The acquisition phase of the Henderson experiment was followed by a reversal $(S_1 + S_2 -)$ condition (not reported here), and not by a within-S phase, so it was impossible to determine from this experiment whether a within-S PRE might be demonstrable with percentages of reward to S_1 smaller than 50. An experiment to test this possibility has been conducted by Galbraith (1966). She employed, in this experiment, a technique for getting away from the differential brightness effects that seem to occur when black and white alleys are used in the within-S experiment. This technique, reported by Kolesnik and Amsel (1966), involves the use of two different stimulus alleys, as before, but instead of one alley being black and the other white, both alleys are black *and* white. In one alley, the left side of the floor and left wall are painted black while the right side of the floor and right wall are painted white, whereas in the other alley the color relationship is reversed. Discrimination experiments conducted in these alleys seem to produce response differentiation almost as quickly as do such experiments conducted with black and white alleys, and with none of the disadvantages of Color $\times$ Reinforcement interactions that are so often seen when the black and white alleys are used (Amsel *et al.*, 1966).

Three groups were run in the Galbraith experiment: $S_1 50-S_2 100$; $S_1 25-S_2 100$; and $S_1 0-S_2 100$. From our present point of view the interesting questions are: (a) Will the $S_1 50$–$S_2 100$ group show results in extinction similar to those obtained using black and white alleys? (b) If the answer to (a) is affirmative, will the pattern of extinction results change in the $S_1 25$–$S_2 100$ group? It is clear from the earlier results of Henderson (shown in Fig. 12) that differential responding to stimuli, one associated with 25% and the other with 100% reward, is greater than to stimuli associated with 50% and 100% reward, respectively. If this increased differentiation is not so great that response to S_1 is virtually extinguished by the end of differential percentage training, the main effect might be to increase the degree of control exercised by the two external stimuli in extinction and to produce a within-S PRE. The result of the Galbraith experiment, shown graphically as Fig. 21, suggests that this is not what happens.

The acquisition data of the Galbraith experiment replicate the comparable Henderson groups almost exactly: the 50–100 group shows (a) the early facilitation of running to $S_1 \pm$ in the goal and later reversal, (b) the extended facilitation in the middle running measure, and (c) no suggestion of faster extinction to S_2 than to S_1. The 25–100 group also shows the early facilitation to $S_1 \pm$ in the goal measure and a clear subsequent reversal, Ss running faster to S_2 than to S_1. There is again no suggestion of differential responding in extinction even in the goal measure, where there was a clear difference in responding in acquisition. Another very interesting finding is that, even after 0–100 training there is no sharp drop in extinction responding to $S_2 100$ at the first point, characteristic of between-S CRF extinction. This experiment provides substantial confirmation of many of our earlier findings, despite the use of somewhat different discriminative stimuli.

c. Experiments in Which Different Responses Are Required to $S_1 \pm$ and $S_2 \pm$. It is apparent that we have had only limited success, at best, in producing a within-S PRE in same-phase experiments by manipulating only the visual properties of the S_1 and S_2 alleys and related differential rewarding events. Another approach to making external control of persistence effects more powerful in within-S experiments has been taken in some experiments conducted by Rashotte (1966). The difference between this approach and the earlier ones is that it requires the subject to make different responses to S_1 and S_2 in the acquisition phase of a within-S PRF experiment.

Rashotte begins with the hypothesis that during within-S acquisition s_F becomes conditioned to the *specific* response made to $S_1 \pm$ and that *this response* is subsequently evoked by s_F during extinction to both S_1 and S_2. He argues that, insofar as the response evoked by s_F does not compete with the response made to S_2, responding to S_2 should be main-

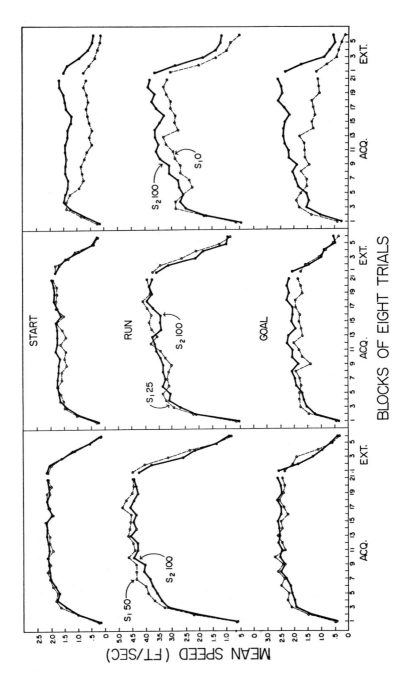

Fig. 21. Data from an experiment by Galbraith (1966) showing within-S acquisition and extinction performance under three conditions of percentage reward to S_1 in a split-alley apparatus.

tained. If, on the other hand, incompatible responses are learned to S_1 and S_2 in acquisition, s_F should elicit responses that are compatible with responses to S_1 but not with responses to S_2, and a within-S PRE should emerge in extinction.

Two experiments were conducted. In the first, two within-S groups and their between-S controls formed a design shown as Fig. 22. The $\text{Run}_1/\text{Run}_2$ condition was one in which two running responses differed with respect to the confinement and color of the alley, the white alley being very narrow, the black wide. The $\text{Climb}/\text{Run}_2$ group involved stimulus-response conditions approximating those of the Ross experi-

DESIGN OF RASHOTTE EXPERIMENT

	$\text{RUN}_1 / \text{RUN}_2$		$\text{CLIMB} / \text{RUN}_2$	
	ACQ.	EXT.	ACQ.	EXT.
(CC) BETWEEN $\underline{S}$	$R_1{}^{\ddagger}/R_2{}^{\ddagger}$	$R_1{}^{-}/R_2{}^{-}$	$C{}^{\ddagger}/R_2{}^{\ddagger}$	$C{}^{-}/R_2{}^{-}$
(PP)	$R_1{}^{\pm}/R_2{}^{\pm}$	$R_1{}^{-}/R_2{}^{-}$	$C{}^{\pm}/R_2{}^{\pm}$	$C{}^{-}/R_2{}^{-}$
(PC) WITHIN $\underline{S}$	$R_1{}^{\pm}/R_2{}^{\ddagger}$	$R_1{}^{-}/R_2{}^{-}$	$C{}^{\pm}/R_2{}^{\ddagger}$	$C{}^{-}/R_2{}^{-}$
(CP)	$R_1{}^{\ddagger}/R_2{}^{\pm}$	$R_1{}^{-}/R_2{}^{-}$	$C{}^{\ddagger}/R_2{}^{\pm}$	$C{}^{-}/R_2{}^{-}$

Fɪɢ. 22. An outline of the basic features of experiments by Rashotte (1966) in which two different responses, as well as two different stimuli, were associated, within Ss, with two different percentages of reinforcement. In the between-S (control) groups the two responses were associated with the same reinforcement percentage, which was varied only between groups.

ment. Of course, the within-S groups were under PRF for one response and CRF for the other, while the between-S groups were either under CRF for *both* responses or under PRF for both. Under these conditions, Rashotte found the usual precipitous drop in extinction responding in the between-S CRF group compared to the PRF group, a clear indication of the usual PRE even though two responses were mixed in acquisition and extinction. He also found clear evidence of a PRE in both within-S groups, the difference being only that in the $\text{Run}_1/\text{Run}_2$ group the two extinction curves were together and looked like PRF curves for two blocks of trials before the continuous curve separated and extinguished more rapidly, whereas in the Climb/Run₂ condition the separation occurred after the first extinction block.

Figure 23 presents the data from the second experiment of the Rashotte study, which included, in addition to the two within-S groups of the first experiment, a B/W group where the response was identical to the two stimuli, as in our earlier within-S studies. The results here are similar to the comparable within-S groups of the first experiment and the additional B/W group replicates our earlier findings of a GPRE when only stimulus color is manipulated.

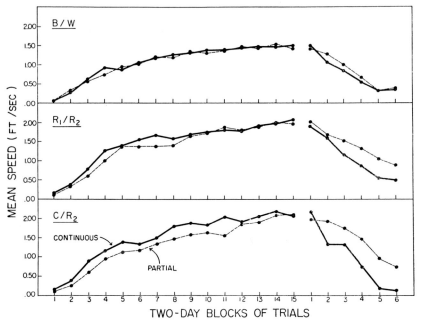

FIG. 23. Data from Experiment 2 of the Rashotte (1966) study showing a within-S PRE in the R_1/R_2 and C/R_2 groups, but not in the B/W group.

Two studies in this section have provided some evidence of a within-S PRE (or breakdown of the GPRE). In both cases there are indications that the within-S PRE differs from the between-S PRE in at least one respect: it *develops* during extinction, as compared with the between-S PRE which, in our studies at least, is marked by a sharp difference in responding at the first extinction point. If this difference in extinction effects is genuine and characteristic of the two procedures, it would seem to point to at least some involvement of primary stimulus generalization in the GPRE. The reasoning behind such an assertion, developed by Rashotte, depends on the idea that some specific, relatively weak, strength of r_F generalizes to S_2 in acquisition and that, therefore, some particular weak strength of s_F is conditioned to approach in within-S acquisition. As long as r_F strength to S_2 does not go above this value in extinction, responding to S_2 (the continuous stimulus) stays up with responding to S_1, providing a GPRE in early extinction trials. Once extinction progresses, however, and r_F to S_2 becomes stronger, an aversive reaction to S_2 sets in and S extinguishes faster to S_2 than to S_1, which has been evoking a much stronger r_F in acquisition and has therefore been a stimulus for persistence in the face of stronger r_F ($s_F \rightarrow$ approach).

The explanation for the differences among the three groups of Rashotte's Experiment 2 in these terms would hinge on the amount of generalization of r_F from W to B, from Run_1 to Run_2, and from Climb to Run_2 in acquisition. It is reasonable to suppose that the degree of generalization would, for the order given, be decreasing, and that the duration of the GPRE in extinction would also, therefore, follow this order.

2. A More Direct Approach to the Study of the Mediating Properties of r_F–s_F

As I suggested earlier, there is another more direct way of studying the hypothesis that s_F acts as a powerful mediator of persistence effects in within-S experiments. The procedure that Rashotte and I employed in this new type of study borrows rather heavily from a procedure developed by Logan (1960), which he terms *discontinuously negatively correlated reinforcement* and which we will abbreviate DNC. The DNC procedure, as Logan developed it, is to run rats in an alley and to reinforce them at the end only if they take longer than a certain number of seconds to get to the goal. This procedure is, of course, somewhat analogous to the differential reinforcement of low rates (DRL) types of schedule used by Skinnerians in the operant conditioning situation. We have used this DNC method as the kind of response required of an animal to one of the two stimulus alleys. In the other stimulus alley S runs the alley for CRF in the usual way. In our terminology, therefore, the procedure would be designated S_1DNC–S_2100, the percentage of reinforcement to S_1 being dependent on the success the animal has in learning to run slowly to S_1.

From our point of view, the situation is one in which the subject must learn to run slowly in the presence of S_1 to cues signaling frustration if he is to be rewarded. It was our hope when we started these experiments that this particular procedure would yield patterns of responding to S_1 that would be idiosyncratic; that each S would learn a different pattern of responding to S_1, and that these patterns would be Ss' means of delaying for the 5 sec necessary to receive a reward at the end of that alley. If s_F cues do in fact control such responding in this kind of situation, and if we find subjects who show very different patterns of responding to S_1 and S_2 in the acquisition phase of this kind of an experiment, we are then in a position to look at the within-S extinction performance of such animals and determine whether, under extinction conditions, the response pattern learned to S_1 transfers to S_2 under conditions of continuous nonreward.

Several subjects have now been run under these conditions and Fig. 24 shows the data from a single S who seems to show quite clearly the

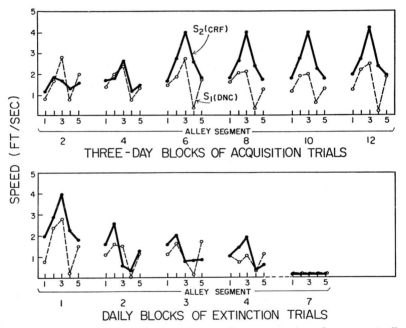

Fig. 24. Acquisition and extinction of a running response in a five-segment alley when reward is continuous for response to S_2 and discontinuously negatively correlated with response to S_1.

kinds of effect we anticipated. These data are presented here, not as evidence that our position has been supported by such experiments, but rather to indicate that the technique does seem to have some promise.

In these experiments we use the five-segment alley and take five response measures. The advantages of using such an alley for these experiments should be clear: it allows the plotting of a profile for each

S showing speed of response on the ordinate and segment of the alley on the abscissa. One thing is clear in these experiments: for most of the Ss a profile of responding does emerge on S_1 (DNC) trials which is quite different from the profile on S_2 (CRF) trials. The S_2 response profile is almost always the same and can be described as an inverted V. As might be expected, speeds are greatest in the middle segment and fall off toward the start and goal. The profile to the DNC stimulus is interesting in that it departs from this inverted-V conformation. In the case presented (Fig. 24), DNC performance at the end of acquisition can be described as a flatter profile of response measures with a sharp drop in speed at Measure 4, the segment just before the goal measure. The DNC profile does not, however, tell the whole story. Rashotte, who conducted these experiments, reports, as Logan had earlier, that each animal seems to adopt a rather specific mode of adjustment to the DNC situation in this within-S type of experimentation. The important thing to determine in the long run is whether the particular response pattern of an animal to S_1DNC conditions, a pattern clearly not in evidence to S_2 during acquisition, does tend to emerge in extinction to S_2. This kind of phenomenon, if established, would seem to require an explanation in terms of some sort of mediational process activated by the extinction procedure.

V. Summary and Concluding Comments

In this chapter I have had the opportunity to bring together for discussion the findings from several experiments conducted in our laboratory over the past two or three years. The experiments also have in common (a) that they were suggested by a conditioning-model theory of positive and negative incentive effects, and (b) that they involved within-subject comparisons of the effects of differential percentage or differential magnitude of reward: they were, in a sense, within-subject partial reinforcement experiments.

After reviewing the kind of theorizing on which the experiments were based, I have tried to make the case that the kinds of phenomena observed in differential reward training can best be described in terms of three behavioral dimensions—intensity (vigor), persistence, and direction (choice)—and have suggested that a profitable study of vigor effects could be made in procedures defining within-subject acquisition, and that persistence effects, particularly the transfer of persistence effects, could be inferred from extinction following within-subject acquisition. The experiments presented were, then, selected because they seemed to have something to say about vigor effects in differential reward training and persistence effects in extinction following such training.

The acquisition findings suggest that there are differences in patterns of response intensity to stimuli that signal partial reward and stimuli that signal continuous reward within the individual subject. These patterns of intensity differences in the within-subject partial reinforcement experiment are in some respects similar to, but in many respects different from, comparable patterns in between-subjects experiments. Some interesting acquisition findings were also reported from an experiment that varied, within subjects, not percentage of reward, but magnitude of reward. Certain differences between the within-subjects percentage of reward and magnitude of reward findings suggested that, although conflict (or uncertainty) is a factor in response to a stimulus signaling lesser percentage of reward, it does not seem to be a factor affecting response to a stimulus signaling lesser magnitude of reward in within-subjects experiments.

An analysis of extinction findings from within-subjects experiments brought to light one major difference between these and the typical between-subjects extinction result: under ordinary circumstances it is difficult, if not impossible, to demonstrate a within-subject partial reinforcement extinction effect. Our results and those of others suggest that this is due to a generalization of the PRE in extinction from the stimulus signaling partial reward to that signaling continuous reward. It would seem that there are two possible explanations for this generalized partial reinforcement effect in within-subject experiments: primary stimulus generalization and secondary (mediated) stimulus generalization; and these alternatives were evaluated in the light of current available evidence. It was pointed out that these are not incompatible interpretations of a generalized partial reinforcement effect. The weight of our earlier evidence on this issue seemed to favor an interpretation in terms of mediated generalization, but some more recent experiments indicate that the issue is still very much an open one, requiring further experimental investigation and theoretical analysis.

REFERENCES

Amsel, A. A three-factor theory of inhibition: An addition to Hull's two-factor theory. Paper delivered at Southern Soc. for Phil. and Psychol. Meetings, Roanoke, 1951.

Amsel, A. The role of frustrative nonreward in noncontinuous reward situations. *Psychol. Bull.*, 1958, **55**, 102–119.

Amsel, A. Frustrative nonreward in partial reinforcement and discrimination learning: Some recent history and a theoretical extension. *Psychol. Rev.*, 1962, **69**, 306–328.

Amsel, A. Partial reinforcement acquisition and extinction effects under within-subject and between-subject conditions. Paper presented at Psychon. Soc. Meeting, Niagara Falls, 1964.

Amsel, A. On inductive versus deductive approaches and neo-Hullian behaviorism. In B. B. Wolman (Ed.), *Scientific Psychology*. New York: Basic Books, 1965. Pp. 187–206.

Amsel, A., MacKinnon, J. R., Rashotte, M. E., & Surridge, C. T. Partial reinforcement (acquisition) effects within subjects. *J. exp. Anal. Behav.*, 1964, **7**, 135–138.

Amsel, A., & Prouty, D. L. Frustrative factors in selective learning with reward and nonreward as discriminanda. *J. exp. Psychol.*, 1959, **57**, 224–230.

Amsel, A., Rashotte, M. E., & MacKinnon, J. R. Partial reinforcement effects within-subject and between-subjects. *Psychol. Monogr.*, 1966, **79**, No. 20 (whole No. 628).

Amsel, A., & Roussel, J. Motivational properties of frustration: I. Effect on a running response of the addition of frustration to the motivational complex. *J. exp. Psychol.*, 1952, **43**, 363–368.

Amsel, A., & Surridge, C. T. The influence of magnitude of reward on the aversive properties of anticipatory frustration. *Canad. J. Psychol.*, 1964, **18**, 321–327.

Amsel, A., & Ward, J. S. Motivational properties of frustration: II. Frustration drive stimulus and frustration reduction in selective learning. *J. exp. Psychol.*, 1954, **48**, 37–47.

Amsel, A., & Ward, J. S. Frustration and persistence: Resistance to discrimination following prior experience with the discriminanda. *Psychol. Monogr.*, 1965, **79**, No. 4 (Whole No. 597).

Berlyne, D. E. *Conflict, arousal and curiosity*. New York: McGraw-Hill, 1960.

Bitterman, M. E., Fedderson, W. E., & Tyler, D. W. Secondary reinforcement and the discrimination hypothesis. *Amer. J. Psychol.*, 1953, **66**, 456–464.

Bloomfield, T. M. Two types of behavioral contrast in discrimination learning. *J. exp. Anal. Behav.*, 1966, **9**, 155–161.

Brown, J. S. *The motivation of behavior*. New York: McGraw-Hill, 1961.

Brown, R. T., & Logan, F. A. Generalized partial reinforcement effect. *J. comp. physiol. Psychol.*, 1965, **60**, 64–69.

Capaldi, E. J. Partial reinforcement: A hypothesis of sequential effects. *Psychol. Rev.*, 1966, **73**, 459–477.

Elam, C. B., Tyler, D. W., & Bitterman, M. E. A further study of secondary reinforcement and the discrimination hypothesis. *J. comp. physiol. Psychol.*, 1954, **47**, 381–384.

Estes, W. K. The statistical approach to learning theory. In S. Koch (Ed.), *Psychology: A study of a science*. Vol. 2. *General systematic formulations, learning, and special processes*. New York: McGraw-Hill, 1959. Pp. 380–491.

Ferster, C. B., & Skinner, B. F. *Schedules of reinforcement*. New York: Appleton, 1957.

Galbraith, K. Within-subject acquisition and extinction performance under three conditions of percentage reward to the partial stimulus in a split alley apparatus. Master's thesis, Univer. of Toronto, 1966.

Goldstein, H., & Spence, K. W. Performance in differential conditioning as a function of variation in magnitude of reward. *J. exp. Psychol.*, 1963, **65**, 86–93.

Goodrich, K. P. Performance in different segments of an instrumental response chain as a function of reinforcement schedule. *J. exp. Psychol.*, 1959, **57**, 57–63.

Grice, G. R., & Hunter, J. J. Stimulus intensity effects depend upon the type of experimental design. *Psychol. Rev.*, 1964, **71**, 247–256.

Haggard, D. F. Acquisition of a simple running response as a function of partial and continuous schedules of reinforcement. *Psychol. Rec.*, 1959, 9, 11–18.

Hebb, D. O. Drives and the C.N.S. (conceptual nervous system). *Psychol. Rev.*, 1955, 62, 243–254.

Henderson, K. Within-subjects partial-reinforcement effects in acquisition and in later discrimination learning. *J. exp. Psychol.*, 1966, 72, 704–713.

Hull, C. L. *Principles of behavior.* New York: Appleton, 1943.

Hull, C. L. *A behavior system.* New Haven: Yale Univer. Press, 1952.

Humphreys, L. G. The effect of random alternation of reinforcement on the acquisition and extinction of conditioned eyelid reactions. *J. exp. Psychol.*, 1939, 25, 141–158. (a)

Humphreys, L. G. Acquisition and extinction of verbal expectations in a situation analogous to conditioning. *J. exp. Psychol.*, 1939, 25, 294–301. (b)

Humphreys, L. G. Extinction of conditioned psychogalvanic responses following two conditions of reinforcement. *J. exp. Psychol.*, 1940, 27, 71–75.

Humphreys, L. G. The strength of a Thorndikian response as a function of the number of practice trials. *J. comp. physiol. Psychol.*, 1943, 35, 101–110.

Jenkins, H. M. The effect of discrimination training on extinction. *J. exp. Psychol.*, 1961, 61, 111–121.

Jenkins, W. O., & Stanley, J. C., Jr. Partial reinforcement: A review and a critique. *Psychol. Bull.*, 1950, 47, 193–234.

Kendler, H. H., Pliskoff, S. S., D'Amato, M. R., & Katz, S. Nonreinforcements versus reinforcements as variables in the partial reinforcement effect. *J. exp. Psychol.*, 1957, 53, 269–276.

Kolesnik, B., & Amsel, A. A "split-alley" technique for equating brightness in a visual discrimination task. *Psychon. Sci.*, 1966, 5, 187–188.

Lachman, R. The model in theory construction. *Psychol. Rev.*, 1960, 67, 113–129.

Lawrence, D. H., & Festinger, L. *Deterrents and reinforcement—the psychology of insufficient reward.* Stanford: Stanford Univer. Press, 1962.

Logan, F. A. A micromolar approach to behavior theory. *Psychol. Rev.*, 1956, 63, 63–73.

Logan, F. A. *Incentive.* New Haven: Yale Univer. Press, 1960.

MacKinnon, J. R. Acquisition and extinction performance to one discriminandum as a function of reward value associated with the other. Doctoral thesis, Univer. of Toronto, 1965.

MacKinnon, J. R. Personal communication, 1966.

Martin, B. Reward and punishment associated with the same goal response: A factor in the learning of motives. *Psychol. Bull.*, 1963, 60, 441–451.

Miller, N. E. Liberalization of basic S-R concepts: Extensions to conflict behavior, motivation, and social learning. In S. Koch (Ed.), *Psychology: A study of a science.* Vol. 2. *General systematic formulations, learning, and special processes.* New York: McGraw-Hill, 1959. Pp. 196–292.

Mowrer, O. H. *Learning theory and behavior.* New York: Wiley, 1960.

Pavlik, W. B., & Carlton, P. L. A reversed partial-reinforcement effect. *J. exp. Psychol.*, 1965, 70, 417–423.

Pavlik, W. B., Carlton, P. L., & Hughes, R. A. Partial reinforcement effects in a runway: between- and within-Ss. *Psychon. Sci.*, 1965, 3, 203–204. (a)

Pavlik, W. B., Carlton, P. L., & Manto, P. G. A further study of the partial reinforcement effect within subjects. *Psychon. Sci.*, 1965, 3, 533–534. (b)

Pavlov, I. P. *Conditioned reflexes.* (Translated by G. V. Anrep) London & New York: Oxford Univer. Press, 1927.

Peckham, R. H., & Amsel, A. The within-*S* demonstration of a relationship between frustration and magnitude of reward in a differential magnitude of reward discrimination. *J. exp. Psychol.,* 1967, **73,** 187–195.

Rashotte, M. E. Frustrative factors in persistence: Within- and between-*S* comparisons. Doctoral thesis, Univer. of Toronto, 1966.

Ross, R. R. Positive and negative partial-reinforcement extinction effects carried through continuous reinforcement, changed motivation, and changed response. *J. exp. Psychol.,* 1964, **68,** 492–502.

Skinner, B. F. *The behavior of organisms: An experimental analysis.* New York: Appleton, 1938.

Spear, N. E., & Pavlik, W. B. Percentage of reinforcement and reward magnitude effects in a T maze: Between and within subjects. *J. exp. Psychol.,* 1966, **71,** 521–528.

Spence, K. W. The nature of discrimination learning in animals. *Psychol. Rev.,* 1936, **43,** 427–449.

Spence, K. W. *Behavior theory and conditioning.* New Haven: Yale Univer. Press, 1956.

Spence, K. W. A theory of emotionally based drive (D) and its relation to performance in simple learning situations. *Amer. Psychologist,* 1958, **13,** 131–141.

Spence, K. W. *Behavior theory and learning.* Englewood Cliffs, N.J.: Prentice-Hall, 1960.

Theios, J. The partial reinforcement effect sustained through blocks of continuous reinforcement. *J. exp. Psychol.,* 1962, **64,** 1–6.

Theios, J., & Blosser, D. An incentive model for the overlearning reversal effect. *Psychon. Sci.,* 1965, **2,** 37–38.

Theios, J., & Brelsford, J. Overlearning-extinction effect as an incentive phenomenon. *J. exp. Psychol.,* 1964, **67,** 463–467.

Tyler, D. E., Wortz, E. C., & Bitterman, M. E. The effect of random and alternating partial reinforcement on resistance to extinction in the rat. *Amer. J. Psychol.,* 1953, **66,** 57–65.

Wagner, A. R. The role of reinforcement and nonreinforcement in an "apparent frustration effect." *J. exp. Psychol.,* 1959, **57,** 130–136.

Wagner, A. R. Effects of amount and percentage of reinforcement and number of acquisition trials on conditioning and extinction. *J. exp. Psychol.,* 1961, **62,** 234–242.

Weinstock, S. Resistance to extinction of a running response following partial reinforcement under widely spaced trials. *J. comp. physiol. Psychol.,* 1954, **47,** 318–322.

Weinstock, S. Acquisition and extinction of a partially reinforced running response at a 24-hour intertrial interval. *J. exp. Psychol.,* 1958, **56,** 151–158.

A SEQUENTIAL HYPOTHESIS OF
INSTRUMENTAL LEARNING[1]

E. J. Capaldi

UNIVERSITY OF TEXAS
AUSTIN, TEXAS

I. Introduction

A. PURPOSES

According to the present hypothesis, performance on some trial Tn is regulated extensively by stimuli contributed from earlier or preceding trials in the series (such as Tn-1, Tn-2, and so on). Although not itself unique, the emphasis given this proposition within the present framework and particularly the auxiliary or supporting assumptions entertained in connection with it are distinctive. Several terms may be used to describe the present approach, such as sequential, trial-dependent, and intertrial. (The respective opposite terms are nonsequential, trial-independent, and intratrial.) We understand these several terms to be roughly synonymous and to mean that the stimulus complex, and therefore performance, on Tn is determined by the specific order of occurrence of earlier trials in the series. It seems probable that few if any current

[1] This work was supported in part by National Institute of Child Health and Human Development Research Grant HD 00949-02.

hypotheses would deny this. For example, many current theories would expect performance on Tn to differ as a function of the following two circumstances: Tn-1 rewarded, Tn-2 nonrewarded versus Tn-1 nonrewarded, Tn-2 rewarded. Nevertheless, earlier writers (e.g., Katz, 1957; Lawrence, 1958; Surridge & Amsel, 1965) have tended to distinguish sharply between intertrial and intratrial theories. From the present point of view, qualitative distinctions of the type that have been drawn are not entirely satisfactory; we tend to view the differences between the two approaches as one of degree or emphasis. Obviously, however, the differing emphases are considered important, and for this reason terms such as sequential will be employed, even though, as we will attempt to show later, such terminology is not particularly appropriate for differentiating the two approaches, except in a general way.

This paper has two purposes, one general, the other specific. The general purpose is to clarify the sequential mode of theorizing insofar as possible. This clarification can be accomplished in part by the more specific purpose, which is to apply the present hypothesis to a variety of learning situations. However, the more general purpose can be accomplished more feasibly in some respects by a variety of other devices. One such device is to break down or minimize the more or less qualitative characteristics normally advanced to distinguish between sequential and nonsequential hypotheses. Another is to apply the present hypothesis to a variety of experiments designed within a nonsequential framework and used to support nonsequential hypotheses. We shall attempt to show at various places in this paper that such "nonsequential" experiments can be given a sequential interpretation.

In line with the more specific purpose, earlier sections of this paper will deal with the reward variables: magnitude of reward; delay of reward; and nonreward. Later sections will use an issue we have raised and touched upon previously (Capaldi, 1965) as a springboard or framework for introducing and interpreting a variety of other learning phenomena, including relearning, pattern learning, the successive acquisition and extinction of habits, and still other classes of data. The issue itself is whether the response decrement accompanying repeated nonreward is due to "extinction" rather than to a progressive change in the stimulus complex (generalization decrement). We understand by the term extinction that nonreward results in either the unlearning of previously established S-R connections or the learning of new S-R connections, or both. On the basis of available data, particularly unpublished data from our laboratory, we feel reasonably confident that not all of the response decrement accompanying repeated nonreward is due to extinction; the conditions under which extinction occurs and indeed the extent to which it occurs constitute, however, an open question. It should be noted at this point that in earlier sections of this paper we shall employ such terms as extinction and resistance to extinction in the way they are ordinarily used in the literature. In later sections of the paper, ordinary usage will be dropped in favor of what is considered to be more precise usage.

Sequential and nonsequential theories normally emphasize different classes of independent variables. Considering partial reward (PR), for example, a nonsequential theory such as the dissonance hypothesis (Lawrence & Festinger, 1962) suggests that resistance to extinction (Rn) is regulated by total number of nonrewards regardless, apparently, of their sequence or order. Where the dissonance hypothesis sees the sequence of nonrewards as irrelevant, the present hypothesis sees number of nonrewards as irrelevant. That is, the present view suggests that Rn is extensively regulated by the number of nonrewards occurring in succession (N-length) with total number of nonrewards acting to limit the size of the N-length or the number of the N-lengths that may be employed in a particular reward schedule. Differing emphases of this sort are of course inevitable, for it is one of the functions of theory to suggest which variables are and which are not significant. An investigation viewed as important in one context may be seen as irrelevant or trite in another.

We raise these matters mainly to indicate that in order to be understood, sequential investigations typically require a somewhat different mental set than do nonsequential investigations. Questions that are entirely reasonable and straightforward in a nonsequential context may seem bizarre in a sequential context, and vice versa. For example, it makes perfectly good sense to ask, in a nonsequential context, if Rn is increased by increased magnitude of PR. A question of that sort could not, however, be raised in a sequential context. A sequential theorist would want to know, for example, if large reward preceded or followed nonreward? This concern, often a detailed concern with the specific order of occurrence of trials, is characteristic of the present approach. Thus a sequential orientation is in some respects a great deal of trouble and often requires painstaking attention to details considered irrelevant in other approaches.

B. Sequential versus Nonsequential Theories

1. *Functional Similarity*

A great deal of what follows depends on an understanding of the specific sense in which the present hypothesis may be called an intertrial, as opposed to an intratrial, hypothesis. Accordingly, we will deal with this issue at the outset. Initially an attempt will be made to show that the distinction between the two modes of theorizing is not qualitative. Following that, what in our view appear to be the quantitative differences between the two approaches will be considered. According to a variety of sources in the literature (e.g., Katz, 1957; Lawrence, 1958; Surridge & Amsel, 1965), intertrial and intratrial theories differ as follows.

(1) Intertrial theory assumes that a portion of the stimulus complex occurring on Tn is determined by Tn-1, whereas intratrial theory makes no such assumption.

(2) Intertrial theory assumes that the stimuli related to Tn-1, and so on, are conditioned on the subsequent trial (Tn), whereas intratrial theory assumes that conditioning always occurs on a trial.

Our view is that neither of the foregoing propositions constitutes a satisfactory or accurate statement of the differences between the two modes of theorizing.

It appears (e.g., Surridge & Amsel, 1965) that the stimulus trace mechanism (Hull, 1952; Sheffield, 1949) constitutes an example of intertrial theorizing, whereas the mediating or anticipatory reaction hypothesis (r_g-s_g) constitutes an example of intratrial theorizing. Let us deal initially with the trace conception.

It is generally recognized, in connection with the trace, that on the basis of the reward outcome on Tn-1 stimuli are occasioned that perseverate briefly and that may be conditioned to the instrumental response occurring on Tn. Thus the trace conception conforms with propositions 1 and 2. Consider now the mediating reaction. Does mediating reaction theory imply that the stimulus complex on Tn is totally independent of the reward outcome on Tn-1? It appears not. A demonstration of this is relatively simple. Assume that the strength of r_g on Tn-1 is zero and that Tn-1 culminates in reward. Clearly on Tn-1 there will be no r_g and consequently no s_g. However, on Tn-1 the animal eats (R_G) and consequently on Tn there will be evoked a small r_g that produces its characteristic s_g. Thus, as can be seen, the mediating reaction position assumes that the stimulus complex on Tn will be some function of the reward outcome on Tn-1. Let us now deal with the second of the two distinctions. Does the mediating reaction position assert that the stimuli occasioned on Tn-1 (that is, s_g) will be conditioned on Tn-1, only on Tn-1, and not on Tn? Again it appears not. Recognize first that the stimulus s_g could not be conditioned to the instrumental response on Tn-1, since the instrumental response was "executed" before s_g came into existence. Clearly, however, s_g

can and should be conditioned to the instrumental response on Tn, since both s_g and the instrumental response occur simultaneously. Thus it can be seen that both the trace mechanism and the mediating reaction mechanism provide that a stimulus occasioned by events on Tn-1 will become conditioned to the instrumental reaction on trials following Tn-1.

From a functional standpoint, stimulus traces and mediating reactions are quite similar, as the considerations just advanced indicate. What then is the distinction between intertrial and intratrial theorizing? Let us consider two properties normally assigned to traces and mediating reactions, properties that we shall call temporality and responsivity, respectively. Although temporality will be considered first, the present view is that the distinction between the two modes of theorizing lies ultimately in assumptions entertained in connection with responsivity.

2. Temporality

The trace is assumed to dissipate rapidly. That is, events occurring on Tn-1 are considered capable of influencing the stimulus complex preceding Tn if and only if the intertrial interval (ITI) separating Tn-1 and Tn is short. Mediating reactions, however, are considered able to bridge long time gaps—how long, and what the effects of ITI might be on r_g and consequently s_g, are issues that do not appear to have been directly raised in the literature. A common, indeed almost universal, view is that intertrial or sequential theorizing may be feasible under short ITIs (traces), but not under long ITIs (mediating reactions). On the basis of earlier discussion the error of this view is obvious. First, mediating reactions could in fact form the basis of a sequential hypothesis. Moreover, since the mediating reaction is considered to be relatively unaffected by ITI it could be incorporated into a sequential hypothesis that is more general than one employing the trace notion. What prevents the mediating reaction from being regarded as an intertrial rather than an intratrial mechanism? The answer seems to lie in assumptions entertained in connection with the second of the properties to be considered, responsivity.

3. Responsivity

Responsivity has two distinguishable aspects, magnitude and latency. Magnitude of responsivity may be said to be high when the stimuli contributed by previous trials have a strong effect on current performance. Attributing a depression effect, for example, to the frustrative stimuli occasioned by one or two small rewarded trials following an "expectation" of large reward (e.g., Crespi, 1944) constitutes an instance of high magnitude of responsivity.

Latency of responsivity may vary between zero and one. Let us contrast latency of responsivity in traces and mediating reactions by consulting Table I, which shows the effects of administering six learning trials (Tn-5 through Tn), of which the initial four are rewarded (R) and the fifth nonrewarded (N), when latency of responsivity is one (traces) and when it is somewhere between one and zero (mediating reactions). Latency of responsivity is said to be one in the trace because the stimulus trace occurring on a given trial is totally determined by the reward outcome on the previous trial. Thus, for example, the stimulus trace preceding Tn-4 is that of reward (S^R) because Tn-5 was a rewarded trial. And the stimulus trace preceding Tn is that of nonreward (S^N) because Tn-1 was a nonrewarded trial. In other

TABLE I

REWARD OUTCOME AND RESPONSIVITY

Trial	Reward outcome	Trace	Mediating reaction
Tn-5	R	—	—
Tn-4	R	S^R	s_g^1
Tn-3	R	S^R	s_g^2
Tn-2	R	S^R	s_g^3
Tn-1	N	S^R	s_g^4
Tn		S^N	s_g^{4-x}

words, latency of responsivity is one when "carry-over effects" (e.g., S^R or s_g) are entirely due to the last trial in the series (Tn-1) and the carry-over effects are entirely independent of earlier trials in the series, such as Tn-2. Hull and Sheffield in their consideration of the trace appear to have assumed responsivity to be one or very close to one.

The mediating reaction presents a slightly different picture. First, it becomes progressively stronger as a function of prior rewards—this increased strength is represented in Table I as s_g^1, s_g^2, and so on. It is to be understood that s_g^2 is produced by a stronger mediating reaction (two prior rewards) than is s_g^1 (one prior reward). Another index of the low responsivity normally assigned mediating reactions is that the nonrewarded trial (Tn-1) reduces the strength of the mediating reaction by a slight (and, on the basis of current information, indeterminate) amount (s_g^{4-x}) rather than converting it to the equivalent of S^N, namely, s_{ng}.

In order for a theory to utilize sequential variables practically, it is apparently necessary to assume, first, that magnitude of responsivity is high, and second, that latency of responsivity is high. It could be argued, for example, that Hull introduced the trace conception when the highly similar mediating reaction mechanism was already at hand merely to provide for high magnitude and latency of responsivity, properties he, and subsequently others, did not believe to be characteristic of mediating reactions. Let us attend to Table II, which is a 2×2 contingency table showing two levels of responsivity (high–low) and two levels of temporality (long–short). Table II shows that the mediating reaction (Hull, 1930) is normally considered to possess low responsivity in connection with long temporality, whereas traces are assigned high responsivity in combination with short temporality. The present assumption is one of high responsivity in combination with long temporality. Apparently, as Table II shows, the assumption

TABLE II

RESPONSIVITY AND TEMPORALITY

| Temporality | Responsivity | |
	High	Low
Long	Present assumption	Mediating reactions (Hull)
Short	Stimulus traces (Hull-Sheffield)	Not assumed (?)

of low responsivity and short temporality has not been entertained as yet. We shall say one further word on this subject, thus anticipating a topic to be dealt with at greater length later in this paper: The notion that the mediating reaction is acquired slowly and extinguishes slowly (that is, has low responsivity) seems to be based on an analogy between the mediating reaction on the one hand and the instrumental reaction (R_I) on the other. Normally it appears to be assumed that if R_I is weak, r_g is weak, and if R_I is strong, r_g is strong. Generally, then, it appears to be assumed that R_I and r_g possess roughly similar, or even closely identical, learning and extinction rates. This assumption is far from necessary; indeed we specifically reject it, assuming instead that expectancy learning (that is, r_g) occurs more rapidly than instrumental learning (R_I).

C. SALIENT BACKGROUND ASSUMPTIONS

It seems desirable for a variety of reasons to consider several salient background assumptions of the hypothesis. One of the systematically more important assumptions is that each condition of immediate reward, delayed reward, and nonreward occasions a specific internal stimulus (Capaldi, 1966a). Further, successive reward events, such as successive nonrewards, also provide specific stimuli (Capaldi, 1964). Like all stimuli, these are conditioned to the instrumental reaction on rewarded trials. A "hard" principle of reinforcement is entertained. That is, it is assumed that the limit to which associative strength may grow is an increasing function of reward magnitude. This assumption, it will be recognized, was entertained and then rejected by Hull (contrast Hull, 1943, with Hull, 1952) and has been more or less universally rejected in recent years. Later, an attempt will be made to demonstrate that a hard principle of reinforcement constitutes a viable theoretical position.

Nonreinforcement is assumed to occasion inhibition (I); the asymptotic value of I is assumed always to be less than that of associative strength, and the limit to which I may grow is a function of two variables: magnitude of reward and duration of nonrewarded confinement. Normally, however, I will not be emphasized; other mechanisms of the present hypothesis do much of the theoretical work assigned to I in alternative formulations. Currently, I is regarded as a relatively rare phenomenon; it may be generated only when the same stimulus is repeatedly and consistently associated with nonreward. Thus I is probably generated only following considerable training. It is also assumed that, as a mechanism for producing response decrement, I is probably considerably less important than generalization decrement. The present treatment draws heavily on the Spence (1936) theory of discrimination learning. In theoretical figures, I is represented by a dotted line, H (associative strength, or habit) by a solid line.

D. STIMULUS SPECIFICITY

It was assumed in the foregoing that each goal event supplies the organism with a specific internal stimulus (stimulus specificity hypothesis). This notion would not be particularly useful for deductive purposes in the absence of further specification of certain relationships between the stimuli involved. Only first steps, shown in Fig. 1, have been taken in this direction. Figure 1 shows a two-dimensional surface on which we have attempted to represent the way the various stimuli are ordered relative to each other; that is, the figure indicates the placement of these stimuli on the continuum or surface relative to one another.[2] It should be borne in mind that Fig. 1 presents only salient

[2] Distance between the various stimuli shown along the front face of the continuum are the same for all theoretical figures in this paper. However, the distance between

stimulus points and that intermediate stimuli occupy intermediate points on the continuum. Although the sort of information shown in Fig. 1 is useful for a variety of purposes, it has obvious limitations. Generally, Fig. 1 can be used to yield deductions concerning the order (e.g., in extinction) of one group relative to another. More precise deductions require a specification of 'the relative distances between adjacent points on the continuum, and so on. Specifications of this sort may or may not be feasible on the basis of current experimental information; in any event, we have not attempted to go very far in this direction. In rare cases, that is, in certain zones of the delay of reward portion of the continuum, it is not possible on the basis of current information to determine the relative position of one stimulus to another. Why this is so will become clear later.

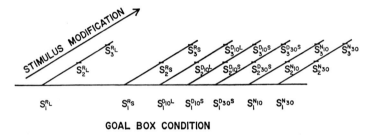

GOAL BOX CONDITION

Fig. 1. Stimulus continuum, showing the relative position of the stimulus consequences of immediate reward, delayed reward, and nonreward: the effect of a given reward in the goal box is shown along the front face of the continuum (goal box condition); the effect of successive rewards of the same type (stimulus modification) is shown running from front to back.

A review of the experimental evidence supporting the assumptions contained in Fig. 1 is not feasible in this section. The evidence is extensive and, generally speaking, scattered throughout later portions of the paper. For the moment the object is to make clear the functional implications of the assumptions contained in Fig. 1. It should be indicated at the outset that the notation used in Fig. 1 is cumbersome and normally needs to be employed only in special circumstances. We shall generally use a simpler notation where possible. For example, when referring simply to immediate reward, delay of reward, and nonreward, we shall write S^R, S^D, and S^N, respectively. The stimuli shown at the extreme left of the continuum,

---

stimuli for stimulus modification are greater in Fig. 1 than in subsequent theoretical figures for purely technical reasons, namely, to provide reasonable depth in the figure.

S_1^{RL} and S_1^{RS}, represent respectively the stimulus consequences of a single large and a single small magnitude of immediate reward. Thus, for example, following the consumption of a large immediate reward on Tn-1, the functional stimulus at the beginning of Tn would be S_1^{RL}. The stimulus S_1^{RL} will be conditioned to R_I on Tn provided Tn culminates in reward. And as indicated, the limit to which associative strength may grow is an increasing function of increasing reward magnitude on Tn. The stimuli S_2^{RL} and S_2^{RS} represent respectively the consequences of receiving two consecutive large or small rewards. The change undergone by the stimulus as a function of receiving two (e.g., S_2^{RL}) or three (e.g., S_3^{RL}) rewards of the same magnitude and delay or, in the case of nonrewards, of the same confinement duration in the goal box (S_1^{N10}, S_2^{N10}, and so on) is termed stimulus modification (Capaldi, 1964). Stimulus modification is assumed to occur according to a simple positive growth function. It is not to be expected that stimulus modification will be the same for all goal box conditions, that is, for immediate reward, delay of reward, and nonreward. Indeed stimulus modification may be a function of the apparatus employed. For example, an investigation by Capaldi (1964) employing the runway indicated that stimulus modification was complete in about 30–40 trials, whereas an investigation by Jensen (1964) using the discrete trial bar-press response suggested that modification might be occurring for about 100 trials. For convenience, the modification undergone by stimuli is shown in Fig. 1 for only three trials (S_1^{RL}, S_2^{RL}, S_3^{RL}). For non-rewarded stimuli, the modification process may continue for far longer, whereas for rewarded stimuli it might be complete following a relatively small number of trials. These are empirical matters to be determined by relevant experiments. Our major empirical and theoretical efforts thus far have been directed at determining the relative position of the various stimuli located along the front face of the continuum (goal box condition).

The stimulus S_1^{D10L} represents the stimulus consequent of a single 10-sec delay of large reward. It might be said then that the limiting case of a small magnitude of immediate reward is a short delay of a large magnitude of reward. The stimulus S_1^{D10S} represents the stimulus consequent of a single 10-sec delay of small reward, the stimulus S_1^{D30S} the stimulus consequent of a 30-second delay of small reward. Where on the continuum is the stimulus consequent of a 30-second delay of large reward (S_1^{D30L}) to be placed? This is difficult to say in the absence of a specific experimental investigation, since longer delays (such as 10, 30, and 60 seconds) drive the stimulus rightward on the continuum, whereas larger rewards drive it in the opposite direction. Thus it cannot be determined a priori whether a longer delay of large reward should be placed to the left or right of a shorter delay of small reward. The procedures for determining issues of this sort are, however, relatively straightforward. One of these, employing resistance to extinction (Rn) as a measure, is particularly clear. Other methods will be considered throughout the paper.

Consider a partial delay of reward investigation or one in which reward is given immediately on some portion of the trials and following a delay on the remaining portion of the trials. Assume that two groups are used and that on all trials, immediate or delayed, the magnitude of reward is the same. Let one group receive a 10-second delay of reward ($S^{D_{10}}$ conditioned to R_I), the other group a 30-second delay of reward. The H acquired at the stimulus points $S^{D_{10}}$ and $S^{D_{30}}$ respectively will generalize along the continuum ($\overline{H}$). In extinction the stimulus S^N occurs, that is, the stimulus consequence of some nonreinforced confinement duration in the goal box. Since S^N lies closer to $S^{D_{30}}$ than to $S^{D_{10}}$, it will receive more $\overline{H}$ from $S^{D_{30}}$ than from $S^{D_{10}}$. Accordingly, S^N will evoke a more vigorous response following training under a 30-second partial delay than following training under a 10-second partial delay. We can expect, therefore, that the 30-second partial delay group will show greater Rn than the 10-second partial delay group. Within the present framework, Rn is generally, a measure of the $\overline{H}$ supplied to S^N, and the $\overline{H}$ supplied is a function of several variables, one of the more salient of course being proximity along the continuum. Let us return to the matter of magnitude of delay versus length of delay, which led to the present discussion. It now can be indicated that if a 10-second delay of small reward occasioned greater Rn than a 30-second delay of large reward, this finding would suggest that $S^{D_{10}}S$ lies to the right of $S^{D_{30}}L$ on the continuum.

Regarding the nonreinforced portion of the continuum, it is assumed that the longer the goal box confinement duration on the nonrewarded trial (e.g., 10 seconds, 20 seconds, or 30 seconds, or longer) the farther rightward on the continuum is S^N driven. Thus it could be said that the limiting case of a long delay of small magnitude of reward is a short confinement duration on nonrewarded trials. As Fig. 1 shows, the stimulus consequent of a 30-second nonrewarded confinement ($S_1^{N_{30}}$) is placed to the right on the continuum of the stimulus consequent of a 10-second confinement on nonrewarded trials ($S_1^{N_{10}}$).

The continuum shown in Fig. 1 could be extended to include the stimulus consequences of punishment (S^P). We have not done so because punishment will not specifically be dealt with in this paper. Recent evidence (e.g., Banks, 1966; Brown & Wagner, 1964) suggests rather clearly, however, that S^P should be placed to the right of S^N, stronger punishments being placed increasingly farther to the right. That is, the limiting case of a long nonrewarded confinement appears to be a relatively mild punishment.

II. The Reward Variables

A. PARTIAL REWARD

1. Extinction

A detailed application of the present hypothesis to Rn following different numbers of training trials under different schedules of PR has already been attempted (Capaldi, 1966b). A familiarity with that treatment or with another by Capaldi (1964) would prove helpful to an understanding of the present discussion, although such prior familiarity is not necessary. Mainly the attempt will be made here to expand on those prior treatments by dealing with some previously considered topics more deeply or in a different way, by dealing with issues not previously raised, and by introducing several recent sources of confirming experimental evidence not then available.

When dealing with Rn following PR, it seems absolutely necessary to consider separately small and large numbers of acquisition trials. This is because there appears to be a schedule of reward $\times$ number of acquisition trials interaction such that the schedule producing the lesser Rn following a relatively small number of training trials produces the greater Rn following extensive training. A theory of PR that hopes to be general must account for both these effects using the same general principles. The treatment of small numbers of training trials will begin by employing a more or less abstract emphasis designed to explicate the general expectations of the hypothesis given certain general circumstances. Subsequently, the hypothesis will be applied to selected data in the area.

2. Small Numbers of Acquisition Trials

a. Theoretical Analysis. From the present viewpoint it cannot be said that 10, 20, 30, or 40 acquisition trials constitute a small number; that determination depends on factors other than number of training trials per se. Most obviously it depends on the learning rate parameter (F). Given a particular learning rate, it would then depend on the number of times the internal stimuli characteristic of reward (S^R) and of nonreward (S^N) are conditioned to R_I. The number of such conditionings will in turn depend on schedule of reward. The following terminology is adopted. Number of acquisition trials refers to the actual number of trials administered, independent of schedule of reward. N-length is defined as the number of nonrewarded trials that occur consecutively prior to a rewarded trial. In terms of the present hypothesis, training level is specified in terms of the number of times a particular N-length occurs. Another variable determining Rn is the number of different N-lengths contained in a particular schedule. In the schedules NR, NNR, and NNNR, N-length is one, two, and three, respectively. In the schedule NRNNR two different values of N-length occur (one and two).

Available data on rats in runways suggest that the major variable determining Rn following relatively brief acquisition training is the number of occurrences of N-length. Consider the two illustrative schedules (1) NRNRNR and (2) RNNNRR.

Each schedule contains three rewarded trials and three nonrewarded trials. Under schedule 1 there are three conditionings of S_1^N (S_1^N-R_I), under schedule 2 one conditioning of S_3^N (S_3^N-R_I). Employing Hull's (1943) equation for habit strength, assuming F, the growth parameter for H, = .25, and using other assumptions to be found elsewhere in connection with, for example, the shape of the generalization gradients (Capaldi, 1964; Capaldi, 1966b), the theoretical situation following training under schedules 1 and 2 is as shown in Fig. 2. The height of the vertical line

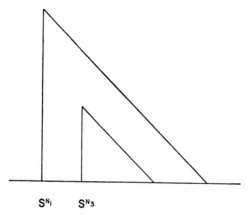

S^{N_1} S^{N_3}

Fig. 2. The effect of delivering three reinforcements at S_1^N versus one reinforcement at S_3^N when F = .25.

above S_1^N represents the amount of H accumulated at that stimulus point in group 1 (three conditionings, 56.25 units) and, correspondingly, the vertical line above S_3^N shows that 25 units of H (one conditioning) have been accumulated at that stimulus point in group 2. According to the present hypothesis, Rn is determined by the amount of generalized H ($\overline{H}$) supplied to the higher values of S^N occurring in extinction, such as S_{10}^N. It can be seen in Fig. 2 that these higher values of S^N are supplied more $\overline{H}$ from S_1^N (group 1) than from S_3^N (group 2). Thus group 1 should show greater Rn than group 2.

b. The Value of F. Rn following limited acquisition training will depend heavily on the value of F. Consider an extreme case. If $F = 1.00$, Rn will be determined exclusively by N-length, being greater, of course, the longer the N-length. If, as in the example given in the preceding paragraph, F has a moderate to large value, a shorter N-length that occurs more frequently will tend to produce greater Rn than a longer N-length that occurs less often. At the other extreme, where F is exceptionally small, it becomes possible for Rn to be greater following consistent reward than following partial reward. Consider a consistent group and a 50% partial group, each of which receives ten acquisition trials. If the partial schedule contains an N-length of five, we have nine conditionings of S^R in the consistent group as opposed to one conditioning of S_5^N in the partial group. It is intuitively obvious that as F decreases from a value of 1.00, it becomes possible for the nine conditionings at S^R to outweigh the one conditioning at S_5^N in supplying the higher values of S^N with $\overline{H}$, and thus in determining Rn. To determine what in fact should occur in extinction following limited training, it is necessary to have an estimate of F. For any value of F, Rn should undergo an orderly and predictable series of changes as a function of training level (Capaldi, 1964; Capaldi, 1966b).

Investigations from the Bryn Mawr laboratory employing fish (e.g., Longo & Bitterman, 1960) have shown Rn to be greater following consistent reward than following PR. These data suggest that F is small, either in fish or under the experimental conditions used at Bryn Mawr. Fortunately, as shall be seen when extended PR training is considered, independent evidence is available which suggests that F is indeed small in the Bryn Mawr investigations. The general principles just presented will now be applied to specific investigations dealing with relatively small numbers of training trials.

c. Experimental Evidence. Capaldi and Hart (1962) found that a 50% alternating schedule of N and R trials produced greater Rn than a 50% irregular schedule, following either 18 or 27 acquisition trials. The alternating group received 8 reinforcements at S_1^N in the 18-trial investigation and 12 at S_1^N in the 27-trial investigation, whereas the irregular group received either 2 reinforcements at S_2^N (18 trials) or 3 at S_2^N (27 trials). These results illustrate, as indicated earlier, that following limited training Rn is determined by number of occurrences of N-length. An examination of the reward schedules employed in Bacon's (1962) investigation, which showed, following 10 acquisition trials, that Rn increased as percentage of reward increased, indicated the following (Bacon, personal communication): The 70% group received three reinforcements at S_1^N; the 50% group, one at S_2^N and one at S_3^N; and the 30% group, one at S_7^N. Thus, Bacon's results indicate that following limited training, Rn is determined primarily by number of occurrences of N-length. A doctoral dissertation by Spivey (1964) demonstrated this even more clearly. Spivey used a 2×2 factorial design with two levels of percentage of reward (30% versus 70%), two levels of occurrences of N-length (one versus three) and, like Bacon, only 10 acquisition trials. Spivey found Rn to be independent of percentage of reward; however, number of occurrences of N-length increased Rn.

It is doubtful if, aside from the present hypothesis, any current hypothesis is capable of dealing with the experimental results just presented. The dissonance hypothesis (Lawrence & Festinger, 1962), which relates Rn to number of N trials, is obviously not supported by the small trial data. The frustration hypothesis (Amsel, 1958; Spence, 1960), as indicated by Black and Spence (1965), encounters difficulty in attempting to deduce differential Rn following relatively small numbers of training trials. The discrimination hypothesis (e.g., Gonzalez & Bitterman, 1964) appears unable to account for the small trial data. According to the discrimination hypothesis, Rn should be an increasing function of the difference between the acquisition series of events and the extinction series of events; thus the discrimination hypothesis, like the present hypothesis, identifies N-length as a variable controlling Rn. Following relatively brief training, however, long N-length groups tend to extinguish faster than short N-length groups, a finding deducible from the present hypothesis but not, apparently, from the discrimination hypothesis.

Investigations (Capaldi, Hart, & Stanley, 1963; Capaldi & Spivey, 1963; McCain, 1964; Spence, Platt, & Matsumoto, 1965) showing that following a relatively few training trials intertrial reinforcement (ITR) is capable of eliminating the increased Rn occasioned by PR offer strong support for the present hypothesis. Intertrial reinforcement consists in placing the rat in the baited goal box during the intertrial interval (ITI). The rationale for the ITR procedure provided by Capaldi et al. (1963) is as follows: placing the rat in a baited goal box during the ITI substitutes S^R for S^N; that is, if the previous trial was nonrewarded, the formerly operative stimulus S^N will be replaced by S^R. However, ITR will prevent S^N from becoming conditioned to R_I because R_I did not occur (that is, the S was placed in the goal box). Thus, if in a three-trial schedule RNR, ITR is given in the ITI between trials two and three, S^N is replaced by S^R and accordingly S^N will not be conditioned to R_I. Since the partial reinforcement effect of increased resistance to extinction is dependent, according to the present hypothesis, on the formation of the connection S^N-R_I, it follows that ITR should be capable of eliminating the increased Rn produced by PR. As indicated, ITR has been shown, in a number of investigations, to reduce Rn.

It is relatively clear, however, that the capacity of ITR to reduce Rn is limited to a relatively few PR training trials. Thus, when approximately 40 or fewer PR training trials have been used (Capaldi et al., 1963; Capaldi & Spivey, 1963; Spence et al., 1965) ITR has reduced Rn; however, when extensive training has been employed, ITR has failed to reduce Rn (Black & Spence, 1965; Spence et al., 1965). Unpublished investigations from our laboratory support the published findings in detail. These results are, as Black and Spence suggest, potentially important. That is, Black and Spence (1965) indicate that one interpretation of these results is as follows: intertrial factors such as S^N may regulate Rn in the early training trials; following extended training, however, Rn must be presumed to be regulated by some other factor or factors. They specifically suggest frustration. According to this view, following a number of rewarded trials, nonreward evokes a frustrative reaction and increased Rn is ultimately related to frustration. The implication of this view is that the present hypothesis has only a limited applicability, such applicability being limited to the early PR training trials prior to the development of frustration.

However, Spence et al. (1965) suggested still another interpretation, which does not imply that the applicability of the present hypothesis is restricted to small numbers of PR training trials. This interpretation begins by noting that, as number of PR training trials increases, ITR is of necessity employed increasingly more often. Eventually, perhaps because of discrimination, ITR no longer replaces S^N with S^R. Thus the S^N-R_I connection would be formed and increased Rn could be expected.

It is relatively simple to arrange an experimental test of the alternatives suggested by Spence et al. (1965). Simply stated, the frustration analysis attributes the decreased effectiveness of ITR to an increase in number of rewarded trials. The discrimination notion, however, attributes such decreased effectiveness to the repeated use of ITR. Olivier, in an unpublished investigation from our laboratory, separated these two variables quite nicely. Initially three groups of 12 Ss each were given 96 consistently rewarded trials. The purpose of this training, of course, was to build up a strong r_g, a necessary precondition for the development of frustration. Following this training, 30 additional trials were given, the control group C continuing to receive consistent reward. The remaining two groups were shifted to 50% partial reward. One PR group, PX, received ITR in all ITIs separating non-rewarded trials from rewarded trials (ITR replaces S^N with S^R and therefore increased Rn is not expected), while the other PR group, PY, was a control. Group PY received ITR only following rewarded trials and not following nonrewarded trials. It can be seen that in group PY, S^N is conditioned to R_I. Accordingly, group PY would be expected to show increased Rn. By employing only 30 PR training trials, Olivier had to administer only 7 ITRs. Thus, his experiment separated number of rewarded trials and the increased use of ITR quite effectively. It should be indicated that Olivier's procedure was quite similar, actually identical in most respects, to the procedure used by Capaldi et al. (1963). Indeed the major difference between Olivier's investigation and that by Capaldi et al., was that in the former investigation the 30 PR training trials were preceded by 96 consistently rewarded trials, whereas in the latter investigation, consistent reward training was not given. Differences among Olivier's groups on the last day of acquisition training (last 10 trials) were not significant ($F < 1.00$). The performance of the three groups on each of the three days of extinction (mean speed) is shown in Fig. 3.

The results are the same as those previously reported by Capaldi et al.; group PX failed to show increased Rn running as slow as group C, whereas group PY showed the increased Rn typically produced by partial reward. Analysis of variance indicated that differences between the groups were significant. However, a subsequent Duncan's range test indicated that only the differences involving group PY were

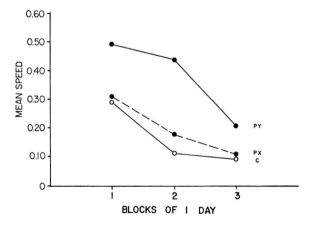

Fig. 3. Mean speed for three groups (see discussion in text) on each of three nonrewarded (extinction) days.

significant. Olivier's results thus suggest that the critical factor responsible for the failure of ITR to decrease Rn following considerable training is not number of rewarded trials per se but, as suggested by Spence et al. (1965), the repeated use of ITR. With repeated use, ITR apparently loses the capacity to replace S^N with S^R. This being so, it follows that under the extended training conditions used by Black and Spence (1965) and Spence et al. (1965) it may be assumed that the S^N-R_I connection was formed, and that the increased Rn observed by them is therefore to be expected, both by the present hypothesis and the frustration hypothesis. Accordingly, in the light of Olivier's results, the finding that ITR fails to reduce Rn following extensive PR training does not indicate that the applicability of the present hypothesis extends only to relatively small numbers of training trials.

3. Extended Number of Acquisition Trials

By extended training is meant that the H values of the various S^Ns conditioned to R_I are at or near asymptote; thus the number of trials required to produce extended training is given by the value of F. When all S^N-R_I connections are asymptotic (or otherwise equal), the hypothesis predicts that Rn will increase as N-length increases. The considerable body of data suggesting that Rn is an increasing function of N-length following extended training falls into two general categories: pattern and percentage. In patterning investigations, percentage of reward is held constant. It has been shown (Capaldi, 1966b) that when rewards and nonrewards are assigned according to some random procedure, N-length tends to increase as percentage of reward decreases. This probably accounts for the extended trial findings of Weinstock (1954; 1958), who found Rn to increase as percentage decreased. Extended trial patterning investigations showing Rn to increase as N-length increases have been reported by Bloom and Capaldi (1961), Capaldi (1964), and Tyler, Wortz, and Bitterman (1953). Capaldi and Stanley (1965) have shown that a higher percentage schedule containing longer N-lengths produced greater Rn than a lower percentage schedule containing shorter N-lengths; that is, the lower percentage actually produced less Rn. Gonzalez and Bitterman (1964) have shown Rn to increase as N-length increased with percentage equated.

Evidence bearing on the schedule of reward $\times$ number of acquisition trials interaction can now be indicated. Lower percentages having long N-lengths produce less Rn early in training (Bacon, 1962; Spivey, 1964) and greater Rn following extended training (e.g., Gonzalez &

Bitterman, 1964; Weinstock, 1954, 1958). Single alternating schedules produce greater Rn than irregular ones following limited training (Capaldi & Hart, 1962) and lesser Rn following extended training (Capaldi, 1958; Tyler et al., 1953). Thus it seems, as the present hypothesis suggests, that the schedule producing the lesser Rn early in training will produce the greater Rn later in training.

Studies from the Bryn Mawr laboratories (Gonzalez, Eskin, & Bitterman, 1963; Gonzalez, Graf, & Bitterman, 1965) using fish and birds have shown Rn to be an increasing function of N-length following extended training. These investigations have employed many more trials than have the rat studies considered earlier (see Capaldi, 1966b). Thus it appears that in the Bryn Mawr studies F was small. Assuming this, it can be explained, as previously indicated, why in other Bryn Mawr studies (e.g., Longo & Bitterman, 1960) consistent reward produced greater Rn than PR in the fish following relatively small numbers of training trials.

Aside from the present hypothesis, only the discrimination hypothesis (e.g., Gonzalez & Bitterman, 1964) has been applied to the extended trial findings in their entirety.

4. Magnitude of Partial Reward

Under irregular PR schedules, increased magnitude of reward produces increased Rn (e.g., Hulse, 1958; Wagner, 1961). According to the present view, associative strength is an increasing function of reward magnitude. Thus, large magnitude of PR (irregular schedule) produces greater Rn than small magnitude because the higher values of S^N occurring in extinction receive more $\bar{H}$ from the S^Ns conditioned by the large magnitude of reward than from the S^Ns conditioned by the small magnitude of reward. From the standpoint of the present hypothesis, the magnitude of PR findings of Hulse (1958) and Wagner (1961) are quite limited; many more experimental variations are possible that bear more directly on the present hypothesis. To mention two, schedule of PR may be varied, and not all rewarded trials in the schedule need be of the same magnitude. As an example of the first, consider the two three-trial schedules (1) RRN and (2) RNR.

S^N is conditioned to R_I under schedule 2 but not under schedule 1. Thus it is possible, in terms of the present hypothesis, that a small magnitude of reward in connection with schedule 2 would produce greater Rn than a large magnitude of reward in connection with schedule 1. Clearly, the present hypothesis does not always expect that under PR a large magnitude of reward will produce greater Rn than a small magnitude of reward.

Indeed there are instances where it may be expected that a large magnitude of PR will reduce Rn. Fortunately, experimental evidence in the form of a doctoral dissertation by Dale Leonard (1966) exists on this point. Leonard's design was a 2×2 factorial, but for the moment consider only two of his groups, (1) SNL and (2) LNS.

Leonard's rats (14 per group) received their daily trials in the straight alley, trial 1 (T1) receiving either large (L) or small (S) reward (two versus twenty-four .045-gm pellets), T2 always being nonrewarded (N), and T3 receiving either L or S reward (8 days of acquisition training). The intertrial interval was about 2 minutes. Three stimuli must be considered: that of small reward ($S^{R}s$), which in group 1 takes on inhibitory properties; that of large reward ($S^{R}L$), which in group 2 takes on inhibitory properties; and S^{N}, which takes on greater H in group 1 than in group 2. Considering S^{N} (conditioned on T3), group 1 should show greater Rn than group 2 (more H); thus the greater the magnitude of reward on T3 the greater should be the Rn. A clear prediction in connection with T1 magnitude, however, is not possible; $S^{R}L$ lies farther than $S^{R}s$ from S^{N} on the continuum (see Fig. 1), but according to an assumption introduced earlier (Section I, C), $S^{R}L$ will take on greater inhibitory properties (I) than $S^{R}s$. Rn will depend on the generalized I ($\bar{I}$) supplied to S^{N} and this in turn will depend, as shown in Fig. 4, on whether distance or amount of $\bar{I}$ is the more important consideration.

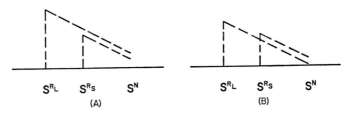

$S^{R}L$ $S^{R}s$ S^{N} $S^{R}L$ $S^{R}s$ S^{N}

(A)   (B)

Fig. 4. The generalization of I from $S^{R}L$ and $S^{R}s$; (A) shows that S^{N} is supplied greater $\bar{I}$ from $S^{R}L$ than from $S^{R}s$; (B) shows the opposite.

Figure 4A shows that S^{N} is supplied more $\bar{I}$ from $S^{R}L$ than from $S^{R}s$, Fig. 4B the opposite. Thus, Fig. 4A suggests that large magnitude on T1 will reduce Rn, Fig. 4B that small magnitude on T1 will reduce Rn. Leonard found that large magnitude of reward on T1 reduced Rn, thus suggesting that the situation shown in Fig. 4A is more nearly correct. Figure 5 presents Leonard's extinction speeds on the first trial of the day (E) and subsequently in blocks of three trials. All 22 extinction trials were administered on the same day. Groups LNL and SNS round out the 2×2 factorial design, giving two levels of reward magnitude on T1 (S or L) and two levels of reward magnitude on T3 (L or S). Specifically the four groups are LNL, LNS, SNL, and SNS.

Since in acquisition large reward on T3 produced faster acquisition speeds than small reward on T3 (T1 magnitude having only a small effect), speed scores were converted into rate measures (Anderson, 1963). A 2×2 factorial analysis of variance over these rate measures indicated that large magnitude on T1 significantly reduced Rn, whereas T3 magnitude had the opposite effect. Note, for example, that group LNS was slowest in extinction (little H for S^N, much $\bar{I}$ from S^R_L), while group SNL was fastest in extinction (much H for S^N, little I from S^R_S). The faster running of group LNL in extinction as contrasted with group SNS is consistent with the findings of Hulse (1958) and Wagner

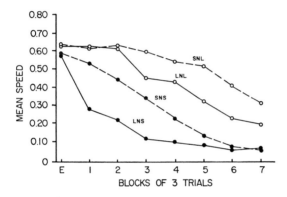

Fig. 5. Mean speed (inches per second) for each of the four groups on the initial nonrewarded trial and subsequently in blocks of three nonrewarded trials.

(1961); that is, these findings show that large reward preceding and following nonreward produces greater Rn than small reward preceding and following nonreward. Leonard's findings, taken together with those of Hulse and Wagner, support the following general conclusions. (1) Large reward following nonreward tends to increase Rn. (2) Large reward preceding nonreward tends to decrease Rn. (3) Schedule of reward and magnitude of reward jointly determine Rn.

It is difficult to determine at this time how other PR hypotheses might attempt to deal with Leonard's data. For example, the frustration hypothesis (Amsel, 1958; Spence, 1960), which relates Rn to the strength of the frustrative reaction, the strength of the frustrative reaction in turn being related to magnitude of reward, might order the four groups in extinction as follows: LNL $>$ LNS $=$ SNL $>$ SNS.

The actual order, of course, was SNL > LNL > SNS > LNS. Perhaps the frustration hypothesis might not wish to accept Leonard's results at face value because the highly ordered trial sequence employed in acquisition may have been anticipated by the rat. Although the ordered trial sequence per se may have influenced the results, it would be well to bear in mind that group LNL showed greater Rn than group SNS, a result similar to that obtained under irregular PR schedules. Another index of the influence of the pattern variable per se might be provided by using smaller numbers of acquisition trials (for example, 6 or 9 in contrast to Leonard's 24). Under limited training it would not be reasonable to assume that the rat would anticipate the trial sequence. It should be indicated that as the number of acquisition trials is progressively reduced, the influence of I is necessarily lessened. Accordingly, under conditions of limited training Rn would not be expected to be a function of T1 magnitude and could be expected to be more or less completely determined by T3 magnitude.

A recent study by Bloom (1966) confirmed and in some respects extended Leonard's findings. Bloom trained 56 rats for four trials each day (ITI = 30 seconds) in a straight alley. Table III gives the order

TABLE III

ORDER OF TRIAL OCCURRENCE EACH DAY[a]

Group	Trial			
	1	2	3	4
I	60N	60R	10N	10R
II	60N	10R	10N	60R

[a] After Bloom (1966).

of occurrence of the trials each day. Group I was always nonrewarded on T1 and confined to the goal box for 60 seconds. On T2 group I was always allowed 60-seconds access to .045-gm J. P. Noyes pellets. In group I, then, the stimulus $S^{N_{60}}$ was associated with large reward and took on relatively substantial H. Note, too, in group I that the 10-second nonrewarded confinement on T3 ($S^{N_{10}}$) was always followed by a smaller reward, 10-seconds access to pellets on T4. Thus, in group I $S^{N_{10}}$ took on relatively weak H. In group II the contingencies were reversed, the $S^{N_{60}}$ occasioned by T1 taking on relatively little H since it was followed on T2 by the smaller reward. However, the $S^{N_{10}}$ occasioned by T3 took on considerable H on T4 since T4 consisted of

60-second access to pellets. Thus, in Bloom's investigation the following "habit" contingencies prevailed for group I and group II.

Group I S^{N60} **H** R_I (strong) S^{N10} **H** R_I (weak)
Group II S^{N60} **H** R_I (weak) S^{N10} **H** R_I (strong)

Following 24 acquisition trials, the groups were extinguished, half the Ss in each group receiving 60 seconds of nonrewarded confinement, the remaining half, 10 seconds of nonrewarded confinement. There were six days of extinction training at four trials each day. The prediction of major current concern in Bloom's investigation was that the specific nonrewarded confinement followed by large reward would produce greater Rn than the nonrewarded confinement followed by small reward. Bloom obtained this result, as can be seen in Fig. 6, which shows

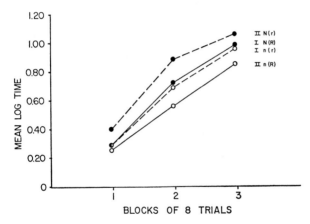

Fig. 6. Mean log time for each of four groups studied by Bloom (1966) during the nonrewarded phase in blocks of eight trials (see discussion in text).

mean log running time in the alley in blocks of eight trials. The group designations in extinction are as follows: group IIn(R) was the group II in original training, which received 10-second (n) rather than 60-second (N) confinement in extinction, and in acquisition (n) was followed by large (R) rather than small reward (r). It can be seen in Fig. 6 that 60-second confinement in extinction (N) produced slower running than 10-second confinement in extinction (n), which replicates previous findings [Capaldi, 1966a; Capaldi & Poynor, 1965]. However, as Fig. 6 shows, if 60-second confinement was followed by large reward in acquisition, it produced faster running in extinction than if it was followed in acquisition by small reward, the same general finding obtaining for 10-second confinement. Bloom reported that 60-second confinement in extinction produced significantly slower running than 10-second confinement in extinction and, of more concern here, that the specific confinement duration associated with large reward in acquisition produced significantly greater Rn than the confinement duration associated with small reward in acquisition. Thus, Bloom's results, like Leonard's, give no support to such general propositions as that a large magnitude of PR produces greater Rn than a small magnitude of PR. This is so because all of Bloom's Ss received both large and small magnitude of reward in acquisition. Thus Bloom's results, like Leonard's, suggest that large reward following nonreward is the critical factor producing increased Rn. This is so according to the present hypothesis, because the specific stimulus occasioned by the nonreward, such as S^N_{10} or S^N_{60}, takes on greater associative strength under large, as opposed to small, reward.

B. DELAY OF REWARD

1. *Introduction*

Delay of reward was among the earliest of the reward variables to come under investigation. Concern was principally in the effects on acquisition of what today is termed constant delay of reward. Under constant delay, reward is delayed on all trials and the value of the delay is the same on every trial. Several excellent reviews of the older literature are available (Mowrer, 1960; Renner, 1964). The major finding in connection with constant delay is that acquisition performance becomes progressively worse as the duration of the delay increases. Among the major hypotheses offered in explanation of this finding was that the limit of growth of associative strength (or, in Hull's (1943) terminology, H) is a decreasing function of increasing delay. It is difficult to understand why the associative strength hypothesis, once generally accepted, has come to be neglected in recent years. It explains a substantial portion of available data and is not particularly incompatible with any major source of evidence.

In recent years, delay of reward has become more or less a theoretical stepchild to partial reward, and on the whole this development has probably been salutary. The early interest in acquisition performance as a function of constant delay has been broadened to include a concern with both acquisition and extinction as functions of varied delay. Under varied delay, the duration of the delay differs from trial to trial. Partial delay may be defined as a special case of varied delay, under which reward is given immediately on some portion of the trials. It can be seen that it is possible to construct a partial delay schedule to correspond to a partial reward schedule simply by replacing non-rewarded trials with delay of reward trials, a tactic adopted in a variety of instances (e.g., Capaldi & Poynor, 1966; Crum, Brown, & Bitterman, 1951).

Certain of the varied delay findings seem to require that the associative strength hypothesis of delay be supplemented by additional assumptions, while other findings seem much more tractable. As an example of the latter, we may consider an application of the associative strength hypothesis to varied delay made by Pubols (1962). Pubols has shown that it is predictable from the associative strength hypothesis that variation between shorter and longer delays should produce better acquisition performance than reward at the mean of the two delays. The deduction is quite simple. It is obvious that the limit of growth of H supported at the shorter of the two varied delays must exceed that supported by the mean delay. Generally, in what follows, we shall be concerned with delay phenomena that seem to require that the associative strength hypothesis of delay be supplemented by additional principles. For a survey of those findings already explained by the associative strength hypothesis of delay, the reader may consult several sources (e.g., Hull, 1943; Mowrer, 1960; Renner, 1964).

2. Extinction Following Constant Delay of Reward

As indicated, the effects of constant delay of reward on acquisition are relatively well known. However, extinction following constant delay presents something of a problem. First, the body of available evidence, although presenting something of a trend, is not entirely consistent. Second, it has been suggested that extinction following constant delay may have to be understood employing principles different from those applied to partial reward (Marx, McCoy, & Tombaugh, 1965). The position adopted here is that all of the reward variables may be understood in terms of the same general set of theoretical principles.

Although most investigators report that constant delay produces greater Rn than immediate reward (e.g., Fehrer, 1956; Marx et al., 1965; Sgro & Weinstock, 1963), some have failed to find such an increasing effect (e.g., Logan, 1960; Renner, 1963). Although additional work is needed, it is difficult not to be impressed by the positive findings. Thus, we shall assume that for some values of delay at least, Rn is greater than for immediate reward. When dealing with the effects of constant delay on Rn in terms of the present hypothesis, two factors are paramount: (1) the relative position on the stimulus continuum of the delay stimulus conditioned to R_I, and (2) the amount of associative strength available at that stimulus point. Since we assume that the limit to which associative strength may grow is a decreasing function of increasing delay, the two factors necessarily oppose each other in producing increased Rn. As the delay becomes longer (10 seconds, 30 seconds or longer), the delay stimulus S^D becomes increasingly similar to S^N, thus supplying S^N with more $\bar{H}$ and thus operating to produce increased Rn. On the other hand, the amount of associative strength supported by the longer delays is, per assumption, necessarily less. This operates to produce decreased Rn. The present hypothesis, then, must determine whether the differential habit factor is overcome by the fact that S^N lies closer on the continuum to S^D than to S^R. The finding that constant delay produces greater Rn than immediate reward forces the assumption that distance does indeed overcome differential H, as shown in Fig. 7A. According to Fig. 7A, constant 30-second delay will produce greater Rn than immediate reward because the proximity factor outweighs the differential H factor.

Obviously, however, the theoretical situation need not be conceptualized as in Fig. 7A. Figure 7B presents a different picture, showing essentially that S^N receives less $\bar{H}$ from $S^{D_{30}}$ than from S^R. According to Fig. 7B, a constant delay of 30 seconds would produce less Rn than would immediate reward.

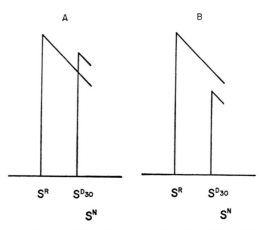

Fig. 7. The accumulation of H and the generalization of H to S^N under consistent reward training (S^R) and under constant 30-second delay of reward training ($S^{D_{30}}$) are shown. Figure 7A shows that consistent reward training should produce less Rn than constant 30-second delay of reward training; Fig. 7B shows the opposite.

Clearly then, in order to deduce that constant delay of reward produces greater Rn than immediate reward, the present hypothesis must assume (as in Fig. 7A) that the proximity factor outweighs the differential H factor (unlike as in Fig. 7B), an assumption that, for the constant delay situation at least, is purely *ad hoc*.

At this stage of theorizing, this sort of *ad hoc* procedure seems mandatory, and it is clear that a good deal of it will be needed in the future. For example, we are unprepared at the moment to assume that the proximity factor will outweigh the differential H factor for all values of constant delay. By way of illustration, it is relatively easy to imagine a delay so long, for example, 100 seconds, that it fails to support any H growth. In that event, despite the proximity factor, a 100-seconds delay would produce less Rn than immediate reward. Thus, according to the present hypothesis, a nonmonotonic function may exist between constant delay and Rn.

It should be understood, however, that the theoretical principles just considered, although relatively vague when applied to constant delay, are not at all vague or indeterminate when applied to a variety of other delay situations. This may be illustrated by Table IV, which anticipates the topic of the next section, partial delay of reward, and broadens the current discussion to include variable delay of reward as well as constant delay of reward. Table IV summarizes a good deal of information about the hypothesis.

The "Stimulus conditioned" column shows the particular value of the stimulus conditioned to R_I, such as S^R (immediate reward), $S^{D_{10}}$, and so on. The row beneath "Reward" gives the particular value of the reward employed in conditioning the stimulus value in question to R_I (as, immediate reward, I; a 10-second delay of reward, $S^{D_{10}}$; and so on). Reading down in the table we have the general theoretical case in which position on the continuum varies (S^R, $S^{D_{10}}$, $S^{D_{30}}$, $S^{D_{60}}$, $S^{D_{100}}$), but

TABLE IV

VARIOUS DELAY OF REWARD SITUATIONS

Stimulus conditioned	Reward				
	I	D^{10}	D^{30}	D^{60}	D^{100}
S^R	X				
$S^{D_{10}}$		X			
$S^{D_{30}}$			X		
$S^{D_{60}}$				X	
$S^{D_{100}}$					X

H is constant (all stimuli are conditioned by means of the same reward, that is, I, or S^D_{10}, or another). Generally, as we go down the
columns, we should expect Rn to increase as shown in Fig. 8.

Reading across in Table IV, we have the general theoretical case in
which position on the continuum is constant (e.g., S^D_{10}), but H steadily
decreases (that is, S^D_{10} will support more H than S^D_{30}, and so on).
Thus, to take but one example, conditioning S^D_{10} to R_I by means of a
10-second delay of reward should produce greater Rn than if S^D_{10} were
conditioned to R_I by means of a 30-second delay of reward. This is

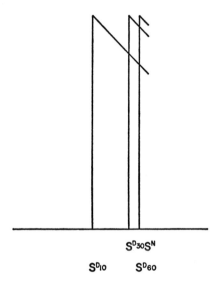

$$S^D_{30}S^N$$

$$S^D_{10} \qquad S^D_{60}$$

Fig. 8. The general theoretical case represented in the figure is one in which
position on the continuum varies. (S^D_{10}, S^D_{30}, S^D_{60}), but all stimuli have the same
associative strength, because they are conditioned by means of the same reward
value, for example, immediate reward, a 10-second delay of reward, and so on.

shown in Fig. 9A and B. Figure 9A shows the situation in which S^D_{10} was
conditioned to R_I by means of a 10-second delay of reward, while Fig. 9B
shows the situation in which S^D_{10} was conditioned by means of a 30-
second delay of reward. Thus S^D_{10} possesses greater H in Fig. 9A than
in Fig. 9B and S^N possesses greater $\bar{H}$ in Fig. 9A than in Fig. 9B. Clearly,
then, the hypothesis expects that Rn will be greater than when S^D_{10} is
conditioned by means of a 10-second delay than by means of a 30-
second delay.

The diagonal in Table IV, running from left to right and labeled with
X's, represents the constant delay case, such as S^D_{10} conditioned by

means of S^{D}_{10} and so on. As previously indicated, the present hypothesis cannot make predictions along the diagonal because two factors vary here: position on the continuum and differential H.

It is, however, entirely possible to entertain predictions from the present hypothesis when *both of these factors vary,* provided they both vary "in concert," that is, in such a way that both operate to produce increased Rn. By way of example, consider two groups trained under a varied delay schedule in which delay is equally often 10 sec or 30 seconds. The experimental situation is arranged so that in one group S^{D}_{30} is conditioned to R_I on the 10-second delay trial (more H), while in the

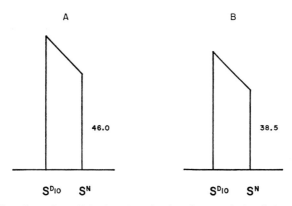

A   B

46.0   38.5

S^{D}_{10} S^N S^{D}_{10} S^N

Fig. 9. The effect of conditioning the stimulus characteristic of 10-second delay of reward (S^{D}_{10}) by means of (A) a 10-second delay of reward, or (B) a 30-second delay of reward.

other group S^{D}_{10} is conditioned to the reaction on the 30-second delay trial (less H). The expected theoretical outcome of such training is represented in Fig. 10. As Fig. 10 shows, the present hypothesis predicts that the group for which S^{D}_{30} is conditioned to R_I by means of a 10-second delay will show greater Rn than the group for which S^{D}_{10} is conditioned to R_I by means of a 30-second delay.

The foregoing discussion serves to illustrate several points of interest. First, constant delay is but one of a number of different delay of reward conditions. Second, the discussion clearly indicates that the present hypothesis employs the sequential mode of theorizing with reference to delay of reward. As will be shown in the following section, recent evidence suggests that sequential factors influence Rn under partial delay of reward. It remains for future investigations to determine if sequential variables influence acquisition and extinction under varied delay of reward.

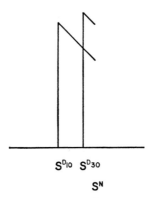

S^D10 S^D30

S^N

FIG. 10. The effect of conditioning S^D_{30} by means of a 10-second delay of reward versus conditioning S^D_{10} by means of a 30-second delay of reward.

3. Extinction Following Partial Delay of Reward

a. *Schedule of Partial Delay.* Capaldi and Poynor (1966) have shown that the present hypothesis is capable of dealing with much of the available data in the area of partial delay of reward (PD). Here we shall attempt to expand on that original treatment. One of the more noteworthy findings in the area of PD is that Rn increases as the duration of delay increases. Thus, while delays of 10 seconds or less fail to increase Rn to a significant degree (Capaldi & Poynor, 1966; Logan, Beier, & Kincaid, 1956), delays of 30-seconds or more produce a substantial increase in Rn (Capaldi & Poynor, 1966; Crum *et al.*, 1951; Logan *et al.*, 1956). Figure 11 presents the theoretically expected outcome for three

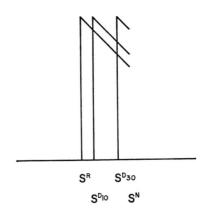

S^R S^D30

S^D10 S^N

FIG. 11. Partial delay of reward (S^D_{10} and S^D_{30}) versus consistent reward (S^R). The figure shows that partial delay of reward represents the general theoretical case in which H is equal with position on the continuum varying.

groups: one trained under immediate reward (S^R conditioned to R_I); one trained under a 10-second delay of reward ($S^{D_{10}}$ conditioned); and one trained under a 30-second delay of reward ($S^{D_{30}}$ conditioned). Since we are dealing with PD, the stimuli S^R, $S^{D_{10}}$, and $S^{D_{30}}$ are conditioned to R_I in the various groups by means of immediate reward, that is, the general theoretical case is one in which Hs are equal in all groups, but position on the continuum varies. It can be seen in Fig. 11 that as delay duration increases, the amount of $\bar{H}$ supplied to S^N increases. It is to be expected, therefore, that Rn will increase as duration of delay increases.

Burt and Wike (1963) report that PR occasions greater Rn than PD. Under PR the stimulus that occurs in extinction (S^N) is directly conditioned to R_I. Under PD the stimulus S^N is a generalized one, since S^D is conditioned to R_I in acquisition. Thus, it follows from the present hypothesis that PR will produce greater Rn than PD. As will be seen later, the Burt and Wike finding has been replicated on several occasions in our laboratory. A study by Cogan and Capaldi (1961) failed to find that PR produced greater Rn than PD. The reasons for this failure are not entirely clear.

Another noteworthy finding under PD is that the sequence of rewards exerts a strong influence on Rn. Thus, for example, Wike, Kintsch, and Gutekunst (1959) report that schedules involving transitions from delayed reward trial to immediately rewarded trials (DI transitions) markedly increased Rn. However, a schedule of PD containing only ID transitions (and no DI transitions) failed to produce greater Rn than immediate reward. How this finding may be deduced from the present hypothesis is perhaps obvious. Where no DI transitions are involved, the stimulus characteristic of delay (S^D) fails to take on H, fails to supply $\bar{H}$ to S^N, and thus Rn cannot be increased. Capaldi and Spivey (1965a) have shown that following a small number of acquisition trials, an alternating schedule of PD produced greater Rn than did a random schedule of PD. It will be remembered that Capaldi and Hart (1962) report a similar finding for alternating and random schedules of PR. (The general interpretation for the PD case is the same as that employed by Capaldi and Hart for the PR case.) It should also be mentioned that Capaldi (in press) has shown that following extensive training, Rn increased as D-length increased (D-length corresponds to N-length) with percentage of delays equated. Specifically, the Capaldi investigation involved a 2×2 factorial containing two percentages of delayed trials (40% and 60%) and two D-lengths (D-lengths = 1 or 3). Percentage of delay had no effect on Rn. However, as previously mentioned, Rn increased as D-length increased. A study by Capaldi and Poynor (1966) showed that when two delays are employed in the same schedule (5 seconds and 60 seconds), Rn is greater when the 60-second delay precedes an immediately rewarded trial than when it does not precede the immediately rewarded trial. Specifically, there were two four-trial schedules each day, one being, for example, $D_{60}IID_5$ (60-second delay precedes immediate reward), the other, D_5IID_{60} (60-second delay does not precede immediate reward).

A recent investigation by Capaldi and Olivier (1966) is interesting in the present context. The design was a 2×2 factorial and it combined elements of PR and PD investigations. Each of the four groups was trained at five trials each day, as shown in Table V. Groups DN and ND are of primary theoretical interest. In group DN, as can be seen, S^N was conditioned to R_I on trial 4 by means of immediate reward. In group ND, however, S^N was always followed by

TABLE V

TRIAL SCHEDULES FOR PR AND PD GROUPS[a]

	Trial				
Group	1	2	3	4	5
NN	R[b]	N	N	R	R
DN	R	D	N	R	R
ND	R	N	D	R	R
DD	R	D	D	R	R

[a] After Capaldi and Olivier (1966).
[b] Symbols: R, immediate reward; N, nonreward; D, a 10-second delay of reward.

delayed reward. Clearly, in group ND, S^N would take on only limited H, since per assumption H is a decreasing function of delayed reward. Thus, S^N possesses greater H in group DN than in group ND, and group DN should show greater Rn than group ND; these were the results obtained. Group NN was most resistent; in this group S_2^N rather than S_1^N (as in group DN) was conditioned to R_I. Thus, as found, the hypothesis expects group NN to show the greatest Rn among the four groups. Group DD showed, as expected, the least Rn. Thus, the Capaldi and Olivier investigation provides further evidence for the influence of sequential factors under PR and PD.

b. Magnitude of Reward in Partial Delay. While there has been some investigation into the effects of magnitude of PR on Rn, apparently the effect of magnitude of PD on Rn has gone unnoticed. We have been unable to find in the literature a magnitude of PD investigation. It should be indicated that a magnitude of PD investigation is necessarily more elaborate than a magnitude of PR investigation. Under PR, magnitude of reward need be varied, indeed can only be varied, on the rewarded trials, there being by definition no reward on the nonrewarded trials. Under PD, however, magnitude of reward may be varied on the delay trials as well as the immediately rewarded trials. In dealing with PD, then, there are two separate considerations. First, what is the effect of magnitude of reward on the immediately rewarded trials, magnitude of reward on the delay trial being constant? And second, what is the effect of magnitude of reward on the delay trials, magnitude of reward on the immediately rewarded trials being constant?

In order to simplify matters, we shall deal with the case of PD in which trials are given in an irregular or random fashion. This should not be taken to imply that sequential factors are unimportant in dealing with magnitude of PD. However, once the general principles of the hypothesis are made evident in connection with irregular schedules, it should be possible to determine the influence of sequential factors in a magnitude of PD investigation, both from the general considerations advanced in this paper and by a specific consideration of the treatment given to sequential factors in magnitude of PR.

Consider the first case, magnitude of reward on the delay trials constant with magnitude of reward on the immediately rewarded trials varied. This essentially is the same case we have when dealing with magnitude of PR. Under these conditions S^D would take on more H when R_I is conditioned by a large magnitude of immediate reward than when R_I is conditioned by a small magnitude of immediate reward. Accordingly, it can be expected that under a PD schedule Rn will increase along with an increase in the magnitude of reward on the immediately rewarded trials.

Consider now the second case, magnitude of reward on the immediately rewarded trials constant with magnitude of reward on the delayed trials varied. The hypothesis expects that as magnitude of reward on the delayed trials increases, Rn will tend to decrease. This follows because the larger the magnitude of the delayed reward, the more it is driven leftward on the continuum (see Fig. 1). In common-sense terms, a large magnitude of delayed reward is less like a nonreward than is a small magnitude of delayed reward. Accordingly, S^N will be supplied more $\bar{H}$ from a small magnitude of delayed reward than from a large magnitude of delayed reward. These matters are shown in Fig. 12, which presents graphically what has just been said. The stimulus S^{Ds} is the stimulus consequent of a small magnitude of delayed reward, while the stimulus S^{DL} is the stimulus consequent of a large magnitude of delayed reward.

From what has been said, it follows that the greatest Rn should be given by a small magnitude of reward on the delayed trial, and a large magnitude of reward on the immediate trial. Conversely, the least Rn should be given by a large magnitude of reward on the delayed trial and a small magnitude of reward on the immediate trial. Investigations concerned with the effects of magnitude of reward in PD are badly needed.

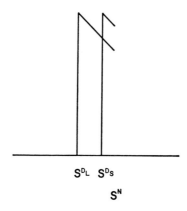

$S^{D}L$ $S^{D}s$

S^{N}

FIG. 12. Schema showing that when a small magnitude of delayed reward ($S^{D}s$) and a large magnitude of delayed reward ($S^{D}L$) possess equal H (as in a partial delay schedule), S^{N} is supplied greater $\overline{H}$ from $S^{D}s$ than from $S^{D}L$.

C. MAGNITUDE OF REWARD

Four general topics will be treated under reward magnitude: extinction following consistent reward; extinction following varied magnitude of reward; acquisition performance as a function of reward magnitude; and shifts in reward magnitude. Magnitude shift investigations fall into two distinct classes, nontransfer shifts and transfer shifts. In a nontransfer shift investigation, a shift, for example, large to small reward is such that S has not previously experienced the small reward. In a transfer shift investigation, however, S has previously been trained under the small reward. Transfer shift investigations supply perhaps the best single source of support for a generalization decrement hypothesis as applied to reward magnitude.

1. Consistent Reward: Extinction

A small magnitude of consistent reward has been shown to produce greater Rn than a large magnitude of consistent reward (e.g., Hulse, 1958; Wagner, 1961). Note first of all that different internal stimuli are conditioned under the different magnitudes; $S^{R}L$ under the large magnitude, $S^{R}s$ under the small magnitude. Since S^{N} lies closer on the continuum (Fig. 1) to S^Rs than to S^Rʟ, it will be supplied more $\overline{H}$ from the former stimulus than from the latter stimulus. On this basis, the Hulse-Wagner finding is interpretable within the present framework. In commonsense terms, a shift from large reward to nonreward occasions greater stimulus change than a shift from small reward to nonreward.

A complication enters into this deduction, however, since it is assumed that the limit of growth of H is an increasing function of reward magnitude. Considered alone, the differential H factor implies increasing Rn as a function of increased magnitude of reward. Thus, as with constant delay of reward (Section II, B, 2), it is necessary to assume in connection with consistent reward that the similarity factor outweighs the differential H factor in determining Rn. This is illustrated in Fig. 13, which shows that S^N is supplied more $\overline{H}$ from S^Rs than from S^Rʟ despite the presence of more H at S^Rʟ.

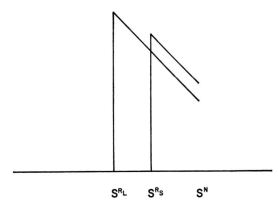

Fɪɢ. 13. The $\overline{H}$ received by S^N from S^Rʟ and from S^Rs when training occurs under consistent reward.

2. Varied Magnitude of Reward

When magnitude of reward is varied between two values, such as 9 pellets (S^R₉) and 1 pellet (S^R₁), Rn is greater than when reward is given either at the mean of the two values (5 pellets, S^R₅) or at the preferred of the two values (9 pellets, S^R₉) (e.g., Logan *et al.*, 1956; Yamaguchi, 1961). These findings, as shown in Fig. 14, are deducible from the present hypothesis. Actually, according to the present hypothesis, there are three reasons why varied magnitude training tends to produce increased Rn: (1) As shown in Fig. 14, S^R₁ has more H than S^R₅; this occurs because S^R₁ is sometimes conditioned by means of a 9-pellet reward, whereas S^R₅ is, of course, always conditioned by means of a 5-pellet reward. (2) S^N will be supplied more $\bar{H}$ from S^{R_1} than from S^{R_5} alone or from S^{R_9} alone. (3) The $\bar{H}$s separately supplied by S^{R_1} and S^{R_9} under varied magnitude training will summate at S^N. There is no summation of course in the mean or preferred magnitude group.

Figure 14 illustrates the three major principles to be considered in deducing the effects of varied magnitude training on Rn.

(1) Varied magnitude training should produce increasing Rn as the smaller of the two magnitudes becomes increasingly smaller; that is, 9–1 training should produce greater Rn than 9–2 training, and so on.

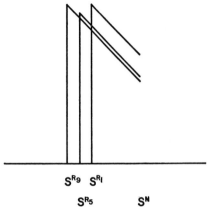

$$S^{R_9} \quad S^{R_1}$$
$$S^{R_5} \quad\quad\quad S^N$$

Fig. 14. Under varied magnitude of reward (9 pellets and 1 pellet), S^N receives $\bar{H}$ from two sources, S^{R_9} and S^{R_1}, whereas under mean magnitude of reward (5 pellets, 5–5 training), S^N receives $\bar{H}$ only from S^{R_5}.

(2) Due to summation, varied magnitude training should tend to produce increasing Rn as the larger of the two magnitudes becomes smaller; that is, as Fig. 14 shows, there will be greater summation at S^N when S^{R_1} and S^{R_5} summate than when S^{R_1} and S^{R_9} summate. Strictly speaking, however, this deduction must be considered with reference to H values. If all H values are equal, the deduction plainly holds, but in many instances the H values will not be equal, particularly when the larger magnitude is fairly small, for example, 5 pellets. Consider 1–5 training versus 1–10 training. Under 1–10 training both S^{R_1} and $S^{R_{10}}$ may tend to take on a higher value of H than will S^{R_1} and S^{R_5} under 1–5 training, because a 10-pellet reward may support a higher terminal limit of H growth than a 5-pellet reward. This consideration leads to the third of the present principles.

(3) Varied magnitude training will tend to produce greater Rn as the larger of the two magnitudes becomes increasingly larger, provided that the increasingly larger magnitudes produce habits of different strength.

It is clear that since the processes listed in paragraphs 2 and 3 tend to affect Rn in somewhat opposite ways, the findings in the varied magnitude area may turn out to be quite complicated; quite possibly, nonmonotonic functions may prove to be the rule. As we shall see, preliminary indications from our laboratory are consistent with this observation.

Results reported by Yamaguchi (1961) and by Beier (reported in Logan, 1960) suggest that under varied magnitude training, Rn increases as the smaller of the two magnitudes becomes smaller. Yamaguchi found 9–1 training to produce greater Rn than 8–2 training, and Beier found 13–1 training to produce greater Rn than 10–4 training. From the viewpoint of the present hypothesis, however, the meaning of these results would be clearer if the larger of the two magnitudes were held constant across groups.

The present hypothesis suggests that varied magnitude training (say 20–2) will produce greater Rn than training at the smaller of the two magnitudes (that is, 2 pellets, 2–2 training). This deduction follows on two counts: S^R_2 will take on greater H when rewarded by 20 pellets than by 2 pellets and under 20–2 training summation will occur at S^N. Since results of this sort are not contained in the literature, we recently ran three groups of 10 Ss each in our laboratory: 20–2, 2–2, and 20–20. There were 20 acquisition trials and group 20–2 received the smaller and larger rewards on an irregular basis. Figure 15 shows that Rn was greatest to least in the order 20–2, 2–2, and 20–20, thus confirming the present hypothesis.

On three separate occasions in our laboratory, Robert Godbout com-

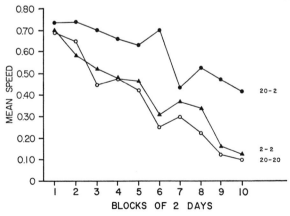

FIG. 15. Mean speed for each of three groups in blocks of two days (see text for discussion).

pared 6–2 training with 20–2 training. Each of these unpublished investigations contained five Ss per group. In the start and run sections of the alley, 6–2 and 20–2 training produce negligible differences in Rn. In the goal section, however, in two of the three investigations 6–2 produced faster absolute speeds than 20–2, although differences were not significant. In the third investigation, the speeds of 6–2 and 20–2 were interlaced across trials (goal section). These results may mean that although summation is operating to produce greater Rn in 6–2 than in 20–2, the H differential favors 20–2 over 6–2. If these conjectures are correct, 8–2 or 10–2 training may well tend to produce greater Rn than 20–2 training (H differentials minimized without too greatly affecting summation). Full-scale investigations along these lines are currently being conducted in our laboratory by Robert Godbout and Thomas Pyle.

Two other variables that the present hypothesis suggests may tend to influence Rn under varied magnitude training should be mentioned. One is the sequence of rewards. Under 20–2 training, for example, there are four types of trial-to-trial transitions: 2–2, 2–20, 20–2, and 20–20. A transition from a 2-pellet trial to a 20-pellet trial (S^{R_2} conditioned strongly by means of a 20-pellet reward) should theoretically have the greatest increasing effect on Rn. On the other hand, a transition from a 20-pellet trial to a 2-pellet trial should have the least increasing effect on Rn. The remaining transitions should affect Rn in an intermediate manner (2–2, 20–20). Possibly, then, the sequence variable may turn out to affect Rn under varied magnitude training as it does under PR training.

Number of acquisition trials is the second of the two variables that may tend to affect Rn under varied magnitude training. The reasoning here is the same as that applied to PR when small numbers of training trials were considered (Section II, A, 2, b and c). The first relevant observation is that constant reward training involves the conditioning to R_I of a single stimulus (such as S^{R_2}), whereas varied magnitude training involves the conditioning of two stimuli (such as S^{R_2} and $S^{R_{20}}$). Since, when number of acquisition trials are equated, there must necessarily be more conditionings of S^{R_2} in the constant magnitude group than of either S^{R_2} or $S^{R_{20}}$ in the varied magnitude group, it is possible, particularly if the learning rate (F) is slow to intermediate, that when number of training trials is small, the differential H attributable to more reinforcements at S^{R_2} might outweigh such factors as summation in the varied magnitude group in determining Rn.

3. Magnitude of Reward: Acquisition

In the influential Spence (1956) model, habit (H), drive (D), and incentive motivation (K) are related to reaction potential (E) as:

$$E = H(D + K) \tag{1}$$

The acquisition model employed here draws heavily on the Hull and Spence models, particularly the Spence model. However, it includes some differences that are demanded by the structure of the present approach. Some of these differences, which on occasion are only a matter of emphasis, follow.

(1) Spence uses a contiguity principle in instrumental conditioning whereas, as already indicated, a reinforcement principle is used here.

(2) In the Spence model the H of R_I is independent of reward magnitude, whereas the limit of growth of H is assumed in the present formulation to be an increasing function of reward magnitude.

(3) We assume that each magnitude of reward occasions a distinctive stimulus. Thus, we tend to emphasize rather strongly that different stimuli are conditioned to the reaction under different magnitudes of reward. We may represent the S-R connection established under a large magnitude of reward as $_{S}R_L H_{R_I}$, or more simply H_L. Correspondingly, the S-R connection established under a small magnitude may be represented as $_{S}R_S H_{R_I}$, or more simply H_S.

The Spence model contains the equivalent of H_L and H_S. Spence assumes different r_gs as a function of different reward magnitudes. Since the value of s_g is specific to the value of r_g and s_g becomes conditioned to R_I ($_{s_gL}H_{R_I}$ and $_{s_gS}H_{R_I}$), the correspondence between the two models is apparent. The correspondence is not complete, however, because the two models entertain different assumptions in connection with the changes undergone by s_g or S^R when reward magnitude is shifted upward or downward. These matters will be considered in the succeeding section.

(4) In the Spence model the value of K is an increasing function of reward magnitude. The present model also assumes that reward magnitude "energizes" habits. However, rather than an incentive concept (K) related to the strength or vigor of a response (r_g), we employ a Hullian (e.g., Hull, 1952) stimulus intensity mechanism (V) related, of course, to the vigor or intensity of the stimulus (S^R_S, S^R_L, and so on) (see Capaldi & Poynor, 1966). Spence (1951, 1956) was the first to suggest that the energizing aspects of reward magnitude could be represented through V rather than K; that step first suggested by Spence is taken here.

Several reasons exist for preferring V to K. Recent evidence (e.g., Beck, 1963; Grice & Hunter, 1964) is favorable to a V assumption; thus its inclusion in a theoretical system is warranted. At the same time, the inclusion of V and K in the same theory runs the danger of redundancy, since V can be employed whenever K can be employed, but apparently not vice versa. This, of course, is because any stimulus, including rewarded stimuli, may be seen as having an intensity component, but not all stimuli can be seen as having an incentive component. Evidently, then, it is desirable to subsume K under V, as perhaps we should do, since at present strong reasons for not doing so do not seem to exist.

Too, drive (D) could be seen as exerting its effects through V (that is, the intensity of the drive stimuli S_D), which leads to still further theoretical simplification. We would write, representing the stimulus intensity component of drive as V_D and of reward as V_R,

$$E = H(V_D + V_R) \qquad (2)$$

And we would write, representing the stimulus intensity component of external stimuli (such as light and auditory signals) as V_E,

$$E = H(V_D + V_R + V_E) \qquad (3)$$

Thus we would replace the three separate concepts of D, K, and V with the single concept of stimulus intensity, or V. Under the present scheme, we would recognize only three different sources of stimulus intensity. With these principles in mind, we are prepared to deal with the effects of shifting reward magnitude.

4. Shifts in Reward Magnitude

a. *Successive Contrast Effects.* The present treatment is exclusively concerned with successive contrast effects, the circumstance in which an S is trained under one magnitude of reward and one magnitude only, and is shifted following some number of trials to some other magnitude of reward. Early investigation (e.g., Crespi, 1944) suggested the presence of so-called positive and negative contrast effects. A positive contrast effect is said to occur if a group shifted from small reward to large reward performs better than a large magnitude control group. Correspondingly, a negative contrast effect would consist in poorer performance by a downward shift group relative to a small magnitude control group. Many investigations (e.g., see Spence, 1956) have failed to observe a positive contrast effect. A negative contrast effect, on the other hand, has been observed rather frequently (see Spence, 1956).

Hull's 1943 statement was what might be called a habit interpretation of reward magnitude, suggesting as it did that the limit (M) to which associative strength might grow is an increasing function of magnitude of reward. Hull, and subsequently others, abandoned a habit interpretation in favor of what is generally called today an incentive account of reward magnitude. The incentive emphasis was seen as a necessary step in view of the rapid performance changes accompanying shifts in reward magnitude. The present approach lies somewhere between what might be called the habit approach on the one hand and the incentive approach on the other. Although the habit emphasis may come as a surprise to some at this date, the transfer shift data to be presented later appear to implicate strongly the sort of associative mechanisms postulated by the present hypothesis.

We may understand the dual habit-incentive character of the present hypothesis by recognizing first that each magnitude of reward produces an associated and distinctive stimulus (large magnitude, S^{R}_{L}; small, S^{R}_{s}). When reward is shifted, the value of the associated stimulus changes in a direction corresponding to the currently prevailing reward magnitude. Consider a nontransfer reward shift from large magnitude to small magnitude. The change in stimulus from S^{R}_{L} to S^{R}_{s} has two major effects, one "incentive" (actually intensity) in character, the other associative in character.

(1) Incentive: Stimulus intensity (V) is reduced from large (S^{R}_{L}) to small (S^{R}_{s}), thus reducing the value of reaction potential (E).

(2) Associational: The stimulus S^{R}_{s} has only a generalized capacity to evoke the instrumental reaction (R_I), since R_I had been previously conditioned to the stimulus S^{R}_{L}. The negative contrast effect is due to such generalization decrement, as may be seen in the more formal presentation of these ideas that follows.

b. *Magnitude Shift Hypothesis (Nontransfer Shifts)*. We posit that

$$E_L = (H_L \times V_L) \quad \text{that is, } S^{RL}\, \mathbf{H_L}\, R_I \tag{4}$$

which represents the reaction potential, habit, and stimulus intensity under large magnitude of reward. We may write, for small magnitude of reward,

$$E_S = (H_S \times V_S) \quad \text{that is, } S^{Rs}\, \mathbf{H_S}\, R_I \tag{5}$$

For purposes of simplicity of exposition, assume that the stimulus change from S^{R}_{L} to S^{R}_{s}, or vice versa, is completely accomplished on the basis of a single experience with the new reward magnitude (responsivity is 1.00). Let the H values be asymptotic with $H_L = 100$ and $H_S = 90$. Let $V_L = 2.0$ and $V_S = 1.0$. Assume that 70% of the H available at S^{R}_{L} generalizes to S^{R}_{s} and vice versa. The values of E on and immediately after the reward shift trial for groups shifted from large to small reward (group L–S) and from small to large reward (group S–L) are given in Table VI.

It can be seen that group L–S should show a negative contrast effect ($E = 70$ versus 90 for control). Group S–L should show an immediate improvement in performance ($E = 126$ versus 90 for control).

Note too that while the hypothesis expects a negative contrast effect, it suggests that a positive contrast effect cannot occur. This is because H and V cannot exceed the limit, appropriate to the new reward magnitude, these values in the example being respectively 100 and 2.0.

According to the hypothesis, the following three variables should exert a strong effect on performance shifts: responsivity, generalization decrement, and the learning rate F.

(1) Stimulus change, or responsivity: The effect of speed of stimulus change in a downward shift group is entirely clear. If responsivity $= 1.00$, a negative contrast effect must occur on the first postshift trial, since of course there must be some generalization decrement. If, on the other hand, responsivity is low, a negative contrast effect need not occur. This is because generalization decrement is small from trial to trial, as are losses in V, and at the same time habit strength is accumulating on each of the postshift trials. For reasons of this sort, in an investigation by Gonzalez, Gleitman, and Bitterman (1962) a group that was gradually shifted from 32 pellets to 2 pellets failed to show a negative contrast effect. The effect of responsivity on upward shifts is somewhat less straightforward because although high responsivity means greater V, it also means greater generalization decrement. Within wide limits, however, the greater the responsivity, the faster the performance change when reward is shifted from small to large.

TABLE VI

E Values on and after the Shift Trial

Group	On shift trial	After shift trial
L–S	E = (100 × 2) = 200	E = (70 × 1) = 70
S–L	E = (90 × 1) = 90	E = (63 × 2) = 126

(2) Generalization decrement: The greater the generalization decrement, (a) the larger the negative contrast effect, (b) the faster will it occur, and (c) the greater the number of trials required to overcome it. The first two of these predictions were nicely confirmed by DiLollo and Beez (1966), who shifted rats to 1 pellet following training under either 2, 4, 8, 16, or 20 pellets. Generally speaking, the larger shifts produced greater response decrement and produced it sooner. Unfortunately, training was discontinued prior to the time the negative contrast effect was completely overcome; thus, the results were not relevant to prediction (c). As regards upward shifts, greater generalization decrement should, of course, increase the number of trials required to reach the baseline of the control group.

(3) Learning rate F: Other things equal, the slower the learning rate, the larger the negative contrast effect, and the greater the number of trials required to overcome it. With rapid learning, negative contrast effects will either fail to occur or be overcome in a relatively few trials; for example, if $F = 1.00$ and responsivity $= 1.00$, the negative contrast effect would occur on the first postshift trial and be overcome on the second postshift trial. The larger the value of F, the faster the upward shift.

The present hypothesis contains what may appropriately be regarded as several unique implications. For example, other current hypotheses do not appear to suggest that the learning rate parameter will affect the speed and extent of performance shifts. What little evidence there is appears to support the present hypothesis. Bower, Fowler, and Trapold (1959), employing escape from shock, failed to observe a negative contrast effect. Original learning in that investigation was extremely rapid, being virtually complete in about five trials ($F =$ about .50). On the other hand, investigations reporting negative contrast effects (e.g., Crespi, 1944; Spence, 1956) showed much slower original learning rates.

Homzie and Ross (1962) and Rosen and Ison (1965) observed slow and gradual shifts in performance for changes in liquid rewards. The present hypothesis would deal with these findings by assuming that responsivity is lower for liquid as opposed to solid food rewards. This assumption needs to be confirmed by independent sources of evidence.

According to the present hypothesis, negative contrast effects can and should occur following only a few training trials. This follows because some generalization decrement is always to be expected. Gleitman and Steinman (1964) report a negative contrast effect following as few as 12 training trials. Presumably a negative contrast effect will occur following even fewer training trials. Actually a negative contrast effect has been obtained in our laboratory following as few as six training trials. In that investigation, however, F was fairly large (about .25). Determinations of this sort seem theoretically important inasmuch as they appear to bear on the adequacy of hypotheses (e.g., Amsel, 1958; Crespi, 1944) that relate the negative contrast effect to disappointment or frustration, the magnitude of such disappointment or frustration being related in turn to the strength of the expectancy for large reward.

c. Previously Established S-R Connections: Transfer Shifts. An explanation of the relevance to the hypothesis of the shift investigations to be treated in this section requires that we anticipate the topic of the next section, extinction as a process. It has long been assumed that the nonreinforcement of a reaction produces extinction in one of two general senses: the already established S-R connection is weakened, or a new S-R connection is formed that opposes the already established one. These processes may be labeled as unconditioning and counter-conditioning, respectively. An extinction theory may assume one or the other or both of these processes.

In our work on extinction, however, it has generally not been necessary to call upon either process. Rather, as stressed in earlier portions of this paper, it is assumed that over a series of nonreinforced trials the stimulus situation undergoes an orderly and progressive series of changes, namely, S_1^N, S_2^N, and so on. Since, generally speaking, later stimuli in the series such as S_{20}^N, possess a more limited capacity to evoke R_I than earlier stimuli in the series (generalization decrement), the progressive response decrement accompanying successive nonrewards can generally be understood quite nicely without unduly stressing extinction. Moreover, it is relatively obvious that a generalization decrement interpretation generally contains a great many implications for transfer phenomena that an extinction model either fails to contain or contains only in a more limited way. A major proposition following from a generalization decrement interpretation, for example, is that the associations formed during original learning are neither lost nor opposed in some subsequent interpolated reward (or nonreward) phase. Rather, the response occurs with less vigor because the stimulus situation has changed. It follows that if we reinstate the stimuli that evoked the reaction in acquisition, that reaction will occur, and will occur strongly. Many phenomena exhibit an extreme lability of this sort; an outstanding example is perhaps the behavior exhibited under a simple single alternating schedule of reward. Often the animal will refuse to traverse the runway on the nonrewarded trial, and on the succeeding rewarded trial the response will occur with great vigor.

Let us look at this sort of reasoning in terms of mediating reactions (r_g-s_g) and equate the stimuli produced by reward and nonreward that are assumed here (S^R_s, S^R_L, and so on) with the response-produced stimuli of the classical mediating reaction (such as s_{gs} and s_{gL}). The following propositions are generally accepted in connection with the current view of mediating reactions: (1) over a series of rewarded trials r_g is acquired slowly and grows progressively stronger; (2) r_g will occur on nonrewarded trials; and (3) r_g is extinguished on nonrewarded trials and will grow weaker over a series of nonrewarded trials until finally it may become completely extinguished. This sort of analysis has been employed on several occasions (e.g., Logan et al., 1956; Moltz, 1957).

The present view of mediating reactions is quite different. The differences between our position and the currently accepted view of mediating reactions is probably related to the type of experimental data each emphasizes. For example, the currently accepted view of mediating reactions appears to assume that since R_I is acquired and extinguished more or less slowly, the progressive changes in R_I reflect like changes in r_g. On the other hand, we tend to emphasize, for example, the alternation situation, in which the response may occur with considerable vigor on rewarded trials and with considerably less vigor on nonrewarded trials, thus suggesting that the mediating reaction may have one value, such as r_g, following rewarded trials, and another quite different value, such as r_{ng}, following nonrewarded trials. We assume, then, that in a variety of situations the mediating reaction quickly mirrors the currently prevailing reward condition, and that if the conditions of reward change, the value of the mediating reaction will change appropriately (responsivity is high).

Note that even if we were to assume here the occurrence of extinction in either of the two general senses considered earlier, the present view of mediating reactions would continue to possess implications not contained in the generally accepted view. For example, according to the generally accepted view, it is r_g that is extinguished, and thus the s_g-R_I connection. According to the present view, however, it would be r_{ng} that is extinguished, and thus the s_{ng}-R_I connection (S^N-R_I in previous terminology). Clearly, according to the present view, neither r_g nor the all-important connection s_g-R_I can undergo direct extinction (because r_g and thus s_g do not occur in the nonrewarded phase), and thus s_g would retain some capacity to evoke R_I, the reduction in capacity being a result of generalized extinction, that is, generalization from s_{ng} to S_g.

An experiment by Vogel, Mikulka, and Spear (1965) is relevant to the present view. These investigators found that a depression effect occurred despite an intervening nonreward phase prior to the reward shift phase. The investigation was conducted as follows. Two groups were trained under consistent reward, one group receiving large reward, the other small reward. Following this training, the groups were extinguished (that is, nonrewarded). Finally both groups were shifted to small reward, whereupon the group given large reward in original training showed a depression effect. Moreover, Vogel *et al.* varied the number of interpolated nonrewards, there being as many as 75 nonrewarded trials in one condition. They report that the magnitude of the depression effect was little influenced by number of interpolated nonrewarded trials.

If, as the generally accepted view of mediating reactions maintains,

r_g was extinguished during the nonrewarded phase, it could be expected that the two groups would perform about equally well during the retraining phase. But this was not the case; the group retrained under the same reward magnitude as in original training performed better than the group given different reward magnitudes in retraining and original training. This finding suggests that some associative connection survived the intervening nonrewarded phase and that this associative connection is based on the stimulus consequences of reward. Fortunately, it can be shown that the Vogel et al. (1965) results are not due to the particular reward magnitudes employed. Logan (1960) performed the opposite experiment, obtaining similar results. In Logan's investigation, as in the one by Vogel et al., the groups were given either large or small reward in original training, followed by a nonrewarded phase. In the retraining phase, however, both groups were shifted to large reward rather than to small reward as in the Vogel et al. investigation. In this instance, the group originally trained under large reward performed better in the retraining phase than the group originally trained under small reward. The transfer effect, therefore, is independent of the particular reward magnitudes employed and depends on a correspondence between reward magnitudes in original training and retraining.

A recent investigation by Wagner and Thomas (1966) is relevant to the present hypothesis. Groups originally trained under either large or small reward (Phase I) were shifted to small reward (Phase II) and then to large reward (Phase III). As in the "extinction" investigations considered earlier, the group originally trained under large reward performed better in the retraining phase than did the group originally trained under small reward. Thus, not only will associations formed in original training persist through an interpolated series of nonrewards, but they will persist through an interpolated series of rewards of different magnitude.

We have performed a variety of transfer shifts in our laboratory, including the one reported by Wagner and Thomas. Our results were the same as those reported by Wagner and Thomas. One of these transfer shifts is of particular theoretical interest because it appears to suggest quite clearly that the negative contrast effect is due to generalization decrement. The experimental design is shown in Table VII. In phase I (each phase comprised 15 trials), 30 rats received large reward, 30 rats small reward. In Phase II, 15 rats from the large reward group continued to receive large reward while the remaining 15 were shifted to small reward. The same was true for the small reward group; that is, 15 continued to receive small reward while 15 were shifted to large reward. The training received by the groups in Phases III and IV is also shown. Hereafter, it is to be understood that the designation LSLS means large reward in Phase I, small reward in Phase II, large reward in Phase III, and small reward in Phase IV. In Phase II, group LSLS showed a negative contrast effect. Indeed, as mentioned in the preceding section, in a previous investigation in this series conducted under conditions almost identical to those of the experiment under discussion (same runway, same strain of rats, and same E), a negative contrast effect was shown following only six training trials. The important question for present purposes is the performance of group SLSL in Phase III: Will it or will it not show a negative contrast effect?

TABLE VII

SUCCESSIVE MAGNITUDE SHIFTS

Phase			
I	II	III	IV
L	L	L	S
L	S	L	S
S	S	S	L
S	L	S	L

According to the present hypothesis, group SLSL should not show a negative contrast effect in Phase III, because $s_g s$ (in present terminology, $S^R s$) was conditioned to R_I in Phase I and remains so conditioned despite the occurrence of large reward in Phase II. As previously shown, according to the present hypothesis, the negative contrast effect is due to generalization decrement (from $S^R L$ to $S^R s$). But since $S^R s$ was directly conditioned to R_I in Phase I and remains conditioned throughout Phase II, there cannot be any generalization decrement in Phase III and, therefore, there cannot be, according to the present hypothesis, any negative contrast effect in Phase III. The performances of group SLSL and its control (SSSL) in Phase III are shown in Fig. 16. It can be seen that group SLSL not only failed to show a negative contrast effect (unlike group LSLS in Phase II), but it approached its baseline control slowly and only over a number of trials. These results support the present hypothesis in suggesting that the negative contrast effect is due to the generalization decrement encountered in going from $S^R L$ to $S^R s$. They show that if $S^R s$ is previously conditioned to R_I, a shift in reward magnitude from large to small will not occasion a negative contrast effect.

E. J. Capaldi

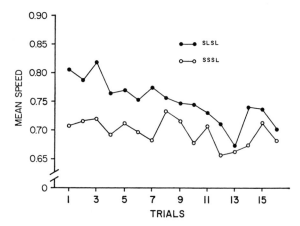

Fig. 16. Mean speed for each of the four groups during the third phase of training (trials 31–45).

III. Nonreward: Extinction or Generalization Decrement

A. BACKGROUND CONSIDERATIONS

1. Definitions

The introduction of continuous nonreward following some sort of acquisition training is commonly termed extinction. Thus, the term extinction is used to refer to both an operation, nonreward, and a process, namely, unconditioning or counterconditioning. Extinction is employed in yet another sense; that is, it is often used to describe the behavior itself, as, an extinguished response. For present purposes it is necessary to distinguish clearly between these several usages. Hereafter, the term extinction will be used to refer to a process, unconditioning or counterconditioning. When reference is to an operation, the operation will be specified, as, nonreward or continuous nonreward. The decreased reactivity accompanying continuous nonreward will be referred to as response decrement. One issue that concerns us here is whether the response decrement accompanying continuous nonreward is to be explained primarily in terms of a theory of extinction or a theory of generalization decrement.

Investigations that use continuous nonreward following some sort of acquisition training are not always concerned with either the process of extinction or a specific theory of extinction. This is particularly true of most investigations along this line conducted within the present framework. Normally we employ continuous nonreward in order to gain information about the specific kinds of S-R connections established during acquisition. However, even this statement is too narrow. Within the present framework, nonreward is used to provide information in connection with a number of theoretical issues, most of which have little to do with extinction per se. By way of example, consider an investigation described earlier by Capaldi and Hart (Section II, A, 2, c). Two groups were trained for a small number of trials (18), one under a single alternating schedule of reward, the other under an irregular schedule of reward. Following this training both groups were shifted to continuous nonreward. It was found that over the series of nonrewarded trials the single alternating group showed less response decrement than the irregular group. This differential response decrement was then used to make the following inferences.

(1) Following a rewarded trial the stimulus is S^R, following a nonrewarded trial S^N. Implied in a statement of this sort is that responsivity is high.

(2) The stimulus S^N is conditioned to R_I more often in the alternating than in the irregular group, and therefore S^N will possess a greater capacity to evoke R_I in the alternating than in the irregular group. Implied in this statement is that S-R connections are strengthened only on rewarded trials.

(3) Since nonreward occasions the stimulus S^N, and since S evokes R_I more strongly in the alternating than in the irregular group, it follows that over a series of nonrewarded trials the alternating group should show less response decrement than the irregular group. Thus Capaldi and Hart employed the lesser response decrement exhibited by the alternating group relative to the irregular one to provide support for at least three propositions: (a) that reward and nonreward occasion distinctive stimuli; (b) that conditioning occurs only on rewarded trials; and (c) that responsivity is high. Generalizing from this example it may be said that within the present framework continuous nonreward is used in connection with a number of theoretical issues. At the same time it is true that one issue appears repeatedly. That is, we often employ continuous nonreward to determine the character, quality, and kind of stimuli that are conditioned to R_I in the acquisition phase.

2. Stimulus Emphasis

The broadest characterization of the present approach to learning phenomena is that it strongly emphasizes the stimulus. This statement requires clarification, since of course all learning approaches recognize and are interested in stimuli. The difference in stimulus emphasis between the present and other approaches may be summarized in the following two general statements. (1) We assume that the various classes of stimuli that control behavior have only begun to be identified. (2) It is typical of a variety of approaches that the attempt to explain behavior is given in nonstimulus rather than in stimulus terms.

One resultant of the present stimulus emphasis is the view that the current approach to mediating reactions needs to be broadened; a step taken in recent years, particularly by Spence and Amsel, who emphasize not only anticipatory consummatory reactions (r_g) but anticipatory frustration (r_f) and anticipatory punishment (r_p). But these are goal events; the present view is that the same sort of logic that has been applied to r_g can be usefully applied to other classes of mediating reactions, including reactions that are not related to goal events per se. Generalizing, it could be said that any stimulus to which the organism reacts (such as visual and auditory) can serve as the basis of a mediating reaction—and thus those stimuli can be internally reinstated on subsequent trials. This view has the following theoretical implication: a stimulus interpretation of a variety of phenomena can be provided where previously a nonstimulus interpretation was deemed mandatory. This may be illustrated in connection with secondary reinforcement. Consider the well-known Bugelski (1938) investigation. It may be remembered that Bugelski trained rats to depress a lever, lever depression being accompanied by food reward (S^R) and an audible click (S^C). Thereupon, the animals were divided into two groups and nonrewarded, one group with and the other without the click. The click group showed less response decrement over the series of nonrewards than did the nonclick group. Hull's (1943) interpretation of this finding was that the click, by being paired with reward, took on reinforcing properties (secondary reward) and so maintained the response over the series of nonrewarded trials. The present interpretation is as follows. The stimulus consequences of reward (S^R) and of click (S^C) occasioned by a given trial, such as Tn-1, were reinstated internally on the succeeding trial, Tn, and conditioned to the bar press reaction (R_B). This can be represented as follows.

During the nonreward phase for both groups the stimulus complex preceding each trial includes S^N; for the click group, however, it includes S^C, whereas for the nonclick (S^{NC}) group it includes S^{NC}. Since the stimulus complex $S^N + S^C$ possesses a greater capacity to evoke R_B than the stimulus complex $S^N + S^{NC}$ (less generalization decrement), we are able to deduce on straightforward *associational* grounds Bugelski's finding that the click group showed less response decrement over a series of nonrewarded trials than did the nonclick group. It can be seen that a straightforward associational interpretation can be substituted for the nonstimulus, motivationally oriented secondary reward type interpretation. This was accomplished by assuming that clicks (and of course other types of nonrewarded stimuli) occasion mediating reactions (and thus internal stimuli) in the same general way as do rewards and punishments. With these general ideas before us we turn to a consideration of several specific phenomena.

B. Successive Acquisitions and Extinctions

1. *Major Findings and Hypotheses*

The procedure of subjecting a reaction to a rewarded series of trials followed by a nonrewarded series of trials, and so on, is commonly termed the successive acquisition and extinction of reactions, a terminology we will use here. The literature in this area presents a particularly conflicting and confusing set of experimental findings, which has yet to be integrated theoretically. In this section we shall introduce a stimulus interpretation that appears capable of bringing a high degree of order into the area. The major findings appear to be the following.

(1) Acquisition rate seems to increase over successive acquisitions (e.g., Lauer and Carterette, 1957), although there is evidence that most of the improvement occurs on the first reacquisition (North & Morton, 1962).

(2) Response decrement rate (which corresponds to what others have called extinction rate), when observed over successive nonrewarded sessions, has been shown to: (a) remain constant (North & Morton, 1962); (b) increase (Bullock & Smith, 1953; Perkins & Cacioppo, 1950); (c) decrease (Lauer & Estes, 1955; Lauer & Carterette, 1957).

Two major hypotheses have thus far been advanced in connection with the successive acquisition and extinction of reactions. According to Hull (1952), we have essentially a discrimination situation. The aftereffect of reward signals reward and the animal runs rapidly, whereas the aftereffect of nonreward signals nonreward and the animal runs slowly. Logan and Wagner (1965), in considering Hull's view, suggest that the North and Morton finding (response decrement rate remains constant) is understandable since in that investigation a 24-hour intertrial interval was employed. With 24-hour intervals, aftereffects could be expected to dissipate and thus in the absence of a discriminable cue response decrement rate would remain constant. The present view is similar to the Hullian hypothesis in suggesting that basically a discrimination between reward and nonreward is involved. The present view differs from Hull's hypothesis, however, in a number of respects, one of which is that the cues of reward and nonreward do not dissipate with time. Thus, in order to explain findings of the North and Morton variety we find it necessary to postulate something other than cue dissipation.

The second major hypothesis thus far presented to deal with the successive acquisition and extinction of reactions is that of the habituation of competing responses (Lauer & Carterette, 1957; Lauer & Estes, 1955). This view is based on an analysis provided by Weinstock (1954). It is suggested that nonreward evokes varied behaviors and that eventually (that is, provided a sufficient number of nonrewards are given), the varied behaviors or competing responses "habituate" or drop out. Once the competing responses habituate they will, of course, fail to interfere with the ongoing locomotor reaction. Thus it follows that over a number of successive nonrewarded sessions, response decrement (literally, extinction) will fail to occur and response decrement rate will decrease. As indicated, Lauer and Estes and Lauer and Carterette provided experimental evidence in favor of the habituation hypothesis.

2. Current Hypothesis

a. *Similarity to Partial Reinforcement.* The similarity between the successive acquisition and extinction of reactions and partial reinforcement has been remarked upon by a number of writers (e.g., Lewis, 1960; Logan & Wagner, 1965). Essentially both experimental situations provide the animal with sequences of rewarded and nonrewarded experiences. The habituation hypothesis was itself first formulated in connection with partial reward (Weinstock, 1954). It is not surprising, therefore, that the principles of the present hypothesis, formulated originally in connection with partial reinforcement, can now be applied to the successive acquisition and extinction of reactions. This has already been done to some extent. That is, the reward shift investigation of Vogel et al. (1965) and of Logan (1960) treated in the previous section fall in this category. Essentially these investigations show that if the same magnitude of reward is employed in reacquisition as in acquisition, reacquisition occurs faster than if a different magnitude of reward is employed. As indicated, findings of this sort are deducible from the present hypothesis (and Hull's as well), although how they may be made compatible with the habituation hypothesis is unclear.

It should be clear, however, that many of the principles covered earlier, particularly those in connection with partial reward, can be applied to the successive acquisition and extinction of reactions. This is particularly true in connection with N-length. However, in order to understand the current findings in the area we shall have to introduce an additional consideration, that of temporal discrimination. As will become clear later, it is virtually impossible to consider N-length without considering temporal discrimination, and vice versa.

b. N-length. Let R-length refer to the number of rewarded trials that occur consecutively without interruption by a nonrewarded trial. An investigation into the successive acquisition and extinction of habits can be characterized in terms of its R-length and in terms of its N-length. We are concerned now with the case in which R-length is constant, N-length varies, *and the intertrial interval between all trials is constant.* Let us say that for group 12 N-length = 12, while for group 24 N-length = 24. In the former group S_{12}^N will take on associative strength, while in the latter group S_{24}^N will take on associative strength. In both cases $S_1{}^N$, $S_2{}^N$, and so on will be supplied $\overline{H}$. However, $S_1{}^N$ lies farther from S_{24}^N than from S_{12}^N (see Fig. 17); thus lower values of S^N will receive less $\overline{H}$ when N-length = 24 than when N-length = 12. We arrive at our first general principle. *The longer the N-length the less the $\overline{H}$ supplied to lower values of S^N ($S_1{}^N$, $S_2{}^N$, and so on) and, therefore, the less vigorous the reaction that will be evoked by these stimuli.* This state of affairs is illustrated in Fig. 17. Note that Fig. 17

$$S_1^N \qquad S_{12}^N \qquad S_{24}^N$$

FIG. 17. Earlier S^Ns in the series receive less $\overline{H}$ from S_{24}^N than from S_{12}^N (see discussion in text).

does not show $\overline{H}$ from S^R to S^N (for reasons of simplicity) and that it suggests that response strength should increase from S_1^N to S_{12}^N (or S_{24}^N, in the case of group 24). It also suggests that if N-length is short, a sufficient amount of $\overline{H}$ will be supplied to lower values of S^N to evoke a vigorous reaction. Indeed, a close examination of the present hypothesis will show that it is entirely possible for response decrement rate to decrease over successive nonrewarded sessions. This is because S_{12}^N, for example, acquires more $\overline{H}$ with each reacquisition and thus $\overline{H}$ would tend to reduce response decrement at S_1^N, S_2^N, and successive lower values over a series of nonrewarded sessions.

c. Temporal Considerations. The treatment just presented assumed that all rewarded and nonrewarded trials were given at the same intertrial interval. In practice this does not always occur. For example, in the investigations by Perkins and Cacioppo (1950) and by Bullock and Smith (1953), the R-length was given initially (massed trials) followed by the N-length (massed trials) and then the experimental session was terminated until the following day. Thus, the last nonreward in the series was separated from the next reward in the series (the R-length of the next day) by a quite different intertrial interval than were all the remaining trials. Those investigations in which response decrement rate increased over nonrewarded sessions contrast sharply with that of, for example, North and Morton (1962), in which all intertrial intervals were equal (24 hr) and response decrement rate remained constant over nonrewarded sessions. We assume, as shown in Fig. 18, that time as such is discriminated by the rat and acts as a powerful stimulus generalizing to other "times." This hypothesis was first suggested by Capaldi and Poynor (1966). Figure 18 shows that if the 30-second value of S^N takes on H, it supplies $\overline{H}$ to the 24-hr value of S^N, and vice versa.

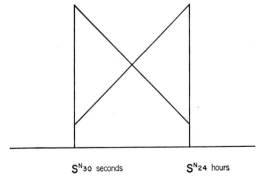

S^N30 seconds S^N24 hours

FIG. 18. A nonreinforced stimulus that has an age of 30-seconds supplies generalized $\overline{H}$ to the 24-hour age of the nonreinforced stimulus, and vice versa.

In investigations of the Bullock and Smith and Perkins and Cacioppo variety, the ITI between nonrewarded trials followed by nonrewarded trials differed from the ITI separating the last nonrewarded trial in the series (call it S_x^N) from the initial rewarded trial of the reacquisition series. Thus S_x^N will supply less $\overline{H}$ to S_{x-1}^N, and so on, than would otherwise be the case. In common-sense terms, S_{short}^N is a signal for nonreward and the animal responds slowly, whereas S_{long}^N is a signal for reward and the animal responds rapidly, and there is little generalization from S_{long}^N to S_{short}^N. However, if all S^Ns are either long or short (to continue with common sense) the rat is less able to determine (more generalization) if the S^N cue is a signal for reward or nonreward; therefore, it runs fast. This analysis assumes that time represents a potent stimulus for the rat. Is such an assumption justified? Since we could find little justification for the assumption in the literature aside from the inferences supported from an analysis of the successive acquisition extinction literature per se, we ran the experiment about to be described. As will be seen, it confirmed the inference about time as a stimulus, based on the differential response decrement rates obtained in the various successive acquisition and extinction studies. The experiment to be described was conducted by Robert Minkoff.

The purpose of the investigation was to determine if time is an important component of the nonreinforced stimulus. Several previous investigations (e.g., Reynolds, 1945; Teichner, 1952) have shown that Ss trained under one ITI in acquisition and shifted to another ITI in the nonrewarded phase show greater response decrement than Ss for which the ITI is the same in the acquisition phase and the nonrewarded phase. Although such investigations are relevant to the current concern, they are far too general for present purposes. Minkoff's study differed in a variety of particulars from these early investigations. For example, in acquisition Ss did not receive a single ITI but an equal number of short and long ITIs.

Let $^{30}S^N$ represent the 30-second age of S^N; that is, a 30-second ITI elapses between a nonrewarded trial and the beginning of the subsequent trial. Let $^8S^N$ represent the 8-minute age of S^N. The experimental hypothesis was that if a series of nonrewards are given at the same age of the S^N as conditioned to R_I in acquisition, less response decrement would occur than if the series of nonrewards are given at a different age of S^N. The hypothesis was tested as follows. Two groups of rats ($N = 10$ per group) were trained in the straight alley at five trials per day under an identical sequence of rewarded and nonrewarded trials (RNRNR). (Four Ss were lost in acquisition because of sickness or death.) There were six days of acquisition training. Both groups received two 30-

second and two 8-minute ITIs daily. For one group, the 30-second ITIs occurred between the N and the R trials ($^{30}S^N$ conditioned to R_I) with the 8-minute ITIs occurring between R and N trials. For the other groups the 8-minute ITI occurred between N and R trials ($^8S^N$ conditioned to R_I), while the 30-second ITI occurred between R and N trials. In the nonrewarded series (five trials per day for three days) the ITI was either 30 seconds or 8 minutes. Half of each acquisition group received the 30-second ITI, the remaining half the 8-minute ITI. The experimental design then was a 2×2 factorial. The four groups may be designated as (A) $^{30}S^N$-$^{30}S^N$; (B) $^{30}S^N$-$^8S^N$; (C) $^8S^N$-$^8S^N$; and (D) $^8S^N$-$^{30}S^N$. It was expected that groups A and C ("same" groups) would show less response decrement over the series of nonrewards (direct conditioning) than the "different" groups B and D (generalized temporal stimulus). Differences between the groups in the run section

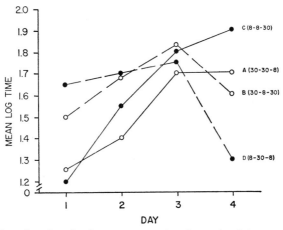

Fig. 19. Mean log time in the runway section for each of four groups (A, B, C, and D) on the initial three nonrewarded days and on the nonrewarded day (4) on which the intertrial interval was reversed (see discussion in text).

on the last day of acquisition were not significant ($F < 1.00$). The performance (mean log times) of each of the groups on each of the three days of decrement training (run section) is shown in Fig. 19, where it can be seen that on the initial two days of decrement training the "same" groups ran faster than the "different" groups; by day 3, however differences were small. The differences on the initial two days of decrement training were significant. On day 4 (to the right of the vertical line in Fig. 19) all Ss received five nonrewarded trials. However, for each group the ITI was the opposite of that in decrement training.

Thus, on day 4 for each of the groups the temporal value of S^N was the same as that in acquisition (groups ${}^{30}S^N\text{-}{}^8S^N\text{-}{}^{30}S^N$ and ${}^8S^N\text{-}{}^{30}S^N\text{-}{}^8S^N$) while for the remaining groups the temporal value of S^N was different (${}^{30}S^N\text{-}{}^{30}S^N\text{-}{}^8S^N$ and ${}^8S^N\text{-}{}^8S^N\text{-}{}^{30}S^N$). It can be seen that on day 4 the "same" groups ran faster than the "different" groups, this difference being significant. In other words, a "return" to the same temporal value of S^N as conditioned to R_I in acquisition produced faster running despite an intervening nonrewarded phase.

On the basis of Minkoff's results, it seems clear that the time elapsing between trials is an important component of the stimulus context. Call this the temporal stimulus; it is a portion, and apparently an important portion, of the total stimulus context conditioned to R_I on rewarded trials. The experimental results suggest that there is great generalization decrement between temporal stimuli. Thus, if one temporal value of S^N is conditioned to R_I, the ability of the other temporal values of S^N to evoke R_I is limited. This fact has important implications for a variety of experimental situations. Its meaning for the successive acquisition and extinction of reactions in particular is clear and provides our second important general principle.

In the successive acquisition extinction situation, if the temporal value of the stimulus associated with the last nonreward in the series (which is conditioned to R_I) is the same as that associated with earlier non-rewards in the series, the ability of the earlier nonrewarded stimuli to evoke R_I will be greater than if the two temporal values differ.

On the basis of what has been said in this section it is clear that more response decrement can be expected (1) when N-length is long and (2) when the ITI separating the last nonreward of the nonreward series and the first reward of the reward series is different from the ITIs separating the earlier nonrewards of the nonrewarded series.

In the Bullock and Smith and Perkins and Cacioppo experiments condition 2 prevailed and an increase in the response decrement rate was observed. In the North and Morton experiment all ITIs were constant and the response decrement rate remained constant over trials. In the Lauer and Carterette experiment N-length was short (12) and the response decrement rate decreased. Thus in a general way, the two principles introduced in this section appear to be confirmed by the existing evidence.

d. Inhibition. The principles covered thus far are adequate in a general way to deal with the existing literature. In one specific respect, however, they are not adequate. They do not tell us why an increase is sometimes observed in the response decrement rate over successive nonrewarded sessions (Bullock & Smith, 1953; Perkins & Cacioppo, 1950) and thus suggest that an additional principle is needed. Let us see why this is the case. Let S_x^N be the last nonreward in the series and let S_{x-y}^N symbolize all earlier nonrewards in the series. The stimulus S_x^N differs from S_{x-y}^N in two ways: it is a different temporal stimulus; that is, it occurs at different ITIs than S_{x-y}^N, and it is, of course, a later value of S^N (e.g., S_{24}^N) than S_{x-y}^N (S_{23}^N, . . . , S_1^N). In the initial nonrewarded session the ability of S_{x-y}^N to evoke R_I is based on stimulus generalization from the rewarded stimuli (S^R). In the subsequent nonrewarded sessions, however, the ability of S_{x-y}^N to evoke R_I is based not only on stimulus generalization from S^R but on stimulus generalization from S_x^N. And even granting that the amount of generalization from S_x^N to S_{x-y}^N is small (because of the different temporal stimuli involved), nevertheless some generalization occurs and the response decrement rate should decrease on the whole rather than increase.

Thus, in order to account for the increased response decrement rate over successive nonrewarded sessions, some sort of inhibitory process apparently must be postulated. We shall assume, for purposes of simplicity in exposition, that the various stimuli occasioned by the nonrewards in the series (S_1^N, S_2^N, and so on) possess an equal amount of such inhibition.

e. Experimental Analysis of N-length. This in mind, we may proceed to examine an investigation conducted in our laboratory by Dale Leonard employing the discrete trial lever situation. There were two groups ($N = 11$ per group), one of which received an N-length of 12 (group 12), the other an N-length of 24 (group 24). The experiment was conducted as follows: the daily session began with seven rewarded trials (R-length $= 7$) followed by the appropriate number of nonrewarded trials (N-length $= 12$ or 24) followed by nine rewarded trials (R-length $= 9$). Following the last rewarded trial the daily experimental session was terminated. All the ITIs of a daily session were the same (30 seconds). The investigation is interesting for the following reasons. (1) It employed many more nonrewarded sessions (20) than the typical investigation in the area. (2) It allowed a test of the different predictions generated by the Weinstock-Estes-Lauer habituation hypothesis and the present hypothesis. (3) It allowed a test of the specific predictions occasioned by the present hypothesis with reference to N-length. (4) The experiment is relevant to the hypothesis presented earlier, that the decreased response decrement rate observed in the Lauer and Estes and Lauer and Carterette investigations was due to the short N-lengths employed.

Figure 20 illustrates the theoretical state of affairs postulated by the present hypothesis *at the termination of training* for N-lengths of 12 and

24. Stimulus generalization from S^R to the various S^Ns is not shown in Fig. 20 since it is equal for both groups. Inhibition is represented by the dotted line running parallel to the x axis. Figure 20 suggests that in the early trials of the nonrewarded series, group 12 should respond faster

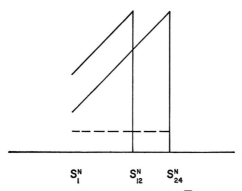

$$S^N_1 \qquad S^N_{12} \qquad S^N_{24}$$

FIG. 20. Schema showing that the effective amount of $\overline{H}$ available to the earlier S^Ns in the series from either S^N_{12} or S^N_{24} is reduced in the later stages of training by I (dotted line).

than group 24. This prediction was confirmed, as may be seen in Fig. 21, which presents bar-press speeds for the first six trials of each nonrewarded session. Figure 21 also shows that over successive nonrewarded sessions group 12 pressed faster (that is, response decrement rate decreased), whereas group 24 pressed slower (that is, response decrement rate in-

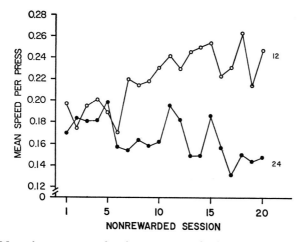

FIG. 21. Mean bar-press speeds of group 12 and of group 24 on the first six trials of each of the 20 nonrewarded sessions (see text for detailed discussion).

creased). The decreased response decrement rate of group 12 may be explained as follows: in the initial nonrewarded sessions the response was evoked by $\bar{H}$ from S^R. In subsequent sessions S_{12}^N steadily accumulated H, and the $\bar{H}$ from S_{12}^N to $S_1{}^N$, and so on, outweighed the accumulating inhibition at these points because S_{12}^N is relatively close to $S_1{}^N$, $S_2{}^N$, and so on. In group 24, however, the $\bar{H}$ from S_{24}^N to the lower values of S^N is less considerable (greater distance) and the accumulating inhibition outweighed the accumulating $\bar{H}$. These results, then, support the expectations of the present hypothesis in connection with N-length. They also suggest that the "habituation" of competing responses is not an important factor in successive acquisitions and extinctions. Actually we have in the present investigation one of those relatively rare instances in which two hypotheses predict diametrically different results. Thus, the habituation hypothesis would expect group 24 to show greater decreased response decrement rate than group 12, because group 24 received more nonrewards than group 12 and thus had the greater opportunity for habituation to occur. As may be seen in Fig. 21, the results were opposite to the predictions of the habituation hypothesis and, as previously indicated, in line with the predictions of the present hypothesis.

Figure 22 presents bar-press speeds for group 24 on the first and last six trials of each nonrewarded session. As may be seen, in the earlier nonrewarded sessions (1–5) more response decrement occurred on the last six trials than on the first six trials. Any theory would, of course, expect a result of this sort. The present interpretation of this finding is as follows: S^R supplied the principal source of $\bar{H}$ in the early nonrewarded

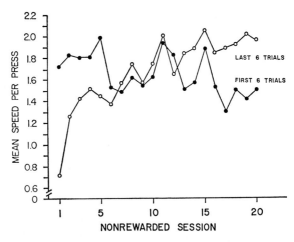

FIG. 22. Mean bar-press speeds of group 24 on the first and last six trials of each nonrewarded session (see discussion in text).

sessions, and since S^R supplies less $\overline{H}$ to the higher than to the lower values of S^N, it is to be expected that response decrement would become greater over the successive nonrewarded trials of each session. In the later nonrewarded sessions (13–20), however, there was less response decrement on the last six trials than on the first six trials, a finding that is not only predictable from the present hypothesis (see Fig. 20), but is probably not deducible (at least not in any simple way) from any current theory of extinction. That in the later sessions the animals became faster in a particular session as they received more nonrewards follows from the assumption that with successive presses the stimulus situation changed in an orderly and progressive fashion (S_1^N, S_2^N, and so on), and that later stimuli in the series (S_{20}^N, S_{21}^N, and so on), since they were closely followed by reward, possessed a greater capacity to evoke the bar-press reaction than earlier stimuli in the series. The results shown in Fig. 22 thus supply one of the more graphic bits of evidence supporting the N-length assumption.

Another matter of interest brought out in Fig. 22 is that over successive nonrewarded sessions (1 through 20) the response decrement rate decreased for the last six trials but increased for the first six trials. The increase for the first six trials represents the greater influence of inhibition relative to the weak $\overline{H}$ supplied from S_{24}^N, whereas the decrease in response decrement rate for the last six trials reflects the accumulating $\overline{H}$ at S_{24}^N. In common-sense terms, the animal "knows" that S_1^N, S_2^N, and so on, will not lead to reward, and so presses slowly. However, over successive nonrewarded sessions he gradually learns that S_{24}^N leads to reward and so when stimuli roughly similar to S_{24}^N are operative (such as S_{20}^N) he presses relatively fast. The results presented in Fig. 22 illustrate that it is too simple to talk about a gross measure of response decrement rate; the rate may actually be different for different segments of the nonrewarded series. In order to increase our knowledge about the successive acquisition and extinction of reactions it is necessary to turn to the patterning situation. From an analysis of patterning behavior, several additional principles of importance emerge regarding the successive acquisition and extinction of reactions. Another generality in connection with patterning should be mentioned. As will be seen, the results of patterning investigations are entirely consistent with those concerned with response decrement following training under various conditions of reward (such as magnitude and delay).

C. PATTERNING BEHAVIOR

1. *Patterning as a Variety of Successive Acquisitions and Extinctions*

If the rat is provided with a regular sequence of rewarded and nonrewarded trials, it may respond appropriately on each kind of trial. For example, when reward and nonreward alternate, the rat runs rapidly on the rewarded trials, slowly on the nonrewarded trials (e.g., Capaldi, 1958; Tyler *et al.*, 1953). Figure 23, taken from an investigation by Bloom and Capaldi (1961), shows the performance of two groups of rats in a straight alley on each day of training (12 trials per day), one group trained under a single alternating schedule of reward (R_1N_1, and so on), the other group under a double alternating schedule of reward ($R_1R_2N_1N_2$, and so on). Initially we shall view patterning as an instance of the successive acquisition and extinction of reactions. From this point of view, both the R-length and the N-length of the single alter-

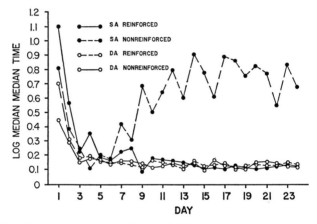

FIG. 23. Reinforced and nonreinforced trial running times on each of the acquisition days (see text for details of experiment). These are plotted on the basis of the log median median time for each *S* on each day.

nating group are one, while both the R-length and the N-length of the double alternating group are two. We may say, then, that the administration of ten trials under an alternating schedule involves five nonrewarded sessions (N-length of one) and five acquisition sessions (R-length of one). The times shown in Fig. 23 are plotted in terms of reinforced and nonreinforced trials separately. Note that the single alternating group eventually ran slowly on its nonrewarded trials, whereas the double alternating group ran rapidly and nondifferentially on both rewarded and nonrewarded trials.

Using language characteristic of the successive acquisition-extinction situation, it may be said of the single alternating group that in the early trials (days 1–6) it showed a decrease in the response decrement rate; beyond day 6, however, a steady increase occurred in the response decrement rate. The double alternating group, on the other hand, showed only a decrease in the response decrement rate.

The relevance of the patterning situation to the successive acquisition and extinction of reactions may be made more manifest by considering the performance of rats trained under a regular 33% schedule $(N_1N_2R_1)$. Figure 24 shows unpublished regular 33% data collected by Hart in our laboratory. There were ten trials a day in the straight alley, confinement duration of N_1N_2 and R_1 trials being 30 sec. The initial daily trial was always rewarded. Note in Fig. 24 that the rats ran slowly on the N_1 trial and rapidly and nondifferentially on the N_2 and R_1 trials. The behavior of the regular 33% group corresponds in impor-

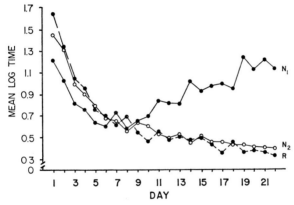

Fig. 24. Mean log time on N_1, N_2, and R trials on each day of training (complete discussion in text).

tant essentials to the behavior of Leonard's group 24 dealt with extensively in the immediately preceding section. Consider for the regular 33% group that the N_1 trials represents the initial portion of each nonrewarded session (as did the first six nonrewarded trials in Leonard's group 24) with the N_2 trials representing the last portion of each nonrewarded session (last six trials of group 24). From this point of view, both the regular 33% group and Leonard's group 24 were similar: on the later training days performance was better on the later nonrewards of the series than on the earlier nonrewards of the series. Thus, in both instances (considering later nonrewarded sessions) the response decrement rate increased for the early nonrewards of the session and decreased for the later nonrewards of the session.

Theoretical gradients of habit strength (solid line) and inhibition (dotted line) are presented below for the double alternation situation

(Fig. 25A) and for the regular 33% situation (Fig. 25B). For convenience, all stimulus points are presented along the front face of the continuum in Fig. 25A and B, a procedure that introduces but slight theoretical distortion. Figure 25A shows that in the double alternation situation H is directly acquired at $S_1{}^R$ (reward occurs on the following trial) and at $S_2{}^N$, while at $S_2{}^R$ and $S_1{}^N$ inhibition is directly acquired. At both $S_2{}^R$ and $S_1{}^N$ there are two sources of $\overline{H}$ (from $S_1{}^R$ and $S_2{}^N$) and these summate (Hull, 1943). Thus, the associative strength differences at the various stimulus points shown in Fig. 25A are small; too small, apparently, to permit differential running on rewarded and nonre-

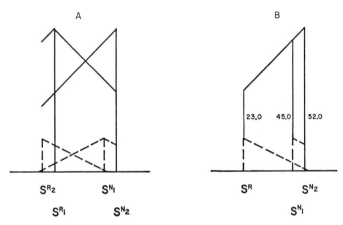

FIG. 25. The H and I tendencies and their generalization under a double alternating schedule of reward. (A) It can be seen that the summation of two generalized habit tendencies at $S^R{}_L$ and at $S^N{}_1$ provides a relatively flat zone of H and thus precludes pattern running. (B) The H tendencies and the I tendencies and their generalization under an N_1N_2R schedule of reward.

warded trials. Under the regular 33% schedule, however, as Fig. 25B shows, $S_1{}^R$ receives $\overline{H}$ from only one source ($S_2{}^N$). Moreover, $S_1{}^R$ directly acquires inhibition, and a source of H is not available from $S_2{}^R$. It can be expected, therefore, that running will be slow in the presence of $S_1{}^R$ (that is, on the N_1 trial). Figure 25B as drawn shows a slight difference in H values between the points $S_1{}^N$ and $S_2{}^N$. We must assume either that the differences shown in Fig. 25B are not large enough to permit differential running on N_1 and N_2 trials or that the gradient extending from $S_2{}^N$ to $S_1{}^N$ is actually somewhat flatter than shown in the figure. Theoretical gradients of habit and inhibition for single alternation training are straightforward; habit is accumulated at S^N and generalizes to S^R, while inhibition is accumulated at S^R and generalizes to S^N.

With these matters in mind we are in a position to state several additional general principles in connection with the successive acquisition and extinction of reactions.

(1) An increase in the response decrement rate may occur when N-length is as short as one (single alternation) or as short as two (regular 33%).

(2) The response decrement rate is affected by R-length. In order to obtain an increase in the response decrement rate with short N-lengths, R-length apparently cannot be greater than one. R-lengths of one supply I and fail to supply $\overline{H}$. When R-length is two, N-lengths of two produce a decrease rather than an increase in the response decrement rate (double alternation). The decreased response decrement rate is occasioned by the $\overline{H}$ supplied by $S_1{}^R$ (or with longer R-lengths such as $S_3{}^R$). The effect on the response decrement rate of R-lengths of greater than two cannot be determined on the basis of available experimental information.

(3) When R-length is greater than one, an increase in the response decrement rate may be observed over successive nonrewarded sessions provided the N-length is long, as in Leonard's group 24. The effect of long N-lengths is to reduce the $\overline{H}$ supplied to earlier S^Ns in the series from the last S^N in the series (for example, S_{24}^N in Leonard's group 24).

A number of other variables are currently known to affect patterning behavior. These will be dealt with following a brief summary of how the present hypothesis deals with successive acquisitions and extinctions in the light of what has been learned from patterning behavior.

Performance over a series of nonrewarded trials is regulated primarily by two factors, $\overline{H}$ and I. Regarding $\overline{H}$, two primary sources may be identified, that from S^R and that from the last S^N in the nonrewarded series ($S_x{}^N$). If $\overline{H}$ from either of these sources is reduced, the response decrement rate tends to increase. A variety of variables can be expected to reduce such $\overline{H}$. If R-length is one, I rather than $\overline{H}$ is supplied to S^N. Under these conditions, an increase in the response decrement rate has been observed with N-lengths as short as one and as short as two. Another way to reduce $\overline{H}$ is to increase N-length; long N-lengths reduce the $\overline{H}$ from $S_x{}^N$ to the earlier S^Ns in the series. Still another way is to separate earlier nonrewards in the series by one intertrial interval while separating $S_x{}^N$ from its rewarded trial by some different intertrial interval; this procedure reduces $\overline{H}$ from $S_x{}^N$ to the earlier S^Ns in the series and thus tends to produce an increase in the response decrement rate.

From the foregoing analysis, it follows that a variety of other variables should influence the response decrement rate. For example, if

S_x^N is followed by large reward, H at S_x^N is greater, the $\overline{H}$ supplied to the earlier S^Ns in the series is greater, and the response decrement rate should tend to decrease rather than increase. If, on the other hand, the R-length preceding (rather than following) the N-length consists of large rewards, less $\overline{H}$ will be supplied to the various S^Ns and the response decrement rate should tend to increase. From this it follows that the greatest increase in the response decrement rate should be observed when the initial R-length consists of large reward and the R-length following the N-length consists of small reward. And generally it follows that any variable which reduces $\overline{H}$ from S^R or from S_x^N will tend to produce an increase in the response decrement rate.

2. Effects of Reward Magnitude

Gonzalez, Bainbridge, and Bitterman (1966) employed alternating schedules in the discrete trial lever-pressing situation. They obtained longer latencies on the nonreinforced trials when reward magnitude was large (six .045-gm pellets) than when it was small (one .045-gm pellet). Leonard, in an unpublished investigation from our laboratory, compared alternation in the straight alley using two .045-gm pellets reward or sixteen .045-gm pellet reward. The two-pellet group showed only slight indications of alternation by the end of training (nine trials per day), whereas the sixteen-pellet group showed definite and statistically reliable patterning. Actually the sixteen-pellet group was significantly slower on nonrewarded trials and significantly faster on rewarded trials than the two-pellet group. Leonard's results may be deduced from the theoretical gradients of habit and inhibition for the large and the small magnitude alternating groups that are shown in Fig. 26A and B.

As previously indicated, Hulse (1958) and Wagner (1961) found less Rn following large as opposed to small magnitude of consistent reward. According to the present hypothesis, the Hulse-Wagner finding follows from the assumption that the S^Ns occurring in extinction receive less $\overline{H}$ from S^R_L than from S^R_S. In other words, both the Hulse-Wagner findings and those in connection with magnitude of reward in the alternating situation receive the same general interpretation within the framework of the present hypothesis (distance along continuum).

3. Effects of Nonrewarded Confinement Duration

Poynor, in an unpublished investigation from our laboratory, trained four groups of 12 rats each in a straight alley (ten trials per day for 18 days). The design was a 2×2 factorial, there being two levels of confinement duration on nonrewarded trials (10 versus 50 seconds) and two levels of confinement duration on rewarded trials (10 versus 50 seconds), reward consisting of free access to a wet mash throughout the confinement interval. Reward magnitude had only a slight influence on the results, presumably because 10 seconds of access to mash is a quite substantial reward. Although 50 seconds of access to mash occasioned slightly slower running on the nonrewarded trials than 10-seconds access to mash, particularly in the goal area, the effect of reward magnitude on the rewarded trials was entirely negligible. However, nonrewarded confinement duration had a substantial effect both on rewarded trial and nonrewarded trial running. First, running on the nonrewarded trials was significantly slower for 50-seconds than for 10-seconds confine-

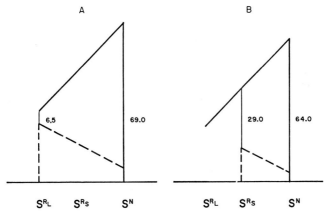

Fig. 26. The H tendencies and the I tendencies and their generalization under single alternating schedules of reward involving large reward (A) and small reward (B).

ment duration ($p < .01$). Moreover, running on the rewarded trials was significantly faster for 50-seconds than for 10-seconds nonrewarded confinement duration (NCD). These results are deducible from the present hypothesis on the basis of two assumptions: longer nonrewarded confinements occasion greater inhibition, and S^R supplies greater $\bar{I}$ to $S^{N_{10}}$ than to $S^{N_{50}}$.

Wall and Goodrich (1964) report that when regular 33% reward is employed in the discrete trial lever-press situation, a clear gradient is obtained, latencies being longest on N_1 trials, shorter on N_2 trials, and shortest on R trials. As indicated, the unpublished study by Hart considered earlier as well as one by Capaldi and Senko (1962), who also employed N_1N_2R schedules, report rather different results, running being slow on N_1 trials, and fast and nondifferential on N_2 and R trials. In the Hart study and the one by Capaldi and Senko, NCD was the same on both N_1 and N_2 trials. We have obtained results, on the other hand, of the Wall and Goodrich variety in our laboratory under rather specialized conditions. Figure 27 shows the results of an unpublished study by Hart in which NCD was, for one group (group 10–50), 10 seconds on N_1 trials and 50 seconds on N_2 trials. For the other group (group 50–10) NCD was 50 seconds on N_1 trials and 10 seconds on N_2 trials. It can be seen in Fig. 27 that group 10–50 performed like the rats of Wall and Goodrich; that is, a gradient effect was obtained, running being slowest on the N_1 trials, faster on N_2 trials, and yet faster on the R trial. Group 50–10, however, performed like the groups

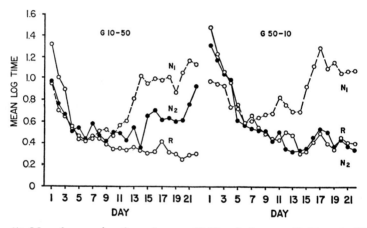

Fig. 27. Mean log running time of groups 10–50 and of groups 50–10 on the N_1, N_2, and R trials of each of the acquisition days (see text for discussion).

of Capaldi and Senko and of Hart, in which NCD was the same on N_1 and N_2 trials. Figure 28 presents theoretical gradients of habit and of inhibition for group 10–50 (A) and for group 50–10 (B).

The principal assumption contained in Fig. 28A and B is that the terminal level of inhibition is greater the larger the nonrewarded confinement duration. The $S^{N_{10}}$ takes on relatively more inhibition in group 10–50 ($S^{N_{10}}$ followed by 50-second NCD), whereas in group 50–10 S^R takes on relatively more inhibition. Under this assumption, as can be seen by examining Fig. 28, a gradient effect is expected to occur in group 10–50 but not in group 50–10. In Fig. 28B, note that two sources of inhibition generalize to $S^{N_{10}}$. These can be expected to summate, reducing the H differences between $S^{N_{10}}$ and $S^{N_{50}}$.

In the bar-press investigation by Wall and Goodrich, in which a gradient effect was also observed, differences in NCD, at least of the type just considered, apparently did not obtain. Presumably, then, the occurrence of a gradient effect in their investigation requires a slightly different explanation. One obvious possibility is that S_1^N and S_2^N are more discriminable stimuli (that is, are separated by a greater distance on the continuum) in the bar-press situation than in the straight alley. That is, as S_1^N and S_2^N become increasingly dissimilar, S_2^N supplies increasingly less $\overline{H}$ to S_1^N and response latencies would become longer in the presence of S_1^N (that is, on the N_2 trial). Presumably a general explanation of this sort is required to account for $N_1 N_2 R$ data reported by Murillo and Capaldi (1961) using human Ss. Human Ss, of course, are capable of discriminating more or less perfectly between N_1, N_2, and R trials. Presumably, this is because humans can count, thus reducing $\overline{H}$ between S_1^N, S_2^N, and S^R.

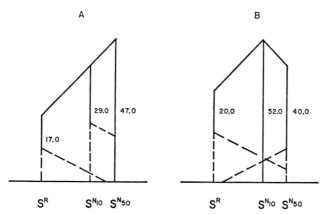

Fig. 28. The H and the I tendencies and their generalization under $N_1 N_2 R$ schedules of reward when (A) N_1 and N_2 are 10 seconds and 50 seconds, respectively, and (B) when N_1 and N_2 are 50 seconds and 10 seconds, respectively.

4. Effects of Delayed Reward

Burt and Wike (1963) reported the results of an investigation of overwhelming importance within the framework of the present hypothesis. Earlier, Cogan and Capaldi (1961) reported that the alternation of delayed reward (20-second delay) and immediately rewarded trials failed to produce patterning behavior. Although Cogan and Capaldi were surprised by their result at the time, their failure to obtain patterning is, in retrospect, entirely understandable; the stimuli $S^{D_{20}}$ and S^R are relatively close together on the continuum and thus afford a difficult discrimination. Burt and Wike replicated the Cogan and Capaldi finding. However, they also included in their experiment two other alternating groups, one of which received 60-second delay of reward, the other 100-second delay of reward. Not only did these groups display patterning but, as could be expected on the basis of the present hypothesis, the 100-second delay group patterned better than the 60-second delay group. What is perhaps even more important, systematically speaking, is that Burt and Wike included in their experiment alternating groups that were nonrewarded, the duration of nonrewarded confinement being varied. One of the nonrewarded groups was confined to the goalbox for 20 seconds, another for 80 seconds, the third for 120 seconds. As in the Poynor investigation treated above (Section III, C, 3), patterning generally improved with longer nonrewarded confinement—that is, the 80-second and 120-second groups that did not differ particularly patterned better than the 20-second group. However, and this perhaps is the finding of greatest interest in the Burt and Wike investigation, the alternating group that received 20-second nonreward patterned somewhat better than the alternating groups that received 100-second delay of reward. What this finding suggests, of course, is that the stimulus S^N_{20} lies to the right on the continuum in relation to the stimulus S^D_{100}. The importance of the Burt and Wike investigation can now be seen; it confirms the implications of the relatively broad portion of the continuum shown in Fig. 1 that extends from S^D_{20} to S^N_{120} and includes as intermediate stimuli S^D_{60}, S^D_{100}, S^N_{20}, and S^N_{80}. Moreover, it confirms for delay of reward what has been shown in investigations from ours and other laboratories for magnitude of reward and duration of nonrewarded confinement—that the results obtained in the single alternation patterning situation are consistent with an entire body of literature concerned with response decrement under nonreward following various kinds of acquisition training, namely, magnitude of consistent reward, partial delay of reward, and partial reward.

5. Effect of Temporal Variables

Capaldi and Stanley (1963) reported approximately equivalent pattern running under alternating schedules when trials were separated by 15 seconds, 2 minutes, 10 minutes, or 20 minutes. Moreover, Capaldi and Spivey (1964a) obtained pattern running under an alternating schedule when trials were separated by 24 hours. However, the patterning was quite poor judged against massed trial standards. Surridge and Amsel (1965), on the other hand, failed to obtain pattern running with 24-hour separation between trials, and Katz, Woods, and Carrithers (in press) obtained increasingly poorer pattern running the longer the intertrial interval (15 seconds, 2 minutes, 10 minutes, or 20 minutes). The reasons for these discrepancies are, at the moment, unclear, but they may be related to the different reward magnitudes and nonrewarded confinement durations used in the various investigations. We have seen, for example, that even with a 30-second ITI, patterning is poor under a two-pellet reward (Section III, C, 2).

Surridge and Amsel suggest the possibility that the stimuli governing patterning behavior may not be those of S^R and S^N, but certain external stimuli such as smell or differential noise preceding rewarded and nonrewarded trials. In another place Capaldi and Spivey (1965b) have advanced considerations suggesting that in runway studies patterning is probably not greatly affected, if it is affected at all, by classes of external stimuli. It should be obvious, too, that the patterning observed in the discrete trial lever press situation by Gonzalez et al. (1966) and by Wall and Goodrich (1964) is probably not regulated by external stimuli. Nor, of course, are the sort of results reported in the unpublished successive acquisition-extinction study by Leonard, which also employed discrete trials in the bar-press situation. Moreover, Bloom and Smith (1965) have reported patterning results in the free response bar-press situation that correspond in many respects to patterning results collected in the runway. Surridge and Amsel (1965) and Katz et al. (in press) suggest that in patterning investigations it might be better to have the reward present on both rewarded and nonrewarded trials. Although this suggestion has merit from some points of view, it may introduce potential complications. For example, following a conventional nonrewarded trial the stimulus is S^N. However, if on the nonrewarded trial the animal sees, smells, or otherwise detects the reward (but of course does not consume it), the stimulus on the succeeding trial may not be S^N but something different. Quite possibly the stimulus may contain components of S^R. In that event, the difficulty of discrimination between "S^N" and S^R would be increased and patterning would be more difficult to obtain. The absence of patterning in the study by Surridge and Amsel and the difficulty in obtaining patterning at 20-minute intervals in the study by Katz et al. may be related to this factor, since in both investigations reward was present in the goal box on "nonrewarded trials."

The attempt has been made to show that patterning is far from being an atypical learning situation. It may be regarded as possessing, in relation to other learning situations, some advantages and some disadvantages; but generally it follows the same laws. One well-substantiated finding in the straight alley is that speed of running tends to increase along with an increase in the intertrial interval. There is no reason to suppose that patterning is entirely exempt from such spaced trial effects, particularly perhaps when the discrimination between S^R and S^N is difficult. Thus relatively poor patterning at some intertrial interval may represent little more than a tendency toward spontaneous recovery. It should also be indicated that patterning represents only one index of the functionality of stimuli such as S^R and S^N at some particular intertrial interval. For example, Weinstock's (1954; 1958) finding that Rn increases as percentage of reinforcement decreases at 24-hour intervals is another such index. Since, as previously shown, N-length tended to increase as percentage decreased, under Weinstock's conditions his finding supports the notion that S^N is operative at 24-hour intervals. Moreover, Capaldi and Spivey (1964b) have shown that ITR reduces nonreward response decrement with 24-hour separation between trials, thus providing another index of the functionality of S^N at 24-hour intervals. Capaldi and Wargo (1963) have shown that following a small number of acquisition trials, alternating schedules produce less nonrewarded response decrement than irregular schedules with 20-minute ITIs. Different dependent variables are not always in agreement, and the evaluation of a hypothesis demands that a variety of factors be considered.

D. RESPONSE DECREMENT INVESTIGATIONS: MODIFIED EXPERIMENTAL DESIGNS

1. *Typical Extinction Design: Defects*

We shall consider certain modifications of the typical extinction investigations which, it is hoped, will be useful in better evaluating the relative contribution to response decrement of extinction on the one hand and generalization decrement on the other. From the present point of view, the usual extinction investigation cannot be used to make inferences about either the process of extinction or the extent to which the response decrement observed is actually due to extinction. As indicated, nonreward itself introduces stimuli into the total stimulus complex. Necessarily, then, there is differential generalization decrement among the several groups in going from the acquisition phase to the nonreward phase. Thus, if differential acquisition treatments in fact produce a differential capacity to resist extinction, in order to evaluate this, the effects of generalization decrement must be equalized. Our interest in correcting what seem to be the deficiencies in the typical extinction design is not casual, and it is likely that at least some of the methods evolved in our laboratory for doing so may fail to achieve general acceptance—nor, of course, should they in the absence of further experimentation. Our interest is not casual, because a good many of the inferences concerning the nature of the learning processes presumed to be operating both in the acquisition and the response decrement phases are based on the assumption that nonreward acts to extinguish S-R connections. If the assumption is faulty, then probably much of the theorizing based on the assumption is also faulty. On the other hand, much of the theorizing contained in this paper is based on the assumption that generalization decrement is a process of greater importance than extinction. If that assumption is faulty, then probably much of the theorizing contained in this paper is also faulty. Our attempts to assess the relative contributions to response decrement of extinction and generalization decrement fall into two general classes, which may be labeled the factorial design and reinstating the acquisition stimuli, respectively.

2. The Factorial Design

Many contemporary theories attribute a differential potency to resist extinction to acquisition main effects (AME). Thus, for example, the claim is often made that acquisition under PR produces a greater ability to withstand the effects of extinction than acquisition under continuous reward or PD. According to the present point of view, statements of this sort are not warranted given existing experimental information. The present hypothesis tends to emphasize that much of the response decrement observed is a result of the interaction between the AME and the response decrement main effect (DME). In the typical design, however, the influence of the $\text{AME} \times \text{DME}$ interaction is not evaluated. We have attempted, therefore, to evolve an experimental design that evaluates separately the effects of the AME and the $\text{AME} \times \text{DME}$ interaction. The assumption is that differences due to the AME reflect the influence of extinction, whereas differences due to the $\text{AME} \times \text{DME}$ interaction reflect the influence of generalization decrement. Consider a specific example of these generalities.

Burt and Wike (1963) reported that response decrement over a series of nonrewards is less if acquisition occurred under PR rather than under PD. In acquisition the stimuli conditioned to R_I under PR and PD are respectively S^N and S^D. In the nonreward phase S^N occurs. Thus, there is more generalization decrement in going to the nonrewarded phase from PD than from PR. Can the generalization decrement be equalized? Apparently it can—or at least a step in that direction is possible—if we recognize constant delay of reward as a legitimate response decrement procedure, as legitimate, that is, as constant nonreward. Given such recognition, we would shift half the Ss in each of the PR and PD groups to constant nonreward, the remaining half to constant delay of reward. And we would be interested in the response decrement exhibited by the PD and PR groups under both response decrement procedures. If, summing over both response decrement procedures, PR in acquisition produced less response decrement than PD in acquisition, apparently we would be justified in assuming that PR produces greater Rn than PD. The effects of generalization decrement would be seen in the AME $\times$ DME interaction; a pure generalization decrement interpretation would expect less response decrement from PR than from PD when the response decrement procedure is constant nonreward, and more response decrement from PR than from PD when the response decrement procedure is constant delay of reward.

3. Reinstating the Acquisition Stimuli

From the present point of view, continuous nonreward following consistent reward is not adequate to extinguish the S-R connection formed in acquisition, that is, S^R-R_I, because S^N and not S^R occurs during the nonrewarded series. At best, the connection S^R-R_I can suffer only generalized extinction. Accordingly, when S^R is re-presented, we would expect it to evoke R_I with considerable vigor. This generally is what is meant by reinstating the acquisition stimuli—presenting, subsequent to a nonrewarded series, those stimuli that presumably occurred during the acquisition phase. From the present point of view, the reacquisition phase of a successive acquisition-extinction investigation involves reinstating the acquisition stimuli. And North and Morton's (1962) finding that an increase in acquisition rate occurs over successive rewarded sessions, and particularly in the initial reacquisition session, supports the notion that the capacity of S^R to evoke R_I was not greatly diminished by the intervening nonrewards. Actually we have previously considered another example of reinstating the acquisition stimuli. It will be remembered that, in the investigation by Minkoff, rats trained under one ITI (e.g., 30 seconds) and subsequently nonrewarded at the 8-minute ITI ran quite rapidly when returned to the 30-second ITI. It can be seen that the procedure of reinstating the acquisition stimuli need not be limited to the successive acquisition-extinction situation, and may be employed in connection with a wide variety of stimuli.

Of course, in order to demonstrate that the improved performance of groups returned to the acquisition stimuli is not due to the change in conditions per se, controls that experience such change but not a return to the acquisition stimuli are required. Fortunately, this control requirement is met by the factorial design. Thus, in what follows, the same factorial design serves to equate for generalization decrement and to reinstate the acquisition stimuli.

4. Specific Experimental Designs

a. *Delay Decrement versus Nonreward Decrement.* Lynch, in an unpublished investigation from our laboratory, gave 40 rats 11 days of acquisition training in the straight alley at six trials per day (30-second ITI). Half the rats were trained under an irregular PR schedule, half under an irregular PD schedule (8-pellet reward), nonrewarded confinement and delay of reward being 30 seconds. Following this training, all *S*s were given response decrement training, half of each acquisition group under constant nonreward, the remaining half under constant delay of reward (six trials per day for six days). Figure 29 shows, for each of the four groups, the mean log times in

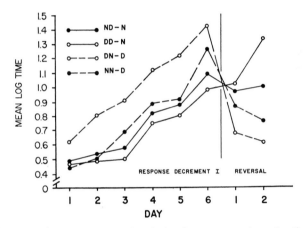

FIG. 29. Response decrement in each of the four groups (see details of experiment in text) in the goal section in the initial decrement phase (days 1–6) and following a reversal of goal box condition.

the goal section on each of the six days of response decrement training (Response Decrement I). Generally, the results are consistent with the expectations of a "pure" generalization decrement interpretation. Note first of all that group DN, the group trained under PD in acquisition and then shifted to nonreward, ran slower than group NN, the group trained under PR in acquisition and then shifted to nonreward. The slower running of group DN relative to group NN is consistent with the findings of Burt and Wike (1963) that PR produces less response decrement than PD when the response decrement procedure is nonreward. Also supporting the expectations of a generalization decrement interpretation is the finding that group DD, the group receiving PD in acquisition and constant delay of reward in response decrement training, ran faster than group ND, the group receiving PR in acquisition and constant delay of reward in response decrement training. It is relatively clear from an inspection of Fig. 29 that the relative amount of response decrement exhibited following training under PR or PD is dependent on the specific kind of response decrement procedure employed, constant nonreward or constant delay of reward. The picture shown in Fig. 29 is supported by the results of a 2 × 2 factorial analysis of variance; the AME × DME interaction was significant ($F = 8.55$; $df = 1.36$; $p < .01$). Somewhat surprising was the failure of the AME to reach a suitable level of statistical significance ($F = 2.60$, nonsignificant). This suggests, providing the AME is taken to reflect the influence of extinction, that extinction per se had little influence upon differential response decrement.

The points to the right of the vertical line in Fig. 29 show the effects of reversing the response decrement procedure for each of the groups (that is, group DN was now given constant delay decrement, and vice versa). Thus, for two of the groups the acquisition stimuli were reinstated (DND and NDN), while the remaining two groups received a change in response decrement training that did not involve a return to the acquisition stimuli (DDN and NND). If the acquisition stimuli retained a capacity to evoke R_I despite the intervening response decrement training, it would be expected that group DND would run faster than its control (group NND), while by the same token group NDN would be expected to run faster than group DDN. A more specific prediction than this is not possible; for instance, group NDN could not be expected to run faster than group NND, because the acquisition stimuli are reinstated for group NDN and not reinstated for group NND. The reason, of course, is that running is affected by the response decrement procedure itself, that is, nonreward produces slower running than delay of reward, and there is no way to determine a priori whether the strength of the reinstated associative connection will or will not override the decrement producing properties of the response decrement procedure per se. A 2 × 2 factorial analysis of variance was applied to the running times on day 2 of reversal training. The results of the analysis indicated that the AME had little effect on performance during reversal training ($F < 1.00$); the AME × DME interaction, however, was highly significant ($p < .01$), suggesting that groups DND and NDN ran faster in reversal than groups DDN and NND. Of course, the DME was also statistically significant ($p < .01$).

It is relatively clear from these results that nonreward did not produce a great deal of extinction. First, in Response Decrement I the

AME was not statistically significant. Moreover, in reversal group DND performed surprisingly well, better than its control NND and better than group DD (Response Decrement I) on its later days of response decrement training. In the absence of further experimentation it is difficult to know just what interpretation to ascribe to the various results shown in Fig. 29. With this in mind, we note that on the second day of reversal training, group NND performed better than group ND on its later days of Response Decrement I training. Can this be taken to mean that in Response Decrement I, six days of non-rewarded training (group NND) produced less diminution in the capacity of the delay stimulus to evoke R_I than did four days of constant delay training (group ND)? Although this interpretation is feasible and suggests that the delay stimulus suffers more extinction when it is directly extinguished than when it receives generalized extinction from nonreward, it is not the only possible interpretation. For example, it is also possible that a change in response decrement procedure per se occasions faster running. Tending to counterbalance the notion that change per se produces faster running is the performance of group DDN in the reversal phase, despite a change in response decrement procedure on the whole, group DDN slowed up in the reversal phase.

Previously in this paper we have employed the concept of inhibition. Inhibition, of course, is an extinction mechanism. The results shown in Fig. 29 are not particularly favorable to extinction interpretations. Obviously, however, as our previous emphasis on inhibition indicates, we are far from prepared to reject extinction as a process altogether, although from the viewpoint of consistency and several other viewpoints as well, the present approach would be far better off without an extinction mechanism. But too many phenomena, such as patterning, suggest the necessity of postulating an extinction process. Moreover, as we shall see shortly, another investigation employing the general factorial procedure produced a significant AME. However, still another investigation in the factorial framework (Capaldi, 1966a) failed to produce a significant AME. Fortunately these investigations appear to fall into a meaningful pattern and it is possible, as we shall see, to hazard a guess as to which conditions will and which will not favor a significant AME. Although not prepared to reject extinction, for reasons already given, we are prepared to hypothesize that for a wide variety of conditions at least, extinction is of secondary importance to generalization decrement, and that nonreward produces considerably less extinction than appears to be normally thought. Extinction is probably of greatest importance in those situations in which the same stimulus (or relatively the same stimulus) is repeatedly associated with nonreward. For example, in the alternation situation, S^R is repeatedly followed by nonreward and under these conditions S^R appears to take on strong inhibitory properties. In continuous nonreward situations, however, extinction is probably of secondary importance. First, as previously indicated, because of the stimulus change factor (different stimuli occur in acquisition and in the nonreward phase) only generalized extinction seems possible. Too, it seems possible that something approaching maximal response decrement occurs on the basis of stimulus change prior to the time that maximal extinction occurs.

b. Delay Decrement. The investigations cited in this section are concerned not only with the issues just considered, but with others as. well. We recognize that in order to identify the AME with extinction as we have done in the foregoing, constant nonreward and constant delay of reward must be shown to be similar in their response decrement-producing properties. If the two procedures produce response decrement in entirely different ways, then the extinction interpretation we have ascribed to the AME is probably not valid. The attempt to establish comparability in response decrement-producing properties of the two procedures encounters the following minor difficulty. Sometimes acquisition treatment x is expected to produce greater response decrement than acquisition training y under both constant nonreward and constant delay of reward (we call this circumstance a nonreversal). Sometimes, however, acquisition training x is expected to produce more response decrement than acquisition training y under one response decrement procedure and less response decrement under the other response decrement procedure (this circumstance is called a reversal). The difficulty alluded to earlier is this: the occurrence of a reversal might be seen as evidence for the proposition that constant nonreward and constant delay of reward produce response decrement in different ways. It is suggested that the occurrence of a reversal where the present hypothesis expects one to occur should not be taken to suggest that response decrement under nonreward and delay of reward are produced by different processes. At the same time, it is recognized that evidence should be provided which indicates that nonreversals will occur where the hypothesis expects them to occur. The general rules for determining when reversals and nonreversals are to be expected are straightforward.

(1) Nonreversals: If acquisition training condition x produces more generalization decrement than acquisition training condition y under all response decrement procedures, nonreversals are to be expected. Consider the truncated portion of the stimulus continuum shown in Fig. 30. Assume that two groups are trained under consistent reward, one receiv-

ing a large magnitude of reward on all trials (S^R_L-R_I), the other a small magnitude of reward on all trials (S^R_s-R_I). The stimuli S^D_{10}, S^D_{30}, and S^N_{10} shown in Fig. 30 will all receive less $\overline{H}$ from S^R_L than from S^R_s. The group trained under large reward should therefore show greater response decrement than the group trained under small reward under all three response decrement procedures, 10-second delay of reward (S^D_{10}), 30-second delay of reward (S^D_{30}), and 10-second nonreward (S^N_{10}). Thus, under the conditions described a nonreversal is expected.

(2) Reversals: If acquisition training condition x involves more generalization decrement than acquisition training condition y under one response decrement procedure and less generalization decrement under the other response decrement procedure, a reversal is to be expected. Thus, as Fig. 30 shows, if one group is trained under a PD schedule

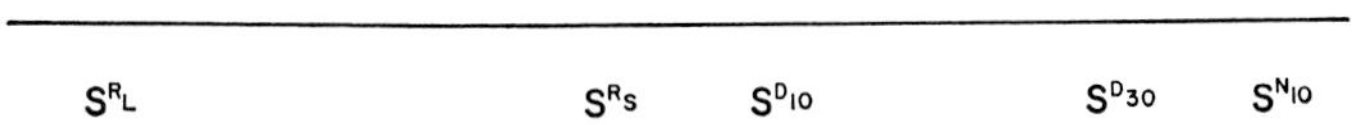

S^R_L S^R_s S^D_{10} S^D_{30} S^N_{10}

FIG. 30. Truncated portion of the total stimulus continuum useful for determining when reversals and nonreversals are to be expected.

in which delay is 30 seconds and the other group under a PR schedule in which nonrewarded confinement is 10 seconds, the PD group should show less response decrement than the PR group when the response decrement condition is 30-second constant delay of reward, and more response decrement than the PR group when the response decrement condition is 10-second constant nonreward. That is, under the conditions described a reversal is to be expected.

We turn now to an unpublished investigation conducted in our laboratory by Waters. In acquisition two groups ($N = 22$ per group) were trained in the runway under identical 45% irregular PD schedules, one receiving 15-second delay on the delayed trials, the other 60-second delay. There were 15 days of acquisition training and a total of 54 trials (ITI $= 30$ seconds). All Ss then received response decrement training under *constant delay* at five trials each day for eight days. In the decrement phase, half of each acquisition group (15- or 60-second delay) received 15-second constant delay (groups 15–15 and 60–15) and the remaining half 60-second constant delay (groups 15–60 and 60–60). The group designation 15–60 is to be understood to mean 15-second delay in acquisition, 60-second delay in the response decrement phase.

A major object in running this particular investigation was to determine if the reversals and the nonreversals expected by the hypothesis could be obtained. Consider first 15- versus 60-second delay in acquisition. It is well established (e.g., Capaldi & Poynor, 1966; Logan *et al.*, 1956) that response decrement under nonreward is less if in acquisition the PD group receives long delay (e.g., 60 seconds) rather than short delay (e.g., 15 seconds). This finding is, of course, predictable from the present hypothesis (see Section II, B, 3, a). Now the present hypothesis also expects that 60-second PD will produce less response decrement than 15-second PD when the response decrement procedure is 60-second constant delay of reward rather than nonreward. We wished to determine if this particular nonreversal expected by the hypothesis could be obtained. On the other hand, the hypothesis expects that the group receiving 15-second PD in acquisition would show less response decrement than the group receiving 60-second PD in acquisition when the response decrement procedure is 15-second constant delay of reward. This result would constitute a reversal of what is obtained under constant nonreward decrement.

Figure 31 presents for each of the four groups the mean log times in

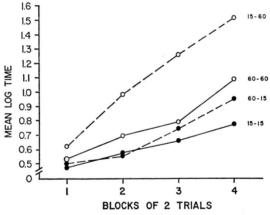

Fig. 31. Response decrement for each of the four groups (details of experiment in text) in the goal section in blocks of two days.

the goal section on each of the eight days of decrement training in two day blocks. Differences between the groups on the last day of acquisition were not significant ($F < 1.00$). It can be seen in Fig. 31 that group 15–60 ran slower than group 60–60, thus duplicating for 60-second constant delay decrement the results previously obtained for nonrewarded decrement following short versus long PD (e.g., Capaldi & Poynor, 1966; Logan *et al.*, 1956). On the other hand, as Fig. 31 shows, group 15–15 ran faster on the whole than group 60–15. Thus, the reversals and nonreversals expected by the hypothesis were obtained. A 2×2 factorial analysis of variance applied to the times shown in Fig. 31 indicated that the AME was significant ($F = 5.11$; $df = 1.36$; $p < .05$), while the AME $\times$ DME interaction was highly significant ($F = 11.03$; $df = 1.36$; $p < .002$). The significant AME suggests that 60-second delay in acquisition produced less response decrement than 15-second delay in acquisition with generalization decrement controlled. Accordingly, it would appear that 60-second delay produces greater Rn than 15-second delay. At the same time, the significant AME $\times$ DME interaction makes it clear that generalization decrement exercised a strong influence over the results.

Another unpublished investigation from our laboratory, this one conducted by Nicholas Wilson, suggests that delay decrement and nonreward decrement are governed by the same general principles by producing a nonreversal where a nonreversal was expected. We have previously covered an investigation by Capaldi and Hart (Section II, A, 2, c) that indicated that following 18 acquisition trials an alternating PR group shows less response decrement than an irregular PR group when the decrement procedure was nonrewarded. Indeed Capaldi and Spivey (1965a), who also used the nonreward decrement procedure, found similarly that an 18-trial alternating PD group showed less response decrement than an irregular control. Thus, the finding is well substantiated that, following 18 acquisition trials, alternating training in acquisition produces less response decrement than irregular training in acquisition when the response decrement procedure is nonreward. The general object of Wilson's investigation was to determine if a nonreversal could be obtained where one was expected. More specifically, Wilson's investigation attempted to determine if delay decrement would produce the same sort of results as nonreward decrement following a small number of acquisition trials under alternating and irregular schedules. Wilson's procedures were identical in most respects to those used by Capaldi and Hart (1962) and Capaldi and Spivey (1965a). Figure 32 shows, for the alternating and irregular groups, the mean log times along the total alley on each of the 13 trials of 30-second constant delay decrement training (delay was also 30 seconds in acquisition). Differences in the decrement phase were highly significant ($F = 34.45$; $df = 1.18$; $p < .001$). Since Wilson obtained a nonreversal when a nonreversal was expected, his results support the notion that delay decrement and nonreward decrement are occasioned by similar processes. Thus, Wilson's finding adds further justification to our use of the AME to reflect the effects of extinction.

c. *Nonreward Decrement.* In a recent investigation (Capaldi, 1966a) rats were given partial reinforcement in the runway in acquisition.

In acquisition there were two major groups of 40 Ss each, one group was confined to the goal box for 60 seconds on nonrewarded trials (S^N_{60}-R_I), the other group for 10 seconds on nonrewarded trials (S^N_{10}-R_I). Both groups, of course, received the same schedule of PR. Response decrement training was by nonreward, half of each acquisition group receiving 10-second nonrewarded confinement, the remaining half receiving 60-second nonrewarded confinement, generating four groups: 10–10, 10–60, 60–10, and 60–60, the first number representing nonrewarded confinement time in acquisition, the second number nonrewarded confinement time in the decrement phase. Following the nine days of decrement training (Response Decrement I), all groups were shifted to the opposite confine-

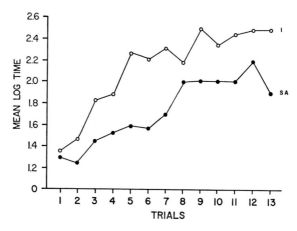

Fig. 32. Response decrement under delay of reward for the alternating and irregular groups (see text for discussion).

ment time (Decrement II). Thus for two of the groups the acquisition stimuli were reinstated (10–60–10, 60–10–60), whereas for two of the groups the acquisition stimuli were not reinstated (10–10–60, 60–60–10).

The mean log times (total alley) for each of the groups on each of the days of Decrement I and Decrement II training are shown in Fig. 33. The AME had little effect on performance, either on the first three days of Decrement I training ($F < 1.00$) or on the last three days of Decrement I training ($F < 1.00$), or on the third day of Decrement II training ($F < 1.00$). The AME $\times$ DME interaction was significant ($p < .01$) for both the first three days of Decrement I training and the third day of Decrement II training. The results shown in Fig. 33 are, of course, quite consistent with the results obtained in the previous factorial investigations considered, although in several ways they add to those earlier results. First, of the several investigations, the one currently being considered shows the least influence of the AME. Note, too, in Decrement I that confinement duration per se influenced performance, 60 second confinement producing slower running than 10-second confinement. And when confinement durations were shifted in Decrement II, performance shifted appropriately, regardless of whether the acquisition stimuli were reinstated, although of course the groups that experienced reinstatement performed better than the groups that did not. A striking example is provided by groups 10–10–60 and 60–60–10; group 10–10–60 slowed up in Decrement II, whereas

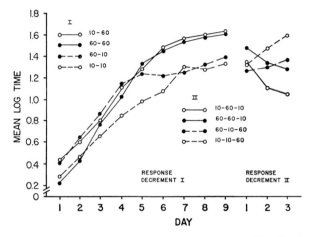

FIG. 33. Response decrement for each of the four groups (details of experiment are given in the text) in the initial nonrewarded phase (Response Decrement I) and following a reversal of nonrewarded confinement (Response Decrement II).

group 60–60–10 speeded up in Decrement II. Such shifts in performance are highly suggestive of the performance shifts accompanying changes in reward magnitude. But here, of course, nonrewarded confinement durations and not reward magnitudes are changed. Results of the sort shown in Fig. 33, which suggest to us that performance changes as a function of changes in goal box condition, require a concept that is somewhat more general than incentive motivation. Seemingly it is not particularly sound to relate the performance shifts shown in Fig. 33 (or even the initial running differences occasioned by confinement duration in Decrement I) to incentive, since nonreward presumably does not involve incentive. Generally speaking, performance would appear to be regulated by variations in goal box conditions on nonrewarded as well as rewarded trials, and if we want to interpret both in similar terms, it seems necessary to use a more general concept than incentive. As previously indicated in this paper and elsewhere (Capaldi & Poynor, 1965), the stimulus intensity (V) concept is not only more general than the incentive concept, but could be thought of as including the incentive concept as a special case. Moreover, the V concept is adequate to deal with the effects on performance of both reward and nonreward (Capaldi & Poynor, 1965).

Thus far we have covered three factorial investigations. One produced a significant AME (Waters), one a substantial, although not significant AME (Lynch), and one (Capaldi, 1966a) found the AME to have virtually no influence on performance during the decrement phase. A comparison of these investigations apparently suggests a hypothesis that is useful in determining when we can and when we cannot expect a significant AME. First, let it be understood that a failure to obtain a significant AME using the factorial procedure could, but does not necessarily, mean that the response decrement being observed is entirely unrelated to extinction. Another interpretation is that although extinction occurs in the response decrement phase, it is not occurring differentially as a function of the differential acquisition treatments. According to this line of reasoning, 10-second nonreward in acquisition increased Rn about as much as 60-second nonreward in acquisition (the Capaldi investigation) and 30-second delay in acquisition increases Rn about as much as 30-second nonreward in acquisition (the Lynch investigation). However, 60-second delay in acquisition produces greater Rn than 15-second delay in acquisition (the Waters investigation). Let us assume that the extinction-producing potency of a particular goal box condition increases as we move rightward on the stimulus continuum shown in Fig. 1. Assume also that this increased extinction-producing potency "asymptotes," or plateaus, quickly, being maximal for an arbitarily chosen 60-second delay of reward. This means in effect that 15-second delay of reward possesses only a slight capacity to increase Rn in relation to 60-second delay of reward or 10-second nonreward, and so on. But 30-second delay possesses a considerable, although not maximal, capacity to increase Rn. This hypothesis accounts for the results obtained in the three factorial investigations we have considered. Note, too, that we could, if we wanted, relate the increasing extinction-producing potency of goal box conditions on the right of the continuum in Fig. 1 to some specific mechanism. For example, it could be assumed that competing responses are greater for a 60-second delay of reward than for a 15-second delay of reward, and that Rn is an increasing function of competing responses. Moreover, it could be assumed that something approaching maximal competing responses is produced by a 30-second delay of reward, and so on. At the moment, however, our own feeling is that, on the basis of existing experimental information, the attempt to relate extinction to some specific mechanism is premature.

IV. Concluding Comments

A primary deficiency of sequential theorizing is that it has been applied thus far only to a relatively restricted number of learning situations. Generally, sequential theorizing seems prepared at the moment to deal with those learning situations in which some single response is made, such as running forward in a runway or pressing a bar. Whether or not a sequential approach will prove to have merit when applied to, for example, selective learning, cannot be forecast at the moment; certainly an attempt should soon be made to deal with relatively more complicated learning phenomena. Another deficiency of sequential theorizing is that even with respect to those learning situations to which it has been applied, some phenomena still resist explanation. For example, the finding that PR produces faster terminal running than consistent reward (e.g., Wagner, 1961) cannot apparently be explained in sequential terms in the absence of additional assumptions. This finding is not limited to irregular PR schedules, but occurs for regular PR schedules as well (Capaldi, Turner, & Wynn, 1962).

On the positive side, the hypothesis appears able to explain many phenomena not deducible from other hypotheses. Moreover, a generalization decrement interpretation has been shown to be applicable to a wide variety of phenomena currently explained in diverse terms, such as associational and motivational. The potential gain here is in terms of parsimony and simplicity. It should be indicated, too, that the present hypothesis seems well adapted to deal with a wide variety of transfer phenomena.

Ultimately, sequential theorizing suggests that nonsequential theorizing and research are limited in scope. It seems possible at this writing that nonsequential theorizing may, in some respects, represent a special case of sequential theorizing. The special case, of course, is that in which great care is normally taken to obscure the more obvious manifestations of sequential variables. As one case in point we might cite the pronounced current tendency to employ irregular PR schedules. From a sequential viewpoint, many of the "control" procedures currently used in fact minimize the effects of the variables that are of actual significance.

REFERENCES

Amsel, A. The role of frustrative nonreward in noncontinuous reward situations. *Psychol, Bull.*, 1958, 55, 102–119.

Anderson, N. Comparison of different populations: Resistance to extinction and transfer. *Psychol. Rev.*, 1963, 70, 162–179.

Bacon, W. E. Partial reinforcement extinction effect following different amounts of training. *J. comp. physiol. Psychol.*, 1962, 55, 998–1003.

Banks, R. K. Persistence to continuous punishment following intermittent punishment training. *J. exp. Psychol.*, 1966, 71, 373–377.

Beck, S. B. Eyelid conditioining as a function of CS intensity, UCS intensity and Manifest Anxiety Scale score. *J. exp. Psychol.*, 1963, 66, 429–438.

Beier, E. M. In F. A. Logan (Ed.), *Incentive*. New Haven: Yale Univer. Press, 1960.

Black, R. W., & Spence, K. W. Effects of intertrial reinforcement on resistance to extinction following extended training. *J. exp. Psychol.*, 1965, 70, 559–563.

Bloom, J. M. Extinction responding as a function of rewarded and nonrewarded goal confinement. Paper read at Southwest. Psychol. Ass., Dallas, 1966.

Bloom, J. M., & Capaldi, E. J. The behavior of rats in relation to complex patterns of partial reinforcement. *J. comp. physiol. Psychol.*, 1961, 54, 261–265.

Bloom, J. M., & Smith, N. F. Stimulus aftereffects of bar pressing. *Psychon. Sci.*, 1965, 3, 23–24.

Bower, G. H., Fowler, H., & Trapold, M. A. Escape learning as a function of amount of shock reduction. *J. exp. Psychol.*, 1959, 58, 484–487.

Brown, R. T., & Wagner, A. R. Resistance to punishment and extinction following training with shock or nonreinforcement. *J. exp. Psychol.*, 1964, 68, 503–507.

Bugelski, R. Extinction with and without sub-goal reinforcement. *J. comp. physiol. Psychol.*, 1938, 26, 121–134.

Bullock, D. H., & Smith, W. C. An effect of repeated conditioning extinction upon operant strength. *J. exp. Psychol.*, 1953, 46, 349–352.

Burt, D. E., & Wike, E. L. Effects of alternating partial reinforcement and alternating delay of reinforcement on a runway response. *Psychol. Rep.*, 1963, 13, 439–442.

Capaldi, E. J. The Effect of different amounts of training on the resistance to extinction of different patterns of partially reinforced responses. *J. comp. physiol. Psychol.*, 1958, 51, 367–371.

Capaldi, E. J. Effect of N-length, number of different N-lengths and number of reinforcements on resistance to extinction. *J. exp. Psychol.*, 1964, 68, 230–239.

Capaldi, E. J. Main effect extinction theory vs. interaction response decrement theory. Paper read at Psychon. Soc., Chicago, 1965.

Capaldi, E. J. Stimulus specificity: Nonreward. *J. exp. Psychol.*, 1966, 72, 410–414. (a)

Capaldi, E. J. Partial reinforcement: An hypothesis of sequential effects. *Psychol. Rev.*, 1966, 73, 459–477. (b)

Capaldi, E. J. Sequential vs. nonsequential variables in partial delay of reward. *J. exp. Psychol.*, in press.

Capaldi, E. J., & Hart, D. Influence of a small number of partial reinforced training trials on resistance to extinction. *J. exp. Psychol.*, 1962, 64, 166–171.

Capaldi, E. J., Hart, D., & Stanley, L. R. Effect of intertrial reinforcement on the aftereffect of nonreinforcement and resistance to extinction. *J. exp. Psychol.*, 1963, 65, 70–74.

Capaldi, E. J., & Olivier, W. P. Sequence of delayed reward and nonrewarded trials. *J. exp. Psychol.*, 1966, **72**, 307–310.

Capaldi, E. J., & Poynor, H. B. Nonreward confinement duration: The complement of reward magnitude. *Psychon. Sci.*, 1965, **3**, 515–516.

Capaldi, E. J., & Poynor, H. B. Aftereffects and delay of reward. *J. exp. Psychol.*, 1966, **71**, 80–88.

Capaldi, E. J., & Senko, M. L. Acquisition and transfer in partial reinforcement. *J. exp. Psychol.*, 1962, **63**, 155–159.

Capaldi, E. J., & Spivey, J. E. Effect of goal-box similarity on the aftereffect of nonreinforcement and resistance to extinction. *J. exp. Psychol.*, 1963, **66**, 461–465.

Capaldi, E. J., & Spivey, J. E. Stimulus consequences of reinforcement and non-reinforcement: Stimulus traces or memory. *Psychon. Sci.*, 1964, **1**, 403–404. (a)

Capaldi, E. J., & Spivey, J. E. Intertrial reinforcement and aftereffects at 24-hour intervals. *Psychon. Sci.*, 1964, **1**, 181–182. (b)

Capaldi, E. J., & Spivey, J. E. Schedule of partial delay of reinforcement and resistance to extinction. *J. comp. physiol. Psychol.*, 1965, **60**, 274–276. (a)

Capaldi, E. J., & Spivey, J. E. Comment. *Psychon. Sci.*, 1965, **3**, 110 and 132. (b)

Capaldi, E. J., & Stanley, L. R. Temporal properties of reinforcement aftereffects. *J. exp. Psychol.*, 1963, **65**, 169–175.

Capaldi, E. J., & Stanley, L. R. Percentage of reward vs. N-length in the runway. *Psychon. Sci.*, 1965, **3**, 263–264.

Capaldi, E. J., Turner, L., & Wynn, W. H. Decremental and facilitative effects in the straight-alley runway under partial reinforcement. *J. comp. physiol. Psychol.*, 1962, **55**, 545–549.

Capaldi, E. J., & Wargo, P. Effect of transitions from non-reinforced to reinforced trials under spaced trial conditions. *J. exp. Psychol.*, 1963, **65**, 318–319.

Cogan, D., & Capaldi, E. J. Relative effects of delayed reinforcement and partial reinforcement on acquisition and extinction. *Psychol. Rep.*, 1961, **9**, 7–13.

Crespi, L. P. Amount of reinforcement and level of performance. *Psychol. Rev.*, 1944, **51**, 341–357.

Crum, L., Brown, W. L., & Bitterman, M. E. The effect of partial and delayed reinforcement on resistance to extinction. *Amer. J. Psychol.*, 1951, **64**, 228–237.

DiLollo, V., & Beez, V. Negative contrast effects as a function of magnitude of reward decrement. *Psychon. Sci.*, 1966, **5**, 99–100.

Fehrer, E. Effects of amount of reinforcement and of pre- and postreinforcement delays on learning and extinction. *J. exp. Psychol*, 1956, **52**, 167–175.

Gleitman, H., & Steinman, F. Depression effect as a function of retention interval before and after shift in reward magnitude. *J. comp. physiol. Psychol.*, 1964, **57**, 158–160.

Gonzalez, R. C., Bainbridge, P., & Bitterman, M. E. Discrete-trials lever pressing in the rat as a function of pattern reinforcement, effortfulness of response, and amount of reward. *J. comp. physiol. Psychol.*, 1966, **61**, 110–122.

Gonzalez, R. C., & Bitterman, M. E. Resistance to extinction in the rat as a function of percentage and distribution of reinforcement. *J. comp. physiol. Psychol.*, 1964, **58**, 258–263.

Gonzalez, R. C., Eskin, R. M., & Bitterman, M. E. Further experiments on partial reinforcement in the fish. *Amer. J. Psychol.*, 1963, **76**, 366–375.

Gonzalez, R. C., Gleitman, H., & Bitterman, M. E. Some observations on the depression effect. *J. comp. physiol Psychol.*, 1962, **55**, 578–581.

Gonzalez, R. C., Graf, V., & Bitterman, M. E. Resistance to extinction in the pigeon as a function of secondary reinforcement and pattern of partial reinforcement. *Amer. J. Psychol.*, 1965, **78,** 278–284.

Grice, G. R., & Hunter, J. J. Stimulus intensity effects depend upon the type of experimental design. *Psychol. Rev.*, 1964, **71,** 247–256.

Homzie, M. J., & Ross, L. E. Runway performance following a reduction in the concentration of a liquid reward. *J. comp. physiol. Psychol.*, 1962 **55,** 1029–1033.

Hull, C. L. Knowledge and purpose as habit mechanisms. *Psychol. Rev.*, 1930, **37,** 511–525.

Hull, C. L., *Principles of behavior.* New York: Appleton, 1943.

Hull, C. L. *A behavior system.* New Haven: Yale Univer. Press, 1952.

Hulse, S. H. Amount and percentage of reinforcement and duration of goal confinement in conditioning and extinction. *J. exp. Psychol.*, 1958, **56,** 48–57.

Jensen, G. D. Number and size of unrewarded blocks as determiners of resistance to extinction. *Amer. Psychologist* 1964, **19,** 534. (Abstract)

Katz, S. Stimulus aftereffects and the partial reinforcement extinction effect. *J. exp. Psychol.*, 1957, **53,** 167–172.

Katz, S., Woods, G., & Carrithers, J. H. Reinforcement aftereffects and intertrial interval. *J. exp. Psychol.*, in press.

Lauer, D. W., & Carterette, T. S. Changes in response measures over repeated acquisitions and extinctions of a running habit. *J. comp. physiol. Psychol.*, 1957, **50,** 334–338.

Lauer, D. W., & Estes, W. K. Successive acquisitions and extinctions of a jumping habit in relation to schedule of reinforcement. *J. comp. physiol. Psychol.*, 1955, **48,** 8–13.

Lawrence, D. H. Learning. *Annu. Rev. Psychol.*, 1958, **9,** 157–188.

Lawrence, D. H., & Festinger, L. *Deterrents and reinforcement.* Stanford: Stanford Univer. Press, 1962.

Leonard, D. E. Effect of magnitude and schedule of partial reinforcement on the acquisition and extinction of an instrumental reaction. Unpublished doctoral dissertation, Univ. of Texas, 1966.

Lewis, D. J. Partial reinforcement: A selective review of the literature since 1950. *Psychol. Bull.*, 1960, **57,** 1–29.

Logan, F. A. *Incentive.* New Haven: Yale Univer. Press, 1960.

Logan, F. A., Beier, E. M., & Kincaid, W. D. Extinction following partial and varied reinforcement. *J. exp. Psychol.*, 1956, **52,** 65–70.

Logan, F. A., & Wagner, A. R. *Reward and punishment.* Boston: Allyn & Bacon, 1965.

Longo, N., & Bitterman, M. E. The effect of partial reinforcement with spaced practice on resistance to extinction in the fish. *J. comp. physiol. Psychol.*, 1960, **53,** 169–172.

McCain, G. The effect of intertrial reinforcement on resistance to extinction. Paper read at Midwest. Psychol. Ass., St. Louis, April, 1964.

Marx, M. H., McCoy, D. F., & Tombaugh, J. W. Resistance to extinction as a function of constant delay of reinforcement. *Psychon. Sci.*, 1965, **2,** 333–334.

Moltz, H. Latent extinction and the fractional anticipatory response mechanism. *Psychol. Rev.*, 1957, **64,** 229–241.

Mowrer, O. H. *Learning theory and behavior.* New York: Wiley, 1960.

Murillo, N. R., & Capaldi, E. J. The role of overlearning trials in determining resistance to extinction. *J. exp. Psychol.*, 1961, **61,** 336–340.

North, A. J., & Morton, M. L. Successive acquisitions and extinctions of an instrumental response. *J. comp. physiol. Psychol.*, 1962, **55**, 974–977.

Perkins, C. C., & Cacioppo, A. J. The effect of intermittent reinforcement on the change in extinction rate following successive reconditionings. *J. exp. Psychol.*, 1950, **40**, 794–801.

Pubols, B. H. Constant versus variable delay of reinforcement. *J. comp. physiol. Psychol.*, 1962, **55**, 52–56.

Renner, K. E. Influence of deprivation and availability of goal box cues on the temporal gradient of reinforcement. *J. comp. physiol. Psychol.*, 1963, **56**, 101–104.

Renner, K. E. Delay of reinforcement: A historical review. *Psychol. Bull.*, 1964, **61**, 341–361.

Reynolds, B. Extinction of trace conditioned responses as a function of the spacing of trials during the acquisition and extinction series. *J. exp. Psychol.*, 1945, **35**, 81–95.

Rosen, A., & Ison, J. R. Runway performance following changes in sucrose rewards *Psychon. Sci.*, 1965, **2**, 335–336.

Sgro, J. A., & Weinstock, S. Effects of delay on subsequent running under immediate reinforcement. *J. exp. Psychol.*, 1963, **66**, 260–263.

Sheffield, V. F. Extinction as a function of partial reinforcement and distribution of practice. *J. exp. Psychol.*, 1949, **39**, 511–526.

Spence, K. W. The nature of discrimination learning in animals. *Psychol. Rev.*, 1936, **43**, 427–449.

Spence, K. W. Theoretical interpretations of learning. In C. P. Stone (Ed.), *Comparative psychology.* (3d ed.) Englewood Cliffs, New Jersey: Prentice-Hall, 1951.

Spence, K. W. *Behavior theory and conditioning.* New Haven: Yale Univer. Press, 1956.

Spence, K. W. *Behavior theory and learning.* Englewood Cliffs, New Jersey: Prentice-Hall, 1960.

Spence, K. W., Platt, J. R., & Matsumoto, R. Intertrial reinforcement and the partial reinforcement effect as a function of number of training trials. *Psychon. Sci.*, 1965, **3**, 205–206.

Spivey, J. E. Influence of small numbers of partial reinforcement training trials on resistance to extinction. Unpublished doctoral dissertation, Univer. of Texas, 1964.

Surridge, C. T., & Amsel, A. Performance under a single alternation schedule of reinforcement at 24-hour intertrial interval. *Psychon. Sci.*, 1965, **3**, 131–132.

Teichner, W. H. Experimental extinction as a function of the intertrial intervals during conditioning and extinction. *J. exp. Psychol.*, 1952, **44**, 170–178.

Tyler, D. W., Wortz, E. C., & Bitterman, M. E. The effect of random and alternating partial reinforcement on resistance to extinction in the rat. *Amer. J. Psychol.*, 1953, **66**, 37–65.

Vogel, J. R., Mikulka, P. J., & Spear, N. E. Effect of interpolated extinction and level of training on the "depression effect." Paper read at Eastern Psychol. Ass., Philadelphia, 1965.

Wagner, A. R. Effects of amount and percentage of reinforcement and number of acquisition trials on conditioning and extinction. *J. exp. Psychol.*, 1961, **62**, 234–242.

Wagner, A. R., & Thomas, E. Reward magnitude shifts: A savings effect. *Psychon. Sci.*, 1966, **4**, 13–14.

Wall, A. M., & Goodrich, K. P. Differential responding on reinforcement and non-reinforcement trials occurring in fixed repeating patterns. *Psychon. Sci.,* 1964, **1,** 193–194.

Weinstock, S. Resistance to extinction of a running response following partial reinforcement under widely spaced trials, *J. comp. physiol. Psychol.,* 1954, **47,** 318–322.

Weinstock, S. Acquisition and extinction of a partially reinforced running response at a 24-hour intertrial interval. *J. exp. Psychol.,* 1958, **56,** 151–158.

Wike, E. L., Kintsch, W., & Gutekunst, R. Patterning effects in partially delayed reinforcement. *J. comp. Physiol. Psychol.,* 1959, **52,** 411–414.

Yamaguchi, H. G. The effect of continuous, partial, and varied magnitude reinforcement on acquisition and extinction. *J. exp. Psychol.,* 1961, **61,** 319–321.

SATIATION AND CURIOSITY:

Constructs for a Drive and

Incentive-Motivational Theory of Exploration[1]

Harry Fowler

UNIVERSITY OF PITTSBURGH
PITTSBURGH, PENNSYLVANIA

The intensification of research on exploration and related phenomena during the past decade or so is certainly significant as an additional ap-

[1] The preparation of this article, together with the program of research reported, was supported in part by grant HD-00910 (formerly MH-04549) from the National Institutes of Health, United States Public Health Service. Grateful acknowledgement is made to the following individuals for their assistance in conducting the experiments reported: Robert Burgess, James Brian, Alan Neiberg, Sandra Senior, and Edward Teitelbaum.

proach to the study of motivation, but particularly so because of the complex of new hypotheses that this approach has engendered. Paralleling the history of developments in the physical sciences (see Conant, 1947), the proliferation of theory alone would seem to reflect rapid progress within both the subfield of exploration and its parent area of motivation. Nonetheless, much of the hypothesizing relevant to exploration, especially as it has pertained to learning based on "novel" or changed stimulation, has been situation- or procedure-specific and seemingly unrelated to any general or unifying scheme of behavior. Thus, in spite of the intense research efforts on exploration, different classes of behavior, such as appetitive and exploratory ones, remain separated by the same, if not increasingly wider, theoretical gaps, with the possibility of a common or similar integrative basis for these behaviors seemingly diminished.

I. Motivational Problems Raised by the Study of Exploration

The absence of concerted efforts toward unifying diverse behavior classes, inclusive of exploration, seems to stem in large part from the difficulties prevalent in the study of exploration. Apart from problems of sensitive and reliable measurement, the investigator has been confronted with the imposing task of precisely specifying the behavior, and therein, of providing for its initial and continued arousal. That early investigators proceeded to study exploration by insuring an absence of known conditions of motivation and reinforcement indicated, however, that the phenomenon was "self-contained" and "autonomously motivated" (Nissen, 1954). With exploration, apparently there was no precipitating condition of deprivation, as with appetitive activities, or of intense stimulation, as with escape and avoidance phenomena. Observations of exploratory behavior seemed to suggest only that it was the novel or unfamiliar stimuli of the animal's surround that provided for the arousal and elicitation, and even the reinforcement of exploration, or of responses instrumental to this behavior.

Within this framework of thought, the difficulty of assimilating the behavior was intensified by the problem that confronted motivational theory, particularly as the concept of drive and the related hypothesis of drive reduction were to be applied to exploration. Indeed, with its formal inception in the early 1950's, the concept of an exploratory drive came under strenuous criticism from drive theorists and critics alike (e.g., Bolles, 1958; Brown, 1953a; Estes, 1958; White, 1959). The criticisms directed at this concept had several bases of departure, but generally they related to the following. First, with its initial application, the concept of an exploratory drive was loosely if not ill-defined; reference to it was sometimes made on the basis of observed variations in exploration that were then circularly explained by the concept. Second, when the concept did receive independent expression, in terms of relatively novel or unfamiliar stimuli, it seemed to engender additional difficulties. That Butler's (1953) and Harlow's (1953) monkeys would perform responses that were *instrumental* to novel or changed visual and tactile stimuli indicated that the exploratory drive, if produced by novel stimuli, was not in fact present during the sequence of responding that led to these stimuli. Furthermore, because these instrumental behaviors were reinforced by the same novel stimuli that produced the drive, it appeared certain that the learning involved depended on an increase in drive rather than on its reduction or termination. Obviously, such a conclusion was not to be reconciled with contemporary theory (e.g., Dollard & Miller, 1950; Hull, 1952).

It is particularly interesting that this reinforcement "paradox" has served in large part as the basis for current theories of optimal stimulation and arousal (see Hebb, 1955; Leuba, 1955). With this type of formulation, both increases and decreases in "drive" are conveniently viewed as potentially reinforcing or motivating, depending on the animal's initial level of stimulation and arousal. This approach may well prove fruitful in the long run, but it should be made clear that the proposed basis for assimilating different behavior classes actually depends on the assumption of fundamental differences among them; for example, the motivational impetus for exploration is assumed to be related to the low arousal of "minimal" stimulation, whereas that for appetitive and escape behaviors dependent on the high arousal of intense intero- or exteroceptive stimuli. Such a bridging of behavior classes may be quite ingenious, but it is not without cost: although variations in exploration or any other behavior are easily (perhaps, too easily) accounted for on the presumption of "too" much or "too" little stimulation and arousal, the lack of operationally specified optimal levels for different types of stimulation in different situations and for different animals essentially precludes meaningful prediction. Coupled with these considerations, and with reference to exploratory phenomena in particular, serious question may be posed regarding the interpretation of minimal stimulation and its effects, and similarly, of the basis for positing *increases* in drive as reinforcing events.

Of these and related issues, fuller discussion will be presented in subsequent sections of this chapter. At this point, however, it is profitable to consider the extent to which the early observations and interpretations of exploratory phenomena alluded to actually called for a recasting of the classical drive position.

A. FOUNDATIONS FOR A DRIVE-INCENTIVE FORMULATION

Criticisms of the drive concept that related to its initial application to exploratory phenomena were certainly more than warranted. Nevertheless, it has generally gone unacknowledged that these criticisms are quite specific; they relate solely to the concept as described earlier, either circularly in terms of behavioral events or independently in terms of relatively novel or unfamiliar stimuli. Quite unrelated to these criticisms are those other, "lesser-known" conceptualizations of exploration that have stressed the animal's "satiation" or "boredom" with familiar and unchanging stimuli, and the related "cue" function that novel or unfamiliar stimuli serve in eliciting approach and investigatory reactions (e.g., Glanzer, 1953a; Myers & Miller, 1954; Rothkopf & Zeaman, 1952). With this type of formulation, as has been elaborated elsewhere (Fowler, 1963; Fowler, 1965), the concept of an exploratory drive obtains tentative operational expression in the length and constancy of the animal's exposure to an impinging stimulus condition, or conversely (and perhaps more meaningfully), with the animal's "deprivation" of a change in stimulation. Correspondingly then, the magnitude of the incentive or reinforcement involved in the learning of instrumental behaviors may be related to the magnitude of the change in stimulation that is provided by the relatively novel or unfamiliar stimuli to and for which the animal responds.

Apart from any theoretical issue regarding the nature of reinforcement, and the related fact that the foregoing two propositions can be offered in rebuttal to the charge of inapplicability of the drive-reduction hypothesis (Dollard & Miller, 1950), it should be recognized that the two propositions also provide the format for a drive and incentive-motivational interpretation of exploration analogous to that espoused by Hull (1952) and Spence (1956) for appetitive actions. In effect, performances based on exploratory "rewards" may be treated as motivationally dependent on both the animal's satiation (constancy or length of exposure) to an initially experienced stimulus condition and the change in stimulation that subsequently obtains with the animal's investigation of a relatively novel stimulus or surround. Because of the different operations suggested for the drive and incentive (or reinforcement) constructs, the proposed formulation successfully circumvents the difficulties attendant on earlier conceptualizations of exploratory motivation, wherein both activating and reinforcing properties are ascribed to novel stimuli. Equally important, the formulation finds satisfactory agreement with the experimental literature.

Together with the now well-established observation that moderate changes in visual, auditory, and tactile stimulation can serve as effective reinforcers (see Berlyne, 1963; Fowler, 1965), several studies offer evidence that instrumental response frequencies for light onset are, within limits, higher over increasing intensities of the reinforcing stimulus (e.g., Henderson, 1953; Henderson, 1957; Levin & Forgays, 1959; Stewart, 1960). From these studies, it is not determinable whether the effective reinforcement variable is the extent of the change in illumination rather than the particular intensity or brightness employed. However, other research showing light offset to be reinforcing (see Kiernan, 1964), and a recent investigation by McCall (1965) that successfully separates the effects of initial and consequent intensity from amount of change, indicate that extent of change in stimulation is of prime import in determining response rate. Further supporting evidence on the magnitude of stimulus-change reinforcement derives from still other studies that have varied visual incentives or light increment and decrement for monkeys (e.g., Butler, 1954; Butler & Woolpy, 1963; Moon & Lodahl, 1956), or the complexity of visual or tactile stimuli, or both, for rats (e.g., Barnes & Baron, 1961; Zimbardo & Miller, 1958).

Findings relating to the effects of stimulus exposure (or stimulus-change "deprivation") also support the formulation, although these data are far less extensive than those on stimulus-change reinforcement. For example, studies by Butler (1957) and Fox (1962) have shown that instrumental response rates by monkeys for general visual incentives, or for light-onset reinforcement in particular, are progressively heightened over increasing hours of deprivation of the visual incentives; and furthermore, that response rates are generally lower across deprivation groups when ambient light in the test chamber is augmented (Fox, 1962). Similar results on the effect of light deprivation have been reported for rats (Premack, Collier, & Roberts, 1957), but for these animals it has also been noted that response rates progressively increase with time between light-reinforcement sessions, irrespective of a light or dark pretest maintenance condition (Premack & Collier, 1962). This finding may suggest that the constancy and length of preexposure, rather than light deprivation per se, are the more effective determinants of performance. Accordingly, response rates for light onset are found to be higher for mice given pretest exposure to darkness or constant light rather than to regular or irregular patterns of light approximating the reinforcement condition (Kish & Baron, 1962).

B. NEEDED EFFORTS TOWARD ADDITIONAL OPERATIONAL SPECIFICATION

In generally illustrating a performance dependency on both the extent of the animal's deprivation of a change in stimulation and the magnitude of stimulus variation contingent on such performance, the noted research offers a fairly substantial base for the suggested formulation. However, it would be premature to conclude from these studies that conditions of stimulus-change deprivation may occasion the learning of responses that are instrumental to stimulus-change reinforcement, and thus that a required boundary property of the proposed drive concept has been established. Not only has the relationship between conditions of stimulus-change deprivation and reinforcement gone unassessed; in addition, other investigations have successfully demonstrated a reinforcement effect without the prior imposition of periods of deprivation (in the latter instances the animal was merely transported from its home quarters to the test apparatus). Furthermore, since the deprivation studies noted have typically utilized periods of deprivation ranging over hours, the concept of an exploratory drive—at least one that is defined in terms of the animal's satiation or exposure to relatively unchanging stimulation—can only attain operational specification in terms of lengthy periods of exposure.

Some evidence relating to the effects of short-term exposure would seem to derive from studies bearing on spontaneous alternation wherein exposure periods have varied over minutes rather than hours. Thus, Glanzer (1953b) has reported that, for rats exposed to one arm of a T maze and then permitted to choose between the arms, the tendency to alternate or select the relatively novel arm is greater if exposure to the initial arm lasts 15 or 30 minutes than for only 1 minute. Relevant to this finding is the general observation that rats' preference for either arm of a T or Y maze, prior to any exposure at all, is typically within the limits of chance expectancy (Dember & Fowler, 1958). And, in an unpublished study that simulated Glanzer's but controlled for the possibility of a confinement factor (that is, the rat's avoidance of the confines of its initial exposure condition rather than any "monotonous" stimulation), the author found that, with confinement time equated at 5 minutes by partial exposure to a mid-gray brightness, selection of the unfamiliar (for example, white) arm was progressively heightened over exposure periods of 0, 1, 2, or 4 minutes to the brightness (in this case, black) of the initial arm.

As illustrative of the effects of short-term exposure as the alternation data may be, the unfortunate problem remains that these findings are unsatisfactory behavioral criteria by which to assess a drive-motivational concept. For example, it cannot be concluded from the alternation data that the animal's initial exposure provides a basis for the learning of a response that is instrumental to the termination or reduction of the satiation-drive effect presumed to be operative, because it cannot be determined that, subsequent to the animal's initial exposure, the change in stimulation provided by the relatively novel arm reinforced rather than, as a cue, simply elicited the behavior of approaching and investigating the unfamiliar arm. Thus, there has remained the need for additional operational specification of a satiation-drive concept, that is, for demonstrations of the effectiveness of differential short-term exposure in providing for varied levels of performance that are acquired on the basis of stimulus-change reinforcement.

II. A Program of Research on Short-Term Exposure and Stimulus-Change Reinforcement

In view of the limitations of the available research, a program of study was undertaken in 1962 that was generally aimed at isolating the motivational determinants of exploration, or more specifically, of performances based on exploratory "rewards." Because the suggested formulation stresses the import of the relationship between (a) those conditions of exposure experienced by the animal prior to its exploration and (b) those novel or changed stimulus conditions that the animal subsequently obtains upon exploration, in the four experiments to be reported these two conditions were structured as the enlarged start and goal compartments, respectively, of a runway apparatus. Thus, the studies have been directed primarily at determining the effect on rats' runway performance of varied lengths of exposure to different brightnesses of stimulus inserts employed within the start and goal compartments.

The adoption of the runway technique for purposes of assessing the effects of short-term exposure and stimulus-change reinforcement was based in part on its suitability for the proposed formulation; in addition, such a technique could provide a convenient empirical bridge between the seemingly disparate content areas of alternation behavior and operant light-reinforcement. For example, whereas the T-maze alternation study provides the animal with an initial exposure to one arm and then permits, via choice, response to the unfamiliar arm, the runway technique requires that the animal proceed directly to the novel goal compartment after its exposure in the start area. Hence, while utilizing both the exposure and change characteristics of the alternation study, the runway technique affords a more sensitive latency assessment of individual performance (and thereby of within-group variability) as opposed to the nominal choice measurement of the alternation paradigm. Furthermore, with the novel or changed stimulus condition made contingent on the animal's approach to and entry into the goal, the reinforcement contingency of the operant light-onset study is met. Yet, because of the discrete-trial arrangement provided by the runway procedure, conditions of initial and subsequent exposure can be precisely maintained for each trial-response or for blocks of responses, thereby precluding such loss or diminution of the relative novelty of the incentive or goal condition as may readily obtain in a free-responding context. Finally, in contrast to general exploratory-behavior studies, which have typically recorded frequency of entries into delineated areas of an "open field," the runway technique provides a single novel compartment, thus avoiding the assessment problem of determining whether frequency of areas entered or the amount of time spent in one area—presumably in order to investigate that area thoroughly—is the more valid index of the exploratory tendency.

A. GENERAL METHOD FOR THE RUNWAY EXPERIMENTS

Because of the similarity of method for the four studies to be reported, full details of the general procedure and control operations are presented first, with the specific design and any procedural changes that may be relevant to a particular study reported separately in the following sections. Readers already familiar with the general method as reported elsewhere (Fowler, 1963) may refer directly to the individual experiments.

1. *Subjects*

Subjects for all the experiments were experimentally naive male albino rats of the Sprague-Dawley strain that were generally received from the supplier (Badger Research Corp., Madison, Wisconsin) at about 70–90 days of age. The Ss were housed individually in the experimental room under both controlled temperature (68°–76° F) and an artifically illuminated day-night cycle, the dark phase occurring from 8 A.M. to 10 P.M. Throughout the course of each experiment all Ss had continuous access to food and water in their home cages; at no time was a condition of food or water deprivation experimentally imposed.

2. *Apparatus*

The apparatus was an enclosed straight alley (uniformly $5\frac{1}{2}$ inches high) with enlarged start and goal compartments (each 9 inches square) and a narrow runway (2 ft long by 4 inches wide). The alley had a transparent Plexiglas top and a hardware cloth floor, with opaque guillotine doors located at the beginning, end, and middle of the runway so as to divide it into two 1-ft segments. Except for its Plexiglas top, the entire apparatus was painted a flat black, matching the brightness of a tar-paper sheeting located beneath the hardware cloth floor.

To effect a particular change in brightness at the goal (for example, to white), the inner goal-box walls (except for the end wall) were lined with sheet metal inserts painted the appropriate brightness. Because the end wall of the goal compartment was visible from the alley and start compartment, it was kept black to match the start and alley brightness, thereby requiring that S's perception of a change in brightness be contingent on its approach to and entry into the goal.

An infrared photoelectric system was used to record the time taken by S to traverse successive portions of the runway. The latencies were recorded on two 0.01-second precision timers that started and stopped consecutively with the opening of the start-box door and S's interruption of two photobeams, one located 2 inches outside of the start box and the other 1 inch in front of the goal box.

To facilitate training of the Ss, four straight alleys of the dimensions and characteristics specified above were employed. These alleys were positioned laterally adjacent to one another, and were enclosed on three sides by the generally homogeneous mid-gray walls of the experimental room and on the fourth side by the back of a large control panel, also mid-gray. General illumination of the alleys was provided by three 100-W bulbs that were operated off a 100-V source. The bulbs were mounted 1 ft apart on a 1- by 4-ft translucent Plexiglas shield that hung directly over and 3 ft above the middle doors of the four runways.

3. General Procedure

Except where otherwise noted, training of the Ss occurred a week after their receipt from the supplier. During the initial week, each S was handled 3–5 minutes daily at a time coincidental with S's planned training trials. Training for all Ss occurred during the dark phase of the day-night cycle, the light panel above the apparatus being the sole source of room illumination during testing.

For each training trial, S was removed from its home cage and placed directly into the start compartment of one of the four alleys, where it was detained for a specified period of time, prearranged to vary across groups. Ten seconds prior to the end of S's period of start exposure, S was gently removed from the apparatus, raised, held to E's shoulder for a mental count of 5 seconds, and then returned directly to the same start compartment, the entire operation requiring about 10 seconds. (As elaborated later, this procedure was introduced to preclude the confounding effect across groups of Ss of differential time between S's handling-transportation to the apparatus and the start of its run following the imposed period of start exposure.) Immediately after S's handling and return to the start compartment, the start-box door was raised, permitting S to run to the goal. If S did not run and interrupt each photobeam within a specified time criterion (initially, 3 minutes per photobeam), S was removed from the apparatus and returned to its home cage. Typically, S did run and when it interrupted the second photobeam, the middle door of the alley was closed behind it, the goal-box door being lowered when S moved completely into the goal compartment. Following a specified period of detention at the goal, which began with S's interruption of the second photobeam, S was removed from the apparatus and returned directly to its home cage.

At the end of each trial the latencies from the two timers were recorded and subsequently transformed to speed scores (10/time in seconds). When S failed to run within a specified time criterion, its latency score was equated with the criterion time for the uninterrupted photobeam(s) and the speed-score transformation was made as usual. Hereafter, the speed-score transformations of the latencies obtained from the two timers will be referred to as start and run speeds.

4. Control Operations

Certain aspects of the general runway procedure peculiar to the current set of experiments are to be noted. First, to control for possible differences among the four runways that were employed, the same runway was used for a particular S throughout its training, but to the extent possible, all four runways were equally distributed in their usage among the members of any group. Second, as described earlier, each S was handled 5 seconds immediately prior to the start of its run on every trial. This handling procedure was instituted on the basis of results from a previous investigation (Fowler, 1963; see also Black, Fowler, & Kimbrell, 1964), which showed not only a marked motivational (that is, activating) effect of handling-transporting an S from its home cage to the apparatus, but also an apparent reinforcement effect relating to the temporal dissipation of the effects of handling-transportation. Consequently, in experiments where differential periods of time elapse between S's handling-transportation to an apparatus and the start of its observed response, as for example in the present set of experiments with the imposition of different periods of start-box detention, control operations are mandatory. However, because S's transportation to an apparatus of the present type is not easily precluded, the effect of the transportation variable was equated across Ss through the imposition of an additional 5 seconds of standardized handling immediately prior to the start of each S's run. For the present apparatus and general procedure, such additional handling has been shown to offset differential effects of the transportation variable (Fowler, 1963).

One other aspect of the procedure must be noted. As indicated in the apparatus description, Ss were generally trained to run from a black start compartment to a brighter (for example, white) goal. Accordingly, no attempt was made to counterbalance the direction of the brightness change contingent on S's run. Although this procedure places a limitation on the generality of the findings, it was deemed advisable for the initial three experiments in view of the results of a pilot investigation in which brightness preferences among 12 Ss that had been tested for a week in the apparatus described were assessed. When permitted daily 10-minute periods of free access from the alley to the start and goal compartments, one of which was white and the other black (counterbalanced both over Ss and test days), each S showed a pronounced preference for the black compartment in terms of frequency of entry and time spent in that compartment. Hence, Ss of the initial three experiments were required to run to a less preferred (brighter) stimulus condition at the goal in order to preclude the operation of an aversion or "escape" conditioning effect.

B. Expt. I: Short-Term Exposure as a Determinant of Performance

The major purpose of the first experiment was to assess the effect of differential exposure to a homogeneous stimulus condition that is regularly imposed upon S immediately prior to its opportunity for exploration. Thus, Experiment I sought to determine whether the concept of an exploratory drive could be operationally expressed in terms of the length or amount of S's exposure (satiation) to the stimulus condition prevailing prior to its exploration of a relatively novel surround. Based on the functional properties that are typically ascribed to a drive-motivational concept, such a demonstration requires, within the confines of the present experimental arrangement, that the presumed drive operation (exposure to the start compartment) provide the basis for acquisition of the runway response, and further, that increasing values of the exposure variable relate positively to performance level.

A secondary purpose of the experiment was to assess the effect of differential exposure to the relatively novel stimulus condition (that is, the goal condition) that S explores subsequent to its initial condition of exposure in the start compartment. On the basis of the proposed operation of stimulus exposure as a defining condition of the satiation-drive concept, extended exposure to the change in visual stimulation afforded at the goal should also be productive of satiation and possibly, for this reason, of a lowered performance level. Such an effect, however, is not critical for the proposed concept since its manifestation is integrally dependent on the availability and occurrence of competing reactions (such as efforts to turn away from the novel stimuli, retrace, escape from the apparatus) that are presumably elicited and conditioned during S's extended exposure to the novel stimuli at the goal.

1. *Design*

For training, 36 Ss were randomly assigned to nine groups of four Ss each, comprising a 3×3 factorial design of 1-, 3-, and 7-minute exposure to the start compartment prior to an S's run on each trial, and 0-, 1-, and 3-minute exposure to the goal compartment following S's runway response. In actuality, the 0-minute goal condition constituted a period of about 5–10 seconds, the time required to remove S from the apparatus subsequent to its interruption of the final photobeam and entry into the goal compartment.

The nine groups were maintained on their different start- and goal-exposure times throughout the course of 200 training trials. Trials were administered one per day for the first 10 days and thereafter two per day at an intertrial interval of 1 hour. For trials 1–140, all Ss were run from a black start compartment to a white goal, the experimentally imposed condition of potential reinforcement being the change in brightness at the goal. To assess the reinforcement effect that did occur, as was evident in the acquisition of the runway response, half the Ss of each group were subsequently trained on an extinction procedure. Thus, for trials 141–200, the Ss of each group were randomly assigned to two equally numbered subgroups, one of which was run from a black start to a black goal (the white goal-inserts being changed appropriately) and the other continued as before, that is, run from a black start to a white goal.

2. *Results*

Mean start speeds in consecutive blocks of 20 trials are presented for the three start-exposure conditions in Fig. 1. The reinforcement effect evident in the progressively faster speeds that obtained over the course of training is statistically attested to by the fact that, from trial 101 on, the mean start speed for each S of every group was faster than S's speed at the beginning of training (trials 1–40). However, differences among the start-exposure conditions as well as among the goal-exposure conditions and the interaction of the start- and goal-exposure variables were all unreliable throughout the course of training. Furthermore, when each group was subdivided after trial 140, with half of the Ss being trained to run from a black start to a black goal and half continued as before to a white goal, the difference that obtained between the two goal-brightness conditions was also unreliable.

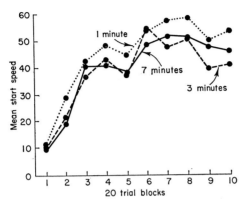

Fig. 1. Mean start speeds in consecutive blocks of 20 trials for the 1-, 3-, and 7-minute start-exposure groups.

In contrast to the start-speed data, group mean run speeds diverged over the course of training such that, from trial 101 on, between-group differences were significant ($F\ ^8\!/_{27} = 2.31,\ p < .05$). Figure 2 presents these data in consecutive blocks of 20 trials for the three start-exposure conditions. As shown, run speeds during the latter half of training (trials 101–200) related positively to start-exposure time: both dif-

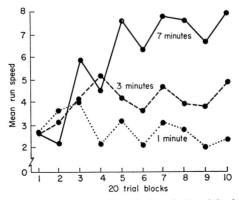

Fig. 2. Mean run speeds in consecutive blocks of 20 trials for the 1-, 3-, and 7-minute start-exposure groups.

ferences among the start-exposure conditions and the linear trend within these data were significant (F $^2\!/_{27} = 3.35$, $p = .05$, and F $^1\!/_{27} = 6.50$, $p < .025$, respectively). Because the residual trend after extraction of the linear component was nonsignificant ($F < 1$), the relationship between runway performance and start-exposure time is best described (within the range of values employed) as an increasing linear function. Such a relationship, however, does not attest to the presumed motivational nature of the exposure-time variable (that is, to its anticipated function of providing the basis for acquisition of the runway response). For, as with the start-speed data, no significant difference in run speed obtained between the two goal-brightness conditions when, with subsequent training (trials 141–200), half the Ss of each group were run from a black start to a black goal and half continued as before to a white goal.

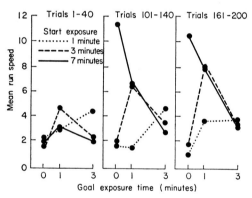

Fig. 3. Mean run speeds at various stages of training for the 1-, 3-, and 7-minute start-exposure groups as a function of goal-exposure time.

Mean run speeds for the start-exposure conditions are presented at various stages of training in Fig. 3 as a function of goal-exposure time. Although differential goal exposure per se did not affect running performance at any stage of training, this variable did interact significantly with start-exposure time from trial 101 on (F $^4\!/_{27} = 2.70$, $p = .05$). As shown in Fig. 3, progressively faster run speeds obtained over the course of training for the shorter goal-exposure groups of the longer start-exposure conditions, specifically the 0- and 1-minute goal-exposure groups of the 7-minute start condition and the 1-minute goal-exposure group of the 3-minute start condition. Mean run speeds for all other subgroups remained relatively constant throughout the course of training. Accordingly, trend analysis of the data for trials 101–200 showed that the relationship between performance and both the start- and goal-exposure variables was most adequately described by an increasing linear start- by decreasing linear goal-exposure interaction (F $\frac{1}{27}$ $= 7.51$, $p < .025$). All other components of this interaction failed to yield significance.

3. *Discussion*

In part, the data seem effective in highlighting the significance of stimulus exposure as a performance determinant, and thus they offer some support for the interpretation outlined. As anticipated, longer exposure to the initially experienced stimulus condition (the start compartment) resulted in faster runway performance, whereas extended exposure to the relatively novel (goal) condition that was subsequently explored produced poorer performance, at least among those start-exposure conditions for which a learning effect was clearly evident and a performance decrement therefore possible. Nonetheless, the interpretation of a satiation-*drive* effect is severely restricted both by the lack of group differences in start speed and the failure of those Ss subsequently run from a black start to a black goal to extinguish. Several factors suggest themselves as possible determinants of these effects.

First, it is most conceivable that group differences in start speed were offset or obscured by the 5-second handling imposed on each S immediately prior to the start of its run. As noted previously, the effect of handling has been shown to be a potent source of motivation for the runway response (particularly its initial or start component), and the temporal dissipation of such an effect concurrent with S's run, presumably its source of reinforcement (Fowler, 1963). Considered together with the relatively moderate influences that may be exerted by exploratory rewards, the reinforcement deriving throughout training from S's handling could well be sufficient to obscure group differences in start speed and possibly even any extinction effect that might be expected to result by training Ss to run from a black start to a black goal. It seems unlikely, however, that this form of reinforcement, or even others deriving indirectly from handling (such as escape from E or "gentling" of S with its removal from the apparatus) are sufficient to account for all of the results. Particularly absent is an explanatory basis for the progressively faster run speeds that obtained primarily for the shorter goal-exposure groups of the 7-minute start condition.

One explanation of the run-speed data might bear on the role of physical confinement, rather than stimulus exposure, as a determinant of performance, especially since length of confinement to the start and goal compartments co-varied with S's amount of exposure to the brightnesses of these conditions. Thus, the confinement variable relates well to the better performances exhibited by the shorter goal-exposure groups of the 7-minute start condition (in that these Ss had the longest confinement and escaped most quickly) and to the failure of Ss subsequently run to a black goal to extinguish. But the possibility that physical confinement served as a determinant of performance seems negated by the enlarged size of the start and goal compartments, each of which provided greater floor space than the home cage to which S was returned immediately following each trial. Furthermore, because the physical confines of the start and goal boxes were the same, there is no a priori basis for assuming that S would run into the goal rather than back and forth in the alley, for example, in order to reduce or escape confinement in the start box.

An alternative explanation of the run-speed data that accords well with the proposed drive interpretation is that S satiated, not to the start and goal conditions, but instead to extra-alley stimuli or perhaps even to distinguishable characteristics of the apparatus other than its brightness. Although seemingly unlikely, such an effect is actually accorded high probability by the results of investigations assessing "stimulus versus place" components of alternation behavior, wherein extra-maze stimuli have been shown to be particularly influential (e.g., Walker, Dember, Earl, & Karoly, 1955). Furthermore, because of the overhead lighting used in the present experiment, the different walls of the experimental room, although fairly homogeneous in appearance, were nonetheless visible to S when in the start and goal compartments. As such, the sources of motivation and reinforcement underlying the performances observed may well have been S's satiation to the stimulus features of one side of the room and the change in visual stimulation that subsequently obtained with S's running to the goal and viewing the other side of the room. Were this the case, alteration of the goal brightness from white to black would be expected to have little if any effect in extinguishing the runway response.

C. Expt. II: Stimulus-Change Reinforcement and Its Relation to Short-Term Exposure

The possible interpretations of the results of Experiment I led to the main purpose of the second experiment, namely, to reproduce the observed start-exposure effect, but with possible confounding factors eliminated. Thus, to preclude interpretations based on differential time of escape from confinement or on gentling of S upon its removal from the apparatus (or on possible secondary reinforcing effects relating to S's return to its home cage), exposure time at the goal was held constant over all *S*s. Second, extra-alley stimuli were effectively eliminated, or blacked out, by restricting overhead lighting to the apparatus. With these restraints, the potential dependency of runway performance on brightness-change reinforcement at the goal could be assessed in either of two ways: (a) by employing the extinction procedure of Experiment I, cr (b) by manipulating, throughout acquisition training, magnitude of brightness change at the goal. The latter alternative was selected because it could accomplish the same effect as the former and, if successful, could also demonstrate the functional relationship between runway performance and magnitude of brightness-change reinforcement. Specifically then, the aim of Experiment II was to assess the effect on runway performance of varied exposure to a black start compartment followed by constant exposure to a goal that differed in brightness, the extent of this brightness difference being varied across groups.

1. *Design*

For training, 48 *S*s were randomly assigned to eight groups of six *S*s each, comprising a 2 × 4 factorial design of 3- and 7-minute exposure on each trial to a black start compartment prior to *S*'s run and constant exposure to one of the following goal brightnesses: black (B), gray (G), white (W), or a vertically striped (1-inch wide) black-and-white (B-W) pattern. Because the B-W goal condition afforded equal amounts of black and white exposure with *S*'s visual scanning of the pattern, it was used as a comparison condition for the intermediate (G) goal brightness. Again, however, the far wall of each goal-brightness condition was black, making *S*'s perception of the change in visual stimulation at the goal, that is, from the black start and alley to B, G, W, or B-W, contingent upon *S*'s approach to and entry into the goal.

The procedure and general conditions of training were the same as those for Experiment I except that, as noted earlier, overhead lighting was restricted to the apparatus. This was accomplished by enclosing the overhead light panel in a sheet-metal box (10 inches by 20 inches by 4 ft), the only aperture in which was a 5-inch by 4-ft lengthwise slot located along the bottom goal-side of the enclosure. This arrangement provided indirect incident lighting of approximately 2.2 ft-c within the start compartment, 2.8 ft-c within the alley, 3.4 ft-c within the goal compartment, and 0.3–0.5 ft-c at the room walls and control panel adjacent to the apparatus.

Because of the facility of training observed in Experiment I, the criterion times allotted per trial for *S*'s interruption of the start and run photobeams were reduced from 3 minutes to 1 and 2 minutes, respectively. In addition, S's length of exposure to the goal on each trial was set at 1 minute in accord with the generally faster run speeds observed for this condition in Experiment I. Training was conducted for 160 trials administered one per day for trials 1–10, two per day for trials 11–50, and three per day thereafter, the intertrial interval on multitrial days remaining at 1 hour.

2. Results and Discussion

Mean start speeds in consecutive blocks of 20 trials are presented for the several goal-brightness conditions in Fig. 4. As shown, the per-

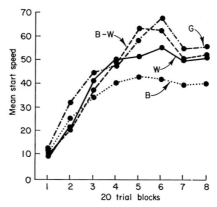

Fig. 4. Group mean start speeds in consecutive blocks of 20 trials for Ss trained to run from a black start compartment to a black (B), white (W), gray (G), or vertically striped black-and-white (B-W) goal.

formance curves increased progressively and diverged over the course of training. For all Ss, mean speeds were again faster at the end of training (trial blocks 7 and 8) than at the beginning of training (blocks 1 and 2), thereby attesting to a reinforcement effect. Analysis of variance of the data for trial blocks 7 and 8 showed further that differences among the goal-brightness conditions were reliable (F $3/40 = 3.10$, $p < .05$), but as indicated by polynomial comparisons, this between-group effect related primarily to a reliable difference between the B goal condition and the others (F $1/40 = 8.28$, $p < .01$); differences among the W, G, and B-W conditions were all unreliable. These results also obtained for trial blocks 5 and 6, which were marked by an unaccountable rise in the performance curves for Ss of the G and B-W conditions. However, the difference between these two conditions and the W condition on trial blocks 5 and 6 was not significant. Similarly, and at any point in training, the difference in start speed between the 3- and 7-minute start-exposure conditions and the start-exposure by goal-brightness interaction were unreliable.

The start-speed data provide some evidence of the effectiveness of restricting overhead lighting to the apparatus. The difference that obtained between the B goal condition and the others shows at least that a change in brightness at the goal afforded better performance than no change. Nevertheless, the improvement in start performance exhibited by Ss of the B goal condition indicates the operation of an additional source of reinforcement, as would be expected from the continued procedure of handling each S immediately prior to the start of its run. For the same reason, the absence of a start-speed difference between the 3- and 7-minute start-exposure conditions, as in Experiment I, is also not surprising.

Mean run speeds in consecutive blocks of 20 trials are presented for the several goal-brightness conditions in Fig. 5. Because of the generally orderly divergence of the performance curves depicted, analysis of the run-speed data was limited to trial blocks 7 and 8. As indicated in Fig. 5, run speed related positively to increasing goal brightness and, correspondingly, to the magnitude of brightness change contingent on S's runway response: differences among the goal-brightness conditions and the "linear" component to these data (assessed over the ordinal positions of B, G, and W, with G and B-W combined) were both highly reliable: $F_{3/40} = 3.59$, $p < .025$, and $F_{1/40} = 9.66$, $p < .005$, respectively. Residual trend components, including a comparison of the G and B-W conditions, were nonsignificant, suggesting that within the

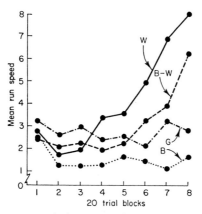

FIG. 5. Group mean run speeds in consecutive blocks of 20 trials for Ss trained to run from a black start compartment to a black (B), white (W), gray (G), or vertically striped, black-and-white (B-W) goal.

confines of the present arrangement runway performance related directly to goal brightness.

Figure 6 presents mean run speeds for the goal-brightness conditions as a function of start-exposure time, during both early and late stages of training. As shown, the direct relationship that obtained over the course of training between run speed and goal brightness derived primarily from the performances of the 7-minute start-exposure groups. Correspondingly, the over-all difference between the 3- and 7-minute start-exposure conditions was reliable, as was the linear component to the goal-brightness by start-exposure interaction (F $\frac{1}{40} = 6.19$, $p < .025$, and F $\frac{1}{40} = 5.10$, $p < .05$, respectively). Residual components of this interaction, including a comparison of the G and B-W conditions, proved unreliable.

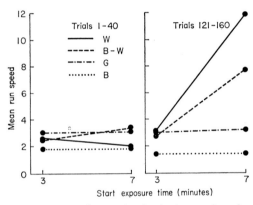

Fig. 6. Group mean run speeds at the beginning and end of training as a function of start-exposure time for Ss trained to run from a black start compartment to a black (B), white (W), gray (G), or vertically striped black-and-white (B-W) goal.

The run-speed data strongly indicate that the absence of an extinction effect in Experiment I resulted, as previously suggested, from S's receipt of extra-alley stimuli or perhaps from S's attending to discriminable features of the apparatus other than the start and goal brightnesses. In either case, with the restricted lighting conditions of the present study, the start-exposure effect observed in Experiment I was replicated and, more important, the acquisition effect was shown to be dependent on magnitude of brightness change at the goal. This dependency is indicated not only by the positive relationship that obtained between run performance and goal brightness, but also by the complete absence of any increment over training in the run performance of Ss of the no-change or B goal condition (see Fig. 5). Taken together with the fact that in Experiment II goal-exposure time was held constant over different goal brightnesses, these findings effectively preclude interpretations based on physical confinement, secondary reinforcement, or gentling variables.

Collectively, the results of Experiments I and II indicate that the stimulus-exposure and brightness-change variables may serve as empirical referents for the operation of both drive and incentive or reinforcement factors. The data satisfy the initial or boundary requirements of the proposed satiation-drive concept in that manipulation of the start-exposure variable provided the basis for differential performance and, as indicated by the performances of the 7-minute start-exposure Ss in Experiment II, for the acquisition of a response that was instrumental to the termination of this exposure. In similar fashion, a reinforcement or incentive factor is called for on the basis of the differential performance effected through manipulation of goal brightness with drive (start exposure) held constant, again as shown in the performances of the 7-minute start-exposure groups. Finally, the interaction of the start-exposure and goal-brightness variables suggests that the magnitude of the incentive-reinforcement effect is dependent on the extent of S's satiation to that condition constituting its initial exposure.

One other aspect of the data requiring comment concerns the apparent operation of an inhibitory or suppression factor. Although less well-documented than the operation of drive and reinforcement factors noted earlier, such an inhibitory effect is indicated by the relatively poorer performances of those 7-minute start-exposure Ss of Experiment I that received extended exposure to the goal and by the intermediate performance level of the B-W group in Experiment II. With the B-W goal condition, visual receipt of the white component should afford maximal change relative to S's previous exposure to black in the start compartment and alley, and should thus provide the basis for performances comparable to those exhibited by Ss of the W goal condition. The intermediate performances of the B-W Ss may suggest, then, that the reinforcing effect of the white component was offset because receipt of the black component provided extended exposure, and hence additional satiation, to this brightness. Based on the presumption that satiation to the goal stimuli may exert an inhibitory effect through the occurrence and conditioning of competing responses, such as S's attempting to turn away from the goal stimuli, escape from the apparatus, or engage in other activities like gnawing and grooming, it is particularly noteworthy that Ss of the no-change or B goal condition showed generally poorer run speeds throughout training than were exhibited by these Ss at the start of their training.

D. EXPT. III: PERFORMANCE SHIFTS FOLLOWING ALTERATIONS OF
STIMULUS EXPOSURE AND BRIGHTNESS-CHANGE REINFORCEMENT

With the isolation in Experiment II of stimulus exposure and brightness change as apparent drive and incentive-defining operations, the main purpose of the third experiment was to assess the presumed motivational or "performance" character of these variables. In particular, attention was directed to the nature of the performance shifts that would occur following alteration of drive and reinforcement conditions, the anticipation being that shifts in performance level would be both relatively abrupt and appropriate to the post-shift performance conditions imposed upon S. Specifically then, Experiment III investigated the effect of independently switching, late in the runway training of different groups of Ss, either the start-exposure or goal-brightness condition that had been imposed on these groups earlier in their training.

1. *Design*

The runway procedure and general training conditions of Experiment III were the same as those for Experiment II, including the control operations of handling each S for 5 seconds immediately prior to the start of its run and of restricting overhead lighting to the apparatus. All Ss were trained for 200 trials administered one per day for trials 1–10, two per day for trials 11–30, and three per day thereafter, the intertrial interval on multitrial days again being 1 hour. Also, as in Experiment II, exposure time at the goal on each trial was held constant at 1 minute for all Ss.

For training, 70 Ss were randomly assigned to three conditions comprising an incomplete 2×2 factorial design of 3- and 7-minute exposure to a black start compartment (3B and 7B), followed by exposure for 1 min to a black or white goal (B or W). Specifically, the three training conditions were 7B-W, 7B-B, and 3B-W, where condition 3B-W, for example, designates 3-minute exposure on each trial to a black start compartment prior to S's run and exposure to a white goal. Again, it should be noted that for any of the three training conditions, the far wall of the goal was black, matching the brightness of the start box and alley and thereby requiring that S's perception of a change in brightness (as in conditions 3B-W and 7B-W) be contingent on its approach to and entry into the goal.

For the first 140 trials, 30 Ss were trained under condition 7B-W and 20 each under conditions 7B-B and 3B-W. Then the Ss of each of these training conditions were randomly assigned to subgroups of 10 Ss each that were either continued on the same training condition or switched to another. Specifically, for trials 141–200, the three subgroups of condition 7B-W were independently assigned to conditions 7B-W, 7B-B, and 3B-W; the two subgroups of condition 7B-B to 7B-B and 7B-W; and the two subgroups of condition 3B-W to 3B-W and 7B-W. By utilizing appropriate subgroups in *separate* 2 × 2 factorial designs of pre- and postshift training conditions relevant to each variable, assessment could thus be made of the dependency of performance on pre- and postshift conditions of start-exposure time (3B-W versus 7B-W) or goal-box brightness (7B-W versus 7B-B).

2. Results and Discussion

Mean start speeds in consecutive blocks of 20 trials are presented for the three training conditions in Fig. 7. As shown, start speeds increased

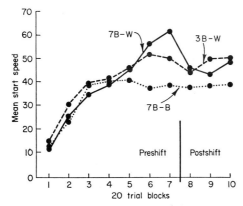

Fig. 7. Group mean start speeds in consecutive blocks of 20 trials for Ss trained under, and then continued on or switched to, a condition of 3- or 7-minute exposure to a black start compartment followed by exposure to a white goal (3B-W or 7B-W), or 7-minute exposure to a black start compartment followed by exposure to a black goal (7B-B).

progressively and diverged over the course of training such that by trial blocks 6 and 7, prior to the shift in training conditions, between-group differences were reliable (F $^2/_{67}$ = 7.65, p < .005). Based on polynomial comparisons, however, the difference on these trials between the 3B-W and 7B-W conditions was not reliable; only the difference between these two conditions and the 7B-B condition proved significant (F $^1/_{67}$ = 12.00, p < .01). These effects were maintained with the shift in training conditions following trial 140. Although, as Fig. 7 indicates, the postshift subgroups representing the 3B-W and 7B-W conditions showed a decrement in start speed for trial blocks 8–10 and, again, did not differ themselves, the difference between these subgroups and those of the 7B-B condition was significant ($F\ \frac{1}{67} = 5.60,\ p < .025$).

The separate performances of the postshift subgroups have not been depicted in Fig. 7 because factorial assessment of the performance relations to pre- and postshift conditions of start-exposure time or goal-box brightness generally showed no reliable effects. This would be expected with the comparison of start-exposure times (3B-W versus 7B-W) because of the reduced number of Ss for this comparison and especially because the preshift difference between the start-exposure conditions was unreliable. In the comparison of goal-brightness conditions (7B-W versus 7B-B) for which a significant preshift difference did occur in the over-all analysis just noted, a reliable "performance" effect was obtained by trials 151–160. Over these trials, the difference relating to postshift conditions of goal brightness was significant and in favor of the 7B-W condition ($F\ \frac{1}{36} = 6.41,\ p < .025$), whereas neither the difference relating to preshift conditions of goal brightness nor the pre- by postshift interaction was significant. This effect was also shown with subsequent training (trials 161–200), but it was not of sufficient magnitude to yield statistical significance. Thus, although the start-speed data provide little information regarding the "associative" or "motivational" nature of the variables under study (a not too surprising fact in view of the typical insensitivity of the start-speed measure), they do match well those data of Experiment II illustrating a partial dependency of start-speed performance on brightness change at the goal.

Figure 8 presents mean run speeds for the three training conditions in consecutive blocks of 20 trials over the first 140 training trials, and then for the postshift subgroups of these conditions in consecutive blocks of 10 trials over the remaining portion of training. As shown, the performance curves for Ss of the three preshift groups diverged over the course of training such that by trial blocks 6 and 7, prior to the shift in training conditions, the difference between the 7B-W group and the other two combined was highly significant ($F\ \frac{1}{67} = 41.12,\ p < .001$), whereas the difference between the latter two was unreliable. Because the 7B-W condition represents a cell common to the comparison of both start-exposure time (3B-W versus 7B-W) and goal-box brightness (7B-W versus 7B-B), the noted difference in run speed satisfies well the initial difference necessary for assessment of performance shifts relating both to the start-exposure and goal-brightness variables.

Figure 8 shows that, with the alteration of training conditions following trial 140, the shifts in performance of the affected subgroups were

both rapid and appropriate to their newly imposed conditions of training. Indeed, all performance shifts were complete by the second block of
10 trials following alteration of the original training conditions: for trial
block 9 (trials 151–160), differences relating to the postshift conditions
of both start-exposure time (3B-W versus 7B-W) and goal-box brightness (7B-W versus 7B-B) were highly reliable ($F\ \frac{1}{36} = 18.63,\ p < .001$
and $F\ \frac{1}{36} = 19.95,\ p < .001$, respectively), whereas differences relating to
the preshift conditions of these variables, and their respective pre- by
postshift interactions, were unreliable in each case. As indicated in Fig.
8, these effects were maintained with high reliability throughout the re-

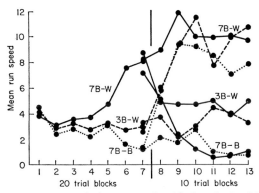

Fig. 8. Group mean run speeds in consecutive blocks of 20 trials for Ss trained
under a condition of 3- or 7-minute exposure to a black start compartment followed
by exposure to a white goal (3B-W or 7B-W), or 7-minute exposure to a black start
compartment followed by exposure to a black goal (7B-B); and in consecutive blocks
of 10 trials, for those Ss that were continued on the same condition or switched to
another.

maining portion of training (trials 161–200): for the postshift differences in start-exposure time and goal-box brightness, $F\ \frac{1}{36} = 9.76,\ p$
$< .005$, and $F\ \frac{1}{36} = 29.89,\ p < .001$, respectively. Correspondingly, over-
all analysis of the data on these trials showed that the difference between
the 7B-W subgroups and those of the other two conditions combined
was again highly significant ($F\ \frac{1}{67} = 30.94,\ p < .001$), and that the difference between the latter two conditions (3B-W and 7B-B) was significant as well ($F\ \frac{1}{67} = 4.26,\ p < .05$).

The observed performance shifts accord quite well with the presumed
motivational or "energizing" nature of the drive (start-exposure) and
incentive (goal-brightness) factors suggested as being operative. The
data are, of course, not sufficiently critical to dismiss possible associative
features of these variables; for example, it might easily be argued that
the performance shifts were only complete after some 10–20 trials—suffi-

cient time presumably for the complete acquisition (or extinction) of a new (or old) response tendency. This consideration notwithstanding, the rapidity of the performance shifts *relative* to the lengthy acquisition of some 100 training trials required for the obtainment of differences among the original training conditions (see Fig. 8) adequately fulfills the necessary energizing requisite of the motivational assumption.

Aside from the significance of the foregoing findings, the runway data are noteworthy with respect to their substantiation and extension of the results of Experiments I and II. The reliable differences noted in the comparison of start-exposure (3B-W versus 7B-W) and goal-brightness (7B-W versus 7B-B) conditions reaffirms the generally positive relationship existing between these variables and runway performance. And, on the basis of the complete absence of any acquisition effect for the no-change, 7B-B condition (see Fig. 8), the data again illustrate effectively the reinforcement dependency of performance on brightness change at the goal. With the present findings, this dependency is illustrated in still another way, namely through the rapid and appropriate decrement in performance that obtained for the subgroup of the 7B-W condition that was switched to the no-change or *extinction* condition of 7B-B. Coupled with the results presented above and those of Experiment II, assessing the effect of magnitude of brightness change at the goal, this observation leaves little doubt that the failure to obtain a comparable extinction effect in Experiment I related primarily, if not completely, to the general overhead lighting that prevailed in that experiment, and presumably then to the imposition of extra-alley cues.

Finally, the extinction performance of the 7B-B postshift subgroup, and similarly, the progressive decline in performance of the group maintained on the 7B-B condition throughout training, both suggest that extended exposure at the goal to those visual stimuli constituting original exposure, that is in the start compartment and alley, produces an inhibitory effect that may operate through the eliciting and conditioning of competing reactions. Because these competing reactions, like turning away, retracing, or attending to other parts of the apparatus (notably the guillotine doors, at which the 7B-B Ss were observed to gnaw) would also result in different or changed stimulation, the strengthening of these competing behaviors accords well with the reinforcement interpretation offered of runway performance itself.

E. EXPT. IV: STIMULUS EXPOSURE AND ITS RELATION TO CONDITIONS OF REARING AND MAINTENANCE

In showing that performance is relatively independent of prior conditions of stimulus exposure and brightness change (that is, prior *train-*

ing conditions), the results of Experiment III in no way preclude the possibility that, at any point in training, performance will also be influenced by those stimulus conditions that S experiences prior to its introduction to the apparatus. In fact, such an influence may be anticipated on the basis of the operational definitions suggested for both the drive (satiation) and incentive (change) constructs. That is, S's preapparatus exposure, such as in its home cage, can be viewed as a temporal extension of the stimulus condition to which S is exposed just prior to its exploration, or opportunity for exploration, of a change in stimulation; consequently, such exposure should constitute a significant determinant of runway performance. For example, if S were maintained in a black home cage and then on each training trial S were exposed to a black start compartment prior to its run to a white goal, the satiation accrued to black would presumably be considerable and should lead to heightened runway performance. On the other hand, if the training procedure of running S from a black start to a white goal were the same, but S were maintained instead in a white home cage, the satiation accrued to black would be considerably less, and the magnitude of the reinforcing change in stimulation at the goal would possibly be offset by the similarity of the goal and home-cage stimuli.

In the preceding three experiments, preapparatus, or home-cage, experience presumably had little consequence because of its constancy across Ss and because the metallic gray brightness of S's home cage represented a value intermediate to the black and white brightnesses of the apparatus. In the present experiment, however, an effort was made to assess the effect of the home-cage or maintenance brightness imposed upon S throughout the course of its training and to determine whether there would be any residual effect of early maintenance (that is, rearing) brightness.

1. *Design*

Upon receipt from the supplier, 120 30-day-old Ss were reared until 80 days of age in individual laboratory cages that were painted either black (B), gray (G), white (W), or all three of these brightnesses separately on the three inner walls of the cage (the fourth wall was the hardware cloth front). Again, the last-mentioned composite brightness (C) served as a comparison condition for the intermediate G brightness. Assignment of the Ss to these four rearing brightnesses was random with the restriction that there were 40 Ss each in the B and W conditions and 20 each in the G and C conditions.

On the day prior to the start of training, which began when all Ss were 81 days of age, half of the Ss of the B and W rearing conditions

were reversed to and maintained on the other of these conditions for the
duration of the experiment; maintenance conditions throughout training for all other Ss remained the same as their respective rearing conditions. Thus, there were 20 Ss in each of six different rearing-maintenance conditions: B,B; B,W; W,W; W,B; G,G; and C,C. For training,
the Ss of each of these rearing-maintenance conditions were randomly
assigned to four subgroups of five Ss each which comprised a 2 × 2 factorial design of 3- and 7-minute exposure on each trial to a black (B)
or white (W) start compartment prior to S's run and constant exposure
for 1 minute to a goal that was of the other brightness. In this experiment,
then, the direction of the brightness change contingent on S's run and
entry into the goal (that is, B start to W goal or W start to B goal), was
counterbalanced specifically to control for any secondary reinforcing
effects of goal brightness that might derive from the association of a
similar home-cage brightness with S's ad lib eating and drinking.

The general training procedure was the same as that employed previously, including the control operations of handling each S for 5 seconds immediately prior to the start of its run and of restricting overhead
lighting to the apparatus. All Ss were trained for 140 trials, administered one per day for trials 1–10, two per day for trials 11–20, and
three per day thereafter, the intertrial interval on multitrial days again
being 1 hour. To accommodate Ss trained to run from a W start to a B
goal, two of the four alleys were completely repainted white, with black
wall inserts being used to effect the appropriate goal brightness. Again,
however, the far wall of the goal was the same brightness as the start
and alley, so that the change in brightness that S experienced was contingent upon its run and entry into the goal.

2. Results and Discussion

Figure 9 presents mean start speeds in consecutive blocks of 20 trials
as obtained under the four conditions of training, that is, 3- or 7-minute
exposure to a B or W start compartment prior to S's run on each trial to
a goal of the other brightness. As shown, start speeds increased progressively and diverged over the course of training such that differences
among the four training conditions were evident. Analysis of variance of
the data for trial blocks 6 and 7 showed that the difference in favor of
the 7-minute start-exposure condition was quite reliable (F $\frac{1}{96}$ = 6.96,
$p < .01$), but that in favor of the W to B (W-B) training condition only
marginally so (F $\frac{1}{96}$ = 3.02, $p < .10$), with the interaction of the start-
exposure and training-condition variables being nonsignificant ($F < 1$).

The fact that the direction of the brightness change contingent upon
S's run had only a marginal effect on performance is somewhat surpris-

ing in view of the early pilot work to the research program, which showed a pronounced black preference for Ss given free exploration in the apparatus. On the other hand, the absence of such a preference might well relate to the imposed balance of rearing and maintenance brightnesses across Ss of the present experiment, or to the typically noted insensitivity of the start-speed measure; that is, the obscuring effect exerted on start performance by the required control operation of handling each S immediately prior to its run. The latter alternative would seem more probable both in view of the run-speed data to be presented and of the fact that statistical analysis of start speeds also showed no significant effect of rearing-maintenance brightness, or of the interaction of this variable with any other.

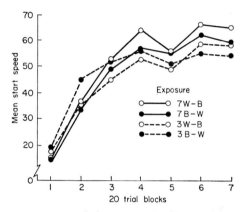

FIG. 9. Group mean start speeds in consecutive blocks of 20 trials for Ss trained under a condition of 3- or 7-minute exposure to a black or white (B or W) start compartment followed by exposure to a goal of the other brightness.

Mean run speeds for Ss of the several rearing-maintenance conditions are presented in consecutive blocks of 20 trials in Fig. 10. To simplify description of these conditions and their relation to the brightness conditions of training (that is, B start to W goal or W start to B goal), the rearing-maintenance conditions have been designated as follows: same (S), both rearing and maintenance brightness the same (for example, B) as the start brightness; different-same (DS), rearing brightness different (for example, W) but maintenance brightness the same (that is, B) as the start brightness; intermediate (I), both rearing and maintenance brightness an intermediate G; intermediate-composite (IC), both rearing and maintenance brightness a composite of B, W, and G, the comparison condition for I; same-different (SD), rearing brightness the same as, but maintenance brightness different from, the start brightness; and finally, different (D), both rearing and maintenance brightness different from the start brightness.

Figure 10 shows that run speeds increased progressively over the course of training and diverged such that by trial blocks 6 and 7 speeds were fastest for *S*s whose maintenance brightness was the same as that of the start box, (the S and DS groups), slowest for *S*s whose maintenance brightness was different from that of the start box (the D and SD groups), and intermediate for the *S*s maintained on the intermediate G and composite brightness conditions (the I and IC groups). Because polynomial comparisons within the analysis of variance of run speeds over trial blocks 6 and 7 showed that the two groups (for example, S and

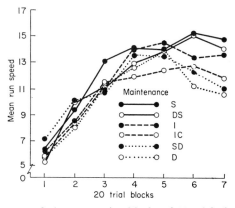

FIG. 10. Mean run speeds in consecutive blocks of 20 trials for the several rearing-maintenance groups. See text for an explanation of group designations in relation to the brightness conditions of training.

DS) at each of the three levels of maintenance—start-brightness similarity were not different ($F < 1$ in each case), the two groups at each similarity level were combined for purposes of trend analysis. As applied to the ordinal positions of same, intermediate, and different maintenance brightnesses (relative to start brightness), trend analysis showed that the "linear" component was reliable ($F \ 1/96 = 4.46, p < .05$), but that any residual component was not ($F < 1$). Collectively, these results indicate that by the end of training runway performance was independent of prior rearing brightness (since S and DS and, similarly, D and SD were not different), but that such performance related directly to the degree of similarity in brightness of *S*'s maintenance condition and the start compartment from which *S* was constantly run.

The results of the analysis of variance also showed that reliably faster run speeds were obtained under the W-B than the B-W training condition (F $\frac{1}{96}$ = 4.42, p < .05), but that the difference between the 3- and 7-minute start-exposure conditions, although consonant with the findings of the previous experiments, was not reliable. The absence of a significant start-exposure effect might seem attributable to the limited temporal extent of such exposure relative to S's almost 24-hour exposure to its maintenance brightness. For example, for Ss maintained in a black home cage, the imposition of an additional 3- or 7-minute exposure to black in the start compartment prior to S's run on each trial to a white goal might be expected to have little if any differential effect. Such an interpretation, however, would not apply to the performances of those Ss trained under the same brightness conditions, that is, B start to W goal, and maintained instead in a home cage that was white; nor does the interpretation accord with the fact that the interaction of the maintenance and training-brightness variables, as well as that for any of the variables studied, was also nonsignificant. Nonetheless, the present findings are not necessarily at variance with those of the previous studies. Although not statistically reliable, the difference in run speeds between the 3- and 7-minute start-exposure conditions was at least consonant in its direction with previous findings; furthermore, such a difference did obtain reliability in the measurement of start speeds. Thus, when considered together with the previous findings consistently showing a reliable run-speed difference but always an unreliable start-speed difference, the present results may suggest that, for whatever reasons, the effect of the start-exposure manipulation was displaced to a forward portion of the response chain where it could be more easily reflected in start than in run speeds—in spite of the typical insensitivity of the start-speed measure. Certainly the conditions of rearing and maintenance peculiar to the present investigation afford such a possibility.

The results of the present study are not so illuminating that they preclude additional study of the relationship between start-exposure time and maintenance brightness, investigations in which, for example, the range of start-exposure times is extended bidirectionally to lower and higher values and maintenance brightness is altered during the course of training. Nevertheless, the findings seem sufficiently clear to warrant the following observations and conclusions. First, it should be recognized that, irrespective of maintenance brightness, the training conditions of the present study, like those of the previous investigations, were such that S acquired a response that was instrumental to a goal brightness that provided change relative to the brightness of S's start compartment and not to that of its maintenance condition. Second, Ss maintained on the D and SD conditions did not fail to acquire the response. The effect of maintenance condition was only to augment or deplete the strength of the acquired runway response, this performance effect being directly related to the degree of similarity in brightness of the maintenance and start-exposure conditions. Taken together, these observations indicate that conditions of exposure, such as S's maintenance condition, that are relatively distant in time from the change in stimulation contingent on the observed response are less effective determinants of the performance of that response than conditions, such as start-box exposure, that are more proximally related.

The foregoing conclusion seems to obtain support also from the observation that terminal runway performance was unaffected by rearing brightness, the condition of exposure most distant in time from the assessed point of training. In this regard, special note must be made of the performances of the SD and DS groups at the beginning of training, when the brightnesses of the rearing conditions to which the Ss of these groups had been exposed for some 50 days prior occupied a more proximal relationship to the brightness conditions of training. As indicated in Fig. 10, the initial performances of the SD and DS groups (that is, on trial block 1) were significantly different (F $\frac{1}{96}$ = 3.99, $p < .05$), but reversed relative to the positions these groups occupied at the end of training.[2] That is, the initial performances of these groups related to the degree of similarity in brightness of their *rearing* and start-exposure conditions, as opposed to the comparable relationship that obtained at the end of training between *maintenance* and start brightness. Thus, in the final analysis, the results of the present study seem to augment the findings of the previous investigations, indicating that performances instrumental to a change in stimulation are dependent not only on the similarity and duration but also the recency, or temporal proximity, of those stimulus conditions to which S is exposed prior to its exploration or opportunity for exploration of the novel or changed stimulus condition.

III. On the Logical and Empirical Structure of a Theory of Exploration

In showing how conditions of prior stimulus exposure may affect performances based on stimulus-change reward—indeed, in suggesting a dependency of this reward on such exposure—the results of the reported experiments seem sufficiently structured to permit formal elaboration of the formulation initially outlined. Before any attempt at meaningful

---

[2] Although over-all group differences on trial block 1 were unreliable, the noted rearing difference (that is, between SD and DS) was maintained at a marginal level of confidence when these two groups were combined with the S and D groups, respectively (F $\frac{1}{96}$ = 3.28, $p < .08$).

formalization can be made, however, it is necessary to consider those earlier efforts at theorizing, in order to illuminate specifically the line of departure that is adopted by the present formulation and the manner in which this formulation integrates certain "basic" concepts germane to exploratory phenomena. Moreover, such a review may bring to the fore the problems attendant on the delineation of exploration, a consideration that acquires particular import when it is noted that the reported experiments, although purportedly on exploration, have little if any direct bearing on the assessment of this behavior. Our course with the following, then, will be to treat the nature of exploration, its relation to early motivational interpretations, and the manner in which these interpretations may be successfully accommodated within a drive and incentive-motivational theory formulated on the basis of the reported findings.

A. THE NATURE OF THE EXPLORATORY RESPONSE

As was noted in the introduction to this chapter, studies on exploratory behavior have, for the past ten or more years, been representative of a unique classification in the realm of animal investigation—a classification characterized by research on a behavior that has been left unspecified. Thus, studying the behavior has simply meant observing the performance of animals that were not or had not been subjected to known conditions of deprivation or intense stimulation, or to the objects and events that "satisfied" these conditions, or both. In this respect, then, the operational delineation of exploratory phenomena that has prevailed has been representative merely of a "wastebucket" classification. This orientation and the underlying difficulties attendant on precise specification of the behavior seem to stem largely from the absence, or apparent absence, of any "goal" object or event that can be associated with exploration. Unlike appetitive activities, for example, which may be sufficiently delineated and thereby studied on the basis of the animal's receipt and consumption of food and water, exploratory phenomena appear devoid of any consummatory aspect. Indeed, the apparent absence of a consummatory "climax" for the behavior has even lead some theorists (e.g., White, 1959) to conclude that exploratory phenomena are beyond the realm of contemporary theory.

Apart from consummatory considerations, the problem of delineating exploratory phenomena might be viewed with respect to a resolution on the basis of a presumed *effect* of exploration, that is, the commonly held position that exploratory behaviors have the prime function of altering or changing those stimuli currently impinging upon the organism. Thus, exploration as a label may be relegated to those behaviors that are instrumental to the animal's receipt of relatively novel or changed stimuli, in which case the observed runway performance reported in the present experiments would illustrate and deserve the term exploration. Unfortunately, the effect of changing the animal's stimulus field is not exclusively representative of exploratory or, perhaps more appropriately, "novelty-seeking" behaviors. Such an effect appears common to most behavior classes, such as food-seeking, and pain-escaping. Furthermore, the analysis finds particular difficulty with the fact that a perceptible change in the animal's stimulation may result via the proprioceptive or "feedback" component of any response.

While itself unsatisfactory, the instrumental analogue suggests an extension by which the nature of the exploratory response might be adequately delineated—and as a consummatory reaction. Such an extension derives from the fact that the paradigm and findings of the reported experiments closely parallel those of instrumental reward conditioning: in brief, both illustrate that the strength of the instrumental response progressively increases (or decreases) over trials when the reinforcer is presented (or withheld); that performance relates positively to the extent or magnitude of imposed conditions of deprivation and reinforcement; and that performance is relatively independent of prior conditions of training. The essential difference between the two cases appears to relate only to the particular performance variables that are manipulated; that is, in place of food deprivation and food reinforcement, the described experiments utilized stimulus exposure (stimulus-change deprivation) and stimulus-change reinforcement. Thus, in its entirety, the comparison suggests that, within the confines of the conditioning paradigm employed, the change in stimulation that was made contingent on the animal's instrumental running response may appropriately be viewed as the "goal" object of this behavior and, further, that the consummatory action involved in this context is the animal's response at the goal to the change in stimulation that obtained. Although not assessed or even considered within the reported experiments, this consummatory action would presumably have reference to responses of orienting toward, attending to, perceiving, or (perhaps most descriptively) "ingesting" the change in stimulation that prevailed at the goal.

By implicating exploration as a consummatory reaction to relatively novel or changed stimuli, the preceding analysis suggests that the nature of this behavior should be adequately reflected in the findings of those studies that have made the particular change in stimulation being investigated (that is, the novel or unfamiliar stimulus configuration) directly available to S rather than, as in the present research, contingent on some instrumental act. Such a paradigm is exemplified by many studies wherein attention has been directed to those features and aspects of the animal's stimulus field that call forth and direct behavior in the absence of any apparent motive or condition of reinforcement, or both—studies in which, for example, novel or changed stimuli represent, or are introduced as, a portion of the animal's immediate environment. In a review of this literature, the author has elsewhere (Fowler, 1965) noted that, with regard to an account of the nature of exploration, the research is significant in two respects. First, through the variety of measures and test procedures that have been used in these investigations (such as choice scores, frequency measures, time in contact, and indices of the direction and ordering of locomotor activity) the term exploration has come to acquire specific reference to behaviors such as orienting to, locomoting toward, peering at, sniffing, contacting, or manipulating (or combinations of these activities toward) particular objects and stimulus configurations. Second, and equally important, the findings of this research have provided the basis for a generally descriptive empirical tenet: animals, both rodents and primates, will respond to (that is, explore in the sense just described) a change in the complex or pattern of stimulation presently or recently impinging upon them and, within limits, the animal's response will be stronger the greater the extent or magnitude of the change in stimulation afforded.

Note should be made that the term "change" or "change in stimulation" as used in this tenet has broad and inclusive reference to the commonly investigated variables of relative novelty and unfamiliarity and to factors such as *complexity, surprisingness, incongruity,* and *asymmetry,* all of which have been empirically isolated as effective determinants of the exploratory reaction. That is, the effect of these variables in eliciting such responses as orienting and attending is subsumed, by definition, under a broad and generally descriptive response-to-change effect. In this regard, however, the possibility of conceptually treating these variables as instances of a single or unitary stimulus-change construct should be considered. For example, with receipt of a complex stimulus configuration, the animal encounters change relative to its immediate prior experience, and also via its perceptual commerce with the variety of stimulus elements comprising the complex configuration. Accordingly, the complex, asymmetrical, or incongruous pattern or object may be viewed as a stimulus composite that provides numerous features of change.

A second point of consideration relating to the response-to-change tenet is the qualifying phrase "within limits" used in describing a positive relationship between the magnitude or extent of the change in stimulation afforded and the strength of the response elicited. Although this relationship derives from the finding that exploration is increasingly pronounced over larger discrepancies between the presently or recently impinging stimuli and the novel or changed stimulus condition that is introduced (e.g., Dember & Millbrook, 1956; Dember & Fowler, 1959; Dewsbury, 1965; Montgomery, 1953), recognition must be given to the dimension of stimulus intensity that may be involved with this type of manipulation. That is, changes in an upward direction of increasing intensities of stimulation can approach an aversion threshold, as is evident with the animal's escape and avoidance of bright lights, loud noises, and the like (see Lockard, 1963). Apart from the effect of a too-intense change in stimulation, however, some evidence also exists that a too-novel change, in the sense of bizarre, strange, or unexpected, may elicit fear and thereby reduce or even preclude exploration, at least as long as the fear persists. Perhaps best illustrating this effect are those "spontaneous" fears that Hebb (1955; but see Butler, 1964) reports for chimpanzees confronted with a clay model of the human head or the anesthetized body of a fellow chimpanzee. Collectively, these data require that reference be made to the determinants of the exploratory reaction as "mild" or "moderate" changes in stimulation.

In total, the descriptive account of exploration that derives from studies of the animal's specific response to novel or changed objects and conditions accords quite well with the proposed delineation of exploratory behavior as a consummatory reaction of orienting to, attending to, and perceptually ingesting the change in stimulation that is made directly available to the animal or contingent on its instrumental act. Thus, the response-to-change tenet is of particular significance in illustrating, even with the qualifications noted, that the relationship between exploration and its eliciting condition of stimulus change is analogous to the relationship between the response of eating and the unconditioned stimulus of food. That is, the positive relation commonly noted between amount or volume of food and strength of eating (more specifically, salivating and chewing) appears adequately reflected in the increased "vigor" or strength of exploration when, as noted but within limits, the magnitude or the extent of the change in stimulation is augmented. Moreover, the consistency in occurrence of the food-deprived animal's unconditioned response to food finds agreement with the relative constancy of exploration that is observed over repeated daily presentations of the novel or changed stimulus condition (e.g., Berlyne, 1955; Berlyne & Slater, 1957; Danzinger & Mainland, 1954; Glanzer,

1961; Howarth, 1962; Montgomery, 1952; Montgomery, 1953).[3] Taken together, these points of similarity argue that exploration may be effectively treated as an *unconditioned* response to change, a view obviously noted much earlier in Pavlov's (1927) specification of the "investigatory reflex."

B. EXPLORATORY MOTIVATION: SATIATION OR CURIOSITY?

The distinction offered between the instrumental and consummatory "components" of exploration (that is, between such activities as bar pressing or running a straight alley for novel or changed stimulus conditions and the specific reactions of orienting and perceptually attending to the change in stimulation) acquires importance for the following reasons. First, the distinction points up that any motivational interpretation of exploratory phenomena, namely, those behaviors occurring in the apparent absence of conditions of deprivation and intense stimulation, must take cognizance of the different functions that the novel stimulus serves with respect to the components of the behavior; that is, that the novel or changed stimulus acts as an eliciting or unconditioned stimulus for the consummatory component and, as illustrated by the findings of the reported experiments, as a reinforcing stimulus for the instrumental component. In this regard, emphasis must also be given to the likelihood previously argued that both components of the behavior will be operative in the context of instrumental conditioning based on exploratory "rewards." Consequently, a further obligation of the motivational analysis is that it have reference to the arousal or activation of *both* of the components of the behavior and even to their possible interrelation. Unfortunately, as is evident with the hypotheses that have resulted from representative subclasses of research on the two components of the behavior (for example, alternation behavior and operant light-reinforcement), current theorizing on each component appears to be relatively independent of the other, most likely reflecting an orientation that has derived from the emphasis initially given to the consummatory component.

[3] On this point it should be made clear that the commonly noted decrement in exploration that obtains with the animal's continued exposure to a novel stimulus (e.g., Adlerstein & Fehrer, 1955; Berlyne, 1955; Glanzer, 1961; Montgomery, 1952; Montgomery, 1953; Thompson, 1953) is in fact consonant with the proposed relationship. With its continued presentation, the novel stimulus should be less effective in eliciting and maintaining exploration since it becomes part of the pattern of stimulation to which the animal is being exposed and therefore no longer provides or adequately represents a change in stimulation. The effect may be viewed as analogous to the decrement in eating that occurs when the hungry animal finally consumes the food available to it.

1. *The Exploratory Response to Change*

With the intensification of research on response-to-change phenomena in the early 1950's, two distinct lines of analysis became evident. One group of investigators (e.g., Berlyne, 1950; Berlyne, 1955; Harlow, 1950; Harlow, 1953; Montgomery, 1952; Montgomery, 1953) maintained that novel forms of stimulation "attracted" or "titillated" the organism so that it would approach and investigate these stimuli; in effect, the animal became "curious" about the novel or changed stimulus and responded to it. This interpretation, in which the novel or changed stimulus is viewed not only as a cue directing the exploratory response but also as the source of motivation or arousal of the behavior, is clearly indicated in Berlyne's account of the phenomenon: "When a novel stimulus affects an organism's receptors, there will occur a drive-stimulus-producing response . . . which we shall call 'curiosity' . . ." (Berlyne, 1950, p. 79). The same assumptions were made with Montgomery's postulation that "a novel stimulus situation evokes in an organism an exploratory drive . . ." (Montgomery, 1953, p. 129), and with Harlow's espousal of both a "manipulation motive" (Harlow, 1950) and a "visual exploration drive" (Harlow, 1953).

Contrasting with proponents of the "curiosity" position, other investigators (e.g., Glanzer, 1953a; Rothkopf & Zeaman, 1952) argued that the animal became "satiated" with or "tired" of stimuli to which it had been or was being exposed, and therefore responded to other stimuli that were novel or unfamiliar. Thus, for these theorists, it was the "tedium" of the familiar stimulus or stimulus pattern that fostered the animal's exploration. This view is explicit in the major postulate of Glanzer's highly formalized account of the phenomenon: "Each moment an organism perceives a stimulus-object or stimulus-objects, A, there develops a quantity of stimulus satiation to A" (Glanzer, 1953a, p. 259). With the related assumption that stimulus satiation reduced the organism's tendency to make any response to A, those stimuli with which the animal had not been or was less satiated (that is, the novel or unfamiliar stimuli) would thus elicit responses of approach and investigation. Essentially the same position was adopted by Rothkopf and Zeaman (1952) with their specification of a "tired" stimulus. In fact, both this conceptualization and Glanzer's seem to derive from earlier statements made by Dennis and Sollenberger (1934) regarding the animal's "negative adaptation" to currently impinging and thus familiar stimuli, and the consequent inability of these stimuli to elicit exploratory reactions.

With its emphasis on the "inhibitory" character of the familiar stimulus, the satiation-type formulation, in comparison with the curiosity position, explained with equal facility the direction or point of focus of the exploratory reaction; with respect to the *manifestation* of the animal's response to change, however, the formulation suffered a major shortcoming. The animal could have a reduced or inhibited tendency to respond to those stimuli with which it was satiated or tired (and therefore a stronger tendency to respond to novel stimuli), but this did not account for the arousal and occurrence of the animal's response to change. Indeed, while Glanzer (1953a) had explicitly proposed that satiation would operate in a decremental or inhibitory capacity, making the animal less active in the face of familiar stimuli, the initial activity or arousal of the animal was left unspecified, or as deriving presumably from other sources of motivation, such as food and water deprivation. Thus, it is particularly noteworthy that, unlike the studies of other investigators, Glanzer's research on exploration (Glanzer, 1953b; Glanzer, 1958; Glanzer, 1961) consistently entailed the use of deprived animals.

Apart from its proposed inhibitory character, however, there is no apparent reason why the satiation concept cannot be assigned motivational or drive properties, as had been the case with the curiosity formulations advanced by Berlyne (1950; 1955) and others. In fact, such a position was given early expression by Myers and Miller (1954), who argued that homogeneous, unchanging, and therefore monotonous stimuli evoked a "drive of boredom" that could be reduced by sensory variety, freedom of action, and the like. Accordingly, for these satiation-*drive* theorists, it was the familiar or unchanging stimuli of the animal's present or recent surround that motivated the exploratory response to change; the novel or unfamiliar stimuli merely served as cues that directed this behavior, much in the fashion that food for the hungry animal served as a cue in directing its behavior, that is, in eliciting the response of eating. In comparison with the curiosity position, then, the satiation-drive formulation may be viewed as differing solely with respect to its ascription of drive or arousal-producing properties to familiar and unchanging stimuli rather than to novel and unfamiliar stimuli. Both formulations, however, accorded cue or directive properties to novel stimuli, thereby agreeing with the empirical generalization that animals respond to a change in stimulation.

With respect to an explanation of the particulars of response-to-change phenomena, the curiosity and the satiation-drive formulations appear to fare equally well. Indeed, they would have to, because both ascribe cue properties to novel stimuli, and whenever a novel stimulus prevails, it can be novel only to the extent that it differs from the stimuli that already comprise or have recently comprised the animal's perceptual field—stimuli, then, that are classifiable as familiar and unchanging. Hence, in any context, the arousal or motivation of the exploratory response may be attributed with equal facility to either novel or familiar stimuli, in accordance with either formulation. The apparent equivalence of the two formulations, however, has not gone uncontested. Quite recently, in a review of these positions, O'Connell (1965) has argued that "titillation" (that is, curiosity) formulations align better theoretically with response-to-change phenomena because in comparison "tedium" (that is, satiation) formulations not only fail to generate unique predictions, but suffer in parsimony as well.

The first point of O'Connell's (1965) argument is well taken: unique predictions regarding response-to-change phenomena should not derive from *either* formulation because of theoretical properties that they have in common, as well as the fact already noted that novelty cannot prevail apart from the animal's current or recent exposure to familiar and unchanging stimuli. The second part of the argument (that regarding the greater parsimony of the curiosity formulation), however, is overdrawn, because it does not derive from the common assumptions of the two formulations but from the descriptive statement by which O'Connell characterizes the two positions: "Titillation theories postulate that new [or relatively novel] stimuli are attractive, while tedium theories state that familiar stimuli tend to cease to control behavior" (O'Connell, 1965, p. 170). This descriptive analysis certainly indicates that the tedium or satiation formulation suffers in parsimony; some additional statement is required to account for the actual elicitation of the behavior directed to novel stimuli. Nevertheless, it should be evident that the characterization afforded the tedium position is representative only of the formulations advanced by Glanzer (1953a) and Rothkopf and Zeaman (1952), wherein a decremental or inhibitory function is ascribed to "satiated" or "tired" stimuli. Indeed, the restrictiveness of O'Connell's description is made conspicuous by the absence of any reference in his review to the position of Myers and Miller (1954), who consider that familiar and unchanging stimuli evoke a "drive of boredom" that can be reduced by sensory variety, freedom of action, and the like. When recognition is given to this viewpoint, together with the cue or directive function that novel stimuli serve within the formulation, it becomes evident that O'Connell's descriptive statement for the titillation or curiosity position, namely "that new stimuli are attractive," is equally representative of the tedium or satiation formulation.

Even so, it might be argued, as O'Connell (1965) and others (e.g., Dember & Earl, 1957) have contended that the curiosity or titillation position can retain greater parsimony merely by eschewing all forms of drive theorizing. Thus, apart from the explicit drive-motivational properties that were posited by the early curiosity theorists, current titillation theorists might account for the animal's approach and investigation of novel stimuli solely on the basis of the "attractiveness" and presumed "eliciting" function of these stimuli, without having recourse to any drive or arousal function. In its simplicity, the elegance of such an analysis suggests that it might equally well be applied to the "eliciting" or unconditioned stimulus function of other configurations and objects, such as food and water. Unfortunately, in this context the interpretation founders because the eliciting function of these objects depends on antecedent conditions of deprivation: animals that have not recently been deprived of food and water typically do not eat and drink. The analogy is instructive, for it illustrates that the unitary assumption of an eliciting function for novel stimuli is not necessarily more parsimonious; rather, it subsumes under the term attractive or eliciting both cue and drive functions, by whatever label. Apparently this confusion has prevailed and been perpetuated only because the eliciting function of novel stimuli, unlike that of food and water, cannot be assessed independently of those antecedent conditions of familiar and unchanging stimuli to which (by definition of the term novelty) the animal must be exposed prior to its confrontation with a change in stimulation.

2. *Performances Instrumental to Stimulus-Change Reward*

Although response-to-change phenomena do not provide a sufficient basis for differentiating the curiosity and satiation formulations, such a basis does prevail when consideration is given to the implication of these formulations for performances that are instrumental to novelty—in particular, instances of learning based on exploratory "rewards." As argued previously with reference to the findings of the reported research, effective analysis of exploratory phenomena must take cognizance not only of the eliciting or unconditioned stimulus function that the novel stimulus serves with respect to the consummatory response to change, but also of its reinforcing function for responses that are instrumental to the change. In part, this obligation receives recognition in the equally representative descriptive statement of the two formulations that novel stimuli are "attractive."

The empirical observation that novel stimuli are reinforcing, however, poses a perplexing state of affairs when taken in conjunction with the noted assumptions of the curiosity formulation. Novel stimuli are apparently to be viewed as unique among classes of reinforcing stimuli, for unlike "positive" reinforcers, such as food and water, which are commonly accorded reinforcing and cue properties, and unlike "negative" reinforcers, such as electric shock and bright lights, which are commonly accorded cue and drive (cf. punishment) properties, novel stimuli possess all three properties. This commitment, which is required only of the curiosity theorist, becomes somewhat alarming when its meaning for performances based on exploratory rewards is noted: responses that are instrumental to novelty are productive of a stimulus condition that is both reinforcing and drive producing. Herein lies the basis, then, for the oft-quoted conclusion that novelty obtains its reinforcing effect through an increase in drive (e.g., Harlow, 1953; Leuba, 1955; Montgomery, 1954). And, as commented earlier, this conclusion has in turn provided the basis for those theoretical formulations which, by reference to optimal levels of stimulation and arousal, posit both increases and decreases in drive as reinforcing events. At this point, some consideration should be given to the logical structure of the inference that underlies these formulations.

The conclusion that reinforcement is accompanied by increased drive certainly derives validly from the empirical observation that novelty is reinforcing and the theoretical premise that novelty is drive producing. Nevertheless, it remains as an unparalleled feat of thinking that this conclusion can be used to foster the claim that classical drive theory is inadequate, when there exists the equally likely proposition that the ascription of drive-producing properties to novel stimuli is erroneous. Confirmation of the latter proposition seems to obtain, moreover, when attention is drawn to the arousal or activation of those performances that are instrumental to change. As illustrated by the findings of the reported experiments, these instrumental performances relate positively to both the animal's length of exposure to an initially experienced stimulus condition and the magnitude of the change in stimulation that is made contingent upon the instrumental act. Accordingly, both the exposure and change variables may be viewed as operational expressions or parameters of "novelty," but this in no way obviates the fact that such novelty does not prevail during the sequence of responding that leads to it. With this consideration, it is evident that the curiosity formulation is without an interpretive basis by which the arousal of the instrumental component of exploration can be explained; for as Brown (1953a; 1961) has cogently argued, if novel stimuli evoke an exploratory drive, this drive is not produced until after the animal has made the response the drive is supposed to be motivating.

In contrast to the curiosity or titillation position, the satiation-drive formulation encounters no difficulty with the same considerations. In fact, the reinforcing function of novel stimuli accords very well with the formulation since the satiation drive, deriving from the animal's receipt of familiar and unchanging stimuli, is theoretically reduced by novelty, and thereby affords the occasion for the learning of responses that are instrumental to changed stimulation. Hence, it follows from this consideration, when coupled with the previous discussion of response-to-change phenomena, that the satiation-drive interpretation satisfies all of the boundary requirements initially proposed for the analysis of exploratory performances, both with regard to the arousal of the two components of the behavior and to the different functions that novel stimuli serve with respect to each of these components.

C. Formalization of the Drive and Incentive-Motivational Interpretation

Because the satiation-drive formulation is patterned after the classical drive interpretation of appetitive performances, it may be expected that the results of the reported studies are capable of full description and therefore formal integration within the framework of those more formalized models that have been advanced for instrumental reward conditioning. It has already been noted that the differences between the paradigm and results of the reported research and those for instrumental appetitive conditioning relate primarily to the performance variables manipulated; that is, in place of food deprivation and food reinforcement, the present studies used short-term exposure (stimulus-change deprivation) and stimulus-change reinforcement. With respect to the relationships that obtained between these variables and others, such as the amount of reinforced and nonreinforced practice, the data, all in all, would seem most satisfactorily accommodated by the behavioral formulation advanced by Spence (1956). Our purpose with the following will be to present the major portions of this formulation for the specific purpose of integrating the obtained findings and of thus providing a basis on which the satiation concept and even the curiosity concept, although redefined, may be formally structured.

1. The Basic Model and Its Application

The major theoretical constructs of Spence's (1956) formulation for instrumental appetitive conditioning are presented within the completely boxed area of Fig. 11. According to the formulation, the excitatory potential of a stimulus complex (S) to elicit a response (R) is a function of the multiplicative interaction of an associative or habit factor (H), operationally defined in terms of the number of training trials, and two motivational or performance factors, drive (D) and incentive (K). These motivational constructs gain respective operational expression in terms of the amount or schedule (or both) of food deprivation that is imposed upon the animal, and of the magnitude (size, weight, volume) of the food reinforcement that is made contingent on the response. Regarding the combination of D and K, the formulation posits that their relationship is additive; that is, increments (or decrements) to D and K will be reflected in an algebraic summation of their effects on performance, as may be empirically attested to by a nonsignificant interaction of the deprivation and reinforcement variables. Finally, the formulation posits that excitatory potential, comprised of the constructs H, D, and K, will be reduced by an inhibitory potential (I) that relates positively to the number of nonreinforced training trials and possibly to the delay in reinforcement following response evocation. Collectively, these constructs operate to produce the *effective* excitatory potential ($\bar{E}$) of the prevailing stimulus complex S—which obtains relevance via the associative factor H—to evoke the response R. (The letter symbols above the boxed area in Fig. 11 are explained in detail in subsections *a–d*, following.)

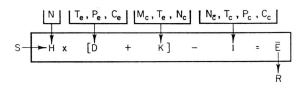

Fig. 11. Diagram, after Spence (1956), summarizing the interrelationships of the major thoretical variables constituting the effective excitatory potential ($\bar{E}$) of a prevailing stimulus complex (S) to evoke an instrumental response (R). The empirical variables presumed to determine the constructs H, D, K, and I are noted at the top of the diagram, with arrows indicating the relevant theoretical construct. See text for further explanation.

The only modifications that appear necessary in order to use the same model to integrate the findings of the reported research relate to an amplification of the specific empirical referents for the theoretical constructs, that is, an elaboration that will permit the inclusion of variables peculiar to exploratory phenomena. In deriving these constructs from the present data and in so applying the model, reference will be made solely to run speeds, primarily because of the apparent obscuring effect exerted on start performance by the control operation of handling *S*s immediately prior to each trial-response. Furthermore, as with the application of the model to instrumental appetitive conditioning, the assumption is made that the theoretical constructs, as summarized by effective excitatory potential $\bar{E}$, bear a linear relationship to running speed.

a. Habit (H). The empirical basis for the H construct stems directly from the progressively faster run speeds that were generally manifest throughout the course of training in each of the experiments reported. Thus, as indicated in the top row of Fig. 11, the associative relationship or habit that develops between the stimulus complex impinging on the animal (in the alley situation) and the response of running down the alley is designated as a positive function of the number of training trials (N). Note, here, that the prescribed S-R association is viewed, not as dependent on reinforcement, but merely on the repeated contiguous occasions of S and R. This supposition derives mainly from the "latent learning" effect of Experiment III, as illustrated by the relatively abrupt and appropriate shift in performance that prevailed for those *S*s that were switched from their original no-change or nonreinforcement condition of training to one of stimulus-change reinforcement (see Fig. 8).

Apart from pointing up its positive character, the findings of the reported studies are of little aid in suggesting a more precise theoretical function relating habit strength to amount of training. This limitation prevails primarily as a result of the difficulty in evaluating runway performance as reflecting speed of *responding* rather than speed of response *evocation*. For example, with the moderate performance influences exerted by conditions of exploratory motivation and reward, it can be expected that runway performance will be especially hampered by competing response influences, such that the acquisition function shows an initially protracted positive inflection (see Figs. 5 and 8). Moreover, at the start of training, the acquisition curve may even show a slight downward deflection, possibly as the result of an initial *eliciting* effect of the novel apparatus (that is, the discernable physical features of the runway) that dissipates or is inhibited as *S* is trained and becomes familiar with the apparatus. Also relevant in this context is the complicating effect of the imposed shift in the distribution of training from one to three trials per day at an intertrial interval of 1 hour. When coupled with the results of Experiment IV (illustrating the effect that can be exerted on early performance by conditions of rearing and maintenance), these considerations indicate that much care must be taken (and perhaps considerable leeway granted) in deriving theoretical functions from the obtained performance curves.

b. Drive (D). To facilitate discussion of both the D and K constructs, the findings of Experiments I–III relevant to the manipulation of start-exposure time and magnitude of brightness change at the goal are summarized in Fig. 12. In the left panel, mean run speeds (averaged within each experiment from trial 151 on) are presented as a function of start-exposure time for *S*s trained under either a no-change (black start to

black goal, B-B) condition or a stimulus-change (B-W) condition, the
two conditions being represented by open and closed data points, respectively. Inclusion of the data from Experiment I under the reinforcement
B-W condition might appear suspect because of the failure in that experiment to isolate brightness change at the goal as the source of reinforcement. However, the fact that extinction did not obtain in that
study indicates that a source of reinforcement (presumably the change
afforded by S's view of different, extra-alley stimuli) was, in fact, operative. Moreover, as shown in Fig. 12, the data points of Experiment I
correspond fairly well with those of Experiments II and III, wherein
the reinforcement effect was successfully isolated. Collectively, these
data are sufficient, when taken together with the relatively abrupt and

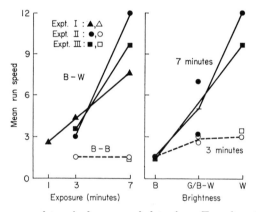

Fig. 12. A summary of terminal run-speed data from Experiments I–III relevant
to the manipulation of start exposure time (left panel) and brightness-change reinforcement at the goal (right panel). See text for further explanation.

appropriate shifts in performance that obtained in Experiment III with
alteration of start-exposure time, to warrant the positing of a satiation-
drive construct (D) that is operationally defined as an increasing monotonic function of the time or length of S's exposure (T_e) to the stimulus
condition that antedates or is concomitant with the observed response.

On the basis of the foregoing considerations, attention may be directed to the theoretical combination of H and D, as reflected by the interaction effects of their empirical referents, N and T_e. Indicative of
the multiplicative relationship posited between H and D in Fig. 11, the
data from Experiments I–III are consistent in showing that with different constant values of T_e, increasing values of N were productive of
diverging performance relationships.

The findings of Experiment IV, although inconsistent with those of

Experiments I–III in showing a T_e effect for run speeds (which did obtain, however, for start speeds), are nonetheless important in demonstrating that the operational base for D should be expanded to include an additional parameter of exposure, namely, the proximity of S's condition of exposure (P_e) to the observed response. The point of reference for positing D as a function of P_e derives not from the fact that runway performance in Experiment IV related positively to the degree of similarity in brightness of S's maintenance (home cage) and start-box condition; such an effect may be accounted for on the basis of the extended T_e that occurred for those Ss experiencing the same brightness in both their home-cage and start-box conditions. Rather, the relevance of P_e obtains indirectly from the fact that S's exposure for approximately 24 hours to a home-cage brightness that was *different* from the start brightness (to which S was exposed for only 3 or 7 minutes) had no effect in counteracting the reinforcing effect of a change in brightness *relative to the start brightness*, and similarly was of little, albeit significant, consequence in reducing the level of runway performance. These observations suggest that the effects of exposure to a particular stimulus condition dissipate fairly rapidly with S's nonexposure to the stimulus condition or, conversely, with S's exposure to some other, different stimulus condition. Thus, it follows that, within an extended temporal period entailing S's receipt of successively different exposures, the condition of exposure that is more proximal to the observed response will be the more effective determinant of the arousal of that response.

The foregoing consideration (that the effects of exposure dissipate fairly rapidly, but not necessarily completely,[4] with S's experiencing of a different stimulus condition) seems to require mention of one additional determinant of D, namely, the constancy of S's exposure condition (C_e). The nature and relevance of this variable may be illustrated by reference to the anticipated effects of exposure to a composite or heterogeneous stimulus condition, such as a start compartment of differing brightnesses, for example, black, gray, and white. As a result of S's commerce with the components of this composite exposure condition (that is, through S's visual scanning of black, gray, and white), exposure to one component should permit nonexposure and, therefore, at least partial dissipation of the satiation accrued to another, previously experienced, component. Hence, apart from the effects of T_e and P_e, satia-

---

[4] The residual influence of a temporally distant condition of exposure seems indicated in the effect that rearing brightness had on performances during the first 20 training trials of Experiment IV. This portion of training represented a period of 1–15 days following alteration of rearing brightness for those Ss that were switched to a different brightness for their maintenance condition.

tion to the condition as a whole or to any of the stimulus components comprising the condition should accumulate more gradually. This expectation obtains formal expression with the statement that the satiation-drive effect relates positively to the constancy or homogeneity of S's condition of exposure. Although the supposition does not bear directly on the findings of the reported experiments, since manipulation of start exposure, for example, had reference only to a homogeneous brightness, it is nevertheless in accord with the intermediate performance levels that were exhibited in Experiment IV by those Ss maintained on the composite (black, gray, and white) home-cage brightness.

Final note on the D construct can be directed to the absence of any performance difference, as indicated in the left panel of Fig. 12, between those 3- and 7-minute exposure groups that were trained under the no-change (B-B) condition. This result is entirely consistent with the commonly ascribed functions of the drive concept both to "energize" behavior and to provide a basis for the acquisition of responses that are instrumental to a reduction or termination of the drive-defining condition. Because such a reduction obtained in the present experimental context with S's receipt of a change in brightness at the goal, those exposure groups of the no-change (B-B) condition were without reinforcement, and thus without a basis on which the runway response could become the dominant member of the behavior hierarchy relevant to the alley situation. Consequently, for these groups, there are no grounds for anticipating that increasing T_e should intensify the runway response rather than some other, presumably more dominant, reaction (such as grooming, gnawing at the apparatus, or attempting to escape) that is selectively reinforced as a result of its differential stimulus consequence. This interpretation might seem inconsistent with the previous treatment of H as a function solely of the number of contiguous pairings of S and R; the inconsistency is dispelled, however, when the operation of reinforcement is recognized as the determinant of excitatory potential, not through the habit factor H but rather through the incentive-motivational factor K.

c. *Incentive* (K). The empirical basis for positing K as an additional determinant of excitatory potential is shown more clearly in the right panel of Fig. 12, where mean run speeds (again averaged from trial 151 on) are presented for the 3- and 7-minute exposure groups (open and closed data points, respectively) as a function of goal-box brightness. (Because, in the designated experiments, the brightness of the start compartment and alley was black, the abscissa also represents increasing magnitudes of brightness-change reinforcement.) As shown, the data from the two experiments obtain close agreement in illustrating that when T_e is held constant, as with the 7-minute condition, increasing magnitudes of brightness change afford reliably higher performance levels. Thus, these data are sufficient, when taken together with the relatively abrupt and appropriate performance shifts that occurred in Experiment III with alteration of goal brightness, to warrant the positing of the additional performance construct, incentive (K), which is operationally defined in terms of the magnitude of the change in stimulation (M_c) that is made contingent on the observed response. Here, the theoretical combination of H and K, as reflected by the interaction effects of their empirical referents, N and M_c, may also be noted. Experiments II and III are consistent in showing that, with different constant values of M_c, increasing values of N also produced diverging performance curves, in accord with the multiplicative relationship between H and K posited in Fig. 11.

While the findings of the reported experiments are satisfactory for positing K and its relation to H, they appear insufficient for specifying anything more than a positive relationship between K and its defining condition M_c. This problem arises primarily because the "intermediate" gray (G) and composite black-white (B-W) values of goal brightness used in determining the reinforcement functions of Fig. 12 derive solely from Experiment II and, with respect to the 7-minute exposure function, these values give quite disparate data points. (For both the 3- and 7-minute exposure functions, the performance levels attained under the G goal condition are represented in Fig. 12 by the lower open and closed data points, and those attained under the B-W condition by the upper open and closed data points; respective G and B-W data points for each exposure condition have been averaged, as indicated by a horizontal "blip," to determine the midpoint of the function.) No clearly valid basis prevails for determining which of the two intermediate goal-brightnesses, G or B-W, is more representative of an intermediate value within the goal-brightness dimension. It can at least be observed, however, that when the G condition is viewed as representing a brightness value that is perceptually closer to black (B), the 3-minute function is not altered and the 7-minute function obtains closer correspondence in depicting performance as a negatively accelerated function of brightness-change reinforcement. The alternative assumption that the B-W condition is representative of a brightness value closer to white (W) only serves to accentuate the discrepancy presently existing between the two functions.

Apart from the data points for the intermediate values of goal brightness, those for the B and W values, respectively, are sufficiently consistent to indicate that the T_e and M_c variables interact in determining performance level. Thus, with respect to the combination of D and K, it seems that their theoretical relationship should take on a multiplicative form, following Hull (1952), rather than the additive relationship posited in Fig. 11, after Spence (1956). In this regard, however, the results that have been met with in the context of instrumental appetitive conditioning are most instructive. Studies using intermediate and high values of D and K (that is, food deprivation and food reinforcement) have consistently failed to show any interaction of the effects of these variables on performance, thereby supporting the assumption of an additive relationship; on the other hand, studies using near zero, if not zero, and intermediate or high values of these variables appear equally consistent in showing the interaction, in agreement with the multiplicative assumption. In a review of this research, Black (1965) has argued effectively that the disparate findings may be readily assimilated under the additive combination rule, if it is further assumed that the drive-defining condition of food deprivation also serves as an empirical determinant of K. Full consideration will be given later to the details of this interpretation and to its implication for the present analysis, together with the relevance of the other empirical variables, T_e and N_c, noted in Fig. 11 as determinants of K. At this point, however, it should be noted that the obtained interaction also derives from the use of near zero, if not zero, and high values of the T_e and M_c variables; as such, the finding is consistent with the results of those studies on instrumental appetitive conditioning wherein a similar combination of values has been used. Thus, although much additional research is required on the relationship of these variables, it is reasonable to suppose that Black's (1965) interpretation of the findings encountered with manipulation of food deprivation and food reinforcement will also apply to performances based on exploratory rewards. Accordingly, the additive combination of D and K is maintained with the K construct being posited both as a function of M_c and T_e, the latter in *summary* of the empirical determinants of D.

    d. Inhibition (I). In contrast to the fairly substantial empirical base that prevails for describing the theoretical composition of excitatory potential (namely, the H, D, and K constructs), that for inhibitory potential I is considerably less evident, in part because of the absence in the present research of any systematic manipulation of those variables relevant to I (as, for example, a delay in reinforcement). Nevertheless, certain aspects of the reported findings seem to call for such a construct, especially in view of those effects that are to be anticipated on the basis of the analysis thus far provided. Here, specific reference may be made to the proposition that exposure to any stimulus condition, including the goal condition that prevails as a consequence of the instrumental act, will produce satiation. In treating the effects of exposure to the goal condition, however, at least three possible conditions must be considered: as expressed in terms of a brightness dimension relative to a start compartment and alley that are black, the goal condition may be (a) the same or similar (for example, black), (b) different (for example white), or (c) both similar and different (for example, a physical or temporal composite of black and white).

When the goal condition is of the same brightness as the start and alley, and thus brightness-change reinforcement is absent, the effect of goal exposure should be to maintain or even amplify D through the extended T_e that obtains under such a condition. However, if this satiation can be reduced or alleviated by differential stimulation resulting, for example, from S's engaging in responses such as turning around, gnawing at the apparatus, grooming, and so forth, then it may be expected that over training these responses will become conditioned to the cues in the situation and, either directly or via their anticipatory occurrence, will compete with the response (R) of running to the goal. With the reported findings, such an inhibitory effect seems evident in the progressively slower speeds that obtained for the no-change (black start to black goal) groups of Experiments II and III (see Figs. 5 and 8). This decrement in runway performance might alternately be viewed as resulting from the decreased "novelty" of the apparatus, that is, the diminished eliciting properties of its distinguishable physical characteristics; even so, recognition must be given to the spaced distribution of training that was employed (over days), and thus to the element of permanence, or learning, that characterizes the decremental effect. The same inhibitory phenomenon also seems evident in the performance decrement that occurred for those Ss of Experiment III that were initially trained on the B-W change condition and were then switched to the no-change B-B condition. This finding in itself, however, is not sufficient evidence for an inhibitory construct, since a switch from the change to the no-change condition should also produce a decrement in the value of K. Nevertheless, when taken together, the performance decrements noted are sufficient to warrant at least tentative positing of an inhibitory construct (I) which, as noted in Fig. 11, relates positively to the number of no-change or nonreinforced training trials (N_c).

The same inhibitory process suggests itself when the effects of exposure to a goal condition that differs from the start and alley condition are considered. Although the change in stimulation that this goal condition provides should be effective in reinforcing the instrumental response, this effect does not preclude the development of satiation to the goal stimuli, as would be expected with S's extended exposure to these stimuli. Consequently, even with a goal condition that is different (that is, provides change), the same theoretical basis prevails for the occurrence and conditioning of competing reactions that may, through their anticipatory occurrence, promote a partial inhibition of performance. This interpretation finds support in the reliably poorer performances of those 3- and 7-minute start-exposure Ss of Experiment I that received extended exposure at the goal. On this basis it is additionally posited that the inhibitory potential I bears a positive relationship to the time or length of S's exposure to the stimulus-change condition (T_c) that is made contingent on the instrumental response.

From the foregoing considerations of the effects of exposure to a goal condition that is either different from or similar to the start and alley condition, two other apparent determinants of I are suggested, albeit in the absence of any direct empirical evidence from the present research. The first of these bears on the temporal proximity of the change in stimulation (P_c) that prevails relative to the instrumental response. Here, reference is specifically directed to the decremental effect that a delay of stimulus-change reinforcement should exert on performance via those competing reactions that may occur and become conditioned during the initial no-change period of the delay. The second variable has reference to the constancy or homogeneity of the stimulus-change condition (C_c) that is made contingent on the instrumental response. As with the similar variable (C_e) suggested as a determinant of D, the relevance of C_c as a determinant of I derives from the consideration that exposure to a complex or heterogeneous goal condition, such as a physical composite of black and white, should afford a more gradual accumulation of satiation to the components of this goal condition, and thus to the goal condition as a whole.

Particular care must be taken with an interpretation of the effects of exposure to a complex goal, however, because of the similarity that may prevail between the components of this goal condition and those constituting S's exposure prior to or during the instrumental response. For example, relative to a start and alley condition that is black, a complex black-and-white goal should afford heightened performance in comparison with a homogeneous black goal, but lowered performance in comparison with a homogeneous white goal. This effect, which relates theoretically to the differential amount of change or extended satiation, or both, provided by the different goal conditions, appears evident in the intermediate performances of those S's of Experiment II that were trained to run from a black start to a vertically striped black-and-white goal. On the other hand, with a start and alley condition that is *gray,* a black-and-white goal condition can be expected to produce heightened performance in comparison with a homogeneous goal that is *either* black or white, in part because of the constancy of these brightness-change conditions (C_c) and the more rapid accumulation of satiation that may obtain with S's exposure to them. Also relevant in this context is the possibility that the complex black-and-white goal will afford greater incentive (K) because of the bidirectional nature of the brightness change provided.

2. *Curiosity Redefined as an Incentive-Motivational Construct*

Although primary emphasis throughout this section of the chapter has been on the drive-motivational effects of satiation, it should be fairly obvious that the incentive-motivational construct K is closely related to the curiosity-drive concept as originally espoused by Berlyne (1950; 1955) and others. Both the K and curiosity-drive concepts obtain operational expression in terms of novel or changed stimuli (M_c), and both are viewed with respect to their motivational influence on performance. By reason of this similarity, it would appear that the curiosity concept can be redefined as an incentive-motivational construct; for the same reason, however, some mechanism must be posited by which the motivational influence of K can be exerted during the sequence of behavior that is instrumental to novel or changed stimulation—otherwise the problem again prevails that the effect of novel or changed stimulation is not exerted until after the instrumental response has been performed.

Resolution of the problem, together with the specific basis for redefining curiosity as an incentive-motivational construct, can be had directly from the analysis afforded K (Spence, 1956) in the context of instrumental appetitive conditioning, that is, by positing the operation of an anticipatory-response mechanism (r_g-s_g). To effect an application of the r_g-s_g mechanism to performances based on exploratory rewards, note must initially be given to certain observations that were made earlier. Thus, it should be recalled that the functional relationships existing between a change in stimulation and the exploratory response that it elicits are quite analogous to those between the eliciting condition of food and the consummatory reaction of eating. That is, comparable to food for the hungry animal, novel stimuli are similarly effective (at least when presented on a spaced basis; see footnote 3) in evoking a consistent response, and within limits, the strength and vigor of this response is greater, the larger the magnitude of the change in stimulation provided. Consequently, when a change in stimulation serves as the incentive or goal condition for an instrumental response—as in the reported experiments—different magnitudes of stimulus-change reinforcement (M_c) should produce different strengths of the goal reaction to that change. Herein, reference is made to the noted "consummatory" component of exploration, general examples of which include orienting to, observing, and perceptually attending to the change, or more specifically, dilation of the pupil, photochemical activity, an opening of the eye, specific head-turning and general movements toward the source of stimulation, a rise in general muscle tonus, and so forth.

It follows from these considerations, that the anticipatory occurrence of the consummatory response to change (R_c) should develop in the same manner as that for the unconditioned goal response of eating. That is, via the action of trace, delayed, or higher-order conditioning, or combinations thereof, R_c should occur in fractional form (r_c) to those stimuli, such as apparatus and drive stimuli S_D, that consistently antedate the stimulus-change reinforcement. (This contention appears supported by the Russian literature, which has shown that when one neutral stimulus consistently precedes another, the first will come to elicit *anticipatory* orienting responses appropriate to the second; see Berlyne, 1960; Berlyne, 1963.) Accordingly, as with the operation of r_g-s_g, the instrumental response can be affected in the following way: through its repeated association with the stimulation characteristic of r_c (i.e., s_c, sensory feedback from anticipatory "investigatory" reactions), the instrumental response can become conditioned to s_c and thus its strength can be influenced by the intensity of s_c. Like that of its counterpart s_g, the intensifying action of s_c derives from several considerations: the stimulus intensity or dynamism effect of s_c itself; the "summation" effect resulting from the conditioning of the instrumental response to s_c together with apparatus and drive stimuli; or quite possibly, the "frustrative-excitement" that may result with the conditioning of r_c to stimuli that are different from the goal and that thus call forth an opposed or different perceptual reaction. With any or all of these considerations, the basis prevails by which the incentive construct K can exert a motivational influence on the instrumental response. Unlike the satiation-drive construct, however, K obtains operational expression in terms of the magnitude of stimulus-change reinforcement (M_c), because it is this variable that is of prime importance in determining the strength and vigor of R_c, the intensity of its r_c-s_c component, and hence, the strength and vigor of the instrumental response. Herein lie the means, then, by which the satiated animal will also become *curious*, that is, will learn to make a specific anticipatory reaction (r_c) to the change in stimulation that has consistently prevailed as a consequence of its instrumental act.

With recognition of the action of r_c ("curiosity") in mediating the effect of stimulus-change reward, full consideration can be given to the interrelation of D and K, in particular, the basis for positing an additive relationship between these constructs and for employing the defining empirical variables of D (such as T_e) as additional determinants of K. It should first be noted that although K exerts its motivational effect through the underlying action of r_c, this interpretation requires that we specify the source of motivation or arousal of r_c. Relevant in this context are those considerations that were offered previously on the drive and cue (or directing) functions of stimuli: although stimuli, such as apparatus and drive stimuli, that repeatedly antedate a change in stimulation can serve as cues to which r_c is conditioned, this cue function in itself does not specify, nor does it necessarily imply, any motivational effect of these cues in evoking r_c. On the other hand, the functional property of the satiation-drive construct is most appropriate. Viewed as an energizing mechanism of behavior or as the basis for heightened reactivity to stimuli, D should exert its motivational effect not only on the instrumental response but also on R_c and its fractional component r_c, and even on those competing reactions presumed to underlie the inhibition that derives from a condition of no change or nonreinforcement. For this reason, the incentive-motivational construct K has reference not only to M_c but also, as indicated in Fig. 11, to those variables, such as T_e, that serve as empirical determinants of D. Furthermore, because the motivational influence of K is established through the conditioning of r_c, we must also acknowledge the dependency of K on the empirical variable N_c (that is, the number of trials on which a change in stimulation is provided and thus the consummatory response elicited and made available for conditioning).

With the positing of T_e and N_c as additional determinants of K, the r_c-s_c analysis offers several implications for the interrelation of D and K. First, as Black (1965) has argued with respect to the theoretical combination of these constructs, it follows that the additive assumption predicts a significant interaction in the performances of groups trained under near zero, if not zero ("0"), and moderate or high (H) values of D and K. As in the reported research, this result should occur because, with three of the four groups comprising the factorial design (namely, 0D-0K, 0D-HK, HD-0K), either the motivational (T_e) or eliciting (M_c) basis for R_c is minimal or absent and thus r_c cannot effectively be conditioned. Hence, for these three groups, comparably low performance levels are to be expected in contrast to the high performance level of an HD-HK group for which both the motivational and eliciting basis of R_c is adequate. (In illustration of this effect, Fig. 12 shows that groups trained under either a condition of 3-minute exposure to the start compartment or no change at the goal consistently exhibited comparably low levels of performance in contrast to the high performances of the 7-minute change groups.) On the other hand, when moderate and high values of D and K are used, the motivational and eliciting basis for R_c should be adequate for all groups of the design; consequently, the performances of these groups should reflect only the algebraic addition of increments to either D or K, in accord with the assumption of an additive combination rule. Although, as noted, this effect has been consistently reported for instrumental appetitive conditioning, its assessment in the context of performances based on exploratory rewards must obviously await studies using moderate to high values of the exposure and change variables.

The other implication of the r_c-s_c analysis is that, while alterations of D and K can lead to abrupt and appropriate shifts in performance, there should nonetheless be some residual but quite transitory effect of the original or preshift training condition. In this context, it may be recalled that the performance shifts observed in Experiment III (see Fig. 8) were not complete until some 10–20 trials following alteration of *either* the exposure or change conditions. This residual or "historical" effect of prior training is to be expected with alteration of brightness change at the goal because of the additional training (N_c or N_c') that is required for the conditioning or extinction of r_c, and consequently, for the development or alteration of K. A comparable historical effect should also result with alteration of the exposure condition, T_e, because r_c is a function not only of N_c but also of the value of T_e and hence of the level of D under which it is acquired. Thus, in contrast to animals trained and tested under low D, for example, animals trained under high D and then tested under low D should enter the test phase with an initially higher value of K, as a result of having previously performed a stronger R_c and having thereby learned a more vigorous r_c. With the imposition of low D, however, the strength of R_c will be considerably reduced and thus the vigor of r_c should rapidly diminish with training to produce a relatively abrupt decrement in performance. The same interpretation prevails, of course, for animals trained under low D and then tested under high D, with the exception that a complete shift in performance is dependent on the learning and performance of a more vigorous r_c.

In total, the r_c-s_c analysis of the action of the incentive-motivational construct K seems to fare quite well in promoting both a satisfactory assimilation of the data and an integrative basis for the seemingly disparate concepts of satiation and curiosity, the latter as noted being redefined as the animal's conditioned anticipatory reaction to stimulus-change reward. In this regard, some point should be made of the discrepancy that exists between the proposed conceptualization and the common-sense or introspective interpretation of curiosity as a nonspecific expectation of something as yet to be experienced. Although scientific concepts are not obliged to be patterned after introspective analysis, it is worth noting that the basis prevails for positing a *general* curiosity.

With the curiosity construct given reference in the present formulation to the animal's *acquisition* of a condition or object-specific anticipatory reaction, it should not be overlooked that the animal's previous history may be replete with conditioned anticipatory reactions of orienting and perceptually attending to each and every novel or changed condition experienced. Thus, it may well be that, as a result of the animal's continuous encounter with stimulus variation (literally a change at every turn), an anticipatory investigatory reaction is conditioned generally in the manner of a learning set. One basis for this conditioning effect would be the ever-present internal stimuli associated with the animal's satiation (exposure) to one stimulus condition prior to its receipt of a different (changed) condition. Hence, through the action of a general r_c, or even, as Brown (1961) has suggested, through generalized anticipatory reactions (quite possibly generalized on the basis of S_D, also), the animal in its initial encounter with a particular surround may be replete with a "general" incentive motivation quite sufficient for the intensifying of approach and investigatory actions.

IV. Some General Implications for Motivational Theory

The foregoing theoretical treatment satisfactorily fulfills the major objective of this paper in illustrating that identity can prevail in the interpretation of performances based on appetitive and exploratory rewards. Because this identity obtains from an extension of classical drive theory, however, it will undoubtedly be asked why any effort should be made to use this particular formulation when, in view of current evidence, it appears to be hampered by so many shortcomings. Several considerations are to be borne in mind in treating such a question. For example, it should be recognized that, although discussion has been conducted within the framework of drive theory, the proposed formulation is actually of the empirical construct variety (see Spence, 1956). Thus, the satiation-drive concept serves merely as a theoretical variable which, when taken in conjunction with the other concepts, is convenient for purposes of integrating findings within the relatively circumscribed area of investigation designated by the conditions and operations defining these concepts. This particular usage of the drive concept in no way precludes alternative conceptions of its functional properties—for example, as a basis for heightened *reactivity* to stimuli rather than as a direct *energizer* of behavior. Certainly the proposal that an exploratory reward exerts its motivational influence on instrumental performance through the conditioning of r_c accords equally well with the former interpretation of the function of the drive operation (cf. Sheffield, 1966). This consideration notwithstanding, the classical concept of drive as an energizer and the related hypothesis of drive reduction as a principle of reinforcement should be considered, if only because, with their potential extension via the proposed formulation to learning based on novel stimuli (a so-called instance of reinforcement through "increased" stimulation) there prevails the alternative issue of the extent to which the classical drive position is in fact hampered by numerous shortcomings. And, on this issue there appears to be some confusion.

A. On the Logic of Drive Theory and Suggested Modifications

Apparently it is seldom acknowledged that the formalization of drive theory in the early 1940's (e.g., Miller & Dollard, 1941) centered for the most part about a simple and relatively unobtrusive inference. Coupled with the observation that even conditions of food and water deprivation produced intense stimuli (such as those associated with the "parching" sensation of thirst and the "pangs" of hunger), the apparent activating or "energizing" effect of strong shocks, loud noises, bright lights, and the like provided an ample base for the general proposition: "Strong stimuli which impel action are drives" (Miller & Dollard, 1941; Dollard & Miller, 1950). Moreover, with the related observation that learning correlated with the reduction of these intense forms of stimulation, the additional inference prevailed that reinforcement was occasioned through drive reduction. It must be noted that these propositions were consistently coupled with the statement that not all drives need be strong stimuli; thus, other conditions of stimulation might exist by which the animal could be brought into action or, with respect to the reinforcement hypothesis, learning might also be occasioned through the reduction of other drive-defining conditions. As a result of this qualification, the major propositions of drive theory logically take on material implications: strong stimuli (S) and strong stimulus reduction (S_r) respectively set the occasion for drive (D) and drive reduction (D_r), that is, $S \supset D$ and $S_r \supset D_r$. In view of the purported shortcomings of the drive position, the rules of deductive logic for materially conditional statements have apparently proved somewhat complicated. From the syllogism that combines the foregoing implications with necessary additional ones (such as that D and D_r respectively set the occasion for action and for the reinforcement of that action that results in D_r) two valid arguments may be deduced: if there is strong stimulation and this strong stimulation is terminated upon some action, then that action will be reinforced; alternately, if no action is reinforced, then strong stimulation *together with* the termination of that strong stimulation upon some action did not prevail. From these arguments, we may consistently expect that the reduction or termination of a strong stimulus will reinforce behavior; but what of those occasions on which the animal "seeks out" stimulation and/or performs acts that are accompanied by increased or even apparently strong stimulation, as in the case of exploration, play, sexual activity, and presumed masochistic action?

In answer to these apparent difficulties, Brown (1955) has cogently argued that increases in stimulation that are contingent on some behavior, even when relatively intense, need not always be categorized as increases in drive. That is, strong stimuli may lose their effectiveness (be "demotivated") as a result of their association with a primary reinforcer (e.g., Pavlov's use of a noxious conditioned stimulus), sensory adaptation, competing stimulation, and so forth. Brown's argument is an effective one, but it must also be emphasized that those occasions of reinforcement that are associated with the "increased" stimulation involved in exploration and the like in no way obviate the basic propositions of the drive position. In fact, any conclusion that these instances of reinforcement conflict with the drive position actually partakes of those *invalid* argument forms that are commonly designated affirming the consequent or denying the antecedent: if some action is reinforced, there must have been strong stimulation together with the termination of that strong stimulation upon the action (but there was not, so the propositions are faulty!); alternately, if there is no strong stimulation together with the termination of that strong stimulation upon some action, there cannot be any reinforcement or strengthening of an action (since there is reinforcement, however, the propositions must again be faulty!). With reference, then, to learning that is based on exploratory, sexual, and similar types of rewards entailing "increased" stimulation (or, more accurately, rewards that do not entail a reduction of intense stimulation), the noted dissatisfaction with drive theory (specifically, with the reinforcement hypothesis of drive reduction) can only be in the sense that the propositions of the theory are not sufficiently broad to incorporate actions productive of "moderate" stimulation. In this regard, it is profitable to ask in what manner the position can be modified or extended so as to include the anomalous behavior patterns. Here, at least three essentially different treatments present themselves.

The first and most extensive modification of the theory finds representation in the provisional statement that "drive is not simply a state, the decreasing of which is rewarding. At high levels, the reduction of drive is rewarding; but at low levels, an increase may be rewarding" (Fiske & Maddi, 1961, p. 22; Leuba, 1955). Formal expression of this modification obtains, of course, with current theories of optimal stimulation or arousal in which the concept of arousal (or activation) is equated with drive as an "energizer," an "energizing mechanism," or the "intensive dimension of behavior" (Fiske & Maddi, 1961; Hebb, 1955; Malmo, 1958; Malmo, 1959). With reference to the Fiske and Maddi (1961) formulation, which has been directed specifically to exploratory and related behaviors, it may be noted that the proposed modification is actually of two forms. First, the defining condition of the drive concept, activation, is broadened to include both strong stimulation and novelty or, in general, stimulus variation and change. Second, in accord with the conceptualization of an optimal level of activation, the mechanism of "positive affect" (cf. reward) is expanded to include both increases and decreases in activation. In effect, then, the motivation of exploratory behaviors is related to the animal's receipt of *minimal* stimulus variation and its consequent efforts to obtain increased variation and change, so as to maintain an optimal level of activation.

Apart from any advantages that the position may hold with respect to the assimilation of data bearing on physiological indices of activation (that is, measures of "arousal"), as a modification of drive theory it seems to engender more shortcomings than solutions. For example, the motivation of exploration is related to the animal's receipt of minimal stimulus variation and thus, by definition, low activation; but, by definition, low activation is synonymous with low drive. Hence, the system suffers a major inconsistency in that exploratory behaviors are energized and intensified only when the energizing or intensifying dimension of behavior, namely, drive or activation, is absent or minimal. Alternately we may note the inconsistency that prevails with the expanded definition of drive as a *positive* function of novelty and stimulus variation; thus, in contradiction to the foregoing, the energizing or drive-motivational basis for exploration obtains with novelty, not with minimal stimulus variation. And, if this definition is maintained, it imposes the same difficulties that were attendant on the earlier formulations of a curiosity drive. Finally, it should be recognized that in many studies, particularly those on alternation behavior, the animal continues to explore, that is, it alternates in its selection of maze arms, when subjected to food deprivation (see Glanzer's research) or even mild intensities of shock (Fowler, Fowler, & Dember, 1959). But, with these conditions of intense intero- and exteroceptive stimulation, and thus already *high* arousal, the animal's choice of the nonexperienced or more novel alternative can only be attributed, within the noted activation framework, to the animal's motive for stimulus variation and hence a heightened level of arousal.

A second and less extensive modification of drive theory is found in Berlyne's (1960; 1963) conceptualization of arousal. As in the preceding type of formulation, Berlyne also describes the animal's behavior as directed to the maintenance of an optimal or intermediate level of arousal, the concept of arousal being similarly equated with drive as an "energizing" construct. In marked contrast, however, the assumption is made that the animal performs in order to *reduce* arousal (drive), where arousal is now viewed as a U-shaped function of both the intensive and the "collative" properties of stimuli, the latter having reference to novelty, incongruity, surprisingness—in general, to stimulus variation and change. Although this formulation dismisses neither the energizing dimension of drive nor the reinforcing action of drive reduction (and thus represents a less severe modification of the theory), two explicit features of the modification are to be noted: first, the defining condition of drive (arousal) is broadened to include both stimulus intensity and stimulus variation or change; second, the theoretical function relating drive to its defining condition is altered such that drive is no longer a positive but rather a U-shaped function of stimulus intensity and variation.

Berlyne's assumptions preclude the inconsistencies noted for the preceding formulation, but other difficulties prevail as a result of them. For example, one may question the truth of the assumption that stimulus intensity and stimulus variation or change represent independent but compatible drive- or arousal-defining dimensions. Coupled with the U-shaped function posited between drive and its defining conditions, this assumption requires that an animal be highly motivated (aroused) when exposed to a stimulus or stimulus condition that is neither too novel nor too familiar, yet is at or near zero intensity. With a view to the other (right) side of the U-shaped function, note should be taken of the positive relationship that prevails between drive and stimulus variation. This part of the formulation is essentially that which Berlyne (1950; 1955) espoused as one of the early curiosity-drive theorists and, as such, it is subject to the limitations previously noted for it.

B. A PROPOSED "NEW LOOK" IN DRIVE THEORY

A third and even less extensive modification of classical drive theory prevails as a consequence of the analysis offered earlier of the reported findings. Specifically, this analysis suggests that the stated positive relationship between drive and its defining condition, stimulus intensity, can remain unaltered, with the only modification required being an extension of those variables that define the drive concept. To utilize the material implication $S \supset D$ in expressing this alteration, the term S, which originally referred to *strong* stimulation, may now be given reference to *stimulation,* the major parameters of which are both intensity (i) and duration (d), so that $S = f(i, d)$. In view of the emphasis given in the analysis of the reported findings to those variables of S's exposure (for example, T_e) as empirical determinants of D, specification of the *duration* of stimulation as a defining condition of D should not evoke much puzzlement. The noted variables of exposure had reference to manipulations of the subject, such as S's time or length of exposure to a particular stimulus condition; conversely, with reference to manipulations of the stimulation imposed on the subject, these variables are most conveniently summarized by d, the duration of those elements of a stimulus complex that prevail prior to the animal's instrumental response. Herein, reference is thus given to all of the noted exposure variables, T_e, P_e, and C_e.

The material implication regarding the hypothesis of reinforcement through drive reduction also remains unaltered, that is, $S_r \supset D_r$, but now of course S_r has reference to a reduction of the intensity or the duration of stimulation, or of both. The coupling of these two parameters obtains the following significance: whereas the reinforcing effect of a reduction in the intensity of stimulation can prevail only with the animal's receipt of a lowered intensity, the reinforcement relating to a reduction of the duration of stimulation may obtain with the animal's receipt of an altered stimulus condition, as through (a) the imposition of new and different stimulus elements, (b) the removal of "familiar" stimulus elements, and/or (c) an increment or decrement in the intensity of the new or prevailing stimulation. The range over which an increment in the intensity of stimulation will be reinforcing is obviously limited by the posited drive-producing effects of intense stimulation (cf. punishment; Brown, 1953b) and the competing escape or avoidance reactions that should develop as a consequence. This range, moreover, should be capable of expansion or contraction depending on the initial intensity characteristics of the stimulation (low or high) that is imposed upon the animal. Herein, integration obtains for the well-substantiated observation that sensory changes in an upward direction (to brighter lights, louder noises, higher concentrations of a substance, and so forth) are productive of a reinforcing effect only when these changes are "mild" or "moderate."

Inclusion of the duration parameter of stimulation as a determinant of drive represents both a slight and elementary modification, but its implications are nonetheless far reaching. For example, with emphasis on time of exposure (or conversely, duration of stimulation), the proposed modification suggests a convergence of classical drive theory with adaptation-level theory (Helson, 1948; Helson, 1959) and the related discrepancy hypothesis that has been advanced by McClelland and Clark (1953). In particular, the position advanced by these theorists in treating the concept of adaptation level as a basis for "affect" finds close agreement with the proposed analysis of exposure as a defining condition of drive. Similarly, the McClelland and Clark interpretation of moderate discrepancies from adaptation level as instances of "positive affect" accords well with the proposed interpretation of moderate changes in stimulation (that is, from the subject's exposure condition) as reinforcing events. Note may also be made of the partial identity that obtains between the posited "negative affect" of extensive or large discrepancies from adaptation level and the heightened drive motivation (i.e., punishment) deriving in the present formulation from sensory changes that are productive of increasingly intense stimulation. Indeed, the major difference between these seemingly disparate formulations is that the present analysis does *not* predict negative affect or heightened drive motivation with pronounced discrepancies in the direction of a lowered intensity of stimulation—a prediction, incidentally, that appears to be devoid of independent substantiation. [Evidence in support of the prediction seems to derive primarily from temperature discrepancies (e.g., Haber, 1958), in which case the negative affect of a considerably lowered temperature can just as easily be interpreted as an *increase* in the intensity of stimulation to the cold receptors.]

The additional consideration offered above that the animal's condition of exposure will vary within an intensity continuum suggests further that the proposed modification is not antagonistic to the conceptualization of an "optimal" level of stimulation. In fact, performances that can be characterized as directed to the maintenance of an intermediate or moderate level of stimulation are actually required by the present analysis because of (a) the reinforcing effect of discrepancies from the animal's condition of exposure, and (b) the central tendency that is to be imposed within any sensory continuum by the limits of very high and very low or zero intensities of the stimulation. Consider, for example, a unitary dimension of stimulation, such as light, on which the animal initially occupies (is exposed to) an intermediate level of the stimulation. The animal may obtain positive affect and thus be reinforced for responses that are productive of increments or decrements in the intensity of such stimulation, but once having received and thus become exposed to these limiting conditions, the animal can only "return to" a more intermediate level. Positive affect should also be occasioned through the animal's receipt of other dimensions of stimulation, but the intensity characteristics of these new dimensions will nevertheless impose the same limits. Hence, with respect to the unitary dimension offered in illustration, the animal's behavior can be described as restricted to the central range of this dimension, or to "lateral" movements (that is, to movements across different sensory dimensions) that will be similarly restricted. Viewed in this fashion, the conceptualization of an optimal level of stimulation or of a preference level thus becomes the special case of a more general formulation.

With the integration of optimal levels of stimulation, it might also be asked whether the proposed modification of drive theory can be made consonant with current notions on arousal; to this question, an affirmative answer is also indicated. The previously voiced dissatisfaction with arousal had reference to the concept as equated with drive, certainly not to the conceptualization of arousal as a neurophysiological reaction. Indeed, the recent work of Berlyne and company (e.g., Berlyne, Craw, Salapatek, & Lewis, 1963; Berlyne & Lewis, 1963; Berlyne & McDonnell, 1965) has been quite significant in illustrating a positive relationship between collative variables (novelty, surprisingness, incongruity, and so forth) and such indices of arousal as EEG frequency, GSR magnitude, and the like. Thus, although any motivational interpretation of exploratory phenomena may be required to assimilate these findings, there is certainly no need to adopt the set characteristic of most investigators in treating arousal as a general energizing mechanism. On the contrary, the fact as indicated by Berlyne's work that arousal accompanies the animal's receipt of change, such as occurs with the imposition of collative variables, suggests that arousal is most appropriately viewed as a *central* component of the animal's consummatory response to change (R_c), heretofore given reference solely in terms of peripheral reactions, such as orienting to, attending to, and perceptually ingesting the change. From this consideration, it follows that the anticipatory occurrence of the consummatory reaction to change (r_c) will comprise both peripheral and central (arousal) components, the latter presumably reflecting a neurophysiological mechanism by which the incentive-motivational construct K exerts its intensifying action on performance.

To conceptualize arousal as a neurophysiological counterpart of incentive motivation does not dismiss completely its relation to drive. As argued previously, the empirical determinants of the satiation-drive construct, specifically the time, constancy, and proximity of the animal's exposure, should also serve as determinants of incentive motivation since the vigor of the consummatory reaction R_c is influenced by D. Thus, the *potential* magnitude of arousal can be viewed as relating positively to D, because greater satiation (that is, exposure) affords the basis for a greater change in stimulation and thereby for a more vigorous reaction to the change, both centrally and peripherally. At an empirical level of observation, then, it can be expected that a positive relationship will prevail between indices of arousal (such as heart rate) and strength of drive, but only at a time when the consummatory reaction or its fractional anticipatory component is in operation. Data relevant to this consideration are not yet evident within the context of exploration. Nonetheless, the findings relating to manipulations of other drive conditions are most instructive. For example, in reporting the unpublished work of Bélanger and Feldman that showed for rats an almost direct relationship between heart rate and hours of water deprivation, Malmo (1959) has drawn attention to the following:

"Particular care was taken to record heart rate under nearly the same conditions of stimulation each time, that is, when the animal was pressing on the lever in the Skinner box or during drinking from the dispenser immediately after pressing. . . . Testing the animal under constant stimulating conditions is a very important methodological consideration. Some exploratory observations indicated that heart-rate measurements taken in a restraining compartment did not agree with those taken under the carefully controlled stimulus conditions provided by the Skinner box" (Malmo, 1959, p. 371).

Quite obviously, Malmo's important "methodological" consideration is recording heart rate at precisely the time when the consummatory reaction or its fractional anticipatory component is operative. This observation should illuminate the confusion that can and has prevailed with an assessment of the relationship presumed to exist between arousal and drive. In this context, consideration might also be given to one other aspect of the findings presented by Malmo (1959), namely, the inverted U-shaped function that obtained between number of bar presses and hours of water deprivation. Typically, this type of finding is taken in support of (actually, as the basis for) the posited optimal level of arousal required for "efficient" performance. Although the data are certainly amenable to such an assumption, there remains the question of a possible *theoretical* basis for this assumption, that is, a basis from which the noted optimal level of arousal can be theoretically deduced rather than inferred from the data as a fundamental principle. The implication of the proposed analysis is relatively straightforward: with arousal viewed as a neurophysiological reaction, the characteristic stimulus component of which should also be representative of an intensity dimension, the possibility prevails that the intensity consequence of high arousal itself may be sufficiently productive of *drive* motivation to impede or inhibit performance through competing escape and avoidance reactions.

It should perhaps be made clear that the preceding discussion of arousal, optimal stimulation, and adaptation level is by no means intended as a final or even formal account of the subjects to which these concepts relate. Rather, the analysis is offered primarily to illustrate the relatively simple modification that can be imposed on drive theory and the potential explanatory power that derives from this extension. In this sense, too, the treatment offered may illustrate the convergence that can obtain for varied and seemingly antithetical accounts of behavior. In proceeding this far, however, it seems fitting to conclude with brief comment on the implications of the proposed modification for some old, if not by now classical problems.

Consideration may first be given to the perennial question of whether there is a need at all for motivational concepts. The implication of the suggested modification is that the problem of choosing between an "active" or "passive" theoretical organism can be successfully side-stepped, for with the initial assumption of a *passive* animal, at least one that is constantly confronted by the motivational impetus of exposure to one configuration or another, there emerges an animal that is continuously active. This activity, however, is not to be construed as action in the sense of heightened locomotor movement, but rather as action in the sense of a behavioral flux. The mechanism underlying this flux should be fairly evident: exposure to one set or complex of stimulus elements should set the occasion for consummatory reactions of attending to and ingesting alterations of the set and, in similar manner, for the occurrence of instrumental behaviors that are temporarily maintained as a result of their stimulus consequence and feedback. The process of behavior selection, however, is self limiting, for the consequence of stimulus alteration and attendance to that change must also be exposure. Herein, behavior runs the gamut from heightened locomotor activity to instances of relative inaction, such as grooming, stretching, scratching, grunting, chirping, specifically vocalizing, sniffing, attending to some insignificant part of the stimulus field, or just plain looking around.

Within this framework of thought, even those basic functionings of the animal take on new significance. As suggested elsewhere (Fowler, Blond, & Dember, 1959), hunger may be viewed as an intense, persistent, and little-changing pattern of stimulation that is dealt with by the animal in the same manner as persistent stimulation of external origin, that is, through the performance of responses that are productive of stimulus variation. Unlike stimulation of external origin, however, which the animal alters by seeking and attending to novel objects and maze arms, hunger is most effectively altered through the animal's receipt and ingestion of food. Even so, the possible stimulus variation relevant to hunger need not derive solely from "gut" considerations, as has long been evident in the known reinforcing effects of nonnutritive, sweet-tasting substances or, more recently, in the preference rats manifest for novel rather than familiar food objects—either nutritive or nonnutritive (Welker & King, 1962). With these and such similar considerations as those offered above in relation to the manifestation of behavior, it comes as no surprise that "need states" and motor activity do not often bear a one-to-one relationship (see Baumeister, Hawkins & Cromwell, 1964). Similarly, as in the now illustrious study by Sheffield and Campbell (1954), there can be little doubt of the discriminative stimulus control that can obtain over the behavior of the deprived animal. Equally important in this regard, however, is the function that these discriminative stimuli serve in providing variation and change, and thereby in eliciting movement via startle and sundry investigatory reactions that can then be strengthened and maintained with the occasion of reinforcement through feeding.

A similar interpretation can prevail for sexual activity. The collective findings of recent studies (e.g., Fisher, 1962; Fowler & Whalen, 1961; Wilson, Kuehn, & Beach, 1963) indicate clearly that the male rat ceases to copulate after extensive mating, not simply because of physical or sexual exhaustion, but even more so as a result of its habituation to the female partner. The effect of changing or altering the female incentive is to elicit renewed investigatory and mating behavior. Through the significance that these findings impart to both the exposure and change variables, they suggest that the initiation and maintenance of sexual activities—as with the preliminary petting and grooming of Nissen's (1953) virginal chimpanzees or the reinforcing effects of copulatory behavior for male rats not permitted to ejaculate (Sheffield, Wulff, & Backer, 1951)—derive not from any need state but from the constancy of the animal's exposure and existence and from the variation or change that is provided by sex play in all its forms, from grooming and petting to consummation with or without the ejaculatory climax.

From this vantage point on those basic needs for food and sex, it is difficult to avoid the "adage" that perhaps even new vintages of research can be contained as well in an old theoretical bottle—unless, of course, our use of that bottle has been of sufficient duration to promote change merely for the sake of change.

REFERENCES

Adlerstein, A., & Fehrer, E. The effect of food deprivation on exploratory behavior in a complex maze. *J. comp. physiol. Psychol.*, 1955, 48, 250–253.

Barnes, G. W., & Baron, A. Stimulus complexity and sensory reinforcement. *J. comp. physiol. Psyschol.*, 1961, 54, 466–469.

Baumeister, A., Hawkins, W., & Cromwell, R. L. Need states and activity level. *Psychol. Bull.*, 1964, 61, 438–453.

Berlyne, D. E. Novelty and curiosity as determinants of exploratory behavior. *Brit. J. Psychol.*, 1950, 41, 68–80.

Berlyne, D. E. The arousal and satiation of perceptual curiosity in the rat. *J. comp. physiol. Psychol.*, 1955, 48, 238–246.

Berlyne, D. E. *Conflict, arousal, and curiosity.* New York: McGraw-Hill, 1960.

Berlyne, D. E. Motivational problems raised by exploratory and epistemic behavior. In S. Koch (Ed.), *Psychology: A study of a science.* Vol. 5. New York: McGraw-Hill, 1963, Pp. 284–364.

Berlyne, D. E., Craw, M. A., Salapatek, P. H., & Lewis, J. L. Novelty, complexity, incongruity, extrinsic motivation and the GSR. *J. exp. Psychol.*, 1963, 66, 560–567.

Berlyne, D. E., & Lewis, J. L. Effects of heightened arousal on human exploratory behavior. *Canad. J. Psychol.*, 1963, 17, 398–411.

Berlyne, D. E., & McDonnell, P. Effects of stimulus complexity and incongruity on duration of EEG desynchronization. *Electroencephalog. clin. Neurophysiol.*, 1965, 18, 156–161.

Berlyne, D. E., & Slater, J. Perceptual curiosity, exploratory behavior and maze learning. *J. comp. physiol. Psychol.*, 1957, 50, 228–232.

Black, R. W. On the combination of drive and incentive motivation. *Psychol. Rev.*, 1965, 72, 310–317.

Black, R. W., Fowler, R. L., & .Kimbell, G. Adaptation and habituation of heart rate to handling in the rat. *J. comp. physiol. Psychol.*, 1964, 57, 422–425.

Bolles, R. C. The usefulness of the drive concept. In M. R. Jones (Ed.), *Nebraska symposium on motivation.* Lincoln: Univer. of Nebraska Press, 1958, Pp. 1–33.

Brown, J. S. Comments on Professor Harlow's paper. In *Current theory and research in motivation.* Lincoln: Univer. of Nebraska Press, 1953. Pp. 49–54. (a)

Brown, J. S. Problems presented by the concept of acquired drives. In *Current theory and research in motivation.* Lincoln: Univer. of Nebraska Press, 1953. Pp. 1–21. (b)

Brown, J. S. Pleasure-seeking behavior and the drive-reduction hypothesis. *Psychol. Rev.*, 1955, 62, 169–179.

Brown, J. S. *The motivation of behavior.* New York: McGraw-Hill, 1961.

Butler, R. A. Discrimination learning by rhesus monkeys to visual-exploration motivation. *J. comp. physiol. Psychol.*, 1953 46, 95–98.

Butler, R. A. Incentive conditions which influence visual exploration. *J. exp. Psychol.*, 1954, **48**, 19–23.

Butler, R. A. The effect of deprivation of visual incentives on visual exploration motivation in monkeys. *J. comp. physiol. Psychol.*, 1957, **50**, 177–179.

Butler, R. A. The reaction of rhesus monkeys to fear-provoking stimuli. *J. genet. Psychol.*, 1964, **104**, 321–330.

Butler, R. A., & Woolpy, J. H. Visual attention in the rhesus monkey. *J. comp. physiol. Psychol.*, 1963, **56**, 324–328.

Conant, J. B. *On understanding science.* New Haven: Yale Univer. Press, 1947.

Danziger, K., and Mainland, M. The habituation of exploratory behavior. *Aust. J. Psychol.*, 1954, **6**, 39–51.

Dember, W. N., & Earl, R. W. Analysis of exploratory, manipulatory, and curiosity behavior. *Psychol. Rev.*, 1957, **64**, 91–96.

Dember, W. N., & Fowler, H. Spontaneous alternation behavior. *Psychol. Bull.*, 1958, **55**, 412–428.

Dember, W. N., & Fowler, H. Spontaneous alternation after free and forced trials. *Canad. J. Psychol.*, 1959, **13**, 151–154.

Dember, W. N., & Millbrook, Barbara, A. Free-choice by the rat of the greater of two brightness changes. *Psychol. Rep.*, 1956, **2**, 465–467.

Dennis, W. J., & Sollenberger, R. T. Negative adaptation in the maze exploration of albino rats. *J. comp. Psychol.*, 1934, **18**, 197–206.

Dewsbury, D. A. Changes in stimulus preference as a function of exposure in an extra-test situation. *Psychon. Sci.*, 1965, **2**, 175–176.

Dollard, J., & Miller, N. E. *Personality and psychotherapy.* New York: McGraw-Hill, 1950.

Estes, W. K. Comments on Dr. Bolles' paper. In M. R. Jones (Ed.), *Nebraska symposium on motivation.* Lincoln: Univer. of Nebraska Press, 1958. Pp. 33–34.

Fisher, A. E. Effects of stimulus variation on sexual satiation in the male rat. *J. comp. physiol. Psychol.*, 1962, **55**, 614–620.

Fiske, D. W., & Maddi, S. R. A conceptual framework. In D. W. Fiske and S. R. Maddi (Eds.), *Functions of varied experience.* Homewood, Ill.: Dorsey, 1961, Pp. 11–56.

Fowler, H. Exploratory motivation and animal handling: The effect on runway performance of start-box exposure time. *J. comp. physiol. Psychol.*, 1963, **56**, 866–871.

Fowler, H. *Curiosity and exploratory behavior.* New York: Macmillan, 1965.

Fowler, H., Blond, Joyce, & Dember, W. N. Alternation behavior and learning: The influence of reinforcement magnitude, number, and contingency. *J. comp. physiol. Psychol.*, 1959, **52**, 609–614.

Fowler, H., Fowler, D. E., & Dember, W. N. The influence of reward on alternation behavior. *J. comp. physiol. Psychol.*, 1959, **52**, 220–224.

Fowler, H., & Whalen, R. E. Variation in incentive stimulus and sexual behavior in the male rat. *J. comp. physiol. Psychol.*, 1961, **54**, 68–71.

Fox, S. S. Self-maintained sensory input and sensory deprivation in monkeys. *J. comp. physiol. Psychol.*, 1962, **55**, 438–444.

Glanzer, M. Stimulus satiation: An explanation of spontaneous alternation and related phenomena. *Psychol. Rev.*, 1953, **60**, 257–268. (a)

Glanzer, M. The role of stimulus satiation in spontaneous alternation. *J. exp. Psychol.*, 1953, **45**, 387–393. (b)

Glanzer, M. Stimulus satiation in situations without choice. *J. comp. physiol. Psychol.*, 1958, **51**, 332–335.

Glanzer, M. Changes and interrelations in exploratory behavior. *J. comp. physiol. Psychol.,* 1961, 54, 433–438.

Haber, R. N. Discrepancy from adaptation as a source of affect. *J. exp. Psychol.,* 1958, 56, 370–375.

Harlow, H. F. Learning and satiation of response in intrinsically motivated complex puzzle performance by monkeys. *J. comp. physiol. Psychol.,* 1950, 43, 289–294.

Harlow, H. F. Motivation as a factor in the acquisition of new responses. In *Current theory and research in motivation.* Lincoln: Univer. of Nebraska Press, 1953. Pp. 24–49.

Hebb, D. O. Drives and the CNS (conceptual nervous system). *Psychol. Rev.,* 1955, 62, 243–254.

Helson, H. Adaptation-level as a basis for a quantitative theory of frames of reference. *Psychol. Rev.,* 1948, 55, 297–313.

Helson, H. Adaptation-level theory. In S. Koch (Ed.), *Psychology: A study of a science.* Vol. 1. New York: McGraw-Hill, 1959. Pp. 565–621.

Henderson, R. L. Stimulus intensity dynamism and secondary reinforcement. Unpublished doctoral dissertation. Univer. of Missouri, 1953.

Henderson, R. L. Stimulus-intensity dynamism and secondary reinforcement. *J. comp. physiol. Psychol.,* 1957, 50, 339–344.

Howarth, E. Activity decrements and recovery during repeated day to day exposure in the same environment. *J. comp. physiol. Psychol.,* 1962, 55, 1102–1104.

Hull, C. L. *A behavior system.* New Haven: Yale Univer. Press, 1952.

Kiernan, C. C. Positive reinforcement for light: Comments on Lockard's article. *Psychol. Bull.,* 1964, 62, 351–357.

Kish, G. B., & Baron, A. Satiation of sensory reinforcement. *J. comp. physiol. Psychol.,* 1962, 55, 1007–1010.

Leuba, C. Toward some integration of learning theories: The concept of optimal simulation. *Psychol. Rep.,* 1955, 1, 27–33.

Levin, H. & Forgays, D. G. Learning as a function of sensory stimulation of various intensities. *J. comp. physiol. Psychol.,* 1959, 52, 195–201.

Lockard, R. B. Some effects of light upon the behavior of rodents. *Psychol. Bull.,* 1963, 60, 509–529.

McCall, R. B. Stimulus change in light contingent bar pressing. *J. comp. physiol. Psychol.,* 1965, 59, 258–262.

McClelland, D. C., & Clark, R. A. Discrepancy hypothesis. In D. C. McClelland, J. W. Atkinson, R. A. Clark, & E. L. Lowell (Eds.), *The achievement motive.* New York: Appleton, 1953, Pp. 42–66.

Malmo, R. B. Measurement of drive: An unsolved problem in psychology. In M. R. Jones (Ed.), *Nebraska symposium on motivation.* Lincoln: Univer. of Nebraska Press, 1958. Pp. 229–265.

Malmo, R. B. Activation: A neuropsychological dimension. *Psychol. Rev.* 1959, 66, 367–386.

Miller, N. E., & Dollard, J. *Social learning and imitation.* New Haven: Yale Univer. Press, 1941.

Montgomery, K. C. Exploratory behavior and its relation to spontaneous alternation in a series of maze exposures. *J. comp. physiol. Psychol.,* 1952, 45, 50–57.

Montgomery, K. C. Exploratory behavior as a function of "similarity" of stimulus situations. *J. comp. physiol. Psychol.,* 1953, 46, 129–133.

Montgomery, K. C. The role of the exploratory drive in learning. *J. comp. physiol. Psychol.,* 1954, 47, 60–64.

Moone, L. E., & Lodahl, T. M. The reinforcing effect of changes in illumination on lever-pressing in the monkey. *Amer. J. Psychol.*, 1956, **69**, 288–290.

Myers, A. K., & Miller, N. E. Failure to find a learned drive based on hunger; evidence for learning motivated by "exploration." *J. comp. physiol. Psychol.*, 1954, **47**, 428–436.

Nissen, H. W. Instinct as seen by a psychologist. *Psychol. Rev.*, 1953, **60**, 291–294.

Nissen, H. W. The nature of the drive as innate determinant of behavioral organization. In M. R. Jones (Ed.), *Nebraska symposium on motivation.* Lincoln: Univer. of Nebraska Press, 1954. Pp. 281–321.

O'Connell, R. H. Trials with tedium and titillation. *Psychol. Bull.*, 1965, **63**, 170–179.

Pavlov, I. P. *Conditioned reflexes.* London & New York: Oxford Univer. Press, 1927.

Premack, D., & Collier, G. Analyses of non-reinforcement variables affecting response probability. *Psychol. Monogr.*, 1962, **76**, No. 5 (Whole No. 524).

Premack, D., Collier, G. & Roberts, C. L. Frequency of light-contingent bar pressing as a function of the amount of deprivation of light. *Amer. Psychologist*, 1957, **12**, 411. (Abstract)

Rothkopf, E. Z., & Zeaman, D. Some stimulus controls of alternation behavior. *J. Psychol.*, 1952, **34**, 235–255.

Sheffield, F. D. A drive-induction theory of reinforcement. In R. N. Haber (Ed.), *Current research in motivation.* New York: Holt, 1966. Pp. 98–111.

Sheffield, F. D., & Campbell, B. A. The role of experience in the "spontaneous" activity of hungry rats. *J. comp. physiol. Psychol.*, 1954, **47**, 97–100.

Sheffield, F. D., Wulff, J. J., & Backer, R. Reward value of copulation without sex drive reduction. *J. comp. physiol. Psychol.*, 1951, **44**, 3–8.

Spence, K. W. *Behavior theory and conditioning.* New Haven: Yale Univer. Press, 1956.

Stewart, J. Reinforcing effect of light as a function of intensity and reinforcement schedule. *J. comp. physiol. Psychol.*, 1960, **53**, 187–193.

Thompson, W. R. Exploratory behavior as a function of hunger in "bright" and "dull" rats. *J. comp. physiol. Psychol.*, 1953, **46**, 323–326.

Walker, E. L., Dember, W. N., Earl, R. W., & Karoly, A. J. Choice alternation: I. Stimulus vs. place vs. response. *J. comp. physiol. Psychol.*, 1955, **48**, 19–23.

Welker, W. I., & King, W. A. Effects of stimulus novelty on gnawing and eating by rats. *J. comp. physiol. Psychol.*, 1962, **55**, 838–842.

White, R. W. Motivation reconsidered: The concept of competence. *Psychol. Rev.*, 1959, **66**, 297–333.

Wilson, J. R., Kuehn, R. E., & Beach, F. A. Modification in the sexual behavior of male rats produced by changing the stimulus female. *J. comp. physiol. Psychol.*, 1963, **56**, 636–644.

Zimbardo, P. G., & Miller, N. E. Facilitation of exploration by hunger in rats. *J. comp. physiol. Psychol.*, 1958, **51**, 43–46.

A MULTICOMPONENT THEORY OF THE MEMORY TRACE

Gordon Bower[1]

STANFORD UNIVERSITY
STANFORD, CALIFORNIA

[1] Research supported by a grant (HD-00954) from the National Institute of Child Health and Human Development. The paper was written during the author's tenure on an NIH special fellowship (F3-MH-8585) as a visitor in the Department of Psychology, University College, London.

I. Introduction

Recent years have witnessed a tremendous surge of research on human memory, particularly as regards short-term or immediate memory. For reviews of this research, the reader is referred to papers by Keppel (1965), Melton (1963), Peterson (1963), Posner (1963), and Postman (1964). Despite the rapid accumulation of factual knowledge about short-term memory, there has not been a corresponding increase in formal theoretical efforts to understand or explain the facts. In this paper a modest attempt is made to begin redressing some of this imbalance of facts over theories.

A particular hypothesis concerning the formal structure of a memory trace will be proposed. The basic idea appears reasonable, probably commonly agreeable, and does not go much beyond conceptions regularly used in discussions of memory by many investigators. However, the chief concern here will be with developing the implications of this idea for a variety of memory experiments. It turns out to have an unexpectedly wide range of implications and, in consequence, provides a common basis for understanding a diversity of memory phenomena. And neither of these virtues of the idea is apparent before its implications are systematically developed. Although some new evidence will be presented in congruence with this hypothesis, it must be admitted at the outset that the marshaling of evidential support on each topic discussed is not our purpose. The purpose, rather, is to demonstrate a common theme running throughout diverse branches of the research tree on human memory. Such a discussion serves its function if all it does is to focus attention on relationships existing among diverse phenomena connected with memory.

Perhaps it is wise to first expose our theoretical bias so that the reader is fairly warned. We take it that the job for a theory of memory is to specify the structures, organization, and rules of operation of a machine (a model) that will behave in a manner that resembles or simulates memory phenomena in important respects. The machine, of course, need not actually be built if its behavior can be forecast by arguments, either verbal, mathematical, or in computer programs.

Advocates of this bias include Miller, Galanter, and Pribram (1960), the computer-simulation theorists, and several British psychologists, notably Broadbent (1958), Craik (1943), Crossman (1964), Deutsch (1960), and MacKay (1956). In general, this approach represents the model organism in terms of an array of information-processing mechanisms, each of which carries out certain elementary operations upon information provided to it. These mechanisms, moreover, are assumed to be organized and sequenced in a way designed to achieve certain results. The job of constructing a completely adequate model of human memory is vast and well beyond available capabilities for quite some time. However, it is possible to artificially segment the over-all problem into subproblems and then try to attack these separately. The basic flaw guaranteed by such a separatist strategy is that the theories so developed will of necessity be incomplete or even vague regarding those aspects of the system not under immediate consideration. Nonetheless, such failings may be acceptable so long as the theory better elucidates the operation of at least a part of the over-all system. It was with this strategy in mind that the present paper was written.

There are many such subproblems; included among them would be such issues as the operation of the short-term store, the transfer of items into long-term storage, the format in which information is represented in storage, retrieval of stored material, and so on. The first two subproblems have been discussed in papers by Atkinson and Shiffrin (1965), Bower (1964), Broadbent (1957), and Waugh and Norman (1965). In those theories, items of information input for storage by the system are treated as unitary elements that queue up in a short-term store for processing by some central program. These theorists then derive the consequences of assuming that the queueing system is governed by certain reasonable principles.

The subproblem to be discussed here is that regarding the format in which information is encoded and stored in the machine. In other words, this paper is concerned with the possible formal structure of a memory trace. To delimit matters further, it will be concerned with the way a memory trace might be functionally characterized by a logician or mathematician, rather than by a neurochemist or neurophysiologist. In our opinion, the past history of theories about the memory trace (see Gomulicki, 1953) contains many hypotheses that have been unprofitably tied to further guesses about the neurological mechanisms involved; and the functional hypothesis is discredited when the postulated neurology is proven incorrect, inadequate, or naive. To limit matters further, the paper will not be concerned with the causes of forgetting. The contending views on this—interference versus autonomous decay—are discussed elsewhere (Bower, 1964; Melton, 1963; Postman, 1964). For what follows here, either view may be adopted without materially affecting the discussion. To repeat, the emphasis here is upon the formal structure of a memory trace—what it "looks like" when it is initially established and during the subsequent course of its disintegration.

A. PERCEPTION, ENCODING, AND THE MEMORY TRACE

It seems reasonable to tie the memory trace of an event to the variables operating in the perception of that event. Within this context, the major assumption seems innocuous: it is supposed that the person does not store the literal input stimulus, but rather some encoded representation of it. The representation stored is either the primary code by which the event is recognized or a secondary code that labels the primary code. In either event, the representation stored is sufficient to the degree that when it is fed into a motor-output system, salient features of the original input event can be reconstructed and output. The general block diagram of the system is shown in Fig. 1.

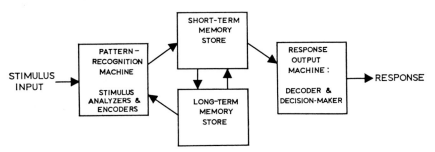

FIG. 1. Block diagram representing the flow of information through the theoretical system. See text for explanation.

It is supposed that the stimulus is first fed into a stimulus-analyzing mechanism, or a pattern-recognition machine. There is no need to give a detailed account of the output from this pattern recognizer, except to assume that it has a particular form. The development of a successful model for pattern recognition is, of course, one of the major enterprises currently in computer-simulation work. Practically all of the more successful programs in current operation (see Nilsson, 1965; Uhr, 1963; Uhr, 1965) employ some variety of "attribute-value" listing to characterize the stimulus. Many submechanisms are designed which measure or identify the value of different properties, attributes, whole—part relationships, or features of the stimulus. In general, the term feature counter will be used to refer to any one of these attribute-analyzing mechanisms. The attributes examined, how many there are, and their possible values all depend, of course, on the program and the population from which the input stimulus is selected and from which it is to be differentiated. However, for present purposes, the important point is that the stimulus is represented in coded form as an ordered *list* of attributes with their corresponding values. This listing will be called the *primary code*. From this point on, the various recognition programs diverge in how this list is used to decide what to call the stimulus; here various principles may enter, such as template matching, discriminant-function analysis, parallel processing with differential weighting of the several features, and the like.

Let us suppose that the primary code may elicit an identifying label and, if so, that this label is fed into the short-term store. If it is subvocalized, the subvocalization constitutes a feedback stimulus that is itself represented in coded form as a list of vocal features (that is, as a list of auditory or phonetic sound features, or as the movements of the speech musculature involved in vocalizing the label). This will be called the *secondary code* of the input stimulus. It consists of a small "program" which, when fed to the motor-output machine, suffices for the speech apparatus to output a verbal label for the stimulus.

It is supposed that what is stored in memory is either the primary code, the secondary code, or both. That is, a memory trace will be represented as an ordered list of attributes with their corresponding values. It will also be referred to as a *vector* of N ordered components.

Perhaps a word of explanation is required for the primary–secondary code distinction and the equivocation about which of the two is stored. The primary–secondary distinction parallels roughly that between filtered sense data and meaning. The property list stored may not be the stimulus as analyzed by the feature counters, but as described or labeled by the vocal subject. Various experimental results, including those on semantic and synonymic confusion in recall of visually presented information, incline one to this view. Perhaps the strongest evidence comes from the experiments of Conrad (1964) and others suggesting that the human short-term memory system operates in terms of either auditory- or phonetic-feature coding of visually presented verbal materials.

Because of the importance of Conrad's results, they will be described in more detail. Two experiments, one on perceptual recognition and one on memory, were done by Conrad. In the recognition experiment, single letters of the English alphabet were spoken over a noisy channel and the listener indicated the letter he thought he heard. The results were arrayed in a confusion matrix with entries indicating how frequently a given letter sent was misidentified as some other letter. In the memory experiment, Ss were presented with strings of six letters presented *visually* at a rate slow enough to be read distinctly. They then attempted immediate recall of the letters in the order presented. Analyzing those cases in which only one error occurred, Conrad derived a recall confusion matrix, indicating how frequently each letter was misrecalled as some other letter. The important point was that the confusion matrices of the two experiments were in substantial agreement. The pattern of confusion errors in recall were substantially like those occurring when the letter sounds were being identified from a noisy auditory channel. The fact that recall confusions of visually presented letters tended to follow the similarities of their auditory (rather than visual) representations suggests that Ss were subvocalizing the letters and storing this auditory code. In terms of the earlier distinction, the auditory or phonetic pattern is the secondary code, whereas the output of analyzing the graphemic (visual) letters is the primary code. In this case, the secondary code is clearly what is stored and it controls the recall. For other stimulus populations, however, the primary code may be stored and control recall. For our purposes here, which are admittedly abstract, it makes little difference which code is stored, so long as the items in a particular experiment are encoded and stored in roughly the same way. For particular conditions it will be supposed simply that each item for storage is represented as a vector of N components, where the same attributes or features are used to encode each item. We will let X_i denote the vector for item i and x_{ji} denote the value of the jth component of X_i. For purposes of simplicity in what follows, it will be assumed that the number of possible values of each component is v, the same for each attribute.

B. Retrieval in Recall

Since we are interested in what this representation implies about recall, we must first specify something about how a given memory trace is retrieved to then guide recall. Generally speaking, recall tests can be classified as either "cued" or "free" recall. In the former case, an explicit cue is either provided (e.g., the stimulus member of a paired-associate item) or is inherent in the serial nature of the task (e.g., ordinal position in a digit-span test); in the latter case, a cue is neither explicitly provided nor can one be easily imagined (e.g., free verbal recall). Presumably in the latter case retrieval is controlled by searching along some temporal dimension of the memory traces and effectively pulling out those items that have occurred "recently" in the past (see Yntema & Trask, 1963).

Since we do not wish to be sidetracked here in specifying an elaborate model for retrieval, we will accordingly restrict ourselves to cued recall experiments where the different cues are distinct. Paired-associates learning with well-differentiated stimuli is the obvious prototype. It is assumed that when a pair A–B is shown for study, S stores a compound vector, denoted (CA, CB), consisting of encoded information about A and about B. It is further assumed that upon the later test with A alone, this input, encoded as CA, is matched successively to the various traces, obtaining the maximum match to the trace (CA, CB). Thus the trace (CA, CB) is retrieved, and the response output will be guided by the vector CB. The main concern is with the forgetting of CB, the response information; retrieval difficulties caused by such factors as loss of stimulus information will be ignored in what follows. In a strict sense, the model presented here applies only to experiments in which such retrieval difficulties are minimized. Since it will be assumed that the stimulus retention and retrieval operate perfectly, the state of the system will be characterized in terms of the state of CB, the vector of response information retrieved on a test trial. At the end of the paper some more complicated retrieval schemes will be considered.

II. Forgetting of Component Information

A. General Effects of Forgetting

Assuming that CB is stored as a vector of information components, then forgetting (from whatever cause) would consist in the blurring, erasure, or change in value of some of the components of the initial vector. As forgetting proceeds and the trace is further degraded, it conveys less and less information about the initiating event B. For simplicity, it is assumed that the loss of the original information in any one component of the vector is an all-or-nothing event. However, since the vector will usually consist of many components, the loss of information in the over-all trace of CB will appear more or less gradual.

In recall, the degraded trace of CB is retrieved and given to the motor-output unit. This unit uses the information in the degraded trace either to construct or to "locate" and generate a response. If the value of a given component of the trace has been erased (for example, re-placed effectively by a question mark), then the output unit lacks a command concerning the value to use there. Assume that it randomly assigns one of the possible values for that component, thus showing complete equivocation regarding responses that differ only in that feature.

One outcome of such a model is that it will show a restricted range of confusion errors in recall. Events that are encoded similarly, with few distinguishing features, will be readily confused in recall. The range or "bandwidth" of the confusion errors in recall will increase directly with the number of components forgotten from the original trace. A few seconds after some input event S's response will convey nearly all the information about the event that has been extracted by his stimulus analyzers; but as the trace is degraded over time, less and less information about the original event is transmitted by the response. In everyday terms, it would be said that S retains the general gist of the event for some time but that he becomes more and more vague or inaccurate about the exact details of it. The trace system is functioning here in the same way that Bartlett (1932) suggested in his "schemata" concepts.

B. The Order in Which Components Are Forgotten

There are two theoretical decisions that must be made about the forgetting of components, and depending on these decisions one of four different variants of the model is obtained. One decision concerns whether the components are forgotten in a strict hierarchial order, from most detailed to most general information, or whether they are forgotten independently regardless of their possible location in a hierarchy of importance. The other decision concerns whether a forgotten value of a component is replaced by a null (guessing) state or is replaced by some other value selected at random.

1. Hierarchial Loss of Components

The hierarchial-loss idea presupposes that the N components of the vector can be strictly ordered in "importance" or specificity of the information conveyed. It roughly corresponds to the information structure utilized by a sorting tree or serial processing system. Figure 2 illustrates a sorting tree for vectors consisting of three binary components. It will correctly partition only 2^3 patterns. A tree of N nodes each with V branches could correctly partition V^N patterns. If S were to partition the response ensemble in this manner, with the first (top) node conveying the most important information and the last (bottom) node the least important, then it is further reasonable to assume that retention of a component would vary directly with its importance to him. Thus, the last component would be forgotten first, then the next to last would be forgotten, and so on.

For purposes of calculating response probabilities at recall, knowledge of the probability distribution of the number of components retained at any time t after input of the N-component vector is needed. Let

$R_i(t)$ denote the probability that exactly i components of the original N are still retained at time t. To derive $R_i(t)$ for this system requires an assumption about forgetting. The simplest assumption is that the components are arrayed in a linear chain, and that after $i - 1$ components have been forgotten, the probability of forgetting the ith

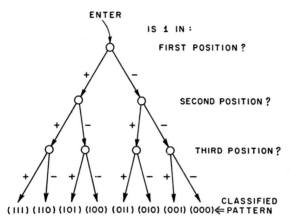

ENTER

IS 1 IN :

FIRST POSITION ?

+ —

SECOND POSITION ?

+ — + —

THIRD POSITION ?

+ — + — + — + —

CLASSIFIED
(I I I) (I I O) (I O I) (I O O) (O I I) (O I O) (O O I) (O O O) ⇐ PATTERN

FIG. 2. A binary sorting tree with three nodes that classifies eight patterns. The stimulus vector enters the tree at the top node and is then shunted by the left or right branch, depending on how it answers the questions at successive nodes.

component is a constant f in each small time unit Δt. This assumption implies the following differential-difference equation

$$R_i(t + \Delta t) = [R_i(t)(1 - f) + R_{i+1}(t)f]\, \Delta t.$$

Converting to differentials in dt and adding in the boundary condition $R_N(0) = 1$, the following system is obtained

$$\frac{dR_i(t)}{dt} = \begin{cases} -fR_i(t), & \text{for } i = N \\ f[R_{i+1}(t) - R_i(t)], & \text{for } 1 \le i \le N - 1 \\ fR_{i+1}(t), & \text{for } i = 0. \end{cases} \tag{1}$$

This is simple "death process" of constant intensity f. The time between successive "deaths" is exponentially distributed, and the time until the kth death has the Erlang (gamma) distribution. By taking successive differences between the cumulatives of the gamma for i and $i + 1$, the number of components retained at time t is found to be distributed as

$$R_i(t) = \frac{(ft)^{N-i}e^{-ft}}{(N - i)!}, \quad \text{for } i > 0. \tag{2a}$$

The absorbing state is $i = 0$, when all components have been forgotten. Its probability is given by

$$R_0(t) = 1 - e^{-ft} \sum_{i=0}^{N-1} \frac{(ft)^i}{i!} = e^{-ft} \sum_{i}^{\infty} \frac{(ft)^i}{i!} \qquad (2b)$$

There are several features of this hierarchial-loss idea that are unattractive. First, the distinction between important and unimportant information components is inexact and fuzzy, and we do not know how to sharpen the distinction. If N bits are required to uniquely specify a member of some ensemble, then all components are needed and are, in this sense, equally important. In Fig. 2, for example, whichever bit is forgotten (erased), the probability of correctly locating the pattern is reduced by a multiplicative factor of ½. So the probability of correct recall is a function only of the number of bits forgotten, and is independent of their location in the hierarchial sorting tree. Second, to use this scheme at all, one is forced to assume a particular forgetting process (such as the Poisson process described earlier) and the entire scheme may mispredict data because the particular forgetting process assumed is incorrect. The alternate scheme, considered in the following section, separates the model of the trace and the law describing forgetting, and thus has the advantage of allocating separate responsibility for mispredictions. Finally, the equations for $R_i(t)$ derived from even the simplest forgetting assumptions (Eqs. 2a,b) are relatively intractable. And since the aim is to apply the general trace model to a variety of situations, the intractability of the hierarchial-loss scheme thwarts that aim. These difficulties do not appear in the alternate scheme, which will now be discussed.

2. Independent Loss of Components

According to the independence scheme, all N information components are equally important and show equal resistance to forgetting. Roughly speaking, this is the information structure appropriate for a classifying system that operates by parallel (rather than serial) processing of information. For immediate purposes, the important point is that component bits of information are forgotten independently and at the same rate. For any particular amount of interpolated material or length of retention interval of time t, $r(t)$ is defined as the probability that the value of any single component of the trace has been retained, and $1 - r(t)$ as the probability that it has been forgotten. Since the total number correctly retained, R, is the sum of N independent component-retention variables, it has the binomial distribution given by

$$P(R = i) = \binom{N}{i} r(t)^i (1 - r(t))^{N-i}, \tag{3}$$

with mean $Nr(t)$ and variance $Nr(t)(1 - r(t))$. One advantage of this scheme is that no particular assumptions about $r(t)$ need be adopted. Also, Eq. 3 is particularly simple to work with in later derivations.

C. INTERPRETATIONS OF COMPONENT FORGETTING

The other theoretical decision regards the interpretation of a component's value after the initial value has been forgotten. According to one view, when the original value of a trace component is forgotten, it reverts to a null state (effectively a blank or question mark). According to the alternate view, forgetting consists in the replacement of the original value of the component by some incorrect, nonnull value. The first assumption can lead to "fuzzy" memories regarded by S with low confidence as to their accuracy; the second assumption will lead to clear but inaccurate memories. On recall, when a null state is encountered, the motor-output unit chooses at random (guesses) among the v possible values at that position in constructing or locating a response. According to the random-replacement view, however, the motor unit never has to guess; it has been tricked by its memory into believing that all components are known.

It is not clear that one of these interpretations will always be more appropriate than the other; on some occasions the first interpretation would seem warranted, and on other occasions, the second. The null-state interpretation corresponds roughly to the decay notion of forgetting and the replacement interpretation to the interference notion; but these are intuitive, not exact, identifications. In what follows, the null-state interpretation of forgetting will be primarily used. This is preferred because it provides a more natural interpretation of confidence ratings of remembered material, and of a possible threshold for recall.

It may be noted that for some purposes, the two interpretations lead to isomorphic prediction equations (for example, for probability of correct recall). However, their implications for performance on recognition tests of memory are different, and it is not yet clear which equations would be more accurate in describing the data. For this reason, in the

discussion of recognition memory, predictive equations for both interpretations will be developed.

D. The Recall Function

Consider the probability of a correct recall in situations in which response omissions are prohibited. This condition is easily satisfied if S
knows the response ensemble and is penalized for failing to respond.
The probability of a correct recall will be a function of the number of
components forgotten and the probability of a correct recall given that
so many components have been forgotten. For the null-state interpretation, let $g = 1/v$ denote the probability of a correct guess on a forgotten component. If i of N bits are retained (and $N - i$ lost), the
probability that all the individual component guesses are correct is
g^{N-i}. For the replacement notion, if any component is changed, the
probability of a correct recall is zero.

The distribution of the number of components retained, according to
the independent-loss scheme, is the binomial given in Eq. 3. Letting
$C(t)$ denote the probability of a correct recall when a test is given at
time t, the recall function is

$$
\begin{aligned}
C(t) &= \sum_{i=0}^{N} P(R(t) = i) P(C \mid R = i), \\
&= \sum_{i=0}^{N} \binom{N}{i} r(t)^{i} (1 - r(t))^{N-i} g^{N-i}, \\
&= [r(t) + g(1 - r(t))]^{N}.
\end{aligned}
\tag{4}
$$

The term $r + g(1 - r)$ is the probability that any given component is
given correctly, either because it is retained or is correctly guessed. The
probability of a totally correct recall is the likelihood that all N components are correct, which is just the factor $r + g(1 - r)$ raised to the
Nth power. If the null-state interpretation of forgetting is used, then
$g = 1/v$. If the random replacement interpretation is used, then $g = 0$
in Eq. 4.

E. The Component-Retention Function

Although Eq. 4 may be tested independently of assumptions about
$r(t)$, it is nonetheless of interest to examine the implications for recall
of particular $r(t)$ functions. Two approaches are available. On the one
hand, one can derive "rational" $r(t)$ functions from more elementary
assumptions; on the other, $r(t)$ may be assumed to have some empirical
shape and its implications for $C(t)$ in Eq. 4 may be determined.

Since short-term memory for elementary units of experimental materials (e.g., a letter or a digit) is being considered, the $r(t)$ function should start at unity when $t = 0$, decrease monotonically with time, and end at some asymptote (possibly zero). Although the discussion here will refer to time elapsed as the effective variable for forgetting, it is a simple matter to interpret the equations in terms that suppose that the effective variable is the amount of interfering material (n) presented between a study and test trial. For most experimental paradigms, t and n are proportional. Thus, writing retention functions in terms of elapsed time involves no commitment to either an autonomous decay or interference view of the causes of forgetting.

A simple theory of $r(t)$ for the null-state interpretation would assume that transitions between the original correct value (state C) and the null-value (state G) form a continuous-time Markov process. Suppose the transition probabilities are as given in the matrix of Eq. 5.

		State at $t + \Delta t$		
		C	G	
State at	C	$1 - f$	f	(5)
time t:	G	c	$1 - c$	

The structure holding the value of this component shows hysteresis with a bias toward the value originally set by the storage operation. In other words, the probability that the structure reverts to the null state in Δt is f; if it has reverted to its null state, then it may return to its original (correct) state with probability c in each Δt. Starting in state C at time 0 the probability that it is in state C (retained) at time t is

$$r(t) = \frac{c}{c + f} + \left(1 - \frac{c}{c + f}\right)(1 - f - c)^t,$$

$$= J + (1 - J)a^t. \tag{6}$$

This gives $r(t)$ as an exponential decay function of time and is the same as the forgetting equation derived by Estes (1955) from his stimulus fluctuation theory. According to Eq. 6, $r(t)$ is concave upward; $C(t)$ is also concave upward with greater concavity for larger N and smaller a values. Figures 3a and 3b show some hypothetical curves of $C(t)$. Those in Fig. 3a have $J = .20$, $g = .25$, $a = .9$, while N is varied from 1 to 4. The curves in Fig. 3b have $N = 4$, $g = .25$, $a = .9$, and the asymptote J is varied from 0 to .9. The asymptotes of the curves decrease as N and $(1 - J)$ increase.

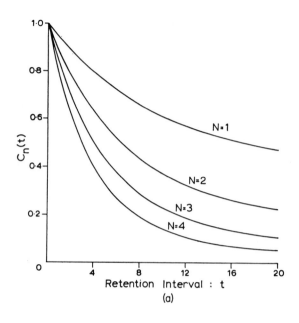

(a)

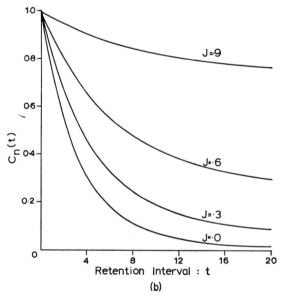

(b)

FIG. 3. Recall function for the exponential $r(t)$ function of Eq. 6. In (a), the number of components N is varied. In (b), the asymptote J of the component-retention function is varied.

The $r(t)$ function in Eq. 6 was based on the null-state interpretation of forgetting. However, a similar equation can be derived for the random-replacement interpretation. In the matrix of Eq. 5, replace the guessing state G by an error state E, and replace c by $c/v - 1$. That is, the correct value is changed with probability f in each Δt; if some incorrect value has been substituted, then it changes with probability c to one of the other $v - 1$ values selected at random. Starting in state C the probability that the structure will be in state C declines exponentially to an asymptote of

$$J' = \frac{(c/v - 1)}{f + (c/v - 1)}$$

If there is no bias toward holding the original value, then $f = c$ and $J' = 1/v$; that is, at asymptote the value of the component is random relative to its initial value. For $c \neq f$, suitable choice of parameters of this replacement scheme will lead to curves identical to those in Figs. 3a and 3b.

The recall curves derived from exponential $r(t)$ functions may be compared to those from linear $r(t)$ functions to note their similarities. A linear $r(t)$ function descending from 1 at rate a to an asymptote of b would have the corresponding recall function

$$C(t) = \begin{cases} [1 - (1 - g)at]^N, & \text{for } t \leq \dfrac{1 - b}{a} \\[2ex] [b + g(1 - b)]^N, & \text{for } t \geq \dfrac{1 - b}{a}. \end{cases}$$

For $N > 1$, successive derivatives of this $C(t)$ function alternate in sign, so the curves have the same concave-upward shape as does the exponential function. For visual comparison to Fig. 3, some hypothetical curves based on the linear $r(t)$ function are shown in Fig. 4 for the parameters $N = 4$ and $g = .25$. For one set of curves, the asymptote b is zero and the decay rate a is varied; for the other set with $a = .04$, the asymptote b is varied. When b is large, the recall function is two-limbed—describing the descent and the plateau. When b is small, the curves look similar to those in Fig. 3 for the exponential $r(t)$ function with small J. Thus, when $C(t)$ has a low asymptote and N is unknown, it would be difficult to discriminate between a linear and an exponential $r(t)$ function. If N is known, then $r(t)$ can be estimated directly from $C(t)$ and its descriptive law thus determined.

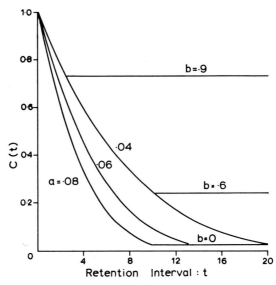

Fɪɢ. 4. Recall functions for the linear function $r(t) = 1 - at$, with asymptote at b. For the curves to the left, $b = 0$ and the rate of decay a varies. The plateaus give the asymptotes when $a = .04$ and the parameter b is varied.

III. New Experiments on Recall

A. Experiment I

The experiments to be reported attempt to test the recall function in Eq. 4. They were carried out at Stanford University with the able and generous assistance of Mr. James Hinrichs. The three experiments are very similar, differing in only minor details. We wished to test Eq. 4 without making assumptions about $r(t)$, the component retention function. This required an experimental situation for which the parameter N, the number of components in the response member of a paired-associate item, could be determined in advance. Given recall functions for several known and different N values, Eq. 4 permits predictions of one N function from any other N function.

1. Method

The method tried to induce a particular encoding and N value by presenting the response ensemble to S in terms of a binary sorting tree. The perceptual layout of the response ensemble for S is shown in Fig. 5. This shows eight push buttons, each with a small jewel light above it. The spatial separations between terminals emphasized their organization in groups of two and then of four on either side. This organization was pointed out to S (with no further comments to use it) and was perceptually emphasized by red tape lines on the board, as indicated in Fig. 5. If S organized and encoded this response ensemble in the way we hoped he would, then the vector description of the memory trace (of the response term) is simple and direct. The eight-alternative ensemble in Fig. 5 consists of $N = 3$ components, each component having two possible values (left or right). Thus for this setup, we would hope that $N = 3$ and $g = 1/v = .50$. The experiment is as much a test of whether this encoding assumption is correct as it is a test of Eq. 4.

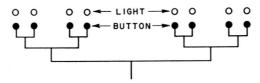

FIG. 5. Spatial arrangement of the eight-response ensemble, with eight push buttons and corresponding jewel lamps. The grouping of the responses into binary clusters was emphasized by red tape lines corresponding to the lines in the figure.

The experimental procedure involved a continuous stream of presentations and tests on single paired-associate items. S first studied a given S-R pair for 2 seconds, and was then tested several seconds later for recall of the response to the stimulus member of the pair. During the retention interval, other pairs were presented for study or for test. Each pair received one presentation, one test, and then was discarded. This procedure is similar to that introduced by Peterson and Peterson (1962).

The stimuli were high-frequency common nouns presented auditorily by a tape recorder at the rate of one every 2.5 seconds. The response was depressing one of the push buttons on the panel before S (see Fig. 5). For an item's first presentation (a study trial), the stimulus word was heard simultaneously with the onset of the light above the correct button. S was instructed to push this button immediately and to associate it with the word heard. After either 1, 3, 5, 7, or 9 interpolated items (some studied, some tested), the target word recurred alone, this time preceded by a brief beep of a tone indicating a recall test. On the test trials, S was allowed 2.5 seconds in which to push the button he recalled as being associated with the test word, being told to guess if necessary.

Each S was run with four different sizes of the response ensemble, with one "list" run for each ensemble condition. The number of response alternatives was either 2, 4, 8, or 16 buttons, representing N values of 1, 2, 3, or 4 binary components of information. Before each list (ensemble condition) began, the appropriate subset of the buttons was indicated to S. For example, an S might have the extreme right-hand pair of buttons in Fig. 5 for his $N = 1$ condition, the right-hand four buttons for his $N = 2$ condition, and so on. When 16 responses were used, a complementary set of 8 was provided below the 8 shown in Fig. 5.

The four ensemble conditions occurred in an order counterbalanced over Ss, and this order will be ignored in data analyses. Each ensemble condition comprised a list containing 10 occurrences of items tested at each of the lags of 1, 3, 5, 7, and 9 intervening items. The particular word lists used with the ensembles were also interchanged among Ss. The Ss were 25 undergraduates fulfilling a service requirement for their Introductory Psychology course.

2. Results and Predictions

The results of interest concern the recall curves, shown in Fig. 6. These show the average percentage of items correctly recalled as a function of the number of items (test or study, or both) interpolated between study and the recall test. Each point is based on 250 observations. The curves decline in an irregular manner with increasing amounts of interpolated material, which is confounded here with retention inter-

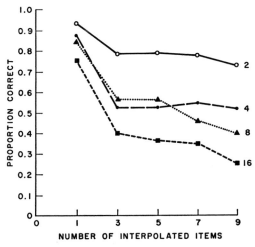

Fig. 6. Percentage of test pairs recalled correctly as a function of the number of items intervening between study and test of the pair. The number of response alternatives is the parameter of the four curves.

val. In general, the curves are ordered from top to bottom in terms of the number of response alternatives. The inversion in two points of the 4- versus 8-alternative curves suggests some misfortunes of sampling variability (not replicated in later experiments), so any reasonable theory may be expected to be somewhat inaccurate in predicting one or another of these curves.

These curves are to be fitted with Eq. 4, where $r(t)$ is to be estimated as a parameter for lags of $t = 1, 3, 5, 7,$ and 9. Since g is constant throughout at $\frac{1}{2}$, set $u(t) = r(t) + g(1 - r(t))$ and write Eq. 4 as

$$C_N(t) = (u(t))^N, \tag{7}$$

where $C_N(t)$ is the recall probability at lag t for ensembles specified by N bits of information. The $u(t)$ parameter is to be estimated to best fit the four observed $C_N(t)$ values at each lag t. Because of the nature of Eq. 7, straightforward least-squares or minimum chi-square procedures lead to seventh-degree polynomials to solve for the $u(t)$ estimate. A more tractable procedure is to minimize the sum of squared deviations about log $C_N(t)$. This leads to the following estimation equation.

$$\hat{u}(t) = \exp \left[\frac{\sum\limits_{N=1}^{4} N \log C_N(t)}{\sum\limits_{N=1}^{4} N^2} \right]$$

The properties of such rule-of-thumb estimates are unknown, but they surely are not the best possible. Their sole advantage is their ease of computation.

The estimates of $u(t)$ obtained in this manner were .940, .798, .791, .772, and .725 for lags of 1, 3, 5, 7, and 9 items, respectively. These $u(t)$ values correspond to $r(t)$ values of .880, .596, .582, .544, and .450, respectively. The irregularity of these $r(t)$ values will be discussed later.

These $u(t)$ estimates were substituted into Eq. 7 for $N = 1, 2, 3, 4$, leading to the predictions displayed in the four panels of Fig. 7. The predictions are generally quite accurate, especially so for $N = 1$ and $N = 4$. The poorest predictions occur at the two inverted points (lags 3 and 5) on the $N = 2$ and $N = 3$ curves, the aberrant points noted before. A chi-square goodness-of-fit test was applied. There are 20 points and 5 parameters, the $u(t)$'s, were estimated, yielding 15 degrees of freedom. The chi-square was 15.11, a value far from significant. It is noteworthy that 84% of this total chi-square was contributed

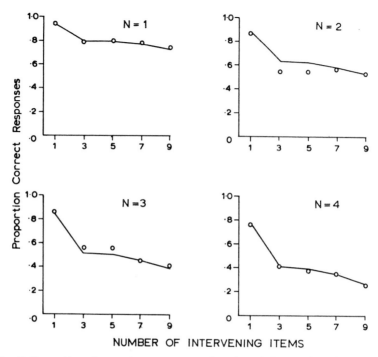

NUMBER OF INTERVENING ITEMS

FIG. 7. Proportion of correct responses as a function of the number of intervening items and N. The line connects the predicted values; the open dots are the observed proportions.

by the two aberrant points on the $N = 2$ and 3 curves. Thus, we may accept the fit of Eq. 7 as satisfactory.

3. Measures and Predictions of Information Retained

Let us consider some further predictions of these data. The theory will in principle tell us the probability that S's recalled response will fall within various sectors of the ensemble relative to the location of the correct response. A problem is to find a convenient way to summarize these "error profiles." The method illustrated here scores the recalled response in terms of information retained, which scores will be denoted as I. A decision was made to calculate I scores according to a hierarchial view of component forgetting. This is an arbitrary scheme, but no better one came to mind for scoring the single response. The customary measure, contingent uncertainty or transmitted information (cf. Garner, 1962), uses the entire input-output matrix and can assign no score to single instances of recalled responses. To illustrate this scoring procedure, consider the eight-response ensemble with the bit clusters being (1, 2), (3, 4) versus (5, 6), (7, 8), and suppose the correct response is 1. Recall of 1 is assigned an I score of 3 bits; recall of 2 is assigned a score of 2; recall of 3 or 4 is assigned a score of 1; and recall of 5, 6, 7, or 8 is assigned an I score of 0 bits. Note that the responses are scored in terms of the number of hierarchial bits retained that would lead to that response. The I scores were so obtained and then averaged over Ss and observations for each N and each lag.

Consider now the derivation of predictions for the information retained scores so obtained. Equation 3 gives the probability that i of N bits are retained and, on the assumption of independent loss, each combination of $N-i$ losses out of N is equally likely. Using this assumption, the expected I score is calculated for retention of i of N bits, and then these are summed, being weighted by the probability that i bits are retained. The procedure will be illustrated with the eight-alternative $N = 3$ case, where the three bits are denoted as a, b, c, going from most detailed to most general (that is, moving from the top of the tree to the bottom in Fig. 5). If the number of bits retained R is 3, then a correct response ensues and the I score is 3 bits. If $R = 0$, then all eight responses are equally likely, and the expected value of I in this case is

$$E(I \mid R = 0) = \tfrac{1}{8}(3 + 2 + 1 + 1 + 0 + 0 + 0 + 0) = \tfrac{7}{8} \text{ bits.}$$

Suppose $R = 2$; then three equiprobable combinations of bits retained are $(a\ b)$, $(a\ c)$, and $(b\ c)$. If $(a\ b)$ is the pair retained, then response 1 and response 5 are equally likely, so the average value of I in this case is $\tfrac{1}{2}(3 + 0) = 1.5$. If $(a\ c)$ are retained, then responses 1 and 3 are equiprobable, so the average I will be 2. If $(b\ c)$ are retained, responses 1 and 2 are equiprobable, so the average I will be 2.5 bits. Since these three possibilities of two bits retained are equiprobable, the average I score when $R = 2$ is

$$E(I \mid R = 2) = \tfrac{1}{3}(1.5 + 2 + 2.5) = 2 \text{ bits.}$$

By a similar line of reasoning from the independent-loss assumption, the average information retained when $R = 1$ may be found to be 1.33 bits for a three-bit ensemble.

Finally, these theoretical expectations of I are used to calculate the expected I score at each N and t value, according to the formula

$$E(I_N(t)) = \sum_{i=0}^{N} E(I_N \mid R_N = i)\, P(R_N(t) = i).$$

Estimates of the distribution of $R_N(t)$ are made by using Eq. 3 along with the previous estimates of $r(t)$ from the mean recall curves.

These curves for $N = 2$, 3, and 4 are shown in the panels of Fig. 8. The curve for $N = 1$ is not shown since it is identical to the percentage-correct recall curve in Fig. 7. The fit of predicted to observed values is fairly good except that the values of the $N = 2$ and $N = 4$ data are often overpredicted, indicating slightly more scattered responding in these cases than even the independence model will allow for. This overprediction could occur if Ss were choosing the "mirror-image" alternative somewhat more than the model predicts. The fit of the model is generally satisfactory, although there is some room for improvement.

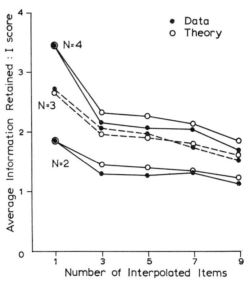

Fɪɢ. 8. Average score of information retained in recall as a function of N and the number of intervening items. The solid dots are the observed averages; the open dots are the predicted values. See text for explanation.

4. Comparison to Simple All-or-None Model

The simple all-or-none model (Bower, 1961a; Estes, 1961) assumes that a memory trace is either completely retained or not at all. It corresponds to the assumption that all N components are tied together so that when one goes, they all go together. When all components are forgotten, it is assumed that S guesses at random among the 2^N alternatives. If $r(t)$ is the retention probability, then the probability of a correct recall of an N-bit response is

$$C_N(t) = r(t) + (1 - r(t)) \cdot 2^{-N}. \tag{8}$$

This equation, in fact, is implicit in the common practice of "correcting" response proportions for guessing.

To compare this model with the multicomponent model, least-squares estimates of $r(t)$ in Eq. 8 were obtained and the recall probabilities in Fig. 6 were predicted by Eq. 8. The fit of these predictions was poor relative to the fit of the multicomponent predictions. The chi-square for goodness of fit was significant ($\chi^2(15) = 28.02$, $p < .01$). The average absolute discrepancy between observed and predicted proportions of this model was .054, about twice as large as the discrepancies for the multicomponent model. Also as would be expected from this outcome, the predictions of information retained, or I scores (cf. Fig. 8), were consistently poorer than the predictions based on the multicomponent model. From these comparisons it may be concluded that the results are inconsistent with the idea that forgetting of the entire vector of information is all or none. However, they are consistent with the idea that individual components of the stored vector are forgotten in all all-or-none manner.

5. The Empirical $r(t)$ Function

The recall curves in Fig. 6 are quite irregular and this shows up, of course, in the $r(t)$ estimates for lags of 1, 3, 5, 7, and 9 interpolated items. Because the list was constructed with interleaved tests and study trials on new items, the intervening events for a particular lag varied in the number of tests versus new-item presentations. A reanalysis of the recall data showed that test trials caused relatively little retention loss, whereas new-item presentations (requiring storage) caused relatively greater retention losses. The differential forgetting due to retrieval versus storage operations is shown in Figs. 9a and 9b. Figure 9a is a plot of recall probabilities against the number of intervening storage operations (new-item study trials) between storage of the target item and its later test. The number of intervening test trials is ignored in these calculations. Figure 9b shows a similar recall function plotted against the number of intervening tests (retrieval operations), with the number of intervening study trials ignored (in fact, permitted random variation). Recall probability declines monotonically with intervening study of new pairs but not monotonically with tests of old pairs; in fact, the latter curves are quite irregular. Since test and study trials occupied the same length of time, these results favor an interference rather than an autonomous decay principle of forgetting. Worded in terms of the model, the main event promoting erasure of component bits of a memory already in storage is the act of storing similar memories (vectors) regarding the same ensemble.

New estimates of $r(n)$ were obtained from Fig. 9a, where n is understood to be the number of intervening first presentations. The estimates

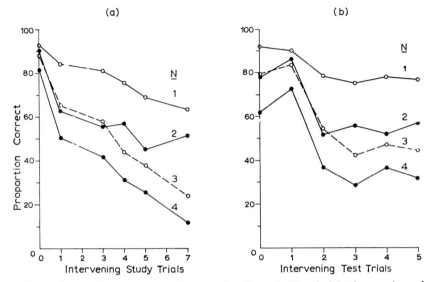

FIG. 9. Proportion correct recalls as a function of N and (a) the number of intervening study trials, and (b) the number of intervening test trials. For each graph, the variable not specified on the abscissa varies randomly over the points plotted.

for $N = 1, 3, 4$ are plotted in Fig. 10. The estimates are similar at each n value; their decline is well described by the straight line $r(n) = .856 - .088n$. Using this fitted $r(n)$ function, the $C_N(n)$ data in Fig. 9a can be fairly well predicted via Eq. 4.

B. Experiments II and III

1. Method

These experiments used the same button-light board and differed from Experiment I in only one major respect. Experiment I had interleaved study trials and test trials in a continuous task; in Experiments II and III the study trials occurred in large blocks followed by a block of test trials measuring recall of several pairs selected from the preceding study block.

In Experiment II a study block consisted in presentation of 12 new pairs (aural words associated to button presses as before) presented at a 3.5-second rate. The test block, preceded by a buzzer, consisted of 5 recall tests; the pairs tested were those presented in positions 3, 5, 7, 9, and 11 in the 12-item list, corresponding to 9, 7, 5, 3, and 1 intervening items before the test block began. The order in which these 5 items were tested was counterbalanced over test blocks. For each response ensemble condition (2, 4, 8, or 16 alternatives), each of 24 Ss had a list consisting of 10 study-test blocks. This then yields recall curves for each N value and each $n = 1, 3, 5, 7, 9$, with 240 observations per point.

Experiment III was similar except the study block consisted of 8 pairs presented at a 2.5-second rate, and 4 of these items were tested for recall in the following test block. The 4 items tested were selected equally often from each presentation position of the preceding 8-item

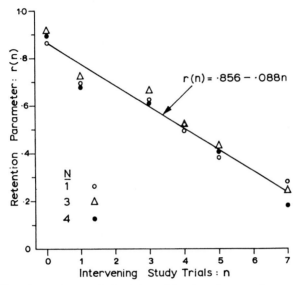

Fig. 10. The $r(t)$ estimates derived from Fig. 9a, where n denotes the number of intervening study trials. The points for the $N = 2$ condition are not plotted. In theory, the three estimates at each n value should be identical.

study block. The order in which items were tested was counterbalanced over test blocks. For each response ensemble condition, each of 24 Ss had a list consisting of 16 such study-test blocks. The recall curves are based on 192 observations per point. As in Experiments I and II, the particular word lists used with the different response ensembles were counterbalanced over Ss.

2. Results and Predictions

The order in which items were tested had practically no effect upon their recall probability. The main exception to this statement is that recall probability of the eighth (last) item in Experiment III was higher when it was tested first rather than later. Except for this point, test order had almost no effect on recall. Consequently, results are pooled over various test orders in what follows.

The average recall probabilities for the two experiments are shown in Fig. 11a and 11b. For each graph, the abscissa is the number of

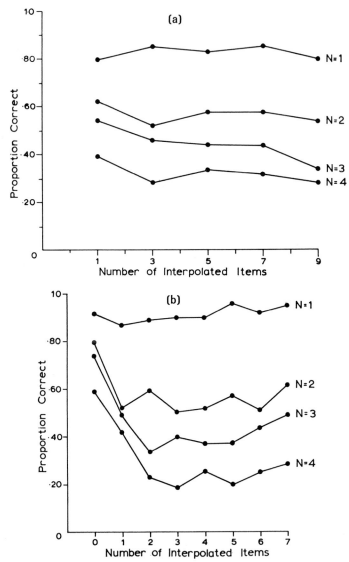

F??. 11. Proportion of correct recalls in (a) Exp. II, and (b) Exp. III, as a function of the number of interpolated study trials before the test block began. The order of testing was counterbalanced and is ignored in these calculations.

items studied between presentation and the start of the test block. The information in the response ensemble is the parameter in each set of curves.

The recall curves of Experiment II in Fig. 11a are essentially flat, but are well separated according to the information in the response. On the other hand, recall in Experiment III (Fig. 11b) shows definite serial position curves (except for $N = 1$) with a marked recency effect and a slight primacy effect. We have no explanation for the difference in recall functions obtained in these two experiments; they differed in several respects, including the number of items per study block, the number of items tested, and the trial rate. Judging from other experiments using a similar procedure (e.g., Murdock, 1963a), the bowed curves in Fig. 11b are the usual result, whereas the flat curves in Fig. 11a are atypical.

The average recall with the two-response ensemble in both experiments is unusually high relative to what would be expected on the basis of the curves for N's of 2, 3, and 4. This, we feel, was probably due to the block, or "short-list," study procedure employed here. Subjects frequently volunteered the information that a simple strategy sufficed to learn the two-response blocks. Since each block (of 12 or 8 study items) contained only half of each response, they could rehearse or concentrate on only those words going with response 1 and ignore the rest. On test trials, any word they did not remember as a 1 would be responded to as a 2. However, they reported that this strategy was of no help for the larger response ensembles and so was not used for them.

To the extent that this strategy is used, the retention parameter for the $N = 1$ data will be higher than for the $N > 1$ data—as indeed it is. This would follow, for example, if it is held that the effective event promoting forgetting is the act of storing other material. By the halving strategy, the number of interfering events for $N = 1$ would be about half of those encountered when $N > 1$. For this reason, Eq. 7 will be tested with only the $N > 1$ data since it can be reasonably presumed that $u(t)$ will be similar in these cases. The surprising fact is that this halving strategy was not used by Ss in Experiment I (none reported it); apparently, the continuous interleaving of study and test trials in that experiment lowered the saliency of such strategies.

In testing Eq. 4 with the $N > 1$ data, recall results are pooled over all lags t because of their essential constancy, and an average retention parameter r is estimated by the same procedure as before. The results of this procedure are shown in Table I. The fit is quite good in both experiments; neither chi-square value is significant, despite the power

TABLE I

AVERAGE RECALL PROBABILITIES

	Experiment II			Experiment III	
N	Observed	Predicted	N	Observed	Predicted
2	.569	.572	2	.575	.572
3	.444	.435	3	.455	.434
4	.323	.325	4	.303	.323
	$\hat{r} = .514$			$\hat{r} = .512$	
	$n = 1200^a$			$n = 1536^a$	
	$\chi^2(2) = .33$			$\chi^2(2) = 3.48$	
	$p > .50$			$p > .10$	

^a Total observations in each proportion.

of the test afforded by the large number of observations. It may be noted that the average recall scores are approximately the same in the two experiments. Attempts to fit the recall curves in Fig. 11b by estimating separate r's at each serial position proved only moderately successful. The general irregularity of the empirical curves prevented a really good fit. Even so, the average discrepancy between observed and predicted proportions was only .03.

3. *Comparison to All-or-None Model*

The fit of the multicomponent predictions in Table I may be again compared to those of the simple all-or-none model. The fit of the latter's predictions are considerably poorer in each experiment, yielding chi-squares (with 2 df) for goodness of fit of 22 and 43, respectively, for Experiments II and III. These chi-squares are 66 and 12 times larger, respectively, than those for goodness of fit of the multicomponent model. Thus, these data again contradict the idea that the total information in the memory trace is lost in an all-or-none fashion; however, the data are consistent with the idea that individual components of the memory vector are lost in an all-or-none manner.

These recall experiments do not, of course, prove that the multicomponent model of memory traces is the only one possible, since few alternatives have been tested against it. The experiments do, however, yield evidence consistent with the vector model and suggest that it is not altogether an idle practice to examine further implications of the model. This is done in the remaining sections of the paper, where we turn to examination of various tests of recognition memory to see what light the model may shed on problems of interrelating performance on a variety of such tests.

IV. Recognition Memory

A. Classification of Recognition Tasks

Some implications of the theory will now be derived for measures of recognition memory. Tests of recognition memory fall naturally into two types. First are *single-stimulus* tests, in which a single unit of learning (e.g., an S-R pair) is shown and S rates this in some way according to its familiarity to him. Often the rating is dichotomous ("Yes, I've seen it before" or "No, I've not seen it before"), but it can be done with as many rating categories as S can handle (for example, the S may be instructed to "Rate on a 7-point scale your adjudged likelihood of having seen this unit before"). The dichotomous judgment may be supplemented by a confidence rating ("Rate on a 5-point scale your confidence that your Yes or No answer is correct"). In data analysis, the yes-no response plus its confidence rating is unfolded and treated in practice as a straightforward rating scale regarding the familiarity of the test unit.

Second are *multiple-choice* tests in which several learning units are shown. These tests take a variety of forms depending on how S is instructed to partition the set of n alternatives. Examples of instructed partitions would be (a) pick the most familiar item; (b) pick the k most familiar of the n; (c) pick the k least familiar of the n; (d) rank order all n on the basis of their judged familiarity; and so on.

Presumably, an S's performance on all these tasks should be interrelated since, in some sense, they are simply different kinds of output from one and the same memory structure. However, development of quantitative models to describe these interrelationships have hitherto proved difficult. In the following, the vector model of the memory trace will be applied to this problem.

B. The Decision Theory Viewpoint

Before proceeding to the main discussion, however, the general viewpoint to be employed will first be presented. The viewpoint is that of statistical decision theory, which has been widely used in dealing with psychophysical experiments on detection and recognition. The best-known model employing decision theory concepts in psychophysics is the theory of signal detectability, or TSD (see Swets, Tanner, & Birdsall, 1961). Egan (1958) was the first to propose the relevance of decision theory concepts to interpretation of performance on recognition tests of memory, and this point of view is now widely accepted (e.g., Bernbach, 1964; Bower, 1964; Murdock, 1965; Norman & Wickelgren, 1965;

Parks, 1966; Pollack, Norman, & Galanter, 1965). The decision-theoretic concepts are used to describe S's judgment "criterion" and how this is manipulated by situational variables.

To illustrate the main concepts, let us consider a yes-no recognition test with single stimuli in which S is to decide whether or not a test item is one he has seen before in a list of items he has just studied. This decision presumably is made on the basis of some "feeling of familiarity" that S experiences when the test item is compared to what he has stored in memory. Let us admit that this feeling of familiarity may vary over a range of values for both previously studied (old) items as well as for novel items not previously seen (new, or distractor, items). Admitting this structure, S's problem is this: given a particular feeling of familiarity produced by a test item, decide from which population of items (old or new) it comes. It is presumed that S resolves this decision problem by choosing a cutpoint or criterion on the familiarity continuum that partitions the range into a region of acceptance and a region of rejection. Test items whose familiarity exceeds the criterion are accepted as old (Respond "Old" or "Yes, I've seen it before"); otherwise the test item is rejected (Respond "New" or "No, I've not seen it before").

If S were to act in a manner approaching that of an optimal decision-maker, several factors would have to be taken into account in selecting the criterion of acceptance. We will discuss later the optimal criterion, but the factors entering into it can be briefly mentioned at once. They are the payoffs and penalties involved for accepting versus rejecting new and old items, and the relative likelihood that a given feeling of familiarity results from an old, as opposed to a new, item. The main components of the latter likelihood are the probability that any test item is old instead of new, and the probability distribution of familiarity ratings given old and given new items. For convenience in the immediate discussion, let x denote the feeling of familiarity, with large numbers representing high familiarity; and let $f_o(x)$ and $f_n(x)$ denote the probability densities of x for old and new items, respectively; TSD assumes that x is a continuous variable and that f_o and f_n are normal density functions. Figure 12a shows possible distributions of $f_o(x)$ and $f_n(x)$, with a particular criterion indicated.

The choice of a criterion determines the "hit rate," that is, the probability that an old item is accepted, $P(A \mid o)$; and a corresponding "false alarm rate," the probability that a new item is accepted as old, $P(A \mid n)$. These represent, respectively, the probability areas of $f_o(x)$ and $f_n(x)$ above the criterion in Fig. 12a. Since the criterion is under S's control and it may vary from one experimental condition to another, a simple measure of hit rate is not by itself an adequate description of recognition memory since it varies greatly according to the criterion involved. An adequate measure can be obtained, however, by noting that as the criterion in Fig. 12a is varied, the hit rate and false alarm rate will covary, constrained in a manner determined by the two underlying density functions. For the particular distributions of Fig. 12a, the covariation of $P(A \mid o)$ and $P(A \mid n)$ is depicted in Fig. 12b. For example, if the criterion were set very low, far to the left in Fig. 12a, then all area under both distributions exceeds the criterion and the point at (1, 1) on Fig. 12b is obtained. If the criterion were set very

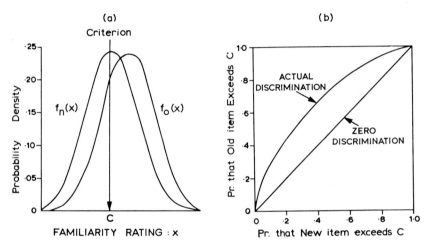

FIG. 12. (a) Hypothetical probability density functions for old (f_o) and for new (f_n) items on the familiarity axis x. A criterion is indicated at C. (b) The covariation of the probability that an old versus a new item exceeds a criterion C as C is varied. The line marked "zero discrimination" would result in case $f_o(x)$ and $f_n(x)$ were identical, so S could not distinguish old from new items.

high, far to the right in Fig. 12a, the point at (0, 0) is obtained. Intermediate criteria lead to intermediate points on the curve in Fig. 12b. The straight line in Fig. 12b labeled "zero discrimination" shows the result obtained when $f_o(x)$ and $f_n(x)$ are identical.

Curves of this kind in psychophysical detection situations are called either receiver-operating-characteristic (ROC) curves or isosensitivity curves. For recognition memory, the terms that have been proposed are memory-operating-characteristic (MOC) curves or isomemory curves. Why isomemory? Because all points falling along this curve represent the same ability to discriminate between old versus new items. If some variable simply moves S's performance from one point to another on the same curve, then that manipulation has affected his criterion (or "response bias") but not his memory or whatever produces discriminability of items along the familiarity axis. Increasing memory, or discriminability, would, on the other hand, have the effect of shifting the entire MOC curve of Fig. 12b toward the upper left-hand corner at (0, 1). From such considerations it follows that a more adequate (that is, criterion-invariant) description of recognition memory is provided either by the entire MOC curve or its parameters.

C. MULTICOMPONENT MODELS FOR RECOGNITION MEMORY

In applying the multicomponent model to recognition tasks, it will be supposed generally that S compares the test stimulus (or stimuli) to the degraded memory trace of the item he holds in store, and depending on the outcome of this comparison (or of several comparisons, if there are several test stimuli), he decides how to respond to the test stimulus (or stimuli). Different models result, depending on (a) the assumptions about the memory trace (for example, whether a null-return or random-replacement interpretation of component forgetting is used), (b) the performance required of S (for example, pick one, rank k, or rate one), and (c) the different decision rules assumed. As in the earlier discussion, the discussion here applies strictly only to tasks that minimize retrieval difficulties, so that, metaphorically, the model-subject knows which memory trace to pull out of its store for comparison to the test stimulus. A convenient prototype would be a modification of the light-board experiments reported earlier: a target pair S_1-R_1 is shown for study, and later S is shown a single test pair S_1-R_x to judge, or is shown several test pairs with different responses paired with S_1, S_1-R_1, S_1-R_2, S_1-R_3, and so on, and is required to choose the correct pairing he has seen before. It is presumed that on the test S retrieves the memory vector (CS_1, CR_1) and compares CR_1 (or its degraded form) to the encoding of the test item, or CR_x. It is assumed that all items are encoded into homogeneous vectors N components in length and that some mechanism compares the values of the N corresponding components of the two vectors.

The outcome to be expected from this comparison process depends on whether forgetting is interpreted as consisting in null-state return or random replacement of a component's value in the original memory trace. If the random-replacement idea is used, then the output of the comparator will be a two-level score, described as M matches (same value in corresponding components) and $N - M$ mismatches (different values in corresponding components). Alternatively, if the null-state idea is used to interpret forgetting, then the output of comparing the test item to the degraded memory trace can be a three-level score, consisting of M matches, $R - M$ mismatches, and $N - R$ question marks. In the latter cases, the original value of the component has been erased and the comparator has nothing (or only a null value) in that position to compare to the value of the test item on that component. Note that in all cases the comparator is deciding simply "same," "different," or "do not know" and is not grading component value-pairs according to how close they are in any metric sense of distance. To apply these ideas to recognition tests, we must first derive from the model the probability distributions of the various scores resulting from the comparator.

1. Distribution of Comparison Scores for Old Items

Consider first the distribution of scores given that the test item is, in fact, old or correct. Thus a degraded memory trace is being compared to what, in effect, it looked like when it was first stored. Recall that the distribution of the number of components correctly retained R is binomial with parameters N and r.

Consider first the null-state interpretation of forgetting. According to this view, the number of matches for an old test item will be exactly R (since all components retained match the test item), there will be no mismatches, and the number of question marks will be $N - R$. Letting M_o denote the matches for an old item, its distribution is the same as R, namely

$$P(M_o = x) = P(R = x) = \binom{N}{x} r^x (1 - r)^{N-x}. \tag{9}$$

The match score suffices to characterize the two-level score in this case.

Consider next the random-replacement interpretation of forgetting. According to this view, the number of matches will be R and the number of mismatches will be $N - R$. Since r denotes the probability that a given component retains its original correct value, the distribution of match scores is given by Eq. 9, and $N - M_o$ is the number of mismatches. But again, M_o completely characterizes the comparison score for the case of an old item.

2. Distribution of Comparison Scores for New Items

a. Representation of Item Dissimilarity. The match scores when new (distractor) items are compared to a memory trace will depend primarily on how different the distractors are from the correct (old) item in question. To get on with the task here, it must be decided how to represent in formal terms this notion of the similarity of a set of distractors to a particular old item.

The most convenient representation found so far is the following: beginning with a known, old target item consisting of N bits, a population of distractors to this target is generated by changing each bit in the original vector to some different value with independent probability d, and leaving the original value of the component the same with probability $1 - d$. The change parameter d then gives a convenient index of the average difference between an old item and a population of distractors generated for comparison with it. In principle, d is under the control of the experimenter (according to how similar he makes the distractors), but it cannot be preset numerically unless S's precise encoding system is known. Thus, experimentally, distractor populations can usually only be rank ordered in similarity, hence in the parameter d. For this reason, with most experimental materials d will serve as a parameter to be estimated from performance curves.

As a consequence of the foregoing independent-change representation, the probability that a given distractor in the population has exactly x changes is given by the binomial law with parameters N and d. The probability distribution of matching scores is to be derived for the case where a degraded memory trace is compared to a distractor selected at random from a population of such distractors. Again the answer differs depending on whether forgetting is interpreted as null state or random replacement of the original value of a component.

b. The Null-State Interpretation. Suppose that the trace has degraded to the extent that R components are retained, whereas $N - R$ components are forgotten (have null values). When an N-component distractor is compared bit by bit to this degraded trace, the outcome may be generally described by the following three-level score: there are M matches, $R - M$ mismatches, and $N - R$ question marks. The probability of M_n matches out of R retained components is binomial with parameters R and $1 - d$. From these considerations, it follows that the unconditional probability of x matches and y mismatches is

$$P(M_n = x \quad \text{and} \quad R - M_n = y) = P(R = x + y) \cdot P(M_n = x \mid R = x + y),$$

$$= \binom{N}{x + y} r^{x+y} (1 - r)^{N-x-y} \binom{x + y}{x} (1 - d)^x d^y, \tag{10}$$

for $x, y = 0, 1, \ldots, N$, and $x + y \leq N$. This is a joint probability distribution of two random variables, the number of matches and the number of mismatches.

For some purposes, it may be assumed that the decision-maker takes account only of the number of matches, thus ignoring the number of mismatches. The marginal distribution of M_n may be obtained from Eq. 10 by summing out y from 0 to $N - x$, namely

$$P(M_n = x) = \sum_{y=0}^{N-x} \binom{N}{x + y} r^{x+y}(1 - r)^{N-x-y} \binom{x + y}{x} (1 - d)^x d^y.$$

The summing is simplified by using the factorial identity

$$\binom{N}{x + y}\binom{x + y}{x} = \binom{N}{x}\binom{N - x}{y}.$$

After summing over y, the marginal probability distribution of M_n is found to be

$$P(M_n = x) = \binom{N}{x}[r(1 - d)]^x[1 - r(1 - d)]^{N-x}. \tag{11}$$

This is a binomial distribution of match scores with parameters N and $r(1 - d)$. The parameter $r(1 - d)$ is the probability that an individual component is both retained in the trace and not changed in the distractor. In fact, the intuitive derivation of Eq. 11 could have proceeded from just this observation without the intervention of Eq. 10 and the summation. As might be expected from the foregoing, the distribution of the number of mismatches is also binomial with parameters N and rd. If the difference parameter d is zero, then the distribution in Eq. 11 reduces to that of Eq. 9 for old items, as it should.

  c. The Random-Replacement Interpretation. Consider next the distribution of M_n implied by the random-replacement interpretation of component forgetting. If there are no null values, then comparisons yield only two-level scores, the number of matches M_n and of mismatches $N - M_n$; thus only the distribution of M_n is of concern.

  To begin the derivation, suppose that R of the trace components retain their correct (original) values, whereas $N - R$ have been changed to some other value selected at random from the remaining $v - 1$ possibilities at each component. Of the R retained components, each has probability $1 - d$ of matching the corresponding component of the distractor. Hence the number of matches from this source will be binomially distributed with parameters R and $1 - d$. If a trace component has been forgotten (replaced in value), then the corresponding component of the distractor may match it with probability $d/v - 1$; that is, with probability d that component was changed in generating the distractor, and with probability $1/v - 1$ the value assigned there will accidentally coincide with the random value replacing the original value of that trace component. Hence, the number of matches contributed by this source is binomially distributed with parameters $N - R$ and $d/1 - v$.

A rigorous derivation can be produced from the foregoing considerations, but an intuitive rationale for the end result is easily provided and is given here. The probability that a given component of the trace will be matched by the corresponding component in the distractor is

$$m = r(1 - d) + \frac{(1 - r)d}{v - 1}.$$

Since the N components are independent, the distribution of the number of matches is binomial, namely,

$$P(M_n = x) = \binom{N}{x} m^x (1 - m)^{n-x},$$

where

$$m = r(1 - d) + \frac{(1 - r)d}{v - 1}, \qquad (12)$$

$$= r - d\left(\frac{r - g}{1 - g}\right).$$

In the last line, g has been substituted for v^{-1}.

The average match score for old items (Nr) exceeds that for new items (Nm) whenever retention exceeds the chance level g. Since for most reasonable forgetting schemes, $r(t) \geq 1/v$ (e.g., Eq. 6 ff.), the average match score will usually be higher for old than for new items.

Having derived the distributions of comparison scores for old and new items, we turn now to their implications for various tasks involving recognition memory.

D. Multiple-Choice Tests

Multiple-choice tests are considered first because the decision rule is simple and obvious in these cases. The rule is to choose that alternative which yields the higher matching score to the memory trace; in case several alternatives are tied for the maximal matching score, then S is presumed to choose among these, possibly with some response bias. This rule is equivalent to the "cross-out" rule that Murdock (1963b) found accurately described Ss' operating strategy on multiple-choice tests, namely, cross out those alternatives known to be wrong and choose at random among the remaining candidates. Viewing the memory trace and the K-encoded answers as points in an N-dimensional vector space, the aforementioned decision rule is the same as one which prescribes choice of that answer-vector having the minimal distance from the memory-vector. Furthermore the rule is equivalent to one based on maximum likelihood wherein the elements are the K Bayesian probabilities that the degraded memory-vector could have arisen given that answer i ($i = 1, 2, \ldots, K$) were the initial input or correct answer. The two-alternative situation will be considered in detail first and discussion of the K-alternative situation will follow.

1. Two-Alternative Forced Choice

Suppose that of the two test items one is in fact old and one new, and that they are presented in a standard display order, such as left–right spatial positions or first–second temporal order. The S's response is designating position A_1 or A_2 as containing the old item. Let $P(A_1 \mid o_1)$ denote the probability of choice A_1 when the old item is in position 1, and $P(A_1 \mid o_2)$ the probability of choice A_1 when the old item is in position 2. These correspond to the hit rate and false alarm rate. Assume that when match scores of the two alternatives are tied, S chooses A_1 with a probability bias b that depends on the payoffs and the probability of an o_1 test trial.

Consider first the null-state interpretation. If x components are retained in the trace, then the match score for the old (correct) alternative will be x, and for the new (incorrect) alternative will be binomially distributed over the values from 0 to x. In case $M_n < x$, the correct alternative will be chosen. In case $M_n = x$, a tie results and the response bias is used. From these considerations, the following expression describes the probability of response A_1 given an o_1 trial:

$$P(A_1 \mid o_1) = \sum_{x=0}^{N} P(R = x)[1 - (1 - d)^x] + b \sum_{x=0}^{N} P(R = x)(1 - d)^x,$$

$$= 1 - (1 - b)(1 - rd)^N. \tag{13}$$

The probability of an A_1 response on an o_2 trial is just the second sum in the first line of Eq. 13, or

$$P(A_1 \mid o_2) = b(1 - rd)^N. \tag{14}$$

These probabilities depend on all four parameters, the bias, the retention, the distractor dissimilarity, and the size of the unit.

The MOC curve in this case can be obtained by eliminating b in Eqs. 13 and 14, yielding

$$P(A_1 \mid o_1) = P(A_1 \mid o_2) + 1 - (1 - rd)^N. \tag{15}$$

Equation 15 describes MOC curves of slope 1 in the unit square. The intercept increases with r, d, and N and has a direct interpretation: it is the probability that at least one of the N components is both retained in the trace and changed in the distractor. The retention and dissimilarity parameters, r and d, enter reciprocally in determining discriminability in performance; better retention can offset increases in similarity of the distractors, and vice versa.

The empirical validity of Eq. 15 is unknown since recognition memory experiments of this type, where b is manipulated, for example, by $P(o_1)$, have not yet been done. For whatever credibility it may lend, it may be mentioned that corresponding forced-choice experiments with signal detection usually lead to ROC curves of unit slope (e.g., Atkinson, Carterette, & Kinchla, 1964a; Atkinson, Bower & Crothers, 1965, Ch. 5).

Consider briefly the random-replacement interpretation of forgetting. In this case, M_n (from Eq. 12) is not constrained by the value of M_o; in fact, M_n may exceed M_o. The probabilities of an A_1 response on o_1- and o_2-type test trials are

$$P(A_1 \mid o_1) = \sum_{x=1}^{N} P(M_o = x)\, P(M_n < x)$$

$$+ b \sum_{x=0}^{N} P(M_o = x)\, P(M_n = x),$$

$$P(A_1 \mid o_2) = \sum_{x=1}^{N} P(M_n = x)\, P(M_o < x)$$

$$+ b \sum_{x=0}^{N} P(M_o = x)\, P(M_n = x). \quad (16)$$

Elimination of the bias parameter (the second sums) from these two equations yields the MOC equation relating $P(A_1 \mid o_1)$ to $P(A_1 \mid o_2)$. It has a slope of 1 and a positive intercept given by the difference between the initial sums in the foregoing two equations. This intercept is the probability that M_o exceeds M_n (leading to correct choices) minus the probability that M_n exceeds M_o (leading to errors). In general properties then, the MOC curves implied by the null-state and random-replacement ideas in this instance are the. same.

2. K-Alternative Forced Choice

In this test, $K - 1$ distractors to the correct alternative are presented; these are to be generated independently according to the usual change rule, each with parameter d. Suppose that x bits are retained so that $M_o = x$. Any distractor with an M_n score less than x is rejected. The probability that a distractor matches all x retained bits is $(1 - d)^x$. Let y_x denote the number of the $K - 1$ distractors that match all x bits; then y_x is binomially distributed with parameters

$K - 1$ and $(1 - d)^x$. If i distractors so match the correct answer, then the unbiased probability that the correct alternative is chosen is $(1 + i)^{-1}$. Thus, when x bits are retained, the probability of a correct choice is

$$P_K(C \mid R = x) = \sum_{i=0}^{K-1} \frac{P(y_x = i)}{1 + i},$$

$$= \frac{1 - [1 - (1 - d)^x]^K}{K(1 - d)^x}. \tag{17}$$

The unconditional probability of a correct choice is the sum over x of Eq. 17 multiplied by the probability that x bits are retained, namely

$$P_K(C) = \sum_{x=0}^{N} \binom{N}{x} r^x (1 - r)^{N-x} \frac{\{1 - [1 - (1 - d)^x]^K\}}{K(1 - d)^x}.$$

This sum can be simplified to the following expression.

$$P_K(C) = \frac{-1}{K} \sum_{i=1}^{K} \binom{K}{i} (-1)^i [1 - r + r(1 - d)^{i-1}]^N. \tag{18a}$$

Unfortunately, no simple closed expression exists for the latter sum. For immediate purposes of qualitative interpretations, however, the unconditional probability in Eq. 18a may be approximated by substituting the average amount retained Nr for x in Eq. 17. The approximation is

$$P_K(C) \simeq \frac{1 - [1 - (1 - d)^{Nr}]^K}{K(1 - d)^{Nr}}. \tag{18b}$$

The critical term in Eq. 18b, $(1 - d)^{Nr}$, is the probability that any given distractor will not be rejected by the Nr bits retained on average in the memory trace. It is the probability that a distractor effectively competes with the correct alternative.

In Eq. 18b, if either retention fails entirely $(r = 0)$ or the distractors are the same as the correct alternative $(d = 0)$, then choice probability is at the chance level of K^{-1}. One failing of the approximation in Eq. 18b is that it does not reduce to Eq. 13 exactly for $b = .5$ and $K = 2$, although Eq. 18a does. Another failing is its indeterminacy when $d = 1$, but in this case the basic theory and Eq. 18a imply that $P_K(C)$ will equal $1 - (K - 1/K)(1 - r)^N$. That is, retention of any one component of the trace suffices to reject all distractors generated with $d = 1$. The $P_K(C)$ is mainly dominated by the K in the denominator, decreasing like K^{-1}. Figure 13 shows several curves for the $P_K(C)$ of Eq. 18b, assuming different values of $(1 - d)^{Nr}$, the average probability that a distractor will pass the matching test and become an effective competitor. The curves decline with K and are ordered by the size of the "acceptance" probability of distractors. These predictions seem qualitatively in agreement with recognition results in which the number and dissimilarity of distractors are varied (e.g., Murdock, 1963b; Postman, 1950; Shepard & Chang, 1963).

Turning next to the random-replacement scheme for the multiple-choice task, $K - 1$ values of M_n are randomly selected from the distribution of Eq. 12 and compared to one value of M_o. The unbiased

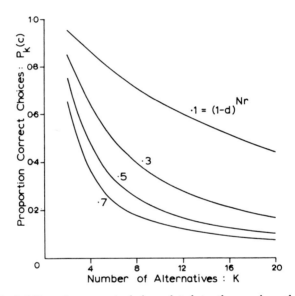

Fig. 13. Probability of a correct choice related to the number of alternatives, where $K - 1$ are distractors. The parameter is the probability that a given distractor will not be rejected by the average number of components retained in the memory tract.

probability of a correct choice is the likelihood that M_o exceeds all $K - 1$ values of M_n plus the sum over i of $(1 + i)^{-1}$ times the probability that i of the $K - 1$ values of M_n tie with M_o. The formal expression is cumbersome, of course. Computations can be substantially simplified by approximating the discrete binomial distributions by continuous normal distributions. This approximation is quite efficient for $N \geq 4$ and more so the closer the match probability (r or m) approaches $\frac{1}{2}$. Let $f_o(x)$ denote the normal density approximation to the distribution of old match scores (Eq. 9) with mean Nr and variance $Nr(1 - r)$. Similarly, let $f_n(x)$ denote the normal density approximation to the distribution of new match scores (Eq. 12) with mean Nm and variance $Nm(1-m)$. Finally, let $F_n(x)$ denote the cumulative probability that a new match score is less than x. With these concepts at hand, the probability of a correct choice in a K-alternative situation may be written as

$$P_K(C) = \int_{-\infty}^{\infty} f_o(x)(F_n(x))^{K-1}\, dx. \qquad (19)$$

This is the integral over x of the likelihood that M_o equals x, whereas all $K-1$ values of M_n are less than x. The previous terms added in the discrete case for $i+1$ ties, and so on, are dropped in the continuous approximation. Equation 19 is identical to that of TSD for cases involving unequal variances and a mean difference of $N(r-m)$ (see Swets *et al.*, 1961).

3. Ranking of K Alternatives

In ranking K alternatives consisting of one old and $K-1$ distractor items, it is supposed that S orders the alternatives strictly in the order of magnitude of their match scores vis à vis the memory trace of the old item. The dependent variable is the rank assigned to the correct alternative. Let $i = 1, \ldots, K$ denote the rank, with 1 being the "most likely correct," and let $P_K(i)$ denote the probability that S assigns the correct alternative to rank i.

Consider first the null-state interpretation of forgetting. According to this view, a distractor can at best only equal (and never exceed) the match score of the correct alternative. If j distractors tie with the correct alternative, then the latter may be assigned any rank from 1 to $j+1$. The likelihood that j distractors will tie M_o given retention of x bits in the trace is binomial with parameters $K-1$ and $(1-d)^x$. No explicit expressions for $P_K(i)$, for any i and K, have been worked out; the same mathematical problems are encountered that required the approximation to $P_K(C)$ in Eq. 18. In fact, $P_K(C)$ in Eq. 18a is just the probability that the correct alternative receives a rank of 1, or $P_K(1)$ in the present notation.

To illustrate the graded test performance of the model when it is ranking, the expressions for $K = 3$ are presented.

$$P_3(1) = 1 - (1 - rd)^N + \tfrac{1}{3}[r(1-d)^2 + 1 - r]^N,$$
$$P_3(2) = (1 - rd)^N - \tfrac{2}{3}[r(1-d)^2 + 1 - r]^N, \qquad (20)$$
$$P_3(3) = \tfrac{1}{3}[r(1-d)^2 + 1 - r]^N.$$

An important implication of these equations is that the probabilities that the correct alternative receives rank 1, 2, or 3 are graded in that order. Equalities of the three probabilities hold only when discrimination is totally absent, either because memory fails entirely $(r = 0)$ or because the test stimuli are identical $(d = 0)$. From these probabilities, one would expect above-chance performance when S is permitted a second guess after an incorrect first choice. The data available (e.g. Binford & Gettys, 1965; Bower, 1964; Brown, 1965) do show this excess information to be contained in second guesses following an error on the first choice.

In applying the random-replacement idea to ranking, the continuous normal approximations introduced before will be used. The probability that the correct alternative receives rank i may be written as

$$P_K(i) = \int_{-\infty}^{\infty} f_o(x) \binom{K-1}{i-1} [1 - F_n(x)]^{i-1} [F_n(x)]^{K-i} \, dx. \qquad (21)$$

This is the integral over x of the probability density that M_o equals x, and that $i - 1$ of the $K - 1$ values of M_n exceed x while the remaining $K - i$ values of M_n are less than x. The final terms in the integral describe the binomial distribution with parameters $K - 1$ and $1 - F_n(x)$. This is the ranking formula for TSD. When the mean value of M_o exceeds that of M_n, then the $P_K(i)$ in Eq. 21 are ordered inversely in magnitude with the rank i. This means that graded performance is predicted by this scheme.

E. SINGLE-STIMULUS TESTS

In single-stimulus tests, S is shown one item, say S_1-R_1 or S_1-R_2, and asked to make an absolute judgment regarding its familiarity to him. As noted before, this judgment may be dichotomous (accept or reject as old) or a continuous rating. Assume that the memory matching process is the same as before, and that the judgment is made on the basis of the outcome of comparing the test stimulus to the memory trace. A two-level outcome occurs for the random-replacement scheme and a three-level outcome for the null-state scheme. For the latter scheme, several alternative decision rules are plausible; for the former, only a single decision rule is plausible, so it is discussed first.

1. Random-Replacement Interpretation: MOC Curves

For the random-replacement scheme, the two-level comparison score is specified uniquely by M, the number of matches. Thus, the judgment of familiarity will be made with respect to M. Of course, M might be transformed in some way before the judgment is made. A simple transformation would take a weighted sum of the number of matches and mismatches for test stimulus i, according to

$$s_i = a \text{ (matches)} - b \text{ (mismatches)} + c,$$

$$= aM_i - b(N - M_i) + c, \tag{22}$$

$$s_i = (a + b)M_i + c'_N.$$

Here, a and b are positive weighting coefficients for matches and mismatches. However, since the M_i are binomially distributed, so will be the s_i (for new and old items); Eq. 22 simply shifts the location and spread of the M_o and M_n distributions without changing the MOC curve implied by them. Thus, decisions on the s_i axis are equivalent to decisions on the M_i axis. In fact, if $\phi(M_i)$ is any order-preserving (positive monotone) transformation of M_i, then M_i and $\phi(Mi)$ are isomorphic decision axes in the sense of implying the same MOC curve.

If M_o and M_n are approximated by continuous normal distributions, the MOC curves are the same as those derived from TSD. The MOC is obtained in theory by sliding a cutoff point C along the axis and plotting values of $P(M_o \geq C)$ against $P(M_n \geq C)$. Some examples of such MOC curves derived from the theory are shown in Figs. 14a and 14b. In Fig. 14a, $r = .7$ and the dissimilarity parameter d is varied; in Fig. 14b, $d = .3$ and the retention parameter r is varied. These MOC curves were obtained from the binomial distributions of M_o and M_n assuming that N equals 20. For such large N values, the MOC curves based on the binomial are indistinguishable from those that arise from normal density approximations. The straight line for $r = .20$ in Fig. 14b arises because $v = 5$ was assumed in plotting these graphs; and it can be shown (cf. Eq. 23 following) that $r = m$ whenever $r = 1/v = g$. The theoretical MOC curves in Figs. 14a and 14b have the same general shape as the empirical curves for recognition memory reported by Bernbach (1964), Egan (1958), Murdock (1965), and Pollack et al. (1965). With freedom to choose the three parameters N, r, and m, the theory will fit the empirical curves fairly well. Such good fits, of course, are only a minimal requirement for any reasonable theory, and do not provide a very stringent test.

In experimental practice, the MOC curve is estimated by plotting the cumulative probabilities that the rating of old versus new items exceeds rating R_i. From an n-point rating scale, $n - 1$ points of the MOC are obtained. Using normal approximations to the binomial distributions, two parameters determine, and thus can be estimated from, the empirical MOC curve (cf. Swets et al., 1961). These estimates are obtained

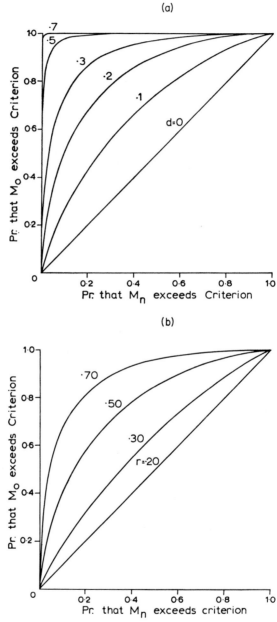

FIG. 14. Memory-operating characteristics for the random-replacement model. In (a) the dissimilarity of the distractors (new items) is varied, with discrimination increasing as d increases; in (b) the average retention of the memory trace is varied. The straight line is obtained when $r = m = g$.

by fitting a straight line to the inverse-normal transformation of the MOC points. The intercept of the straight line estimates the mean difference scaled with respect to one of the standard deviations, such as that of M_o, namely,

$$\theta_1 = \frac{E(M_o) - E(M_n)}{\sigma(M_o)} = \frac{d(r - g)}{1 - g}\left[\frac{N}{r(1 - r)}\right]^{1/2} = K\left[\frac{N}{r(1 - r)}\right]^{1/2}. \quad (23)$$

where $g = v^{-1}$ and $K = d(r - g)(1 - g)^{-1}$. This parameter corresponds to the d' measure of TSD. It determines how far the MOC curve deviates toward the upper left-hand corner at $(0, 1)$, away from the diagonal line. The slope of the fitted straight line in normal-normal coordinates is an estimate of the ratio of the standard deviations, that is,

$$\theta_2 = \frac{\sigma(M_n)}{\sigma(M_o)} = \left[\frac{m(1 - m)}{r(1 - r)}\right]^{1/2} = \left[\frac{(r - K)(1 - r + K)}{r(1 - r)}\right]^{1/2}. \quad (24)$$

This ratio controls the symmetry of the MOC curve about the antidiagonal line from $(1, 0)$ to $(0, 1)$. The MOC curve is symmetric when $\theta_2 = 1$; humped below the antidiagonal line when $\theta_2 < 1$; and humped above when $\theta_2 > 1$. Theoretically, the symmetry depends on the sign of $2K(r - .5 - .5K)$. If this sign is positive, $\theta_2 > 1$; if negative, $\theta_2 < 1$; if zero, $\theta_2 = 1$. Since K depends on the size of $r - g$, it is expected to be positive; so the MOC curve may be expected to be humped above $(\theta_2 > 1)$ when retention is high $[r > .5(1 + K)]$, and humped below when retention is low $[r < .5(1 + K)]$. If curves of one type of asymmetry were consistently obtained regardless of retention probability, such evidence would discredit this model. Obviously with three theoretical unknowns (N, r, K) and only two estimated numbers, θ_1 and θ_2, the theoretical parameters cannot be estimated uniquely on the basis of the MOC curve.

a. *The Optimal Setting of the Criterion.* The MOC curve is derived from category rating data where the category boundaries correspond in theory to different judgment criteria established by S. In the dichotomous experiment, only a single criterion is set. If S were to set his criterion so as to maximize the expected value of the trial outcomes over the experiment, it is easy to show (cf. Swets *et al.*, 1961) that the optimal criterion would be that value C where

$$\frac{P(o)\ P(M_o = C)}{P(n)\ P(M_n = C)} = \frac{W_n - L_n}{W_o - L_o}. \quad (25)$$

In Eq. 25, $P(o)$ and $P(n)$ are the probabilities that the test item is in fact old and new, W_o and W_n are the utilities of the winnings earned by a correct response to old and new items, and L_o and L_n are the utilities of the penalties incurred for an error on old and new items, respectively. The sense of Eq. 25 is that the criterion should be so set that the relative likelihood of a match score of C arising from an old versus a new item equals the payoff differential for new versus old items. If the M_i are interpreted as discrete-valued variables, then C may lie in an interval between two integers; if the continuous normal approximation to the M_i is used, then Eq. 25 determines a unique value of C. The extent to which Ss will approximate in practice this ideal criterion is not known; clearly, their criterion will vary roughly in the manner summarized by Eq. 25. At present it appears difficult to determine how well Ss approximate the criterion in Eq. 25 because the parameters of the M_o and M_n distributions must be estimated before Eq. 25 can be tested. But earlier it was mentioned that a single point or even the entire MOC curve does not suffice to estimate all the parameters of the theory.

b. Alternative Method for Setting Criterion. Parks (1966) has suggested an alternative rule by which Ss set their criterion in dichotomous (yes-no) recognition tasks. The proposal is that S sets his criterion so that his over-all probability of saying "Old" is proportional to the actual proportion of old items in the test series. Letting k denote the proportionality constant and p_o denote the proportion of old test items, the proposal is that C is so chosen as to satisfy the following equality.

$$p_o P(M_o \geq C) + (1 - p_o) P(M_n \geq C) = k p_o.$$

The proportionality constant k is presumed to vary with the payoffs. It is easily estimated, for example, by the sum of hit and false alarm rates on a $p_o = .50$ condition (any other p_o between 0 and 1 would serve as well). Given assumptions about normality and equal variances of M_o and M_n, the same data will also serve to estimate d', the scaled mean separation between M_o and M_n. Having thus estimated k and d', the relation just proposed specifies a unique C for any new p_o schedule, thereby allowing predictions of the hit rate and false alarm rate on this new p_o schedule. Parks reported several sets of recognition memory data in which such predictions were quite accurate. This supports his proposal for how S sets his criterion in the dichotomous recognition task.

2. Null-State Interpretation and Absolute Judgments

Recall that the null-state model of the memory trace yields a three-level comparison score consisting in general of M_i matches, $R_i - M_i$ mismatches, and $N - R_i$ unknowns or question marks. It will be assumed that the decision axis is formed by a linear combination of these three scores. Letting s_i denote the score for test stimuli of type i (old or new), the assumption is that the decision axis is

$$s_i = AM_i - B(R_i - M_i) - C(N - R_i) + D. \tag{26}$$

In this score, A, B, and C are weighting coefficients. For old items in memory $M_o = R_o$, so the second term vanishes, yielding

$$s_o = (A + C)M_o + D'_N. \tag{27}$$

Since M_o is binomially distributed, so will be s_o; Eq. 27 just shifts the mean and spread of M_o. For new (distractor) items $M_n \leq R_n$; thus all terms of Eq. 26 may exist and the full distribution of s_n is given by Eq. 10; that is,

$$P[s_n = (A + C)x - By + D'_N] = P(M_n = x \ \& \ R_n - M_n = y),$$

$$= \binom{N}{x}\binom{N - x}{y}[r(1 - d)]^x (rd)^y (1 - r)^{N-x-y}, \tag{28}$$

for $0 \leq x$, $y \leq N$, and $x + y \leq N$. This distribution of s_n is inconvenient to work with, and the general shape of MOC curves implied by Eqs. 27 and 28 are unknown. This question should be investigated.

A particularly simple scheme arises if, in Eq. 26, B is set equal to zero. When information about mismatches is ignored, the theory leads to a one-dimensional decision axis similar to that of TSD. That is, the decision axis is the match score and M_o and M_n have binomial distributions given by Eqs. 9 and 11, respectively. Using continuous normal approximations to the binomials, the two parameters of the MOC curve will be

$$\theta_1 = \frac{E(M_o) - E(M_n)}{\sigma(M_o)} = d\left(\frac{Nr}{1 - r}\right)^{1/2},$$

and

$$\theta_2 = \frac{\sigma(M_n)}{\sigma(M_o)} = \left[\frac{(1 - d)(1 - r + rd)}{(1 - r)}\right]^{1/2}. \tag{29}$$

The value of θ_2 determines the symmetry of the MOC curve, and it depends on the sign of the quantity $1 - r(2 - d)$. If this sign is positive, then $\mathrm{Var}(M_o)$ exceeds $\mathrm{Var}(M_n)$, $\theta_2 < 1$, and the MOC curve is humped below the antidiagonal; if the sign is negative, then $\theta_2 > 1$ and the MOC is humped above the diagonal; if the quantity is zero, then $\theta_2 = 1$ and the MOC is symmetric. When retention is less than .5, then $\theta_2 < 1$ regardless of d; when retention is greater than .5, the sign depends on d.

Some MOC curves based on the null-state model are shown in Figs. 15a and 15b, wherein d and r are separately varied. The curves are very similar to those for the random-replacement model.

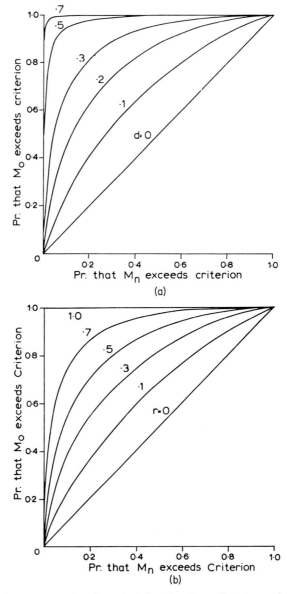

FIG. 15. Memory-operating characteristics for the null-state model. In (a) the dissimilarity of the distractors is varied; in (b) the average retention of the memory trace is varied.

3. Category Discrimination and a Posteriori Probabilities

Before leaving the topic of MOC curves based on rating data, it may be mentioned that the degree to which the various rating categories are used discriminately by S can be estimated by the a posteriori probabilities (see Norman & Wickelgren, 1965). This is the likelihood that an item assigned rating C_i is in fact old. Suppose that there are 7 categories, $N > 7$, and that S sets the six boundaries B_1, B_2, . . . , B_6, as shown in Fig. 16a. The probability of a rating of C_i given an old or

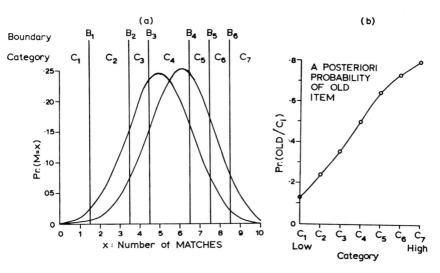

Fig. 16. (a) Possible locations of six boundaries B_i partitioning the M scores into seven categories C_i. (b) The a posteriori probability that the item is old given that a rating of C_i occurs.

new item is just the area of $f_o(x)$ or $f_n(x)$ between boundaries B_i and B_{i-1}. Letting $F_o(B_i)$ and $F_n(B_i)$ denote the cumulative probability that f_o and f_n, respectively, are less than B_i, then the equations for the a posteriori probabilities are

$$P(\text{old} \mid C_i) = \frac{F_o(B_i) - F_o(B_{i-1})}{F_o(B_i) - F_o(B_{i-1}) + F_n(B_i) - F_n(B_{i-1})} \tag{30}$$

For C_1, we interpret $B_o = -\infty$, and for C_7 we interpret B_7 as $+\infty$. Plots of Eq. 30 are shown in Fig. 16b for the boundaries in Fig. 16a. The important point about $P(\text{old} \mid C_i)$ is that in theory it increases monotonically with the rating C_i. This monotonicity property should hold so long as N exceeds the number of categories, whatever the spacing between the category boundaries.

The theoretical expression for the a posteriori probabilities is easily derived, but its relation to the observed curve (derived from category ratings) must be interpreted with caution. The likelihood that an item is old given that it yields a match score of x is

$$P(\text{old} \mid M = x) = \frac{p_o P(M_o = x)}{p_o P(M_o = x) + (1 - p_o) P(M_n = x)}.$$

For example, using the expressions for the null-state model, a logistic or S-shaped curve is implied, namely,

$$P(\text{old} \mid M = x) = (1 + Ab^x)^{-1},$$

where
$$A = (1 - p_o) \left(1 + \frac{rd}{1 - r} \right)^N p_o^{-1}$$

and $b = 1 - d(1 - r + rd)^{-1}$. The logistic increases monotonically with x, of course, thus establishing that property of the expected data. It should be noted, however, that the theoretical curve for $P(\text{old} \mid M = x)$ cannot be directly compared to the observed proportions $P(\text{old} \mid C_i)$ obtained from category ratings. It suffices to note that the independent variables differ for the two functions, the first depending on the unknown M values, and the second on unknown intervals on the M scale (that is, the category boundaries). In principle the observed curve is obtained from the theoretical curve by segmenting or chunking the M scale into n category divisions, and then plotting for each category the value of $P(\text{old } M = x)$ averaged over all x values within that interval or chunk. But unfortunately, the theory does not predict the locations of the category boundaries, so detailed fitting of the theoretical to the observed curve is precluded. Since at best it can be assumed only that the category boundaries are arranged in increasing order on the M scale, the strongest predictions possible are that the observed a posteriori probabilities (a) will have a minimum no less than $P(\text{old} \mid M = 0)$ and a maximum no greater than $P(\text{old} \mid M = N)$, and (b) will increase monotonically with the category rating C_i.

4. The Effect of Too Many Rating Categories

Mention must be made of one complication to the preceding discussion of MOC curves and a posteriori probabilities derived from rating data. Recall that M is a discrete-valued variable ranging over the integers from 0 to N. A complication can arise if the number of rating categories S is requested to use exceeds N, the number of components in the memory trace. This would occur, for example, if $N = 6$ and S were asked to use 10 rating categories, as was done in experiments by Norman and Wickelgren (1965) and Murdock (1965). If such were the case, S would have the choice of either not using some categories at all or else using several indiscriminately. Since instructions are usually interpreted by S to mean that he should use all the categories (cf. Parducci, 1965), he would tend in such a case to use several categories indiscriminately.

There are many idiosyncratic variations on how the categories could be assigned in such cases, but to show the possible effects of this excess of categories, a simple scheme will be used. Suppose that $N = 6$, S is asked to use 10 categories, and he decides to assign M scores to the categories as follows: $M = x$ is assigned uniquely to category C_{4+x}, except that $M = 1$ and $M = 0$ are assigned randomly to categories C_1 through C_5. Figures 17a and 17b show the MOC and a posteriori probability curves that can arise in this case. For these curves, retention is assumed to be generally poor ($r = .26$) and $d = .62$.

As Fig. 17a shows, the MOC curve based on such category assignments yields straight-line segments over that portion of the rating scale that is used indiscriminately. And as Fig. 17b shows, the lower five categories contain no differential information in the sense of giving different a posteriori probabilities. Both curves are similar, in fact, to several re-

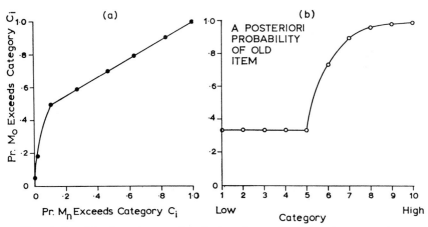

Fig. 17. Possible distortions produced when the number of rating categories (10) exceeds the number of information components in the memory trace (6). In (a) the MOC has a straight-line segment over that portion of the rating scale used indiscriminately. In (b) the aposteriori probabilities are the same for the lower five categories, which are used indiscriminately.

ported by Norman and Wickelgren (1965) for poorly retained material.

The point to be emphasized here is that knowledge or memory of an item is not infinitely divisible, but rather is limited. By simply increasing the number of rating categories, we cannot increase S's resolving power beyond certain limits; if you will, S has a definite "channel capacity" for the amount of information he can transmit about these items by using the category responses. An essentially similar conclusion has been reached about information transmitted by category responses to psychophysical stimuli (cf. Garner, 1962, pp. 87–90).

V. Related Aspects of Recall Performance

The theory will now be used to interpret several features of recall performance. The topics to be discussed in this section include the amount of information transmitted in recall, confidence ratings of the correctness of a recalled response, effects of a possible threshold for recall, the operation of proactive biases in recall, and response latencies. For all topics except the first, the discussion is sensible only in terms of the null-state interpretation of component forgetting since in these cases the model has to "be aware" of how much information has been retained and how much forgotten from a memory trace and, as mentioned earlier, the random-replacement interpretation of forgetting provides no basis for discriminating how much has been retained.

A. The Information Transmitted in Recall

Pollack (1953), Miller (1956), and others have reported data indicating that the amount of information transmitted in recall increases directly with the formal uncertainty of the ensemble of items used as memory materials. The measure of transmitted information is formally derived from the complete matrix of inputs versus outputs (see Garner, 1962, Ch. 3). For present purposes, the input will be the correct response given to the memory system, and the output will be the response recalled by the system. To distinguish these two usages of response, let A_i denote input of alternative i of some ensemble, and R_j denote recall of alternative j of that same ensemble. The data matrix consists of entries $p(A_i, R_j)$ denoting the joint proportion of study-test trials when A_i was "sent" and R_j was "received." In the following, the aim is to derive from the theory the expected information transmission, so as to compare this to some of Pollack's results. The equations used are given by Garner (1962, pp. 56–59).

The transmitted information, or contingent uncertainty, between R and A is defined as

$$U(R : A) = U(R) - U_A(R),$$ (31)

where

$$U(R) = -\sum_j p(R_j) \ln_2 p(R_j)$$

is the uncertainty in the over-all response recall distribution, and

$$U_A(R) = -\sum_i p(A_i) \sum_j p(R_j \mid A_i) \ln_2 p(R_j \mid A_i)$$

is the conditional uncertainty in R when A is known.

Suppose that 2^N response alternatives are used, with memory vectors encoded into N binary components. Let these alternatives be used as correct responses equally often, so that $p(A_i) = 2^{-N}$, and suppose that the various responses are, over-all trials, recalled equally often. Without specific response biases, $p(R_j) = 2^{-N}$. With this structure, it follows that

$$U(R) = -\sum_{j=1}^{2^N} 2^{-N} \ln 2^{-N} = N$$

and

$$U_A(R) = -\sum_{j=1}^{2^N} p(R_j \mid A) \ln p(R_j \mid A).$$ (32)

The task now is to characterize theoretically the probability distribution over the R_j given that a particular A_i is sent. With no output biases, all the distributions turn out to be the "same" in a sense to be defined now. For any given A_i sent, the 2^N possible responses to be recalled can be partitioned into $N + 1$ subsets, denoted $S_0, S_1, \ldots, S_N$, where each member of a given subset has an identical probability of occurrence. The number of response members in subset S_i is $\binom{N}{i}$, and the common response probability for each member of subset S_i is

$$p(R_i \mid A) = [.5(1 - r)]^i [.5(1 + r)]^{N-i} = c^i (1 - c)^{N-i}.$$

Derivation of these statements from the independent-loss model is lengthy and cannot be given here. The input A_i determines which responses belong to which subsets, but the over-all numerical pattern remains the same in theory regardless of the specific input. This partitioning accounts for all the recall possibilities since, summing elements of the subsets,

$$\sum_{i=0}^{N} \binom{N}{i} = 2^N.$$

Also the sum of probabilities of all recall responses is unity since

$$\sum_{i=0}^{N} \binom{N}{i} c^i (1 - c)^{N-i} = 1.$$

Consider a single element of subset S_i, and define U_i^* as the uncertainty associated with recall of this response. It is

$$U_i^* = -p \ln p = -c^i(1 - c)^{N-i}[i \ln c + (N - i) \ln (1 - c)].$$

Since uncertainty measures are additive, the uncertainty of the $\binom{N}{i}$ members of subset S_i is

$$U_i = \binom{N}{i} U_i^*.$$

Finally, the total uncertainty $U_A(R)$ may be obtained by summing U_i over the $N + 1$ subsets to obtain

$$U_A(R) = \sum_{i=0}^{N} \binom{N}{i} U_i^*,$$

$$= \sum_{i=0}^{N} \binom{N}{i} [i \ln c + (N - i) \ln (1 - c)] c^i (1 - c)^{N-i}.$$

But this sum just involves constants times the mean of a binomial distribution. Summing, substituting $c = .5(1 - r)$, and then simplifying, we obtain

$$U_A(R) = N - \frac{N}{2} [(1 - r) \ln (1 - r) + (1 + r) \ln (1 + r)].$$

Using this in Eq. 31 along with Eq. 32, we get the end result

$$U(R : A) = N(.5)[(1 - r) \ln (1 - r) + (1 + r) \ln (1 + r)],$$
$$= Nb. \tag{33}$$

The information transmitted in recall is thus proportional to N, the information contained in the ensemble of correct responses ("messages") sent into the memory system. The proportionality constant b depends on the retention parameter r and behaves sensibly; that is, when $r = 0$ and there is no remembering, responses are completely random and the information transmitted from input to output is zero ($b = 0$); when $r = 1$, the output perfectly maps onto the input and $b = 1$; for $0 < r < 1$, b takes on intermediate values.

Figure 18 shows the fit of Eq. 33 to Pollack's (1953) memory data as summarized in a figure published by Miller (1956). The graph relates the information transmitted in recall to the information characterizing the ensemble of materials used as memory items. The least-squares estimate of b was .64. The straight-line relation provides an adequate description of the data.

B. Confidence Ratings of Recalled Responses

Several investigations (e.g., Atkinson & Shiffrin, 1965; Bower & Hintzman, 1963) have indicated that Ss can give accurate confidence judgments regarding whether the response they have recalled is in fact correct. For example, Fig. 19, taken from the report by Atkinson and Shiffrin (1965), shows an exponential function relating the probability that a recalled response was correct to its confidence rating of either 1 (certain correct), 2, 3, or 4 (very uncertain). The proportion correct in this instance is approximately equal to the reciprocal of the confidence rating. The result indicates the accuracy of S's judgment of the likelihood that his response is correct.

To apply the theory to confidence ratings, begin by supposing that S retains x of N components in the memory trace and responds correctly with probability g^{N-x}. Assume that x and N are known to the decision-maker and a confidence judgment is made on the basis of these numbers. The rule transforming x and N into a confidence judgment will

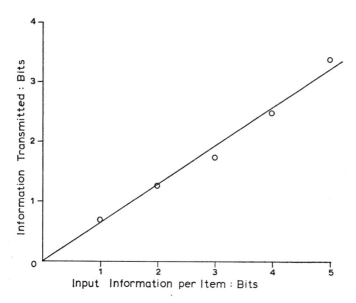

Fig. 18. The amount of information transmitted in recall as a function of the information per item of the materials to be memorized. The open dots are the observed values and the straight line is the theoretical prediction. Data from Pollack (1953) as summarized in a graph by Miller (1956).

depend on the instructed form of the rating scale for S—for example, whether high confidence is to be associated with a high or low number. For example, for the Atkinson and Shiffrin data shown in Fig. 19, the transformation would be something like $z = 1 + A(N - x)$, where z is the confidence rating and A is the weighting coefficient for the number of forgotten components.

Fɪɢ. 19. Proportion correct for those recalled responses assigned a confidence rating of 1, 2, 3, or 4. Based on Fig. 10 from Atkinson and Shiffrin (1965).

Suppose generally that the confidence rating is some monotonic function $f(x)$ of x, the amount retained. It then follows that the probability of a correct response is related to the confidence rating z according to

$$C(z) = g^{N-f^{-1}(z)} = ka^{f^{-1}(z)}.$$

Different choices of $f(x)$ then lead to different $C(z)$ functions. For example, if f is linear, then $C(z)$ is an exponential function; if f is a power function, then $C(z)$ is a Gompertz function: if f is an exponential function, then $C(z)$ is a power function. All of these are more or less reasonable $f(x)$ and $C(z)$ functions.

The important point is not the specific equations derived in this discussion, since they depend on an arbitrary assumption relating confidence judgments to x. Rather the point is that the theory provides a natural means for interpreting such confidence data and indicates, in general, the basis for the fact that Ss judgments about the correctness of a recalled response can be very accurate.

Clarke, Birdsall, and Tanner (1959) have suggested that the distributions of confidence ratings for correct versus incorrect responses can be used to construct what they called the Type-2 operating characteristic. To illustrate, suppose that S is permitted five gradations of confidence in the correctness of his answers, with 5 meaning very high and 1 very low. Then the point for rating C on the Type-2 ROC is obtained by plotting the conditional probability that the confidence ratings exceed C given that the response was correct against the similar likelihood given that the response was incorrect. From an n-point confidence scale, $n-1$ points of the Type-2 curve can be estimated. Clarke *et al.* point out that the Type-2 curve tells us how discriminating are S's confidence ratings, although they admit that theoretical interpretations of such curves are somewhat obscure.

Our reason for raising the point here is because Murdock (1966) has used this method for analyzing a memory (recall) experiment. In his study, Ss were exposed to many blocks of five S-R pairs and after each block were tested for recall on one of the five pairs and required to state their confidence in the correctness of the response they gave. The percentage of correct recalls for the five pairs varied over a large range according to a typical serial position curve. The remarkable result, however, was that the Type-2 operating characteristics were very similar for the five items despite variations in their percentage correct. Roughly speaking, the accuracy of the confidence judgments was almost independent of whether an item on the average was remembered well or ill.

Such Type-2 operating characteristics are easily derived from the multicomponent model for recall. Two conditional probability distributions are involved: the first, denoted $p(x_c)$, is the probability that x bits are retained given a correct response; the second, denoted $p(x_e)$, is the probability of retaining x bits given an incorrect recall. Letting C denote the over-all proportion of correct recalls, the expressions for these conditional distributions are

$$p(x_c) = C^{-1} P(R = x)g^{N-x},$$
$$p(x_e) = (1 - C)^{-1} P(R = x)(1 - g^{N-x}).$$

The first expression weights $P(R = x)$ by the likelihood of a correct recall given x and the second weights it by the likelihood of an error given x. These conditional distributions are skewed away from the binomial from which they derive, but they are unimodal.

If confidence boundaries are aligned in increasing order with the amount retained x, the operating characteristic can be plotted from these two conditional distributions by methods illustrated previously (cf. Figs. 12 and 16a). The foregoing expressions for the conditional distributions imply the following expression for the Type-2 operating characteristic.

$$CP(x_c \geq j) + (1 - C) P(x_e \geq j) = P(R \geq j).$$

The Type-2 curves obtained in theory are asymmetric and are similar in form to those reported by Murdock (1966). However, contrary to Murdock's finding, the theoretical Type-2 curve changes with variations in the retention parameter r. To show this, we may calculate the d' measure of the two distributions, defined here as the mean difference scaled with respect to $\sigma(x_c)$. The relevant quantities are found to be

$$E(x_c) = Nrb, \qquad \mathrm{Var}(x_c) = Nr(1 - r)gb^2,$$

$$E(x_e) = Nr(1 - C)^{-1} (1 - Cb),$$

and

$$d' = \frac{E(x_c) - E(x_e)}{\sigma(x_c)} = K(1 - C)^{-1}\sqrt{r(1 - r)},$$

where $b = (r + g - gr)^{-1}$, $C = b^{-N}$, and $K = (1 - g)(N/g)^{1/2}$. The value of d' increases with r under most circumstances (that is, N and g values); however, the increase in d' appears generally to be of small magnitude relative to the associated increases in C, the probability of correct recall. It is not implausible to suppose that the small increase expected in d' may not appear in empirical estimates provided by a single experiment, as it did not in Murdock's study. It is admittedly a weak defense of a theory to explain away results by appeal to sampling variability, but no better alternative comes to mind in this case. Rather than discard the entire theory on the basis of this one result, it would appear wiser to await replications and clearer elaboration of the conceptual significance of Type-2 operating characteristics.

C. THE RECALL THRESHOLD

We now examine some implications of supposing that a recall threshold exists. The basic idea is that S will not attempt recall unless the amount retained in the memory trace equals or exceeds some threshold number of remembered components. Such a threshold, or criterion, would be operative in recall from very large or poorly defined response ensembles, but it will be shown how a threshold can be introduced, if desired, into recall performance from smaller ensembles. Let T denote the recall threshold; it is to be conceived of as an adjustable criterion that S sets depending on motivational and payoff conditions for recall.

1. The Effect on Recall Probabilities

Since the number of bits retained R is binomial, the probability that a recall will be attempted is $P(R \geq T)$, which is the area at and above the threshold T in the tail of the binomial distribution. The unconditional probability of a correct recall is

$$C(T) = \sum_{x=T}^{N} \binom{N}{x} r^x [g(1 - r)]^{N-x},$$

and this decreases as T increases since fewer recalls will be attempted. The conditional probability of a correct response, given that recall is attempted, is $C(T)[P(R \geq T)]^{-1}$, and this increases directly with T. Several examples of the effect of the threshold upon $C(T)$ and $P(C \mid$ recall) are shown in Fig. 20. The latter relation is similar to that between probability of correct recall and confidence; that is, T measures the "internal confidence" S requires of his memory before he will overtly respond.

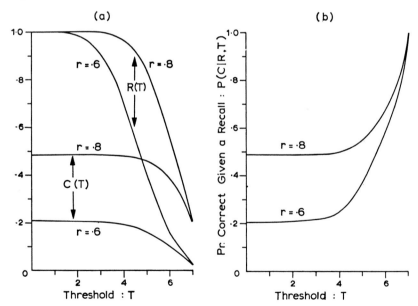

Fig. 20. Threshold effects: (a) the probability $R(T)$ that recall is attempted, and the probability $C(T)$ of a correct recall, plotted as a function of the recall threshold T; (b) the conditional probability of a correct response given that recall is attempted when the threshold is T. The parameter in each set of curves is r, the average retention probability of each component.

2. *The Optimal Criterion*

The optimal setting of the recall criterion will clearly depend on the payoffs for not responding and for responding right or wrong, and on the probability of guessing correctly given particular amounts of retention. Let W denote the utility of the payoff for a correct recall, L the utility of the payoff for an overt error, and u the utility occasioned by not responding at all. Since only the differences in these utilities are important, suppose that they have been so scaled that they all are positive numbers. If S retains x of N components and recalls by guessing on the forgotten components, the probability of a correct recall is g^{N-x}. The expected utility of the payoffs encountered for recalling when x of N bits are retained is

$$EU(\text{recall} \mid R = x) = Wg^{N-x} + L(1 - g^{N-x}),$$

$$= (W - L)g^{N-x} + L.$$

Contrariwise, if S fails to recall at all, his utility is u for certain. If S were to maximize his expected utility, he would attempt recall whenever x is such that $EU(\text{recall} \mid R = x)$ is larger than u, and otherwise would not recall. Thus the threshold should be set at that value T which satisfies the relation

$$(W - L)g^{N-T} + L = u. \tag{34}$$

Solving for T yields the value

$$T = N - \frac{\log (u - L/W - L)}{\log g}. \tag{35}$$

A value of $R \geq T$ should lead to recall; any other should not. Adoption of this recall criterion maximizes the expected utility.

If the utilities of the payoffs are strictly ordered as $W > u > L$, then $T < N$ and some recall will occur. If there is no gain in recalling (that is, $u \geq W$), then $T > N$ and no recall should occur. If u is less than L (a greater penalty for not responding than for overt errors), then Eq. 34 has no solution, but obviously in this case the optimum is at $T = 0$ and S should always attempt recall.

To briefly illustrate the relation between T and the payoffs, consider an example where $N = 4$, $g = .50$, $L = -1$ and $u = 0$; the relation between T and the payoff W for correct recalls is desired. Using Eq. 34 directly,

$$(W + 1)(.5)^{4-T} - 1 = 0,$$

or

$$W = 2^{4-T} - 1.$$

Thus, to force the threshold to be 4 (never recall) requires zero or negative payoff, $W \leq 0$; for $T = 3$ requires $W = 1$; for $T = 2$ requires $W = 3$; for $T = 1$ requires $W = 7$; and for $T = 0$ (always recall) requires $W \geq 15$. Thus, by appropriate choice of the win payoff the optimal setting of the criterion can be varied. Whether Ss in fact set their recall criterion in this optimal fashion is a question for empirical investigation; but Ss probably will approximate it to some extent.

3. Recognition of Unrecalled Items

The existence of a recall threshold implies that S frequently has information in storage that does not appear in recall. Indeed we may suppose that it is just this unused information that is tapped when S chooses the correct item on a recognition test although he was unable previously to recall it. Landauer (1962) and others have reported such results. Of course, the recognition probability for such unrecalled items will be considerably less than for recalled items, but it nonetheless can be considerably better than chance. How much better than chance it is will depend on how high was the recall threshold (which the memory trace failed to pass) and the similarity of the distractors to the correct item on the recognition test.

A particular case will illustrate the influence of the recall threshold upon subsequent recognition of unrecalled items. The probability distribution of R for unrecalled items, when the threshold is T, is given by

$$P(R = x \mid x < T) = \frac{\binom{N}{x} r^x (1 - r)^{N-x}}{\sum_{x=0}^{T-1} \binom{N}{x} r^x (1 - r)^{N-x}}, \qquad \text{for } 0 \leq x \leq T - 1.$$

Suppose the recognition test is an unbiased forced choice between two alternatives, with the distractors generated with dissimilarity d. Then the probability of a correct choice on the recognition test for unrecalled items is

$$P(T) = \sum_{x=0}^{T-1} P(R = x \mid x < T)[1 - .5(1 - d)^x],$$

$$= 1 - .5 \frac{\sum_{x=0}^{T-1} \binom{N}{x} [r(1 - d)]^x (1 - r)^{N-x}}{\sum_{x=0}^{T-1} \binom{N}{x} r^x (1 - r)^{N-x}}. \tag{36}$$

Some curves of this function are drawn in Fig. 21 for different values of the recall threshold T and different retention parameters. The other parameters are $N = 6$ and $d = .5$. The point to be established about Fig. 21 is that the recognition probability increases sharply with the threshold value that prevented recall, reaching higher asymptotes as r increases. High recall thresholds bury more information beneath them than do low thresholds, and this difference appears in recognition tests.

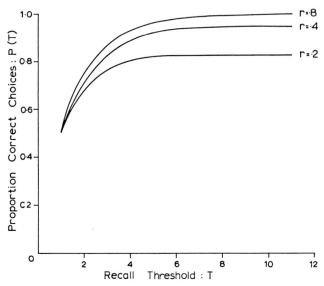

Fig. 21. Probability of correct recognition on a two-choice test for items not recalled when the recall threshold was T. The retention parameter r varies among the curves.

A further point of interest may be mentioned here. Suppose that S has some subjective measure or "awareness" of the size of R even when it is below his threshold for recall. If this subjective measure is proportional to R, then it constitutes available information helping S to predict whether he could recognize the item he is presently unable to recall. A recent experiment by Hart (1965) is relevant to this suggestion. He had his Ss estimate their "feeling of knowing" on items they could not recall. Later multiple-choice recognition tests on the unrecalled items showed that Ss chose correctly more frequently for items they felt they knew (but could not recall) than for items they felt they did not know. In terms of the theory, Ss demonstrated some ability to discriminate among R values falling below the recall threshold. In later experiments, Hart tried various means to induce Ss to try harder, or to make more guesses on the recall test; in our terms, T was lowered. This tended to cause a shrinkage in the differential recognition probability of unrecalled items that S felt he knew versus those he felt he did not know. This shrinkage is expected by the theory (cf. Eq. 36 and Fig. 21).

D. PROACTIVE BIASES IN RECALL

In the previous discussion, it was assumed that in recall the motor-output unit treated null-state components as instances requiring a guess by randomly selecting one of the v values to fill in at that component. But suppose, on the contrary, that the assignment of values to unknown (forgotten) components is biased by the past history of the memory machine. In principle, there are two ways this nonrandomness could be introduced. One way is based upon an accumulation of experience (memories) in which components within the vector become highly inter-correlated (see the later discussion of redundancy). For instance, if the values of components i and j are x_{in} and x_{jn}, then the value of component k over the past history has usually been x_{kn}. It is easy to imagine that such intercorrelations would be used in recalling from a trace in which component k has been forgotten whereas components i and j have been retained. The other method of introducing bias would have the value of a null-state component assigned according to its relative frequency of occurrence in past usage, independent of possible correlations of the value of this component to the values of other components in the encoding system. This notion is similar to the "spew" hypothesis of Underwood and Schulz (1960), where the output of a structure is seen as more or less matching the statistical distribution of inputs to it.

By either method, the bias in component-value assignments will tend to produce leveling or "commonizing" in the recall of the system. The recall of the system would tend to move in the direction of popular stereotypes, away from any uniqueness of the memory trace of the original event. This aspect of the system reminds us of the research on memory distortions carried out by Bartlett (1932) on stories, by Allport and Postman (1948) on rumors, and by Wulf (1922) and many successors on recall of outlined drawings. Riley (1962) gives a fine review of the later work.

Wulf's hypothesis was that the memory of simple outlined figures would tend over time to be autonomously reorganized in the direction of making a "good Gestalt" figure. Thus, local irregularities, small gaps, and slight asymmetries in the original figure would tend to be regularized in recall. Riley's review summarizes the evidence critical to this hypothesis, which is not generally favorable. Of the distortions that do occur in recall, Riley indicates two potent factors determining their direction: first, the way in which S encodes, describes, or labels the stimulus figure upon his initial viewing of it; and second, the proactive influence of similar common figures (popular stereotypes) upon recall of a unique figure, resulting in a commonizing in recall of the unique figure. These same factors are regarded in the present system as important in determining the type of distortions obtained in recall.

If the trace is successively recalled, with long time intervals between successive recalls, what is retained each time is some increasing fraction of the components recalled on the previous occasion. If the forgotten components are filled in by using the bias in a way consistent with the remembered components, the recalled pattern will change progressively over the recall series. Thus, some aspects of the figure may be leveled while other aspects may be "sharpened." The latter case could arise if some unique component is retained and several related forgotten components are assigned values consistent (correlated in the past) with the unique component retained.

These are only qualitative implications of the memory system, and to make them more exact would require more elaboration of the system and its input than can be pursued at present. The important point of this discussion, however, is to show that the system has the potential flexibility to deal with meaningful as well as random distortions in remembering.

E. Response Latencies in Recall

The system delivers reasonable predictions about recall latencies if some elementary hypotheses about processing times in the motor-output unit are adopted. The memory vector retrieved and fed into the motor-output unit consists of, say, x retained components and $N - x$ forgotten components with null values. Suppose that in constructing (or locating) a response to recall, the motor-output unit has to process each of these N components, and each processing takes a variable (small) amount of time. Suppose that the time taken to process a null-state component has probability density function $f_n(t)$ and that the time to process a retained (nonnull) component has density function $f_r(t)$. So much of the structure is relatively innocuous. The crucial assumption, having several important implications, is that the mean processing time is shorter for a retained component than for a null-state component, since in the latter case the motor-output unit has to make an additional (random) decision about what value to assign to the forgotten component. Two immediately obvious predictions from this scheme are that as learning proceeds and more bits are retained, the average response latencies become shorter, and that at any given stage of learning the average latency of correct recalls will be shorter than the average latency of erroneous recalls.

There are several options to filling in details of this system. One option concerns the choice of the elementary processing-time distributions. In the following we make the customary assumption (e.g., McGill, 1963) that $f_n(t)$ and $f_r(t)$ are exponential density functions with rate parameters u_n and u_r, respectively. A second option concerns whether the motor-output unit is viewed as operating by serial or parallel processing of the N-component vector. A serial device would examine the components one at a time in serial order, and the time to respond would be the sum of the separate processing times of the N components. A parallel device would examine all N components simultaneously and the response would finally be initiated only after all N components had completed processing; for such a device the time to respond is determined by the slowest of the N processes. A few features of each system will be derived using exponential density functions for the underlying distributions of f_n and f_r. These latency systems are similar to those investigated by Christie and Luce (1956). The difference is that they assumed that the unit processing time was the same for all units, whereas we must deal with a binomial mixture of two unit-processing distributions.

1. *Serial Processing*

The time to respond with a serial device is the sum of the N separate processing times. Assuming that x components are retained and $N - x$ forgotten, then the total time is the sum of x samples from $f_r(t)$ and $N - x$ samples from $f_n(t)$. Let $M_r(\theta)$ and $M_n(\theta)$ denote the moment-generating functions (mgf) for $f_r(t)$ and $f_n(t)$, respectively. Because independent random variables are being summed, the moment-generating function for the total time in this case is

$$M(\theta \mid R = x) = (M_r(\theta))^x (M_n(\theta))^{N-x}. \tag{37}$$

To obtain the unconditional moment-generating function for the total time, Eq. 37 is multiplied by the binomial probability that $R = x$ and then summed over x, yielding

$$M(\theta) = \sum_{x=0}^{N} M(\theta \mid R = x) \, P(R = x),$$

$$= [rM_r(\theta) + (1 - r)M_n(\theta)]^N. \tag{38}$$

Equation 38 expresses the mgf of the total time in terms of the mgfs of the elementary distributions and the memory parameters r and N.

An exponential density with rate u has mgf of $(1 - (\theta/u))^{-1}$. Substituting these into Eq. 38 yields

$$M(\theta) = \left[r\left(1 - \frac{\theta}{u_r}\right)^{-1} + (1 - r)\left(1 - \frac{\theta}{u_n}\right)^{-1} \right]^N. \tag{39}$$

By evaluating the first two derivatives of $M(\theta)$ at $\theta = 0$, the first two moments are found to be

$$E(t) = N[ru_r^{-1} + (1 - r)u_n^{-1}],$$

$$\text{Var}(t) = N[ru_r^{-2} + (1 - r)u_n^{-2}] + Nr(1 - r)(u_r^{-1} - u_n^{-1})^2. \tag{40}$$

The probability density function corresponding to the mgf in Eq. 39 is not presently known since inversion proves difficult. However, the mean in Eq. 40 gives the conjectured information. Since u_r^{-1} is smaller than u_n^{-1} by assumption, $E(t)$ decreases as the retention probability r increases. Also, since correct responses are more likely to occur when R is high, and high R scores produce faster response times, the conditional mean latency will be less for correct recalls than for errors.

2. Parallel Processing

The cumulative density function (cdf) is easily derived in this case, but little else can be obtained without substantial effort. Suppose there are x samples from $f_r(t)$ and $N - x$ samples from $f_n(t)$, and we seek the cdf of the maximal (largest) element of the two samples considered together. Let $F_r(t)$ and $F_n(t)$ denote the cdfs of the elementary densities $f_r(t)$ and $f_n(t)$. Since all N processes are carried out independently, when x is given the cdf of the time to the last of all N events is

$$F(t \mid R = x) = (F_r(t))^x (F_n(t))^{N-x}.$$

The unconditional cdf is obtained by multiplying the foregoing by $P(R = x)$ and summing, yielding

$$F(t) = \sum_{x=0}^{N} F(t \mid R = x) \, P(R = x),$$

$$= [rF_r(t) + (1 - r)F_n(t)]^N. \tag{41}$$

If an elementary distribution is exponential with rate u, then its cdf is $1 - e^{-ut}$. Such may be substituted into Eq. 41 using the rates u_r and u_n. Differentiating Eq. 41 then gives the probability density function for the total times.

Calculation of even the expected value of t for the cdf in Eq. 41 has proved difficult. It is known to be bounded in the interval

$$u_r^{-1} \sum_{i=1}^{N} \frac{1}{i} \leq E(t) \leq u_n^{-1} \sum_{i=1}^{N} \frac{1}{i}.$$

The upper bound is obtained when all N samples come from the slow f_n density function and the lower bound when all come from the fast f_r density. Each is the mean for a "pure death" process (see McGill, 1963), giving the time until the slowest component has completed its processing. Intuitively, $E(t)$ will be something like r times the lower bound plus $1 - r$ times the upper bound. If so, then the same qualitative implications hold for this system as for the serial processor; that is, response latency decreases as retention increases, and correct responses occur faster on average than do errors in recall.

The times just derived describe only the processing time in the motor-output unit. To these times must be added constants representing stimulus-encoding time, trace-retrieval time, plus apparatus constants. These have not been explicitly mentioned before since they are the same whether the response recalled is correct or incorrect. Differences in retention affect only the processing time of the motor-output system, which is the system under study in the foregoing discussion.

The purpose of this discussion has been to show how the general system makes contact with data concerning recall latencies. The particular assumptions used here (for example, that densities for unit processes are exponential) are to be considered as illustrative. The qualitative implications of the system agree with the findings of several investigations of latency in short-term recall (e.g., Atkinson, Hansen & Bernbach, 1964b; Izawa & Estes, 1965).

3. *Reaction Time and Memory*

For this system, the time to react to a stimulus will consist of the following components: the time for the stimulus-analyzers to encode the input stimulus, the time to retrieve the response trace to this stimulus from memory and send it to the motor-output unit, the time for the motor-output unit to decode the response vector, all plus a constant that depends on physical characteristics of the effectors used and the apparatus. To illustrate a few properties of this system, the serial processing device discussed earlier will be used. For such devices, the processing time is proportional to N, the number of components that are to be processed.

Adding the times for the components just listed, the equation for reaction time T is

$$T = (ET) + (RT) + (DT) + C,$$

where ET, RT, and DT are encoding, retrieval, and decoding times, respectively. If all three processes are carried out by serial devices, each process takes an average time proportional to N. Hence, the average reaction time may be expressed as

$$T = AN + C, \qquad (42)$$

where A is the sum of constants representing rates of encoding, retrieval, and decoding.

The relevance of this reaction-time equation to memory is that correct recall probability, when retrieval and decoding are delayed until some time after input, is also a function of N, namely,

$$P(C) = (u)^N.$$

If N is expressed in terms of the mean reaction time in Eq. 42 the relation between percentage correct recall and T is

$$P(C) = (u)^{T-C/A} = a\phi^T, \qquad (43)$$

where $0 < \phi \leq 1$. Hence, the longer the average time required to identify (name or react to) an incoming stimulus, the poorer should be recall of such units in a memory experiment.

Experiments supporting this conjecture have been reported by Mackworth (1963; 1964). She used different types of input materials, including letters, digits, colors, and geometric shapes, and measured average "reading time" (time for S to rapidly name the members of a series) as well as immediate memory span for each set of materials. It seems reasonable to suppose that the average time to read off k symbols of a given set is proportional to the average reaction time to the individual symbols. Hence, the time taken to read a fixed number of symbols is proportional to T in Eq. 43. Consistent with Eq. 43, Mackworth found that the probability of correct recall of elements of a string of k symbols decreased with their average reading time. Mackworth measured memory span, and the complexities of that measure preclude an exact relation to the $P(C)$ in Eq. 43, which is the retention probability for an individual symbol with a particular lag between its input and recall. However, expected span would clearly be a monotone increasing function of $P(C)$. Hence, Mackworth's data, showing longer memory spans for materials that could be read faster, provides qualitative confirmation of Eq. 43.

In passing, it may be mentioned that the reaction time Eq. 42 is consistent with results reported by Hick (1952), Hyman (1953), and several others investigating multiple-choice reaction time. The finding is that mean T increases with the number of equiprobable response alternatives K approximately as $\log K$. To apply the theory to this situation, assume that N is chosen by S so as to provide a reasonably efficient coding of the K alternative stimuli and responses. That is, K is to be expressed as

$$K = Bv^{N_k}$$

where B is a proportionality constant representing the efficiency of the coding system, $v = g^{-1}$, and N_k is selected by S. For any coding system employing N_k components, the mean reaction time T_k in Eq. 42 is a linear function of N_k. Hence K may be written as

$$K = Bv^{(T_k-C)/A}$$

By taking logarithms of both sides, we find that

$$T_k = b + b' \log K,$$

where b and b' are nonnegative constants. Thus, mean reaction time with K alternatives increases linearly with the logarithm of K. This is approximately the result reported by Hick and Hyman.

The relation just derived follows only if it is likely that the conditions force S to modify his "natural" coding system to deal more efficiently with the set of stimuli and responses actually used in the experiment. Natural coding system here refers to that used and overlearned throughout S's past history in dealing with the entire ensemble of events of which the experimental presentation-set may compose only a small fraction.

VI. Repetition and Redundancy in Trace Formation

A. Alternative Representations of Trace Redundancy

Various information theorists have pointed out that sensory events contain much more information than is required to specify the initiating stimulus uniquely from a known ensemble. In fact, the sensory transmission system is often described (e.g., Attneave, 1954; Barlow, 1959) as a filter that makes use of redundancies to discard part of the sensory inflow of information. And Brown (1959) has suggested that a memory trace of an event will, at least initially, contain some of this redundant or excess information. To the extent that redundant information is stored in a memory trace, accurate recall of that trace will be facilitated.

Within the proposed system there are basically two ways to represent information redundancy in an individual memory trace. Possibly both operate together, but they will be presented as independent methods.

One representation of redundancy supposes that more information components are encoded and stored in the memory trace than are minimally required to select the initiating event from its appropriate ensemble. This will be called the *excess components* idea. The other idea is to represent redundancy in terms of intercorrelations among the component values of a trace; thus, if components i and j are highly intercorrelated, then retention of either one will suffice for recall of both. This will be called the *intercorrelation* idea.

1. *Excess Components*

Here it is supposed that S initially encodes an event and stores it in memory in terms of $N + K$ information components, although in fact only N components are required to reconstruct or select the item from the test ensemble. The number of excess components K is then a measure of the initial redundancy of this individual trace. For simplicity in the following, it is assumed that the $N + K$ components are "interchangeable" in the sense of providing equal information toward selection of the correct response.

If the components are forgotten at the same independent rate, the number of components retained is distributed as

$$P(R = x) = \binom{N + K}{x} r^x (1 - r)^{N+K-x}. \tag{44}$$

One crucial influence of the excess components is that they modify the response rule. Using the null-state interpretation of forgetting, suppose that if N or more components are retained, then the null states are ignored in constructing a response. This means that recall will be perfect until more than K components have been forgotten. Formally, the response function when x components are retained is

$$P(C \mid R = x) = \begin{cases} 1 & \text{if } N \leq x \leq N + K, \\ g^{N-x} & \text{if } 0 \leq x \leq N. \end{cases}$$

Using this response function in conjunction with the retention distribution in Eq. 44, we find that the expression for the unconditional probability of a correct recall is

$$P(C) = \sum_{x=0}^{N+K} P(C \mid R = x)\, P(R = x),$$

$$= \sum_{x=0}^{N} \binom{N + K}{x} r^x (1 - r)^{N+K-x} g^{N-x}$$

$$+ \sum_{x=N+1}^{N+K} \binom{N + K}{x} r^x (1 - r)^{N+K-x}. \tag{45}$$

This expression cannot be appreciably simplified. The second sum is the probability above N in the upper tail of the binomial. The first sum can be rearranged so that it is a constant times one minus the tail of a different binomial distribution.

Some graphs of Eq. 45 are shown in Fig. 22a and 22b. The theoretical

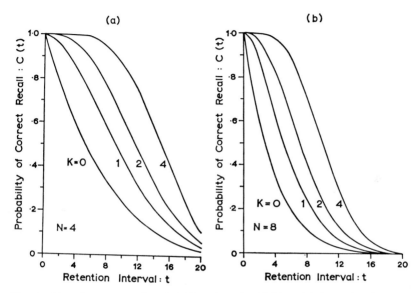

Fɪɢ. 22. The effect on recall probability of storing K bits of information in excess of the N required to specify the response. The $r(t)$ function is a linear descent to zero at $t = 20$. The curves differ in N and K.

values for the curves are $r(t) = 1 - .04t$, $g = .25$, $N = 4$ or 8, and the parameter varying between curves is K, the redundancy or number of excess bits. The average recall probability increases with K. Of more interest is the fact that as K increases, the recall function approaches an S-shaped curve. The initial plateau of the S curve becomes longer as K increases, since K is the number of excess components that can be forgotten before recall begins to fail. The S curves in Fig. 22a and 22b are of interest because such curves have been obtained in several investigations of short-term memory (e.g., Hellyer, 1962; Peterson, 1963).

No detailed discussion of the implications of this redundancy scheme for performance on recognition tests will be given. It is clear that an increase in K will improve recognition generally. This is obvious from Eq. 29, which shows that the scaled mean difference between the match scores of old and new items increases directly with the square root of N, the number of components in the memory trace.

2. *Intercorrelated Components*

An alternative representation of redundancy supposes that some of the components in the memory trace are highly intercorrelated. Two components are said to be correlated (or redundant) if knowledge of the value of one component enables one to predict the value of the other. The advantage of this correlation for memory performance is that both components can be produced if either one is retained. Whereas two independent components have probability r^2 of being both retained, two perfectly correlated components have probability $1 - (1 - r)^2 = 2r - r^2$ of being both retained. Thus, the presence of intercorrelations among the components will increase the amount recalled, and to an extent depending on the number and pattern of intercorrelations.

Although this general approach appears attractive, we confess an inability to develop it to any great extent. There are several decisions to be made in any formal representation. These include the questions of whether nonunity correlations are to be permitted; whether all correlations are symmetric (go in both directions); whether multiple or only pairwise correlations of elements are admitted; and so forth. Even the simplest assumptions—pairwise, symmetric correlations of unity—encounter the basic problem of how to represent conveniently the over-all pattern of intercorrelations existing in a trace. Recall performance will depend on this precise pattern, and a simple index, such as the number or proportion of component pairs correlated, has no unique relationship to recall. The analytic problem is of a kind encountered in graph theory (Harary, Norman, & Cartwright, 1965), where k intercorrelation lines are distributed at random among N points. The connectivity or clustering of the points determines recall when some (random) components are forgotten. Particular cases (patterns) can be enumerated and consequences worked out, but this is neither an elegant nor illuminating attack upon the general problem. The most general statement possible is that such intercorrelations will increase the average retention probability r in some complicated way depending on the amount of redundancy present.

Adding to this analytic difficulty, a possible conceptual difficulty of this approach may be mentioned. An intercorrelation between two components would seem itself to require a memory trace. That is, the correlation represents knowledge derived (remembered) from past experience with a particular population of stimuli, and it seems that such correlative knowledge should be explained rather than taken as a primitive postulate in a theory of the memory trace. Possibly this objection can be sidestepped by supposing that the correlative knowledge does not "reside" in the individual memory trace, but rather is added to it (at forgotten components) when it passes through the motor-output unit. This unit could bias the assignment of values to forgotten components of a trace by reference to the statistical distribution of that component value in other traces it holds in its memory store.

B. The Effects of Repetition

It is well known that repeated study trials on an item increase its retention. To mention just one illustration, in an experiment by Hellyer (1962), S saw either 1, 2, 4, or 8 successive presentations of a verbal item before he began an interpolated activity filling a retention interval of from 3 to 27 sec. Hellyer found that repetitions slowed the rate of decay of recall probability and increased the apparent asymptote of the recall curves. A similar effect can be produced by increasing the duration of a single study interval on an item before interpolated activity begins.

Such effects may be interpreted in the system by supposing that repetitions increase the effective retention parameter. Two general hypotheses may be suggested to account for this increase. One is that repetitions increase the internal redundancy of the memory trace, the notion just discussed. Such increases in internal redundancy would elevate the average retention. However, as was noted before, no specific consequences have been derived from this type of hypothesis.

An alternative and more tractable hypothesis supposes that repetitions or increases in study time result in *multiplexing* of the trace, by which we mean that the whole trace or components of it are copied several times in the memory banks. Suppose that the initial study time or the number of uninterrupted presentations (as in Hellyer's experiment) is such as to allow z copies of a given component to be recorded. If all components are so copied, then the trace system would be best represented as a z by N matrix with identical rows. Assume that the several copies of a component fade out randomly and independently with retention probability r, and that a component's value will be assigned correctly if any one copy of it is retained; then, the more copies made, the greater the probability that at least one is retained, leading to the assignment of the correct value to that component. Let p_z denote the probability that a component represented by z copies is retained; it is

$$p_z = 1 - (1 - r)^z. \tag{46}$$

There are several schemes for generating the z's. A simple and general scheme that contains several special cases of interest is the following binomial process: during the study time available after input of an

N-bit vector, the system makes k attempts to copy each component, each attempt producing a successful copy with probability c. Thus, the total copies available at the end of this period is one (the original input vector) plus $z - 1$ excess copies, where $z - 1$ is binomially distributed with parameters k and c.

The N components will probably be copied differing numbers of times, and for each z value Eq. 46 gives the retention probability of that component. By a derivation too lengthy to include here it may be proved that the distribution of the number of retained components is given by

$$P(R = x)$$
$$= \binom{N}{x}\left[\sum_{z-1=0}^{k} P(E = z - 1)p_z\right]^x\left[\sum_{z-1=0}^{k}(E = z - 1)(1 - p_z)\right]^{N-x} \quad (47)$$

In this expression, $P(E = z - 1)$ is the binomial probability that $z - 1$ excess copies are made, where $z - 1$ ranges in value from 0 to k. The terms inside the two brackets sum to one. Since each forgotten component is guessed correctly with probability g, the recall probability will be

$$P(C) = \sum_{x=0}^{N} g^{N-x} P(R = x),$$

$$= \{\Sigma P(E = z - 1)[g + (1 - g)p_z]\}^N. \quad (48)$$

Substituting into Eq. 48 the expression for p_z and the binomial probabilities and simplifying, we obtain the desired final result, namely,

$$P(C) = [1 - (1 - r)(1 - g)(1 - cr)^k]^N. \quad (49)$$

The parameters k and c represent the rate and efficiency, respectively, of the multiplexing system. If either $k = 0$ or $c = 0$, then no excess copies are made and Eq. 49 reduces to the former expression for recall of a single input copy.

For $c = 1$, each component is copied exactly k times and the forgetting probability is $(1 - r)^{k+1}$. Some hypothetical curves of Eq. 49 with $c = 1$ are shown in Fig. 23a and 23b. In Fig. 23a, the retention parameter $r(t)$ is assumed to decline linearly to zero according to $1 - .04t$. The other parameters are $N = 6$, $g = .25$, and the amount of multiplexing k increases from 0 to 4 across the various curves. The quantity k would be expected to increase with study time or with the number of uninterrupted presentations. The recall functions in Fig. 23a increase with k and become positively accelerated with longer initial plateaus the larger k is. The functions in Fig. 23a asymptote near zero because the $r(t)$

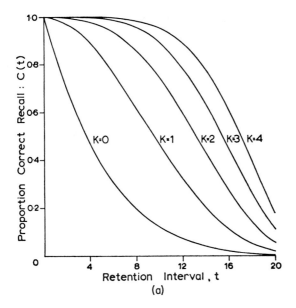

(a)

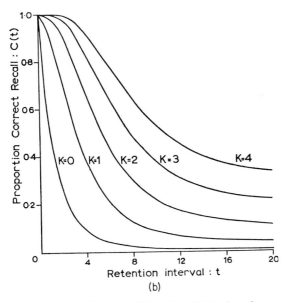

(b)

Fig. 23. The effect on recall probability of multiplexing the trace K times. In (a) the retention function is $1 - .04t$, asymptoting at zero when $t = 25$; in (b) the retention function is $.25 + .75(.8)^t$.

function is assumed to go to zero. Figure 23b shows curves for an $r(t)$ function that has a nonzero asymptote; that is, $r(t) = .25 + .75(.80)^t$. In this case, the asymptote of $C(t)$ increases in approximately exponential fashion with k, the amount of multiplexing. These curves are similar to those reported by Hellyer.

If this scheme were applied to spaced repetitions of an item with interpolated activity between successive presentations, then k would be assumed to be proportional to the number of presentations and c would be interpreted as the probability that a given copy is retained between successive presentations. In fact, c would either equal r or be some simple function of r. By making k (the number of trials) large enough, the probability of correct recall in Eq. 49 can be brought arbitrarily close to unity. Such a system also provides an interpretation of the beneficial effect on retention of overtraining provided after response probability has reached unity. If the intertrial interval is relatively short, then r will be high, and a few copies will suffice to keep short-term recall probability near unity. However, the benefit of extra copies induced by overtraining would appear upon testing at a long retention interval, when r has a lower value.

This multiplexing scheme has been developed because it is a simple way for a memory device to improve its component memory (p_z) without changing the reliability of its single memory units (the copies). That is, by multiplexing and pooling many unreliable memory units, the entire system can become very reliable. The simplest alternative to this scheme is to suppose that the parameters of the single unit change in a direct manner with repetition. For example, in Eq. 6 for $r(t)$, it would be supposed that the asymptote J increases directly with repetition. But auxiliary assumptions would be required to describe such changes.

VIII. Perceptual Recognition of Degraded Stimuli

A. Similarity of Memory to Recognition of Noisy Stimuli

In the following, some possible contacts between this model of memory and results concerning immediate perceptual recognition of stimuli embedded in noise backgrounds are suggested. In the foregoing discussion of memory it was assumed that the input event was faithfully encoded and then was degraded by forgetting. Metaphorically, forgetting introduces "noise" into delayed recognition of the original faithful recording of the input event. A model of perceptual recognition in noise may perhaps be found by analogous reasoning: a particular signal or message is sent over a noisy channel to the N stimulus-analyzers to be encoded, but while in the channel the signal is degraded to various degrees so that what is finally encoded by S bears only a probabilistic resemblance to what was sent.

Several alternative models can be developed along these lines; a promising one, based on a random-replacement interpretation of degradation, will be illustrated. It will be supposed that when sent over a perfectly noiseless channel the signals are encoded into N (say, binary) components. The set of analyzers that actually perform these conversions can, of course, be quite complicated. For example, in speech recognition the input signal is actually a time-varying frequency-amplitude spectrum of very complex nature, and it is a difficult (and as yet, only partially solved) scientific problem to design a system of analyzers that can extract from a population of such signals the relevant phonetic parameters and exclude various irrelevant aspects (such as the speed and intonation of speech). However, available models of speech recognition (e.g., Forgie & Forgie, 1959; Halle & Stevens, 1964; Stevens, 1960) do propose a set of analyzers whose function is to perform by one or another means this conversion of a continuous time-varying spectrum into a discrete listing of the phonetic parameters of the input. Our concern here is not with the nature of the analyzers themselves, but rather with their joint output, considered as a list or vector of N binary components.

When a signal is sent over a noisy channel and then encoded, it will be assumed that some components are faithfully (correctly) recorded, whereas other components are distorted and incorrectly recorded. Let h denote the probability that the component value sent is encoded correctly, and $1 - h$ the probability that the encoded value differs from the one sent. If the encoded representation were to be matched component by component to the item sent (or rather, to what would be the encoding if $h = 1$ and there were no distortions due to noise), the number of matches would be binomially distributed with parameters N and h. In this system, h is a measure of the fidelity of the channel, decreasing as the signal-to-noise ratio is decreased. The h parameter plays the same role as r, the retention parameter of the memory system. The reasonable bounds on h are $.5 \leq h \leq 1$, the lower bound being obtained only when the signal : noise ratio is so low that no information whatever is conveyed by the signal.

Three aspects of this system will be considered. The first concerns the effect on recognition accuracy of the number of alternative signals, wherein selection of a response is from the entire ensemble of possible inputs. The second concerns the effect of experimentally restricting the set of response alternatives after the signal has been received; this restriction has a large effect on the percentage of correct choices (recognition accuracy) almost independently of the size of the ensemble of signals that could have been sent. Finally, the information transmitted by the response will be related to the information contained in the stimulus ensemble. The following discussion will be clarified if a particular experimental situation is taken as a referent. These purposes are served by an experiment on auditory recognition by Pollack (1959): an S with earphones monitors a channel into which white (Gaussian) noise is continuously introduced and at discrete intervals, or trials, a warning signal comes on and is shortly followed by a spondee (a two-syllable word like "backbone," "doorstep," or "hothouse") spoken into the channel by E. The S then selects what he thought he heard from a list of alternatives provided to him.

B. Recognition Accuracy and the Size of the S-R Ensemble

Consider first the accuracy of immediate recognition responses when selection occurs from all possible alternatives. Suppose there are 2^N possible input signals and that E has provided S with a unique identification function relating the correct response to the signal sent, that is, there are 2^N response alternatives. The identification function is in fact a list of paired associates in memory, relating the encoded stimulus to its correct response. The stimulus is encoded by the perceptual system as a vector of N binary components; call this the image for convenient reference. The image may be distorted somewhat from the correct representation of the signal sent. The likelihood that the image is completely accurate is h^N. If it is inaccurate in one or more details and the response alternative corresponding to this inaccurate image is available on the choice test, then it will be chosen and the response identifying the signal sent will not be chosen. Hence the probability of a correct response from an ensemble of 2^N alternatives is just

$$C_N = h^N. \tag{50}$$

Thus, accuracy of recognition declines with the number of alternatives, and declines at a rate depending on the signal-to-noise ratio. This is true; the decline in accuracy with increasing numbers of alternative signals is one of the best-documented facts about perceptual recognition (e.g., Garner, 1962).

C. Restrictions on the Response Set

Consider first the effect of restricting the response alternatives to just two. That is, one of 2^N possible signals is sent, but on the test S is to choose only between this one and a second (distractor), chosen by E at random from the remaining $2^N - 1$ alternatives. It is supposed that the image is matched component by component to the two test alternatives. That alternative yielding the higher match score is chosen; if the match scores of the two alternatives tie, then a random choice is made. The match score of the image to the signal sent is binomially distributed with parameters N and h. The match score of the image to the distractor depends on the particular distractor chosen as well as the number of changes occurring in the image. Depending on these variables, some distractors may be always chosen in preference to the correct alternative, others never, and still others half the time. For the Pollack (1959) experiment, the distractor used was selected at random from the remaining $2^N - 1$ alternatives, and the percentage of correct choices was averaged over the various tests.

To show the calculations from the theory for this experiment, suppose there are four alternative signals $(N = 2)$ and the binary states of each component are labeled 1 and 2. Suppose that the signal sent is (1 1). The four possible images are shown in the first column of Table II; the second column gives the probabilities that each of these images is received when (1 1) is sent. The entries in the next three columns represent the probability that the correct alternative (1 1) is chosen, given that the test distractor is as indicated at the top of the column. Tests involving these three distractors occur equally often, with probability $\frac{1}{3}$. The final column gives the average probability of a correct choice given that a particular image is received, assuming that the distractor is randomly chosen.

TABLE II

PROBABILITY OF CORRECT CHOICE RELATED TO
IMAGE RECEIVED AND TEST DISTRACTOR[a]

Image received	Probability	Test distractor			Average probability of correct choice
		1 2	2 1	2 2	
1 1	h^2	1	1	1	1
1 2	$h(1 - h)$	0	1	.5	.5
2 1	$h(1 - h)$	1	0	.5	.5
2 2	$(1 - h)^2$	0	0	0	0

[a] The correct coding of the stimulus sent is 1 1.

For this case, the over-all probability of a correct choice is seen to be

$$p_2 = h^2 + h(1 - h).5 + h(1 - h).5 = h.$$

Now h is also the probability of correct recognition when the stimulus ensemble consists of only two possibilities. Hence, we conclude that when the response set is restricted to two members, the probability of correct recognition is the same (namely, h) whether the stimulus sent is one of 2 or 4 possibilities.

It would be convenient if this result held for any N, but this unfortunately is not the case. By enumerating the possibilities in tables similar to Table II but for $N = 3$ and $N = 4$, the probability of a correct choice on the binary test is found to be

$$p_3 = \frac{6h}{7} + \frac{h^2}{7} (3 - 2h),$$

$$p_4 = \frac{2h}{3} + \frac{h^2}{3} (3 - 2h).$$

Cases for higher N's have not been enumerated because of the excessive labor involved, so no basis for inducing a general formula is provided.

The important feature to be noticed is that p_3 and p_4 give values that are practically equal to h in the range from .5 to 1.0. They are greater than h by only about 2 or 3 percentage points even at their maximal discrepancy. In practice, such small differences cannot be discriminated experimentally. Hence, to a first approximation we have

$$p_N \simeq h. \tag{51}$$

That is, the probability of a correct identification on a two-choice test is approximately independent of the size of the stimulus ensemble.

Tests of Eqs. 50 and 51 from Pollack's (1959) data are shown in Figs. 24a and 24b for two different signal : noise ratios (different h values). The graph for signal-to-noise (S/N) $= -15$ db is the average of two such conditions run by Pollack (panels 1 and 3 of his Fig. 7). The open circles are the proportion of correct identifications on two-choice tests; their relation to the size of the possible message set is well described by the horizontal line at the mean value. This is the implication of Eq. 51. The black circles depict the proportion correct when the choice is from all 2^N alternatives, and these are well described by the h^N function of Eq. 49. The h parameter was estimated from the mean value of the two-choice points (the horizontal lines in Figs. 24a and 24b); as expected, the h estimate is lower for the lower signal : noise ratio.

The case just discussed involved restriction of test responses to only two of the 2^N possible response alternatives. To a first approximation, the percentage of correct choices was found to be h, relatively independent of the size of the ensemble of possible stimuli. But suppose that 2^i alternatives are present on the test, corresponding to the message sent plus $2^i - 1$ distractors chosen at random from the remaining $2^N - 1$ possibilities. Although exact equations have not been worked

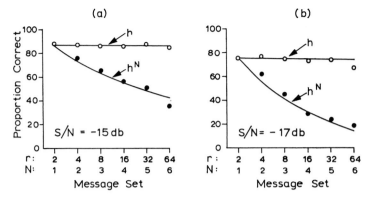

FIG. 24. Probability of correct identification related to the size of the message set r (2, 4, . . . , 64) or the number of bits in the message set $N(1, 2, . . . , 6)$. In each case, the horizontal line and open dots represent the predicted and observed values, respectively, when the choice is restricted to two alternatives. The decreasing curve and black dots are the predicted and observed values when choice is from all 2^N alternatives. The signal : noise ratio (S/N) is indicated on the two figures. Graphs adapted from Fig. 7 of Pollack (1959).

out for the general case, it seems intuitively clear that the theoretical percentage correct will be of the approximate magnitude of h^i when the choice set is restricted to 2^i alternatives. This relation is exact for $N = 2$. The fit of this approximation equation to some of Pollack's (1959) data is shown in Fig. 25. The size of the message set varied from 2 to 64 and, independently, the size of the set of response alternatives was varied from 2 up to the number of possible messages. In general, accuracy decreases with the size of the response set but, holding constant the size of the response set, accuracy is relatively unaffected by the size of the message set. The mean values for each response set (drawn from the middle panel of Pollack's Fig. 2) are indicated by horizontal lines. The value predicted for 2^i response alternatives comes from the formula h^i. With the exception of the 64-response data, the function h^i provides a satisfactory fit to the mean accuracy scores. Pollack mentioned that half of the words in the 64 set were new and relatively unfamiliar to the Ss, so performance to this full set may not be completely comparable to that obtained from subsets of the other (familiar) set of 32 words. That is, in Fig. 25 the experimental points for the 64-message set are usually lower than predicted.

From Pollack's results in Figs. 24 and 25, it is clear that the largest effect is that due to the number of alternative responses and not the number of possible stimuli. In discussing these and similar data, Garner writes:

But one thing does seem very certain, and this is that some sort of matching operation goes on, and that the larger the number of categories to be matched against, the greater the possibility for error or apparently faulty perception. We can say that the perceptual confusions among the set of possible responses increase as we increase the number of such responses, and that these confusions contribute to errors of recognition. We are, in other words, not dealing with relations between stimuli which are present and those which are not—rather we are dealing with relations between responses all of which are present and must be chosen from (Garner, 1962, p. 38).

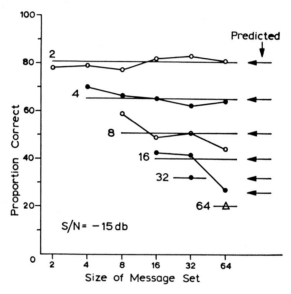

Fig. 25. Probability of correct identification related to the size of the message set. The number beside each horizontal line is the number of response alternatives on the choice test and the flat line is the average of the values for that size of response set. The arrows indicate the predictions of the mean values. Graph adapted from the middle panel of Fig. 2 of Pollack (1959).

The model presented here seems to be an appropriate formalization of Garner's ideas. That is, S is viewed as matching his image (percept) to the image appropriate to each of the available response categories, and selecting that response category whose image best matches the percept. And as the number of response alternatives increases, there is increasing likelihood that some distractor will match the percept better than does the correct alternative.

D. Information Transmitted by Immediate Recognition

To complete this discussion, the theoretical relation between input information and transmitted information will be derived, where choice is from the entire ensemble of 2^N alternatives. The derivation follows lines similar to that for the memory model with the exception that a null-state interpretation of degradation was used there, whereas the present development uses a random-replacement interpretation. As before, when any stimulus A_i is sent, the 2^N response alternatives may be partitioned into $N + 1$ subsets, S_i for $i = 0, 1, \ldots, N$, where each of the $\binom{N}{i}$ members of S_i have the identical probability $h^i(1 - h)^{N-i}$. Following through the derivations as before, we find the contingent uncertainty to be

$$U(R : A) = N[1 - h \ln h - (1 - h) \ln (1 - h)],$$
$$= NJ. \tag{52}$$

Thus transmitted information is proportional to the input information. The coefficient J depends on the fidelity parameter h in a reasonable way: when $h = 1$, $J = 1$; when h attains its lower bound of .5, $J = 0$; and for intermediate values of h between .5 and 1, J is likewise of intermediate value between 0 and 1. To check the validity of Eq. 52, a study on the intelligibility of words spoken over a noisy channel may be considered. Using intelligibility (recognition accuracy) data from an experiment by Miller, Heise, and Lichten (1951), Garner (1962, p. 80) calculated contingent uncertainty scores and plotted them against information input (the logarithm of the size of the message set). The information transmitted increased linearly up to some limit, then leveled off. The slope of the line was lower with lower signal : noise ratios (lower h values in Eq. 52). The leveling off of the functions may be interpreted as reflecting a limiting channel capacity—in our terms, a limiting value of N, N_{max}—for this particular kind of ensemble. Equation 52 implies that the asymptote of transmitted information is JN_{max}, which is lower for smaller signal : noise ratios. This was true for the data plotted by Garner.

The preceding discussion illustrates how the general multicomponent model can be developed to deal with perceptual recognition experiments. The particular model presented requires considerably more exploration and thought. For example, one of its obvious failings is that it cannot handle confidence-rating data when all 2^N alternatives are available on the test. Moreover, it supposes that each feature (component) is recorded faithfully with the same probability h, thus leading to symmetric confusion matrices, but this is a gross approximation sufficient only for certain limited purposes. However, more elaborate alternative models can doubtless be developed along the same general lines. The purpose in carrying through this analysis was to show that a multicomponent theory views memorial and perceptual distortions caused by noise as being characterized by similar principles.

This paper began with the assumption that memory and perception are closely related. The relation of memory to perception was illustrated by Conrad's (1964) experiments showing that recall confusions are similar in manner and distribution to perceptual confusions about a noisy (degraded) stimulus. In this section of the paper, we have returned to and developed that point by treating perceptual recognition in theoretical terms that were first used to describe memory.

VIII. Commentary

A. Related Work

A variety of consequences of the multicomponent representation has now been explored; the general idea seems indeed to have a diversity of implications. To place the theory in somewhat better perspective, recent similar or related work will be briefly discussed. Essentially the same hypothesis about memory has been proposed and researched by Bregman (cf. Bregman & Chambers, 1966). In his experiments, done with explicitly "dimensionalized" geometric figures varying in shape, color, and so on, Ss were shown particular patterns and told to remember the attribute-values conjoined in each pattern. Later tests of memory via reconstruction of the patterns, with additional guesses following errors, established presumptive evidence that S remembered and forgot single attributes of a pattern in an all-or-none manner. Memory test performance to a multidimensional pattern appeared graded, of course, because it was composed of several all-or-none units that could be remembered independently.

The relation of the multicomponent theory to the "one-element" model for associative learning (Bower, 1961a; Estes, 1961) is clear: the one-element model is a special case (namely, $N = 1$) of the multicomponent model. From a survey of research on the one-element model (Bower, 1964), it is clear that it fits learning data best only when there are two response alternatives. With more than two response alternatives, the data typically show "increments," or partial learning that goes on before a learning criterion is reached. Such a pattern of results is the outcome expected by the multicomponent theory.

The multicomponent theory is formally similar to models used by Crothers (1964) and Bower (1961b; 1964) to handle what they called "compound response learning." To illustrate, in one experiment by Bower (1964), Ss learned a 20-item paired-associate list in which the four response members were A1, A2, B1, and B2, consisting of two ordered binary components. Backward learning curves and other analyses of precriterion responses gave presumptive evidence that the (A, B) and (1, 2) components were separately learned and retained in an all-or-none fashion. The precriterion increments in the probability of the correct compound response were apparently related to the learning of one response component before the other. In that experiment, the encoding of the response ensemble was sufficiently obvious to permit a direct decomposition of the total response into elementary components that were being learned and retained in all all-or-none fashion. As for the general multicomponent model, the probability of a correct compound response was equal to the product of the probabilities that the separate components were recalled correctly.

The relation of the multicomponent theory to the stimulus fluctuation theory of forgetting proposed by Estes (1955) and modified by Izawa and Estes (1965) may be noted. Estes proposed that the N_s stimulus elements available when a reinforcement occurs become conditioned to the reinforced response, but during a retention interval any element in the available set may be interchanged with one of the N'_s elements that was not present at the time of the reinforcement. If these intruding elements from the N'_s set have not previously been conditioned, they will tend to lead to the correct response with only a "guessing" probability g. Letting $r(t)$ denote the probability that an element available at the time of reinforcement is still available at time t later, we can write the probability of the correct response at time t as

$$C(t) = r(t) + g(1 - r(t)).$$ (53)

This is obtained by averaging over the N_s elements currently available, of which a number $N_s r(t)$ were available and conditioned at the time of the previous reinforcement and a number $N_s(1 - r(t))$ were unavailable then but have intruded during the retention interval.

The $C(t)$ function in Eq. 53 is the same as the $u(t)$ function of the multicomponent theory in Eq. 7. Moreover, the $r(t)$ function that Estes (1955) derived from stimulus fluctuation theory is the same as Eq. 6 derived earlier from different considerations. Whereas' stimulus sampling theory expresses $C(t)$ as an *average* over the N_s available elements of their probabilities of correct association, the multicomponent theory expresses $C(t)$ as the *product* of the N component probabilities. The response rules are the same when $N = 1$, but not otherwise. For the multicomponent theory, g is a constant and $r(t)$ increases with successive repetitions; for the fluctuation theory, $r(t)$ is a constant and the effective g in Eq. 53 increases with repetitions. But since $r(t)$ and g enter Eq. 53 in exactly the same way, these alternate descriptions are indistinguishable mathematically. Thus it would appear that predictions of *average* response probabilities for the multicomponent theory with $N = 1$ can be made identical to those of fluctuation theory. They will differ, however, in predictions of conditional probabilities of responses over several tests (that is, the RTT paradigm of Estes, 1960).

Finally, the multicomponent model may be compared to the "continuous-strength" model for recognition memory suggested by Egan (1958), Murdock (1965), Norman and Wickelgren (1965), Parks (1966), and developed more formally and extensively in a paper by Wickelgren and Norman (1966). The common approach of these investigators has been to apply to recognition memory essentially the same concepts as used in TSD, the theory of signal detectability (Swets *et al.*, 1961). In terms of specific assumptions, it is supposed that putting an item into the memory store establishes a trace characterized by a numerical "strength" that decreases with forgetting. Whenever this trace is retrieved on a test trial, its strength is subjected to random variations due to noise in the system. These noise variations are presumed to be continuous and the strengths of memory traces so varied are presumed to be normally distributed. Moreover, it is presumed that new items, not previously put into memory, nonetheless have, because of stimulus generalization, a memory trace existing at a certain strength, and these are assumed to be normally distributed. Finally, the average separation between the distributions of strengths of new and old items is assumed to vary with the amount of retention and the dissimilarity of the two sets of items. By such postulations, TSD is carried over for application to recognition memory—specifically, to account for MOC curves.

The main difference between the continuous-strength approach and the theory proposed here is one of strategy. The continuous-strength theory simply postulates a particular decision structure (corresponding to TSD) for recognition memory. In contrast, the multicomponent theory provides a rationale for deriving this decision structure from more elementary assumptions. Because of their wider range of application, these elementary assumptions obtain evidential support from other sources besides the shape of MOC curves for recognition. Also, in providing a rationale for TSD in recognition memory, the multicomponent theory eliminates some of the awkward or inelegant postulations required by the continuous-strength approach.

B. SOME CRITICISMS

In developing a theory, the alternate role of a critic of the developments must also be adopted. There are a variety of criticisms that can be lodged against the specific theory outlined here. Many concern the incompleteness inherent in any initial formulation, or indicate the need to admit further complications to the first simple representation explored (for example, the components may be forgotten at different rates or have different guessing probabilities). Incompleteness or even ambiguity in certain respects is to be expected here since, as mentioned at the outset, the proposal deals with really only one aspect of the memory problem, namely, representing a possible logical structure of the memory trace. But to say that a preliminary theory is incomplete, idealized, or even occasionally ambiguous is not to say that it is dead wrong, but rather than it requires further thought and elaboration. Of the several incompletenesses of the present formulation, two particularly vexing ones will be discussed.

The first concerns the parameter N, the number of information components encoded by the stimulus-analyzers and stored in memory. For a given population of stimulus materials (such as nonsense syllables), what approximately is N? Is N a fixed constant determined by the past perceptual learning of S in dealing with materials of a given type, or is it an elastic variable that can be adjusted on the spot to efficiently encode the limited ensemble of materials that happen to be selected for experimental use? For a given item in a constant ensemble, does N remain stable or does it change systematically over the course of learning? What, if any, difference in N exists for encoding integrated versus nonintegrated strings of symbols (such as DOG versus OGD)?

Such questions cannot be answered now with any definiteness or assurance. They are really questions concerning the operation of the pattern-recognition machine in Fig. 1—whether and how its operations can be modified by knowledge in the memory stores. It will be recalled that at the outset of this paper the operation of the pattern recognizer was left deliberately vague; this vagueness is necessary because no completely adequate model of pattern recognition is known (cf. Gyr, Brown, Willey, & Zivan, 1966, and Uhr, 1965, for a review). The only assumption made about the pattern recognizer was that its output could be characterized as a list of features or information components.

More specific assumptions about its operation can be explored for their consequences in the memory system. For example, a likely assumption is that the pattern recognizer groups or segregates the experimental stimulus materials into elementary functional units (such as alphabetic letters of a trigram), which it treats as the units for encoding and identification. According to this view, presentation of the visual trigram OGD would initiate three separate identification and storage operations. An O would be identified in position 1, leading to storage of the trace (P1, C(O)), where C(O) would be a list of the distinctive phonetic features of saying O to oneself; G and D would be similarly identified and stored in association with markers for positions 2 and 3. Thus, the compound trace system storing OGD would be represented as [(P1, C(O)), (P2, C(G)), (P3, C(D))], where C(O), C(G), and C(D) are vectors describing phonetic features of saying O, G, and D, respectively.

The problem with this naive approach is that the elementary units for storage will change as the material goes from nonsense to meaningful words. Thus, the grapheme DOG, although initially identified in terms of its letters, would be given a secondary phonetic coding, the distinctive features of saying "DAHG," and this shorter secondary code would be stored. Because this code is shorter than the three-letter code, forgetting is less and learning faster. This view agrees with the finding (Underwood & Schulz, 1960) that the pronounceability of a trigram corelates highly with its rate of being learned. However, this view simply assumes that the encoding units change without really explaining why. It does not dispose of the *deus* in the perceptual *machina*. The conceptual problem remains and probably will continue thus until more substantial progress is made on theories of pattern recognition.

C. POSSIBLE RETRIEVAL SCHEMES

1. *Stimulus Confusion Errors*

The second incompleteness of the theory that requires mention regards retrieval of the memory trace. The derivations have proceeded on the naive view that the retrieval mechanism (whatever it is) operates perfectly, always pulling out the appropriate memory trace for recall or comparison to a test stimulus. Moreover, only cued retention tests (such as paired associates with distinctive stimulus members) have been explicitly considered. These simplifications were introduced into the initial formulation to see what types of retention data were explicable in part by assumptions only about the structure of the memory trace. A more complicated but realistic retrieval mechanism for cued retention tests can be elaborated (cf. Bower, 1964). Given storage of the pairs S_1-R_1, S_2-R_2, and so on in terms of compound encoded vectors (CS_1, CR_1), (CS_2, CR_2), and so on, retrieval of the trace to test stimulus S_i is determined by a "similarity" principle. That is, the test stimulus S_i, encoded as CS_i, is matched successively or in parallel to the encoded stimulus members of the traces located in the relevant parts of the storage system. That trace whose encoded stimulus best matches CS_i is retrieved (provided the match score exceeds a criterion) and the response vector of this trace is sent to the motor-output unit. Suppose that this were indeed the retrieval process. If the information in the encoded stimulus CS_1 is perfectly retained, then stimulus S_1 always will retrieve the (CS_1, CR_1) trace. But retrieval errors will occur if the components of the stimulus members are themselves subject to forgetting. In this case, the encoded test stimulus CS_1 would be compared to the degraded forms of CS_1, CS_2, . . . , and a better match may possibly result for an incorrect stimulus. In such cases, the trace that S retrieves would lead to a response best described as a "stimulus generalization" error. The over-all retrieval process when K traces are effective in the relevant memory bank (through which the search is done) is identical in form to the process described in Section IV,D, for multiple-choice recognition tests with K alternatives, except that in the latter case the comparison and matching operations are carried out on the response rather than the stimulus members of the pairs. The likelihood of retrieving the correct trace will vary with (a) the number of alternative traces to be compared, (b) the rate of forgetting stimulus information, and (c) the similarity of the encoded representations of the various stimuli. Let $w(K, t)$ denote the probability that the correct trace, as degraded at time t, is retrieved out of a store holding K traces, and let q denote the probability of correct recall when a trace with an incorrect stimulus member is erroneously retrieved; then the modified recall probability would be

$$C'(t) = w(K, t)C(t) + [1 - w(K, t)]q \qquad (54)$$

In this expression, $C(t)$ is the previous value calculated when retrieval was assumed to be perfect (that is, Eq. 4), $w(K, t)$ is the retrieval probability, comparable to Eq. 18, and $C'(t)$ is the correct response probability when retrieval effects are considered.

Two immediate consequences of Eq. 54 may be mentioned. First, over the course of a short-term memory experiment, K will begin at or near zero and increase as more items are introduced, arriving at some stable asymptote dependent on the net forgetting rate; correspondingly, the correct retrieval probability $w(K, t)$ will decline, and so will $C'(t)$ as a consequence. Thus, immediate recall of the first item in the experiment should be highest, with progressively poorer immediate recall of the second, third, and so forth, item in the series, until K reaches its equilibrium value. Such changes in $C'(t)$ over the experiment have been reported by Keppel and Underwood (1962) and Loess (1964). Second, an abrupt change, in mid-experiment, in the nature of the items to be remembered (as, to a different set of letters) will increase the effective d in Eq. 18, causing an abrupt increase in the correct retrieval probability in Eq. 54. Thus, the first few items after the shift in materials would have higher retrieval and recall probabilities. This effect has been reported by Wickens, Born, and Allen (1963). Both of these effects were interpreted by the experimenters in terms of the accumulation and release of proactive interference; they are interpreted here in terms of changes in the probability of retrieving the correct memory trace. Although the vocabulary used differs, there is in fact very little difference between the two interpretations (proactive interference versus retrieval difficulty) in this instance.

2. Item Recognition

This simple matching scheme may be applied also to the item recognition task introduced by Shepard and Teghtsoonian (1961). In their experiment, S viewed a long series of items (three-digit numbers), half of which were repetitions of items presented earlier. For each item S judged whether or not it had occurred previously (was "old"). Conceived in terms of the present model, the successive items I_1, I_2, . . . , would be encoded and stored as compound vector traces, denoted CI_1, CI_2, . . . , and these traces would decay as previously assumed. For S to decide whether a freshly presented item is old or new, it would be supposed that its encoded representation would be matched successively to the CI_j's in the memory store, and the comparator would report back the maximal match score so obtained. The probability distribution of the maximal match scores would be difficult to derive, but its mean value would clearly be greater for old than for new items, and would also be greater the larger the number of active traces in the store. To make a decision, the maximal match score obtained in a given scan of the memory store would be compared to an adjustable criterion, with the "old" decision arising if the score exceeded the criterion. Such a system would show a decline in recognition rate with time (or intervening items) since a target item was put into it. The system would also show an increasing false alarm rate as the experimental series proceeds, since the more traces in the memory store to be compared to the current (new) item, the greater on the average will be the maximal match score obtained, thus leading to a (false) positive judgment with appreciable probability. Such were the results reported by Shepard and Teghtsoonian (1961). Furthermore, once steady state has been reached (that is, once the average number of effective traces reaches equilibrium), if an item is falsely called old upon its first presentation, it is more likely to be called old on its second presentation than would be an item called new on its first presentation. That is, the similarities between the former item and other items in the store that caused it to be called old upon its first presentation are likely to persist and boost the probability of its being called old again the second time, even though its encoded representation in memory may be forgotten. Such conditional effects of the first response upon the second response to an item have been found in experiments by Melton (cited in Bernbach, 1964). Detailed mathematical investigations of the proposals for this task have not been undertaken, but simulation by Monte Carlo runs could easily be carried through.

3. Noncued Recall

Finally, consider noncued recall tasks, which can be either restricted or unrestricted in order of recall. Examples of the first would be a digit-span test or the single-trigram recall procedure of Peterson and Peterson (1959); an example of the second is free verbal recall of a list of words (Murdock, 1962), where the words may be recalled in any order. Since many different lists and tests are given successively in the typical experiment, it is clear that in retrieval S must be guided by temporal cues, essentially selecting only items from the most recent list. It is clear that Ss can make such temporal discriminations with fair accuracy (see Yntema & Trask, 1963), but the present theory must be expanded before it can account for such phenomena.

Such temporal discrimination among memory traces could be carried out by several methods. One approach would assume that an "arrival-time tag" of some sort is one of the pieces of information stored along with a memory trace. Temporal discrimination among traces would then use only the information provided by this time-tag component. An alternative hypothesis is to suppose that the storage system itself has an inherent means for keeping track of the order of arrival of incoming information.

An example of a simple device that preserves temporal order of item arrivals is a "push-down list," wherein a newly arriving item is placed on the top of a memory list and is the first encountered. A familiar analog is the spring-loaded plate holder commonly found in cafeterias, which operates on a "last in, first out" principle. Consider using such a device to represent storage of temporal recency and spatial-order information in the Peterson and Peterson (1959) task. The S is presented with a series of nonsense trigrams, counting backward and recalling each one after it is presented. The representation would consist in three push-down lists, one for each of the three letter positions. The notion of using a separate list to store the letter in each position is essentially the hypothesis Conrad (1965) proposed to deal with confusions and misorderings in serial recall from short-term memory. To illustrate these concepts, suppose the first four trigrams presented (and then recalled) are XYZ, FLP, DUX, and MLS, in that order. Then the push-down list in memory after presentation of the fourth trigram could be represented as in the accompanying tabular array.

	Letter position		
	1	2	3
Top (last in):	C(M)	C(L)	C(S)
	C(D)	C(U)	C(X)
	C(F)	C(L)	C(P)
	C(X)	C(Y)	C(Z)
	.	.	.
	.	.	.

The C(X) notation denotes the encoded vector of information corresponding to X. Since forgetting degrades the memory vectors to an extent depending on their time in memory, the vectors lower down on the list will usually contain less information than those higher up.

Recall of the most recently presented item is provided by retrieving the top "plate" of the stack. Its integrity for aiding recall would depend on how much degradation of this vector had occurred during the counting-backward activity that followed its input. Such a device could also perform in recalling items at a constant lag back in time; for example, upon presentation of item n, store it, then recall item $n - j$. The processor would simply count down j deep into the stack, retrieve that vector, and output whatever was possible (if anything) on the basis of its degraded information. Recall accuracy, of course, would decline rapidly with the lag j and with the size (complexity) of the experimental items. Slight errors in the count backward would produce recall of items adjacent to the one j back. Such results were reported by Mackworth (1959) and have been repeated in unpublished experiments by the author. Furthermore, if two previously presented items were shown on a test trial, the device could do a creditable job at recognizing which item had occurred more recently in the past. This could be done by its noting the location on the list at which each test item obtained its maximal match score, and then choosing as more recent that one higher up on the list. Forgetting, causing loss of information, would introduce error into locating the items in question, and more so the more components forgotten. Thus, accuracy of judging the more recent of two items would decline as the items grew older in memory. Such results seem qualitatively in line with those reported by Yntema and Trask (1963) for recency discrimination. Again, Monte

Carlo simulations would be needed to investigate further implications of the system.

Turning finally to free recall, the evident complexities of that process prevents any simple hypotheses. Various potent factors have been identified in determining whether a word will be recalled and in what order; such factors include list length, study time, serial position, inter-item associations, word clustering, and approximation of word order to English text. Moreover, over successive practice trials in recalling the same list of words, it is clear that *S*s subjectively organize the items into idiosyncratic patterns, presumably using clusters that facilitate carrying out a systematic search through memory that will retrieve most of the items (Tulving, 1962). We are unable to suggest any sensible retrieval scheme that, in conjunction with the present memory system, would begin to make contact with the complexities of free recall data. The obvious candidate—simply sampling traces from the store and "dumping" them out in recall—gives a gross approximation for some purposes (such as serial position curves, cf. Atkinson & Shiffrin, 1965; Bower, 1964), but it ignores too many of the potent determinants of such recall.

Acknowledgment

Many of the themes developed in this paper were stimulated by attendance at a 1965 summer institute on Mathematical Models for Memory at Cambridge, Massachusetts, sponsored by The Center for Advanced Study in the Behavioral Sciences. The author wishes to express his gratitude to the conference participants for their encouragement and stimulation.

References

Allport, G. W., & Postman, L. *The psychology of rumor.* New York: Holt, 1948.

Atkinson, R. C., Bower, G. H., & Crothers, E. J. *An introduction to mathematical learning theory.* New York: Wiley, 1965.

Atkinson, R. C., Carterette, E. C., & Kinchla, R. A. The effect of information feedback upon psychophysical judgments. *Psychon., Sci.,* 1964, **1**, 83–84 (a)

Atkinson, R. C., Hansen, D. N., & Bernbach, H. A. Short-term memory with young children. *Psychon. Sci.,* 1964, **1**, 255–256. (b)

Atkinson, R. C., & Shiffrin, R. M. Mathematical models for memory and learning. Tech. Rep. No. 79, Institute for Mathematical Studies in the Social Sciences, Stanford Univer., 1965.

Attneave, F. Some informational aspects of visual perception. *Psychol. Rev.,* 1954, **61**, 183–193.

Barlow, H. B. Sensory mechanisms, the reduction of redundancy, and intelligence. In *Mechanization of thought processes.* Vol. II. London: H. M. Stationery Office, 1959. Pp. 535–561.

Bartlett, F. C. *Remembering.* London and New York: Cambridge Univer. Press, 1932.

Bernbach, H. A. A decision and forgetting model for recognition memory. Tech. Rep. No. 64–4, Univer. of Michigan, Math. Psychol. Program, Ann Arbor, 1964.

Binford, J. R., & Gettys, C. Nonstationarity in paired-associate learning as indicated by a second guess procedure. *J. math. Psychol.,* 1965, **2,** 190–195.

Bower, G. H. Application of a model to paired associate learning. *Psychometrika,* 1961, **26,** 255–280. (a)

Bower, G. H. Application of the all-or-none conditioning model to the learning of compound responses. Tech Rep. No. 37, Institute for Mathematical Studies in the Social Sciences, Stanford Univer., 1961. (b)

Bower, G. H. Notes on a descriptive theory of memory. Paper read at second conference on learning, remembering, and forgetting. Princeton, 1964. To appear in D. P. Kimble (Ed.), *Learning, remembering, and forgetting,* Vol. 2. New York: N.Y. Acad. Sci., in press.

Bower, G. H., & Hintzman, D. L. Confidence ratings during paired associate learning. Unpublished manuscript, 1963.

Bregman, A. S., & Chambers, D. W. All-or-none learning of attributes. *J. exp. Psychol.,* 1966, **71,** 785–793.

Broadbent, D. E. A mechanical model for human attention and immediate memory. *Psychol. Rev.,* 1957, **64,** 205–215.

Broadbent, D. E. *Perception and communication.* Oxford: Pergamon Press, 1958.

Brown, J. Information, redundancy and decay of the memory trace. In *The mechanisation of thought processes.* Natl. Phys. Lab. Sympos. No. 10. London: H. M. Stationery Office, 1959.

Brown, J. A comparison of recognition and recall by a multiple-response method. *J. verb. Learn. verb. Behav.,* 1965, **4,** 401–408.

Christie, L. S., & Luce, R. D. Decision structure and time relations in simple choice behavior. *Bull. math. Biophysics,* 1956, **18,** 89–112.

Clarke, F. R., Birdsall, T. G., & Tanner, W. P., Jr. Two types of ROC curves and definition of parameters. *J. acoust. Soc. Amer.,* 1959, **31,** 629–630.

Conrad, R. Acoustic confusions in immediate memory. *Brit. J. Psychol.,* 1964, **55,** 75–84.

Conrad, R. Order errors in immediate recall of sequences. *J. verb. Learn. verb. Behav.,* 1965, **4,** 161–169.

Craik, K. J. *The nature of explanation.* London and New York: Cambridge Univer. Press, 1943.

Crossman, E. R. F. W. Information processes in human skill. *Brit. Med. Bull.,* 1964, **20,** 32–37. (Issue on *Exp. Psychol.*)

Crothers, E. J. All-or-none learning with compound responses. In R. C. Atkinson (Ed.), *Studies in mathematical psychology.* Stanford: Stanford Univer. Press, 1964. Pp. 95–115.

Deutsch, J. A. *The structural basis of behavior.* Chicago: Univer. of Chicago Press, 1960.

Egan, J. P. Recognition memory and the operating characteristic. AFCRC TN 58–51, AD 152650, Hearing and Communication Laboratory, Indiana Univer., June, 1958.

Estes, W. K. Statistical theory of spontaneous recovery and regression. *Psychol. Rev.,* 1955, **62,** 145–154.

Estes, W. K. Learning theory and the new mental chemistry. *Psychol. Rev.,* 1960, **67,** 207–223.

Estes, W. K. New developments in statistical behavior theory: Differential tests of axioms for associative learning. *Psychometrika,* 1961, **26,** 73–84.

Forgie, J. W., & Forgie, C. D. Results obtained from an auditory-recognition computer program. *J. acoust. Soc. Amer.,* 1959, **31,** 1480–1484.

Garner, W. R. *Uncertainty and structure as psychological concepts.* New York: Wiley, 1962.

Gomulicki, B. R. The development and present status of the trace theory of memory. *Brit. J. Psychol. Monogr.,* 1953, Suppl. 29, 1–94.

Gyr, J. W., Brown, J. S., Willey, R., & Zivan, A. Computer simulation and psychological theories of perception. *Psychol. Bull.,* 1966, **65,** 174–192.

Halle, M., & Stevens, K. N. Speech recognition: A model and a program for research. In J. A. Foder and J. J. Katz (Eds.), *The structure of language.* Englewood Cliffs, New Jersey: Prentice-Hall, 1964. Pp. 604–612.

Harary, F., Norman, R. Z., & Cartwright, D. *Structural models: An introduction to the theory of directed graphs.* New York: Wiley, 1965.

Hart, J. T. Memory and the feeling-of-knowing experience. *J. educ. Psychol.* 1965, **56,** 208–216.

Hellyer, S. Frequency of stimulus presentation and short-term decrement in recall. *J. exp. Psychol.,* 1962, **64,** 650.

Hick, W. E. On the rate of gain of information. *Quart. J. exp. Psychol.,* 1952, **4,** 11–26.

Hyman, R. Stimulus information as a determinant of reaction time. *J. exp. Psychol.,* 1953, **45,** 188–196.

Izawa, C., & Estes, W. K. Reinforcement-test sequences in paired-associate learning. Tech. Rep. No. 76, Psychol. Ser. Institute for Mathematical Studies in the Social Sciences, Stanford Univer., 1965.

Keppel, G. Problems of method in the study of short-term memory. *Psychol. Bull.,* 1965, **63,** 1–13.

Keppel, G., & Underwood, B. J. Proactive inhibition in short-term retention of single items. *J. verb. Learn. verb. Behav.,* 1962, **3,** 153–161.

Landauer, T. K. Two states of paired-associate learning. *Psychol. Rep.,* 1962, **11,** 387–389.

Loess, H. Proactive inhibition in short-term memory. *J. verb. Learn. verb Behav.,* 1964, **3,** 362–368.

McGill, W. J. Stochastic latency mechanisms. In R. D. Luce, R. R. Bush, & E. Galanter (Eds.), *Handbook of mathematical psychology.* Vol. I. New York: Wiley, 1963. Pp. 309–360.

MacKay, D. M. Towards an information-flow model of human behavior. *Brit. J. Psychol.,* 1956, **47,** 30–43.

Mackworth, J. F. Paced memorizing in a continuous task. *J. exp. Psychol.,* 1959, **58,** 206–211.

Mackworth, J. F. The relation between the visual image and post-perceptual immediate memory. *J. verb. Learn. verb. Behav.,* 1963, **2,** 75–85.

Mackworth, J. F. Interference and decay in short-term memory. *J. verb. Learn. verb. Behav.,* 1964, **3,** 300–308.

Melton, A. W. Implications of short-term memory for a general theory of memory. *J. verb. Learn. verb. Behav.,* 1963, **2,** 1–21.

Miller, G. A. The magical number seven, plus or minus two: Some limits on our capacity for processing information. *Psychol. Rev.,* 1956, **63,** 81–97.

Miller, G. A., Galanter, E., & Pribram, K. *Plans and the structure of behavior.* New York: Holt, 1960.

Miller, G. A., Heise, G. A., & Lichten, W. The intelligibility of speech as a function of the context of the test materials. *J. exp. Psychol.,* 1951, **41,** 329–335.

Murdock, B. B., Jr. The serial position effect in free recall. *J. exp. Psychol.*, 1962, **64**, 482–488.

Murdock, B. B., Jr. Short-term retention of single paired associates. *J. exp. Psychol.*, 1963, **65**, 433–443. (a)

Murdock, B. B., Jr. An analysis of the recognition process. In C. N. Cofer & B. S. Musgrave (Eds.), *Verbal behavior and learning*. New York: McGraw-Hill, 1963. Pp. 10–22. (b)

Murdock, B. B., Jr. Signal-detection theory and short-term memory. *J. exp. Psychol.*, 1965, **70**, 443–447.

Murdock, B. B. Jr. The criterion problem in short-term memory. *J. exp. Psychol.*, 1966, **72**, 317–324.

Nilsson, N. J. *Learning machines*. New York: McGraw-Hill, 1965.

Norman, D. A., & Wickelgren, W. A. Short-term recognition memory for single digits and pairs of digits. *J. exp. Psychol.*, 1965, **70**, 479–489.

Parducci, A. Category judgment: A range-frequency model. *Psychol. Rev.*, 1965, **72**, 497–418.

Parks, T. E. Signal-detectability theory of recognition-memory performance. *Psychol. Rev.*, 1966, **73**, 44–58.

Peterson, L. R. Immediate memory: Data and theory. In C. N. Cofer & B. S. Musgrave (Eds.), *Verbal behavior and learning*. New York: McGraw-Hill, 1963. Pp. 336–353.

Peterson, L. R., & Peterson, M. Short-term retention of individual verbal items. *J. exp. Psychol.*, 1959, **58**, 193–198.

Peterson, L. R., & Peterson, M. J. Minimal paired-associate learning. *J. exp. Psychol.*, 1962, **63**, 521–527.

Pollack, I. Assimilation of sequentially encoded information. *Amer. J. Psychol.*, 1953, **66**, 421–435.

Pollack, I. Message uncertainty and message reception. *J. acoust. Soc. Amer.*, 1959, **31**, 1500–1508.

Pollack, I., Norman, D. A., & Galanter, E. An efficient non-parametric analysis of recognition memory. *Psychon. Sci.*, 1965, **1**, 327–328.

Posner, M. I. Immediate memory in sequential tasks. *Psychol. Bull.*, 1963, **60**, 333–349.

Postman, L. Choice behavior and the process of recognition. *Amer. J. Psychol.*, 1950, **63**, 576–583.

Postman, L. Short-term memory and incidental learning. In A. W. Melton (Ed.), *Categories of human learning*. New York: Academic Press, 1964.

Riley, D. A. Memory for form. In L. Postman (Ed.) *Psychology in the making: Histories of selected research problems*. New York: Knopf, 1962. Pp. 402–465.

Shepard, R. N., & Chang, J. J. Forced-choice tests of recognition memory under steady-state conditions. *J. verb. Learn. verb. Behav.*, 1963, **2**, 93–101.

Shepard, R. N., & Teghtsoonian, M. Retention of information under conditions approaching a steady-state. *J. exp. Psychol.*, 1961, **62**, 302–309.

Stevens, K. N. Toward a model for speech recognition. *J. acoust. Soc. Amer.*, 1960, **32**, 47–51.

Swets, J. A., Tanner, W. P., Jr. & Birdsall, T. G. Decision processes in perception. *Psychol. Rev.*, 1961, **68**, 301–340.

Tulving, E. Subjective organization in free recall of "unrelated" words. *Psychol. Rev.*, 1962, **69**, 344–354.

Uhr, L. Pattern recognition computers as models for form perception. *Psychol. Bull.*, 1963, **60**, 40–73.

Uhr, L. (Ed.) *Pattern recognition: Theory, experiment, computer simulations, and dynamic models of form perception and discovery.* New York: Wiley, 1965.

Underwood, B. J., & Schulz, R. W. *Meaningfulness and verbal learning.* Philadelphia: Lippincott, 1960.

Waugh, N. C., & Norman, D. A. Primary memory. *Psychol. Rev.*, 1965, **72**, 89:104.

Wickelgren, W. A., & Norman, D. A. Strength models and serial position in short-term recognition memory. *J. math. Psychol.*, 1966, **3**, 316–347.

Wickens, D. D., Born, D. G., & Allen, C. K. Proactive inhibition and item similarity in short-term memory. *J. verb. Learn. verb. Behav.*, 1963, **2**, 440:445.

Wulf, F. Uber die Veränderung von Vorstellungen. *Psych. Forsch.*, 1922, **1**, 333:373.

Yntema, D. B., & Trask, F. P. Recall as a search process. *J. verb. Learn. verb Behav.*, 1963, **2**, 65–74.

ORGANIZATION AND MEMORY[1]

George Mandler

UNIVERSITY OF CALIFORNIA, SAN DIEGO

LA JOLLA, CALIFORNIA

Organization has had a somewhat tattered reputation in the history of modern psychology. Many theorists have talked about it and others have viewed it from a distance—with either affection or alarm—but

[1] The initial experiment on free categorization was presented at the meetings of the Psychonomic Society at Niagara Falls, Ontario, in October, 1964, where the hypothesis of the category–recall relation was outlined. The general model and some preliminary data were discussed at a Conference on the Quantification of Meaning in January, 1965, at La Jolla, California, and at a colloquium at the Center for Cognitive Studies, Harvard University, in February, 1965. The major experimental data were presented at the meeting of the Psychonomic Society in Chicago, Illinois, in October, 1965.

The preparation of this chapter and the research reported in it were supported by Grant GB 810 from the National Science Foundation, Grant APA 64 from the National Research Council, Canada, and a travel grant from the University of California, San Diego.

most of the efforts either to develop a generally acceptable class of variables that might be called organizational or to find a single acceptable measure of organization have tended to be short-lived. This has been particularly true in the area of memory and learning. Perception has fared somewhat better, although the efforts of the Gestalt psychologists to translate perceptual concepts into other areas of psychology have often produced a feeling of failure and ennui. Too often the concept of organization has become the rallying cry for theoretical battles; as a result, its connotation frequently has become emotional rather than scientific. There is no doubt that less strictly drawn battle lines in the 1920's, 1930's, and 1940's might have produced more fruitful attention to organizational concepts on either side of the fence.

Organizational variables have assumed a new importance in human psychology, particularly in the area of human memory. The present paper will be devoted to the illustration of three general principles: First, memory and organization are not only correlated, but organization is a necessary condition for memory. Second, the organization of, and hence memory for, verbal material is hierarchical, with words organized in successively higher-order categories. Third, the storage capacity within any one category or within any level of categories is limited.

Memory as used here comprises memory for specified verbal units—the memory for lists of words; long-term memory—memory extending over periods longer than a few seconds; and memory in free recall—memory for lists of words where no restrictions are placed on the order or time in which a person recalls these words. This chapter will not deal with unintegrated verbal material (such as nonsense syllables), memory for connected passages, short-term memory, nor serial or paired-associate learning. The paradigm to be explored is the free recall experiment in which the subject is presented with a list of words and then asked to recall as many of those words as possible in any order he wishes.

I. The Concept of Organization

In 1940 George Katona wrote a book called *Organizing and Memorizing* in which he elaborated a Gestalt position as it applied to human memory; it is in a sense an unfortunate book, for Katona's preoccupation with grand theoretical points hides many of the book's empirical contributions, and some of his specific theoretical insights were inconsistent with the temper of a period that called for the development of grand general schemes. Hidden among vague generalities—about undefined wholes, inner necessities, and "real" understanding—and general denigrations of the role of prior experience is the assertion that organization is a requirement for successful memorization. He avoids any specific definition of organization, but he does suggest that organization involves the formation and perception of groupings and of their relations. Organization is a process that establishes or discovers such relations. Throughout the book Katona emphasizes the grouping of verbal stimuli as an important variable in memorizing; for example, in one series of experiments he shows how an otherwise "unrelated" sequence of digits is better retained in memory when the digits are regrouped according to categories or principles supplied by the E or S. The notion that memory is limited when grouping is not used and that grouping overcomes such limitations was plainly stated for anyone who cared to pay attention. But for the next decade or two, few psychologists did.

Like his associationist brethren, Katona had little use for mnemonic devices. He neither cared to investigate them nor felt that they really aided memory; they excluded "real understanding." Katona failed to see that all organizations are mnemonic devices; the "real" ones are those chosen by the experimenter or generally agreed to be more "relevant" to the problem. There was not then nor is there now any evidence that the use of socially learned organizations is better than or different from the use of unusual or idiosyncratic ones. Katona also maintained a distinction between rote or senseless memory on one hand and organized or meaningful memory on the other. The former he attacked as "pure" memorization, partly because associationists wanted to make "pure" memorization the basis of all learning or memory. Except possibly in the sense of immediate or primary memory (cf. Waugh & Norman, 1965), it is questionable whether the distinction between rote memory and other kinds can be maintained today (cf. Underwood, 1964).

Following Wertheimer (1921), Katona considered a set of stimuli to be meaningful when the existence and quality of the parts are determined by the structure of the whole. The notion that meaning, and hence organization, can be defined by the relations among the units of the set has persisted and has found its way into modern and more serviceable formulations.

Garner (1962), for example, prefers the term "structure" to "organization," but is obviously talking about the same problem. His very attractive definition of structure is worthy of quotation.

By structure I mean the totality of the relations between events. When we say that a picture composed of randomly located dots is meaningless, we imply that we see no relations between the dots and that, therefore, the picture has no structure. If the same total number of dots is rearranged, however, we can perceive structure and the picture becomes meaningful. . . . Meaning . . . refers to the entire set of relations, not just to the significations of each individual word. A particular word may be meaningful in the sense of signification, but the entire language becomes meaningful only if some structure is perceived in the total set of symbols. I am definitely not implying that meaning as structure is simply the sum of the significations of the individual words, but rather that the structure is itself meaningful (Garner, 1962, p. 141).

Organization and structure are clearly related to the general problem of grouping. G. E. Müller had been concerned with grouping at the turn of the century, as had Selz early in this century; and in 1932 Thorndike had wrestled with the concept of "belongingness"; two events "belong" when it is apparent to the S that "this goes with that." Belongingness defined the boundaries of groupings.

We can propose a general use for the term organization at this point: A set of objects or events are said to be organized when a consistent relation among the members of the set can be specified and, specifically, when membership of the objects or events in subsets (groups, concepts, categories, chunks) is stable and identifiable.

II. The Limits of Memory and the Unitization Hypothesis

The importance of organization and grouping was made obvious to psychologists interested in information processing in two papers by Miller (1956a; 1956b). Miller started with a puzzle. Evidence from a large number of sources had suggested that there were limitations on the capacity of the human organism for processing information; limitations that were observed over a range of tasks from the absolute judgment of unidimensional variables to immediate memory. In all these cases, Miller suggested, the limiting value—the "magical" number—was 7 ± 2. Subjects usually can not distinguish more than about seven alternatives of a unidimensional variable, nor remember more than about seven items from an input list in immediate memory. Given these limitations, some mechanism must be responsible for extending human judgment and memory, since we obviously do remember more than seven items and can judge across a wider range. Miller's solution to this puzzle was, in the case of human memory, the unitization hypothesis.

The unitization hypothesis (Miller, 1956b) states, first, that the memory limit cannot be extended by simply adding more sets of seven items. The second set of seven apparently makes us forget the first and human memory can deal only with seven items at a time. The only way to extend the amount of information is to enrich each item, that is, to increase the amount of information each item conveys. Miller refers to informationally rich units in memory storage as chunks. The input items must be recoded or reorganized into new units or chunks. Miller talks about "grouping or organizing the input sequence into units or chunks" (1956a, p. 93), specifically suggesting that "by organizing the stimulus input simultaneously into several dimensions and successively into a sequence of chunks, we manage to break . . . [the] informational bottleneck" (1956a, p. 95). In summary, organization is absolutely necessary if memory is to exceed the limit of individual items that the system can deal with at any one time. This process of organization involves recoding the input material into new and larger chunks. Memory consists of the recall of a limited number of chunks (that is, about seven) and retrieval of the contents of these chunks.

The influence of this formulation on the area of human learning and memory has been both fruitful and decisive (cf. Mandler, 1967). However, relatively few extensions of the unitization hypothesis in the specific area of human verbal memory are available. Some of these extensions, by Tulving, Cohen, and others, will be discussed later, but first some further elaborations and extensions of Miller's model are necessary.

Miller's 1956 papers suggested that if the number of chunks is limited to about seven, the chunks themselves may contain apparently unlimited informational riches. The following excerpts illustrate Miller's suggestions:

> The span of immediate memory seems to be almost independent of the number of bits per chunk, at least over the range examined to date (1956a, p. 93) . . . . The process if memorization may be simply the formation of chunks, or groups of items that go together, until there are few enough chunks so that we can recall all the items (1956a, p. 95). Since the memory span is a fixed number of chunks, we can increase the number of bits of information that it contains by building larger and larger chunks containing more information than before (1956a, p. 93).

The general import is that there is no limit to the amount of information a chunk may contain. Miller's major suggestion for enriching the information in a chunk was to increase the size of the set of alternatives from which an item is chosen. A second possibility involves a hierarchical arrangement in which the number of items in a chunk is limited to 7 ± 2, just as the number of chunks is initially limited to that

number. This does not imply that memory is limited to 49 items—
seven items with seven items per chunk. Rather, the seven items in a
chunk may in turn be informationally rich—containing again about
7 ± 2 items. This extension of Miller's unitization hypothesis will form
the major theoretical argument of this paper. A hierarchical system
recodes the input into chunks with a limited set of items per chunk
and then goes on to the next level of organization, where the first-
order chunks are recoded into "superchunks," with the same limit
applying to this level, and so forth. The only limit, then, appears to
be the number of levels the system can handle, a problem to be discussed later. It might be noted that whereas Miller's early formulation
advances the general notion of informationally rich chunks, later formulations discuss hierarchical systems similar to the one advocated here
(Miller, 1962, p. 49; Miller, Galanter, & Pribram, 1960).

In the organization of words as items, chunking proceeds primarily
by way of conceptualization or categorization of sets of words. A
further assumption, therefore, is that a category is equivalent to
Miller's chunk.

Given that a limit constrains the number of words that can be
recalled from a category and that a similar limit constrains the number
of subcategories, categories, and superordinate categories that can be
recalled, what is the numerical value of that limit? Miller suggested
"the magical number seven, plus or minus two." As he points out
however, the span for monosyllabic English words is only about five
(cf. also Tulving & Patkau, 1962) and, in fact, the immediate memory
experiment may hide an artifact that spuriously inflates the limiting
value. Since Miller's work there has been a recurrent interest in immediate or short-term memory, dealing with memory effects within
30–60 seconds following input (cf. Melton, 1963). When a S is required
to memorize relatively large sets of words, the mechanism apparently
involves two separate processes: Short-term, or primary, memory
(Waugh & Norman, 1965), which produces recall of the words immediately preceding the output; and organized memory, which typically
includes earlier words from the list (cf. Waugh, 1961). Thus the
number of 7 ± 2 may be made up of two components: 4 ± 1 plus 3 ± 1.
Since the present concern is not with short-term or immediate memory
in the sense of recovering items from some temporary or buffer storage,
it seems likely that the value of items to be recalled per chunk is
below seven; for working purposes, and in light of some of our subsequent data, a value of 5 ± 2 seems more appropriate.

To recapitulate: Given a set of words, a human organism categorizes them and, if the length of the list requires an extended organization, arranges the categories in turn into superordinate categories. When a category contains more than about five words it may, if necessary and possible, again be subdivided into two or more subordinate categories. Thus it is assumed that if recall from a list contains more than five items, then the S has used more than one category and some of his categories contain more than one item. Conversely, if a list of words is categorized into several categories such that each category contains one or more words, then recall should be a direct function of the number of categories used during organization of the list. The experimental data presented in the following discussion pertain directly to the relation between the number of categories used in organization and the number of words recalled.

In the sense of the unitization hypothesis and its elaborations presented in this section, the process of memorization is a process of organization. Katona's formulation thus is correct; memorization or learning depends on organization and the organizational variables (rather than the number of trials, for example) determine memory.

If organization determines recall, then the categories available to a S should also determine the form of his output. Members of categories should be recalled together if the S remembers categories and then their content. Extensive work has been done on this effect of organization and we will briefly review some of the experimental studies on clustering in free recall.

III. Clustering: The Organization of Recall

A large number of studies has been concerned with the tendency for categorized items to cluster during recall. This particular line of research was initiated with an experiment by Bousfield and Sedgewick (1944), who found that Ss instructed to produce all the items in a particular language category (such as birds) would cluster subcategories during recall. In 1953 Bousfield initiated a program of research to investigate further the tendency of members of a category to appear contiguously during recall. In the first experiment (Bousfield, 1953) Ss were given a randomized list of 60 items consisting of four categories (animals, names, professions, and vegetables) with 15 items per category. Following a single presentation Ss listed the items they could recall and Bousfield's data showed conclusively that such recall contained clusters of the categories built into the lists.

It should be noted that in this and almost all subsequent experiments on clustering the categories investigated were only the categories pre-established by the experimenter. Such a procedure presents two serious problems of analysis: first, the problem of the distinction between the discovery and use of these categories, and second, the necessary tendency to ignore any clustering or organization used by the S but different from the organization expected by the E.

Concerning the distinction between discovery and use, consider the following problem. Assume that I make up a list of names of all the people in my acquaintance and then categorize this list into those people who are blood relations, those who are professional acquaintances, and those who are social acquaintances. In my recall of such a list, I would probably cluster these categories according to these three characteristics. If the same list were presented to a total stranger, it is unlikely that his recall would show any significant clustering in terms of my categories. If I were to present the list to a professional colleague, however, we would find some clustering in terms of one of the categories, and if I gave the list to my wife, there would probably be significant clustering for all three categories. Similarly, any pre-categorized list will show clustering to the extent that the S has available the categories that the E has put into the list. On the other hand, the S might know of these categories but may not discover that the list in fact contains them.

Closely related to this difficulty is the possibility that a S may in fact discover the categories but choose not to use them, or he may use some combination of these categories and some of his own construction. In either case the analysis of clustering in terms of the preestablished categories will usually underestimate the actual degree of clustering imposed by the subject.

When, as is usual, the data from a group of Ss are averaged in a typical clustering experiment, the idiosyncratic clusters are never examined. Subjects will be included in the analysis who use their own rather than the experimenter's organization, because of some idiosyncratic preference or because they never discovered the experimenter's categories. In general, then, both final performance and clustering data will contain an inordinate amount of noise and variance.

There is one aspect of these studies that is of general interest and is the point of major emphasis of workers in this field; it concerns those variables that affect discovery and clustering. For example, Bousfield, Cohen, and Whitmarsh (1958) have shown that if the categories contain items with high taxonomic frequency, the recall and clustering values will be significantly greater than for categories with items of low taxonomic frequency. Taxonomic frequency thus is one variable that affects the likelihood that a category will be discovered and used. Similarly it is reasonable to suppose that the discovery and use of highly overlearned categories will produce a more stable organization and therefore better recall than the *ad hoc* categories a S may impose on the material. In a summary of a large program of research on factors that affect the organizational characteristics of free recall, Cofer (1965) arrived at a similar conclusion.

Cofer and his associates have also compared the occurrence of E- and S-defined clusters. Their data suggest that the more "obvious" the E-defined categories or pairs, the less likely it is that idiosyncratic S-defined clusters or pairs will occur in recall; that is, the more likely it is that the E's and Ss' categories coincide. Similarly, Marshall and Cofer (1961) have shown that if word relations have "some prominence," telling the Ss to look for such relations increases the degree of clustering of these pairs in recall.

In summary, the various studies on clustering show that clustering of E-defined categories will occur and that such clustering is a function of the ease with which the S can discover these categories. In addition, important advances have been made to define the variables that will influence the ease of such discovery and, finally, the variety of different conceptual schemes that Ss may use to categorize lists of words is illustrated by the large variety of E-defined schemes that affect clustering. These include categorical, associative, syntactic, and semantic factors, and probably extend to a variety of idiosyncratic schemas that are a function of the individual S's past experience and past word usage.

More immediately relevant to our present interests are those studies that have investigated the relation between the number of categories in a list and free recall from that list. The earliest of these was a study by Mathews (1954); two more recent ones were those of Dallett (1964) and Tulving and Pearlstone (1966). The results obtained in these studies will be discussed after some of our data have been presented and the category–recall relationship has been discussed in greater detail. What should be noted now is that these studies also have used E-defined categories. In addition, they have held list length constant while varying number of categories, and have thereby confounded list length with items per category. Although such confounding is inevitable when list length, number of categories, and number of items per category are varied, it presents some difficulty in interpretation. This point will be discussed later, but as far as E-defined categories are concerned, the same criticism applies to these studies as to the clustering studies. Although in the clustering studies the relation between the discovery and use of categories is a minor problem if the main point of interest is the specification of the variables that will produce organization and clustering, any attempt to specify the relation between recall and number of categories becomes dubious when it is not known whether the S did in fact discover and use the categories built into the list. Only Tulving and Pearlstone paid detailed attention to this problem and demonstrated the occurrence of subjective clustering of objective categories.

It will be the major import of the studies presented here to show just such a relation. The difficulty of some of the prior studies on this topic will be better illuminated in that context, but it seems that one of two conditions must be met in order to be able to demonstrate the relation between categories and recall. The first possibility is to provide the S with the names or labels of the categories and to show him the actual categorical structure of the list. If that is done during input only, one might be fairly certain that an input organization has taken place that is at least similar to that desired by the E. The S may, of course, still impose some of his own category system on the list. If the S is also provided with category labels during the output, we can further be sure that he will remember all the categories specified by the E. Tulving and Pearlstone (1966), for example, have fulfilled these conditions.

Another possibility, the one used here, is to permit the S to impose his own organization on the input. Such a method not only avoids the problems mentioned earlier but also permits us to see how organization proceeds and what the preferred or optimal organizational schemas might be.

IV. Subjective Organization

There have been several recent attempts to investigate the organization that Ss impose on input materials. Tulving (1962) and Seibel (1964) have been most directly concerned with subjective organization in free recall. Tulving's paper raises the question—derived from some of Miller's (1956a) notions—whether or not the improvement in performance in multitrial free recall is a direct function of the increase in organization. In his demonstration study Ss were given a list of "unrelated" words, that is, words not organized by the E. The order within input lists was changed in a random fashion from trial to trial.

Tulving developed a measure of the sequential dependencies in the output of successive trials. This measure, called SO for "subjective organization," evaluated the Ss tendency "to recall items in the same order on different trials in the absence of any experimentally manipulated sequential organization among items in the stimulus list." Tulving concluded "that the Ss do impose a sequential structure on their recall, that this subjective organization increases with repeated exposures and recall of the material, and that there is a positive correlation between organization and performance" (1962, p. 352). A similar conclusion was reached by Bousfield, Puff, and Cowan (1964). Both their measure and the SO measure only evaluate pairwise dependencies and can only tell us that organizational activity is in fact revealed in the output. It is not designed to evaluate the categorical organization by the S, nor can it evaluate the occurrence of organized units larger than pairs.

The last deficiency is a major argument against using either a clustering or SO measure in evaluating the organization imposed by the S. A cluster of two items that occurs in repeated trials does not imply that the category to which the cluster belongs is not in fact larger than two, and this argument applies to an output cluster of any size. A S may in fact produce one or two members of a category, use his written output as a reminder while recalling other items, and then return to the category that he had previously started. For example, a list may contain a "furniture" cluster; the S recalls "table" and "chair," then recalls some other items, checks the list, and on seeing "table" and "chair" may then give additional items from the furniture category.

Finally, the SO and clustering approaches do not tell us what the organization at the time of input was, nor how output and input organization are related to each other or to performance. Tulving (1962) has suggested the need for studying both the input and output phases of free recall. Our experiments are more directly addressed to the relation between organization during input and performance. For the reasons just listed, less emphasis will be placed on the dependent measures of organization developed by Bousfield, Tulving, and others.

Seibel (1964) has reported some initial work in which the subjective organization of the input lists was related to performance and clustering. His Ss were presented with 40 words at a constant rate and were required to write these words on a study sheet containing an array of blank cells. On this sheet Ss could—though they were not instructed to do so—organize the input according to categories of their own choosing. After the presentation of the list, Ss were required to recall at a constant rate. Seibel found that Ss' recall contained clusters that corresponded to the clusters on the study sheet and that performance of the experimental group was superior to the performance of a group that had been instructed to write down the words from the input list in the order in which they were given. The performance of the latter group was indistinguishable from that of another control group whose members did not write down the input list at all. In other words, subjective organization significantly improved recall and affected subsequent clustering in recall.

With this background on prior work on organization and memory, some of our experimental studies can be considered, starting with a recapitulation of a study on free and constrained conceptualization and the relevance of free conceptualization or organization to the problem at hand. This will be followed by a series of six studies on the category–recall relationship. Finally, a brief experiment on organizing and memorizing instructions will be discussed.

V. Free and Constrained Conceptualization

In our discussion of experiments on clustering we have suggested that E-imposed categories may frequently hide the Ss' system of organization. In addition, a procedure that focuses on such categories gives us little information about how the average human organism might go about organizing an input list. Similar arguments can be addressed to the typical experiment in concept learning where Ss are required to attain some concepts specified by the E. Since categories and concepts are, in the present sense, interchangeable notions, an examination of an experiment by Mandler and Pearlstone (1966) on this topic provides the first step in the program of research reported here.

Mandler and Pearlstone argued that the typical concept-learning experiments not only hide important aspects of conceptual behavior but also present the S with an interference paradigm. It is assumed that any set of stimuli will invoke some categorization or conceptualization on the part of the S. The initial categories imposed by the S and those imposed by the E are not likely to be identical. To the extent, then, that the S must suppress, extinguish, or ignore his own system of conceptualization, such activity will interfere with the acquisition of the E-defined conceptual categories.

Subjects were given either free or constrained concept-learning tasks with four different kinds of materials, of which the high frequency words are of particular interest. Subjects in the "free" groups were given a deck of 52 cards, each of which had a word printed on it. They were asked to sort these cards into anywhere from two to seven categories according to any system they wished to use. They were also told that following their first sorting trial they would be given another deck with the same words in a different order and would be asked to sort the words again and to continue in this manner until they had achieved identical categorizations in two successive trials. The Ss in the "constrained" group learned the same category systems as the free Ss by yoking one constrained S with one free S. The constrained S thus was in a typical concept-learning or attainment situation, with the target concepts being those of the yoked free Ss. Following attainment of the concept-sorting criterion, Ss in both groups were asked to recall as many words as possible from the set they had just sorted.

The major relevant findings were that constrained groups needed twice as many trials as free groups to reach criterion in sorting, but that both groups recalled the same number of words, about 20 out of 52. In addition, the various free groups used a fairly stable mean number of categories in sorting, that is, from 4.0 to 4.6, regardless of the materials they were asked to sort.

Thus the assumption that constrained concept learning represented an interference paradigm was supported by the data. Furthermore, numbers of sorting trials did not affect recall; if a stable categorization had been achieved by the two groups, recall was identical.

These findings supported our notion that the free or subjective organization of verbal materials could be fruitfully investigated and that the method used in this experiment provided one approach to the investigation of the organizing behavior of human Ss. We have already mentioned Tulving's (1962) approach to a similar problem; Imai and Garner (1965) have also made the distinction between free and constrained classificatory behavior.

The major finding of the Mandler and Pearlstone study that is relevant here, and the starting point for subsequent experiments, concerned the relation between recall (R) and number of categories (NC) used during sorting. Since Ss in the free group could use any number of categories from two to seven, it was possible to relate these values to free recall performance. Figure 1 shows the observed relation between NC and R for the 10 free Ss. The correlation between these two variables is .95 and the equation for a straight line fitted by the method of least squares has a slope of 5.59 and a y-intercept of —6.0. In other words, Ss remembered on the average 5.6 words for each category and their recall was a direct function of the number of categories used. It was this reassuring suggestion that the category—

recall relation could be directly investigated that launched the following set of experiments.

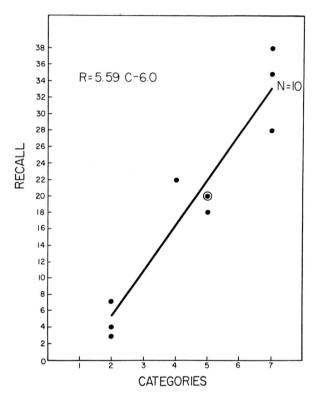

FIG. 1. Recall as a function of number of categories used in Experiment A. Data points are for individual Ss. The equation shown is for the line of best fit.

VI. The Category–Recall Function

The following six experiments are all variations on the theme developed in the Mandler and Pearlstone study, which will be referred to as Experiment A. Free categorization was used to investigate the categorization behavior of the Ss and to establish stable and reliable category systems. Following such free categorization, free recall of the words used in sorting was tested in order to investigate further the category–recall relationship. The general method used in all six experiments will be described first, followed by the specification of the variations incorporated in each of Experiments B to G and the description of the relevant data from these experiments.

A. General Method and Procedure

All Ss received identical basic instructions. They were given decks of cards that they had to sort in successive trials until they had achieved two identical sorts. Subjects were not allowed to put one card into one category and all others in another; apart from this restriction, any method of sorting or categorization was permitted. Following their last criterion sort they were asked to write on a sheet of paper all the words they could recall. They were given enough time to write down all the words immediately available to them. Recall terminated after a pause of about 1 minute with no recall had occurred. During sorting Ss were allowed to proceed at their own speed. However, if a S was not able to reach criterion within about 1¼ hours the session was discontinued. Column 4 of Table I shows the number of Ss in each group who

TABLE I

Summary of Design of Experiments A–G

Exp.	Initial N	Noncontent Ss^a	Noncriterion Ss^b	Ss with more than 7 categories	Final N	Criterion (%)
A	10	2	0	—	10	100
B	70	17	10	—	43	100
C	32	7	12	6	7	100
D	40	8	17	—	15	100
E	39	11	3	5	20	100
F	49	16	8	—	25	95
G	64	19	14	3	28	95

[a] Over-all percentage of Ss who did not use content categories was 26%.
[b] Over-all percentage of Ss who failed to reach criterion was 21%.

failed to reach criterion. This number also contains some Ss who continuously changed numbers of categories and for whom no stable NC (number of categories) value could be determined.

Subjects were seated at a table with a sorting hamper with seven slots slightly larger than the 3- by 5-inch cards on which the words were printed. They were always able to inspect the top card of any category, but they were not allowed to inspect any other card during the sorting task. In some experiments Ss were allowed to use more than seven categories. In these cases the table top was subdivided with chalk lines into an array of 20 compartments. Otherwise the procedure was identical.

The Ss were first-year psychology students of both sexes at the University of Toronto who had not previously participated in any free recall experiments.

B. Materials

Three sets of words were used. The first set, identical with that used in the Mandler and Pearlstone study, consisted of 52 words from a fairly wide range of Thorndike-Lorge values—the *52-range* set. Frequencies ranged from 14 per million to AA. There were 50 nouns, 1 adjective, and 1 adverb, though 20 of the nouns also had verb functions and 3 also had adjective functions. Six different decks were prepared in random order, and *S*s who used more than six trials were given the same decks over again.

The second set of words consisted of *52 AA* nouns, 33 of which also had verb functions and 1 of which also an adjective function. The third set of words consisted of *100 AA* words, the 52 from the previous set plus another 48. Of these 100 nouns, 59 also had verb functions and 1 had an adjective function. They were arranged in six decks just as the first one.

C. Data Analysis and Rationale

It has already been noted that *S*s who did not reach criterion were excluded from our analysis. For Experiments B, C, D, and E, the criterion was the same as that for Experiment A, namely, two identical sorts in succession. The high degree of attrition suggested an attempt to use a less stringent criterion, which was applied in Experiments F and G, where the 100-word vocabulary was used. Criterion was reached when sorting on two successive trials differed for no more than 5 words out of the 100. In other words, a 95% sorting consistency criterion was used instead of 100%.

One other source of *S* loss must be discussed. Since *S*s were told that they could use any sorting or categorization criterion they wished, some *S*s used organizations based on systems other than word content. However, such organizations of words in terms of alphabetizing the initial letters or using word length or counting number of vowels is potentially or actually useless for purposes of recall. When words are sorted according to the alphabet, the *S* need only look at the first letter of the word. Since *S*s were not told that they would be asked to recall the words following the categorization task, such noncontent sorting was fairly frequent. Column 3 of Table I shows the number of *S*s in each experiment (except for Experiment A) who were discarded because they did not use content categories. The over-all percentage of such *S*s was 26%. Since a subsequent experiment showed that additional *recall* instructions prior to categorization did not affect recall, future studies can avoid this source of attrition. If *S*s are instructed to recall, the use of alphabetical and other noncontent categories declines markedly.

Finally, for purposes of initial analysis only those Ss were used who restricted themselves to seven categories or less in those Experiments (C, E, and G) where Ss were permitted to use more than seven categories. The restriction to seven categories in most of our experiments and in all of our analyses arose out of the consideration of the major purpose of the studies. We are concerned with (a) the relation of number of categories to number of words recalled and (b) the number of words that are recalled per category. For present purposes it would have obscured some of our major findings if the task had been complicated by also including category recall. It was felt that with a maximum of seven categories and with several trials during which the S could become thoroughly familiar with his categories, the likelihood that a S would forget a category would be relatively small and that the results would not be a function of both category recall and recall within categories. This reasoning was fully borne out by our data. Using Cohen's (1963) criterion for category recall (that is, counting a category as recalled if at least one member of the category set is recalled), the incidence of failure to recall categories was extremely low. Out of a total of 680 categories appearing in our final protocols, only 13 categories, or less than 2%, did not appear in the recall data. Thus restricting both the Ss and the analysis to seven categories or less assures us that the data presented will present a picture of items recalled per category and will, except in rare cases, not be confounded by problems of category recall. Data on Ss who used more than seven categories will be presented separately.

The "Final N" column in Table I shows, for each of the experiments, the number of Ss included in the analysis in Table II. These Ns include only Ss who reached the criterion, used content criteria in their categories, and used seven categories or less—where that restriction is applicable.

Table II shows, in successive columns: (1) the final number of Ss (N); (2) the mean number of categories used (NC); (3) the mean number of trials needed to reach criterion (T); (4) the mean total recall (R); (5) the correlation between NC and R; (6) the correlation between T and R; (7) the partial correlation between NC and R, holding T constant; (8) the slope of the line of best fit for the NC-R function; (9) the intercept of that line; (10) the mean ratio of repetition (RR) developed by Bousfield to measure clustering (Cohen, Sakoda, and Bousfield, 1954). It is defined as $R/(N-1)$ where R is the number of times a word from a category follows another word

TABLE II

SUMMARY DATA FOR EXPERIMENTS A–G

| Exp. | N | Mean cat. (NC) | Mean trials (T) | Mean recall (R) | Correlations | | | Slope | Intercept | RR[a] | Vocabulary |
					NC–R	T–R	NC–R (T constant)				
A	10	4.6	4.6	19.5	.95[b]	.45	.94[b]	5.6	−6.0	.63	52 Range
B	43	4.4	6.9	23.4	.74[b]	.16	.75[b]	2.9	10.6	.56	52 Range
C	7	4.6	5.4	23.6	.39	.30	.30	1.7	15.7	.56	52 AA
D	15	5.5	6.1	35.3	.70[b]	.24	.73[b]	2.5	21.2	.72	52 AA
E	20	5.0	6.2	28.2	.60[b]	−.22	.61[b]	3.9	8.7	.70	52 Range
F	25	4.2	6.2	38.8	.84[b]	−.02	.86[b]	7.5	7.5	.68	100 AA
G	28	3.7	6.3	40.7	.64[b]	.10	.64[b]	7.2	14.4	.68	100 AA
Median		4.6	6.2		.70+	.16	.73+	3.9	10.6	.68	

[a] Mean ratio of repetition.
[b] $p < .01$.

from that category and N is the total number of words recalled; (11) the vocabulary used in the experiment.

It should be noted that the line of best fit for the NC–R function was obtained from the raw data of all final Ss, even though Figs. 2–4 only show the mean recall for each NC value.

D. Experimental Data

1. *Experiment B*

In order to assure adequate sampling for all values of NC, it was decided to impose one additional constraint on the Ss, namely, to instruct them on the number of categories they were to use. The additional instructions for each of the six NC groups who were told to use from 2 to 7 categories informed Ss that they must use a certain number of categories but that they were free to use any category system within that limitation. Data were collected for 10 Ss in each NC group who reached the sorting criterion. The NC–R relation is shown in Fig. 2

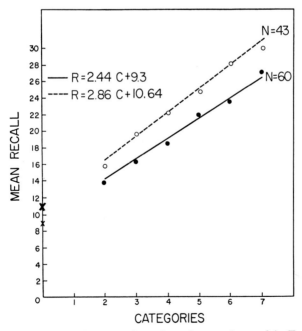

Fig. 2. Mean recall as a function of number of categories used in Experiment B. Filled circles and solid line are for original 60 Ss; open circles and dashed line, for the 43 Ss using content categories only. The equations shown are for the line of best fit.

for these 60 Ss as well as for 43 Ss who only used content categories. The data in Table II are for the latter group. The 17 Ss who used noncontent categories were rectangularly distributed across the NC groups; two came from the 2-NC group and three from each of the others.

The slope of the function is reduced from that obtained in Experiment A. But the straight line fit is obviously excellent. Subjects recall about 2.9 words per category and the y-intercept is positive. It might be noted that comparisons with Experiment A are probably spurious. The N in that experiment is small, the data include points from Ss who alphabetized, and the negative y-intercept is difficult to interpret. The general significance of the y-intercept will be discussed at the conclusion of the experimental discussion.

Table II shows that the Ss used a mean of 4.5 trials to reach criterion. The mean number of categories used is, of course, fixed in this experiment. There is highly significant correlation of .74 between NC and R and the T and R correlation is nonsignificant. The RR is .56.

2. Experiments C and D

It was thought that the constraint imposed on the Ss in Experiment B might have depressed the slope value of the NC–R function and Experiments C and D were conducted with a new, high frequency vocabulary. In Experiment C, Ss were allowed up to 20 categories; in Experiment D the conditions were similar to Experiment A. Unfortunately the attrition due to noncriterion Ss was heaviest in these two experiments, reaching a value of 40%.

In Experiment C, Ss chose more than seven categories more frequently than in the similar unlimited-category Experiments E and G. As a result the final N for Experiment C was only 7. In Experiment D a large number of Ss continued to switch numbers of categories and the final N was only 15.

For Experiment C the slope was 1.7 and the intercept 15.7. The correlation between NC and R was .39 and between T and R, .30.

Experiment D produced another low slope value of 2.5 with a very high intercept of 21.2. The NC–R correlation was .70; the T–R correlation was .24.

In general these two experiments produced the most disappointing results of the series. In trying to remove the constraint imposed in Experiment B, we not only reduced the NC requirement but also provided Ss with a combination of the shortest list of the series (52 words) and the most familiar vocabulary (AA). The possibility exists that these lists were so easily organized that Ss might have used the sorting task to impose organization over and above the obvious associations and clusters apparent in the list. In such a case, the organization produced by the categorization task is not in fact the organization that determines recall, and recall might have been a function of both the overt and other covert organizing schemes.

It should be noted that Experiment D was essentially a replication of Experiment A but produced a less stable, though still highly significant, relationship between NC and R.

3. *Experiment E*

On the assumption that the 52 AA list was too easy for the task in Experiment C, the original 52-range list was used in Experiment E in which Ss were allowed unlimited number of categories. Table I shows that only 5 Ss out of 36 criterion Ss used more than seven categories. The slope of 3.9 for the criterion content Ss is within the expected limits and the intercept is 8.7. The NC and R correlation is .60, and the recall and trials correlation is negative and low at —.22.

Figure 3 shows the NC–R relation for Experiment E. The fitted line

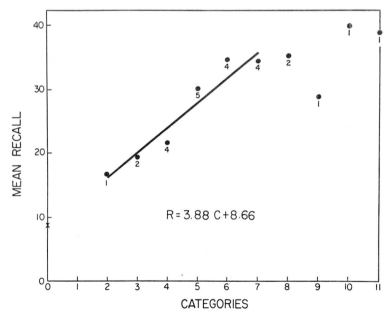

$$R = 3.88\ C + 8.66$$

FIG. 3. Mean recall as a function of number of categories used in Experiment E. Numbers next to data points indicate number of Ss contributing to the mean value shown. The equation is for line of best fit for all Ss using seven categories or less.

is for the *S*s with seven categories or less only. The data for the
other five *S*s are also shown. It is quite clear from inspection of this
figure that the category–recall function does not hold beyond seven categories. In fact, the line of best fit for the five *S*s who used more than
seven NC has a slope of 1.65 with a high intercept of 20.6. In the
previous unlimited category experiment (C), the slope for the comparable six *S*s was 0.88, the intercept was 29.7.

4. *Experiments F and G*

If the 52 AA vocabulary was too easy, in the sense that the list was
relatively short considering the high familiarity of the items, another
way to avoid parallel organizations, that is, those that the sorting
task might not detect, is to increase the length of the list. Experiments
F and G therefore used the 100 AA list, with F restricting *S*s to seven
categories, while G again permitted *S*s to use unlimited NC. At the
same time, the new criterion of two successive trials with only 95%
overlap was introduced. The results are shown in Fig. 4 for the NC–R
relation.

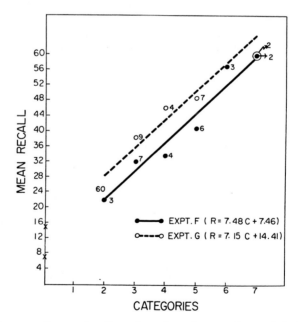

Fig. 4. Mean recall as a function of number of categories used in Experiments
F and G. Number next to data points indicate number of *S*s contributing to the
mean value shown. Equations shown are for the lines of best fit.

The data for Experiment F in Table II are in the expected direction. The slope of the NC–R relation is 7.5 with an intercept of 7.5 and all other values are within the ranges that by now had become fairly stable.

Experiment G produced only 3 Ss who used more than seven categories; the remaining 28 content criterion Ss produced results very similar to Experiment F, with a slope of 7.2, an intercept of 14.4, and other comparable values.

In order to check on the acceptability of the new criterion, 10 of the 25 Ss in Experiment F who had reached the old 100% criterion provided data for a separate analysis. These Ss used a mean of 4.1 categories, 5.8 trials, and recalled 38.7 words. Their slope value was 8.0, the intercept was 6.3. Thus, the data can be said to be quite comparable whether the 100% or 95% criterion is used.

E. SUMMARY OF THE CATEGORY–RECALL RELATION

With Experiments F and G the present program of research terminated, since the relation between NC and R seems to have been fairly stably established under a variety of different conditions.

The consistency of some of the dependent variables is quite remarkable. The last row of Table II shows the median of the major variables of interest. The value of 4.6 categories for median NC is consistent with the Mandler and Pearlstone (1966) data that Ss will, on the average, select about 4–5 categories out of 7. While the range for all Ss is determined at 2–7, the preference for about 5 ± 2 categories during conceptualization seems to be fairly well established. In all the unlimited-category experiments only 20% of the Ss used more than seven categories. The same general level applies if Ss are examined regardless of content or criterion restrictions.

A surprising finding was the general stability of the mean number of trials (T) needed to reach criterion. The median was 6.2, with a range of 4.6–6.3. While the materials used were, of course, quite homogeneous, the stability of this value is still somewhat unusual.

More important for understanding the trials variable is the relation among NC, T, and R. Table II shows that the median value for the correlation between NC and R is .70. This coefficient expresses the major thesis of this paper, that is, that there is in fact a highly significant positive relation between number of categories and recall. The significance level of the individual correlation coefficients also permits an evaluation of the stability of the straight line fit.

It might be argued that the NC–R relation hides a more basic relation between trials and recall. Thus it would have been possible that Ss take more trials the more categories they use and that the more trials they had during which they were exposed to the input list, the better would be their recall. In that case we would expect a high NC–R correlation, mediated by the trials variable.

The column of correlation coefficients for the T–R relation suggests that such an argument is inadmissible. Not only is there a generally nonsignificant, if not negative, relation between trials and recall (median $= .16$), but the NC–R relation remains essentially stable when it is corrected for the mediating effects of trials. The median partial correlation between NC and R with T held constant is .73. Thus trials are an unimportant variable in the particular relations investigated here. (When total time expended during sorting is used instead of number of trials, the relation with both NC and recall is very similar to that obtained with trials.) Subjects need a certain number of trials to reach a criterion of organization, but it is the nature of that organization, not the number of trials needed to produce its stability, that determines recall. In other situations, the apparent effects of trials would, of course, be greater. Thus in a multitrial free recall experiment, organization would develop more slowly with trials, and there would be a much larger correlation between trials and recall, though we would argue that such a relation hides the basic category–recall function. Multitrial free recall will be discussed later in more detail.

The median slope value for the various experiments is 3.9, which is within the range of our hypothesized value of 5 ± 2. On the average, Ss in these experiments add about 4 words to recall for every additional category used, with a range of 1.7–7.5.

The median y-intercept value is 10.6. The theoretical meaning of the y-intercept is somewhat complicated. The straight line function suggests that when Ss use no category they would recall about ten words from the list. This is theoretically meaningless for our purposes, since we assume that categorization is essential for memory and, by definition, words cannot be classified in zero categories. If anything, the value of the intercept might be applicable to the situation where all items in the list are categorized into a single set or category, but the function does not, of course, make that prediction.

It seems reasonable to suggest that the function is in effect discontinuous between 0 and 1, primarily because of the theoretical and empirical lack of interpretation of a zero-category sort. The y-intercept can be used as an estimate of the amount of material recalled on the basis of organizations other than those assessed by the NC variable. It is of course possible, as we have already discussed in relation to the 52 AA vocabulary, for Ss to use two or more concurrent organizational schemas. In that case we would expect the y-intercept to be fairly large and the effect of the NC variable should be interfered with. In fact, such a relation between the slope and the intercept does exist in our data. For the seven experiments there is a rank order correlation of $-.68$ ($p = .05$) between slope and intercept values. This is not artifactual since the intercept could, of course, change with the slope staying constant, and vice versa. It is therefore defensible to use the y-intercept value as an index of concurrent but unevaluated organizational schemas.

One other possible explanation that could be advanced for the category–recall relation needs to be discussed briefly. In all experiments except Experiment B the number of categories used was selected by individual Ss. It could be argued that the category–recall correlation is mediated by some individual capacity such as general intelligence, with the more intelligent Ss selecting more categories and also recalling more words. Such an explanation cannot be advanced for the data on Experiment B, however, where the number of categories to be used was randomly assigned to Ss. The correlation between NC and R in that experiment was .74, above the median for all the studies, and the slope was at 2.9, below the over-all median. We have argued that the latter low figure was due to the additional constraint on the Ss. These data make an explanation based on self-selection less tenable.

F. Clustering and Categorization

The clustering scores (RR) in Table II show a median of .68 and a range of values, as one would expect, generally greater than that found in the clustering of E-defined categories.

Another way to evaluate the clustering behavior of Ss in this situation is to consider clustering scores as a function of NC. In order to be able to obtain relatively stable values, N per NC must be fairly large, and only Experiments B and G provided enough data for such an analysis. Figure 5 shows, for Experiment B ($N = 43$), three values at each NC level: first, the obtained mean ratio of repetition (RR); second, the random RR value determined by randomizing each S's recall protocol; and finally, the maximum value that would be obtained if each S had recalled the words from each category in a single cluster.

Both the limiting values (random and maximum) are affected by NC; both decline, with the random value dropping much more steeply

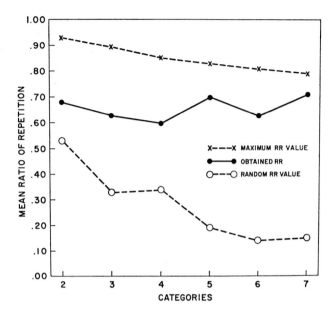

Fig. 5. Mean ratio of repetition (RR) as a function of number of categories used in Experiment B ($N = 43$). Solid line shows observed data; dashed line with crosses shows maximum possible if perfect clustering had occurred; dashed line with open circles shows RR values for a random rearrangement of output.

as a function of NC. The empirical values, however, remain remarkably stable and are essentially unaffected by NC. In other words, as NC increases, Ss diverge more from the random model and approach the maximum or perfect clustering score. The same relationship was found when the clustering data for Experiment G were analyzed.

The clustering data show that the free organization of material produces a very strong tendency for members of the same category to be recalled in a cluster. This tendency apparently increases as the number of categories increases and, of course, as the total number of words recalled increases. With small NC values Ss apparently have more of a tendency (a) to switch from category to category during recall than with large NC values, where categories are recalled in more consistent clusters, or (b) to use categories not evaluated by the categorizing task.

G. Long-Term Memory of Organized Material

Although no plans had been made to retest the Ss in the various experiments, it was discovered during the course of conducting Experi-

ment G that most of the Ss in Experiments C–G had been recruited
from two lecture classes. One half week after conclusion of Experiment
G, the available Ss in these two classes were retested for long-term
recall. It should be noted that these Ss had no information at the time
of the first recall that they would be retested, nor, as a matter of fact,
had the E. The same E who had conducted the original session addressed the students in the two classes, reminded them of the experiment by describing the categorizing task and the recall, and then
asked them to write on a sheet of paper all the words they could
recall from that experiment.

Figure 6 shows the recall data for those Ss whose data were used
in the final analyses of the original experiments and who were avail-

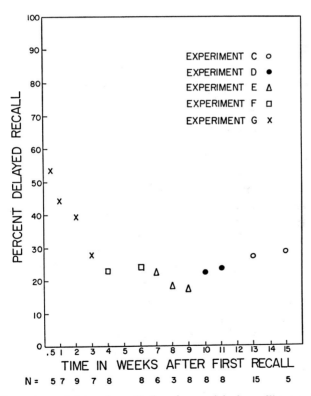

FIG. 6. Percentage of delayed recall (based on original recall) as a function of
time since original recall for Experiments C–G. Bottom line on abscissa shows
number of Ss contributing to each data point.

able at the retest. The figure shows the delayed recall as a percentage
of the number of words the Ss were able to recall during the original
experimental session. This percentage of delayed recall is plotted as a
function of time since the original recall session. Delayed recall drops
very sharply within the first 3–4 days to a little over 50% and reaches
a relatively stable level of 20%–30% after about three weeks. While
few data are available in the literature (cf. McGeoch and Irion, 1952)
on memory decay over long periods of time, these data do seem to be
more similar to long-term memory for connected, meaningful passages,
rather than to the memory for lists. It appears that memory for organized material shows a sharp initial decay, but no further loss, even
after three or four months. The nature of this long-term storage is
further illustrated by category recall. Using a single word recalled
from a category as an index of category recall, percentage of category recall is much more variable than percentage of word recall. However, category recall generally drops from about 90% to about 75%
during the first six weeks, then drops to about 60% in the seventh week,
whereupon it stabilizes at approximately 50%–60%. These figures should
be compared with a category recall of 98% during immediate recall.
It can be argued that the persisting memory of the list over 15 weeks
is to some extent due to the high percentage of recall for the coding
categories.

The importance of the category system for long-term recall is also
supported by the clustering analysis for long-term recall. Even after
14 weeks recall is still clustered relative to a random measure. The RR
for 10 Ss from Experiment C was .24 as against .16 for the random
measure. However, the clustering score declines generally over time
from .56 at ½ weeks to .24 after 14 weeks.

An important additional set of data on the relation between recall
and category size will be discussed after the next section, which will
present a final experiment on the category–recall function.

H. Organization and Recall as a Function of Instructions

The following experiment was conducted for two reasons. First,
having argued that organization is a necessary condition for recall
and having shown that organization was directly related to recall, it
was decided to explore the further step that organization is a sufficient
condition for recall and that asking Ss to remember something implies
that they are instructed to organize. Do instructions to organize have
the same effect on recall as instructions to remember? Second, the
previous series of experiments had shown that recall was apparently

unrelated to number of trials of exposure, that the recall–category relation was independent of number of trials. That demonstration, however, has been only statistical. The next experiment was designed to produce an experimental demonstration of the recall–trials–category relation.

1. Method

In the main study four groups of Ss were run, comprising the four cells of a 2 × 2 design involving the presence or absence of instructions (a) to categorize or (b) to recall material. An additional group was tested for incidental memory. The five groups and the N in each group follow, with "Category" and "Recall" indicating the instructions given: (1) Category-Recall, $N = 21$; (2) Category-No Recall, $N = 21$; (3) No Category-Recall, $N = 19$; (4) No Category-No Recall, $N = 19$; (5) Incidental; No Category-No Recall, $N = 15$. All data were collected in five group sessions, one for each of the experimental groups; Ss were assigned to groups at random. Word lists were presented aurally at a 4-sec rate and had been pretaped for five presentation trials, each of which consisted of a random rearrangement of a 52-word list. The lists were the 52-range lists with five words changed because of their auditory confusability. Subjects in all groups were given booklets consisting of five sheets with seven columns and a final blank sheet. The instructions varied as follows.

(1) Category: Ss were told that this was an experiment in categorizing words and that they were to divide the words into any number of categories from two to seven. After hearing a word, they were to write it in a column and then add to that column any other word that went with it. They were asked to try to use the same organization on successive trials, and were not allowed to look at the category sheet of a previous trial. With a fixed number of trials, aural presentation, and written sorting, this procedure was similar to that used in the previous experiments.

(2) No Category: Ss were instructed to write the first word they heard in the first column, the second word in the second, and so forth, followed by the eighth word in the first column, and so on; and to continue this until the end of the trial.

(3) Recall: Ss were told at the beginning of the experiment that they would have to recall all the words at the end of the experiment.

(4) No Recall: Ss were given no additional instructions.

(5) Incidental: Ss were given the same words, but on a different tape on which each word was followed by a randomly selected digit from one to nine. They were asked to write the words down just as the

No Category group and were told that their task was to remember how often each of the digits appeared. At the end of each trial, they were required to write down their estimate of the number of times that each digit was heard.

At the end of the five trials, all groups were asked to write down all the words from the lists that they could remember.

2. Results

Table III shows the mean number of words recalled by each of the five groups. The only significant result for the four main groups was

TABLE III

MEAN NUMBER OF WORDS RECALLED IN FIVE EXPERIMENTAL GROUPS

Categorization instructions	Recall instructions	
	Present	Absent
Present	31.4	32.9
Absent	32.8	23.5
Incidental condition		10.9

the difference between the No Category-No Recall group and the other three main groups ($p < .01$). The Incidental group performance was significantly below the lowest of the other four groups ($p < .01$). Either organization or recall instruction produce the same level of recall, significantly better than that produced in the absence of instructions. It could be assumed that the No Category-No Recall group was self-instructed and therefore organized to some extent, either because they expected to be asked to recall or more generally because Ss tend to organize material to some extent, even in the absence of instructions. It might be noted that half of the Ss in the No Category-No Recall group reported after the experiment that they expected to have to recall the words. It should be noted, however, that recall instructions produce the same results as organizing instructions, thus supporting our initial hypothesis. When organization is inhibited by directing Ss attention to another task, as in the Incidental group, recall drops to a level about one-third that of the organizing groups. Even in that last group, however, 4 of the 15 Ss reported that they expected to be asked to recall the words.

As far as the category–recall relationship is concerned, it should be noted that all Ss received five trials and identical amounts of time during the input presentation. Any relation between NC and R, therefore, is and must be independent of number of trials.

The change in procedure retarded speed of categorization. Only 3 of the 42 Ss in the categorizing groups reached the criterion of two identical successive trials and two of those Ss used alphabetic organization. But even with these relatively unstable organizational schemas, the same NC–R relationship is discernible as in the previous studies. The correlation between NC and R was .64 ($p < .01$) for the Category-No Recall group and .53 ($p < .02$) for the Category-Recall group. The respective equations for the line of best fit were 3.7 Cat. + 11.2 and 3.0 Cat. + 13.9, respectively. Thus, despite a low level of organization and constant number of trials, we obtained a stable NC–R relation with three or more words added to recall per category.

This last experiment has shown that recall is a function of the number of categories used and that this relation cannot be derived from some mediating effects of number of trials; moreover, the data support the notion that both recall or organizing instructions produce equivalent organization and equivalent recall. Thus, with some of our assumptions more firmly anchored, we can return to the more general problems of the Category-Recall function. In particular, we shall now consider how category size affects recall from that category. Following this discussion we will also be able to evaluate some prior studies on the category–recall relationship.

I. CATEGORY SIZE AND RECALL

How many items can a S recall from a category of a given size? We have already suggested the importance of this problem when we assumed that recall from sets of a given size follows the same general function whether the set is a category made up of word items or whether it is a set of categories from which categories must be recalled prior to word recall. At present we can evaluate only word recall from categories of given sizes, since our experiments were deliberately designed to maximize recall of all the categories. Data of category recall from other investigators will be compared with our data to demonstrate the generality of the relationship.

The basic data for the category size–recall function was obtained from all useable protocols in Experiments B–G. Category size varied from 1, which was permissible if Ss used more than two categories, to 96, which is, of course, only possible for 100-word lists. For each category size, all Ss who used that category size in any experiment were combined into a single group. The data from all available categories are shown in Fig. 7. For purposes of presentation a log scale is used for category size and the number of categories contributing to each value is shown on the abscissa. For large category sizes (beyond

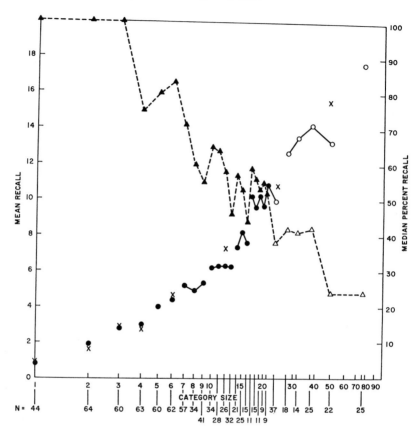

Fig. 7. Mean and median percent recall as a function of category size. Solid line, circles, and left-hand ordinate show mean recall. Triangles, dashed line, and right-hand ordinate show median percent of category size recalled. Open circles and triangles indicate that several category sizes have been combined. For the mean recall function, adjacent points that differ at the .01 level of statistical significance (*t* tests) have not been joined. The abscissa shows category size on a logarithmic scale. The bottom line on the abscissa shows the number of categories observed at each size. Single crosses show data from Tulving and Pearlstone (1966) see text for explanation.

21), data were combined for several sizes and are shown as empty circles. Figure 7 also shows recall as a percentage of category size.

The means shown in Fig. 7 form a fairly stable function of recall as a function of category size. It should be noted that the means of the low values of category size somewhat underestimate actual recall. The medians for category sizes 1, 2, 3, 4, 5, and 6 were 1, 2, 3, 3, 4, and 5, respectively. For the larger values the means and medians agree more closely.

For small category sizes Ss recall close to 100% up to about size three, then drop to about 75% at sizes up to about seven items per category (IPC), after which the percentage function drops rapidly to the 50% level and reaches 25% for very large categories. In other words, the relative recall from categories decays rapidly after the 5 ± 2 level has been passed. For the time being it can be assumed that up to an IPC size of seven, recall is fairly stable. But what of categories that contain more than seven items, and what of category recall as a function of the size of the set of categories? Before dealing with that problem directly, some data from several other studies must be considered.

J. RELATED STUDIES

Tulving and Pearlstone (1966) presented Ss with preorganized lists of varying lengths and varying numbers of items per category (IPC). Category size varied from 1 to 2 to 4 IPC, while list length varied from 12 to 24 to 48 words. Thus different lists contained from 3 to 48 categories—from list length 12 with 4 IPC to list length 48 with 1 IPC. During input, Ss were given category names and after one presentation, they were tested either with (cued) or without (noncued) presentation of the category name. Rather than investigating the relation between recall and number of categories, as Mathews (1954), for example, had done, Tulving and Pearlstone chose to investigate the relation between list length and IPC. They concluded that list length affected the number of categories recalled but not the number of words recalled within a recalled category. Their criterion of category recall was the same as Cohen's (1963), that is, recall of any one member of the category was taken as a criterion of category recall. It must be noted, however, that as list length increased, so did the number of categories within any value of IPC. Thus, category recall increased as a function of list length but also as a function of number of categories to be recalled. Tulving and Pearlstone suggest, in accord with the present orientation, that category recall and recall within a category are independent. So far so good; but they do not raise the question whether or not the mechanism of category recall is the same as the mechanism of word recall within categories. In other words, the number of items recalled from a particular category and the number of categories recalled from a set of categories should—and do—follow the same general function.

Their data permit a reanalysis that tests this proposal.[2] Word recall from categories was obtained from their cued condition in which Ss were given category names, thus assuring category recall, which is necessary to assess recall within a category. Recall per category was obtained from all categories of a given IPC value. This procedure provides values for recall from categories of sizes 1, 2, and 4. If, at the same time, the sets of categories are considered with 3, 6, 12, 24, and 48 categories per list, then the number of categories recalled, as defined earlier, provides data for recall of sets of sizes 3–48. These later values were taken from their Table 2, which shows number of categories recalled for different list lengths and different IPCs under noncued conditions. It is, of course, only in the noncued condition that category recall can be investigated. These values also were averaged for all sets with identical numbers of categories. The resulting data from both analyses for sets of sizes 1, 2, 3, 4, 6, 12, 24, and 48 are shown as crosses in Fig. 7. Despite the different Ss, materials, and procedures used, Tulving and Pearlstone's data fit nicely into the general relation between set size and mean recall shown for our various experiments. This concordance suggests that mechanisms for the recall of categories and of words within categories follow the same general function. Subjects recall a fixed number of words from any category of a particular size, and they recall the same proportion of categories from a set of categories of that size. Thus, although it is reasonable to argue that category recall and recall within categories are independent processes, they do follow the same size–recall function.

Since we are dealing with Tulving and Pearlstone's data, their major finding should be noted. When Ss were given category names during recall, their performance dramatically improved, suggesting that these additional words had been available but were accessible only when the category was also recalled. Interestingly enough, their data failed to show any superiority of cued recall when only three categories were used (list length 12 with 4 IPC). Considering the present argument this is not surprising since cuing for three categories cannot provide much if any advantage over the already high—if not perfect—recall of the three categories. Subjects should be able to recall three categories and cuing does not help. As soon as the number of categories becomes 6 or larger, cuing—the addition of category names—does and should produce significant advantages.

In a summary of an extended program of research on coding behavior dealing primarily with the recall of categorized word lists, Cohen (1966) has discussed the "some-or-none" characteristics of

[2] I want to thank the authors for making these data available to me.

coding behavior. He has shown that under a variety of different conditions Ss will recall a fairly constant proportion of the members of a particular category. His research has dealt primarily with category sizes 3 and 4, and therefore contributes relatively little to the generality of the present data, but some of his data on category sizes 2–5 suggest the same general function as the one shown in Fig. 7. His values are somewhat lower than those in Fig. 7, primarily because his procedure includes data from Ss who recall words from some categories that they have in fact not used in a categorical fashion. Thus, although Cohen points out that Ss recall a constant proportion from a category of a given size if they recall any word from that category, the means for category recall include data from Ss who may have recalled a word or two from a category without having discovered the complete categorical structure of the list. As was pointed out earlier, if Ss do not discover a category, then recall from that category will not follow the general mechanism apparent in category recall. The free conceptualization method insures that Ss not only discover these categories but, in fact, develop them in the first place.

Just as Tulving and Pearlstone did, Cohen distinguishes between category recall and recall within categories. Once a category has been recalled, "performance on these recalled categories appears to be invariant." He notes in passing that Ss recall about 10–14 categories from an 18- or 20-category list. These values are consistent with the function in Fig. 7. Recall within the category of categories is the same process as recall within a category.

In another study Cohen (1963) was concerned with the contrast between the recall of unrelated words and the recall of categories. He found that when presentation time was held constant, the recall of categories—scored as the recall of one or more words from a category—was similar to the recall of unrelated words. He concludes that these data support Miller's (1956a) notion that the recall of chunks should be constant, whether these chunks are single words or categorized groups of words. This general finding supports the assumption that category recall and IPC recall are limited by the same general mechanism, though they may not be influenced by the same variables.

Both Cohen, and Tulving and Pearlstone thus support the general notion that, given a particular category size, recall from that category will be constant if it occurs at all. In general, then, the recall of organized material depends (a) on the number of categories used, which determines the number of categories that will be recalled, and (b) on the size of the recalled categories, which determines the amount to be recalled from each category. When category size is constant, the function is a simple multiplicative one of recalled categories times items recalled within categories, a relationship proposed by Tulving and Pearlstone in their paper.

This position suggests a simple trading relationship between size of the set of categories and the number of items within the categories. When the set of categories is small (6 or less), a large proportion of the categories will be recalled and, if the category is large, a relatively large amount per category will be recalled because of subcategorizing, and the total amount of recall will be large. But if the number of categories is large, the percentage of categories recalled will be relatively small and recall, particularly if the category size is small, will be relatively low. This relationship explains some data on the recall of categorized material.

Dallett, in one of his experiments (1964, Exp. IV), demonstrated a decreasing amount of recall with increasing number of categories. However, by keeping list length constant at 24 and keeping IPC constant within any one list, his lists varied from 2 categories with 12 IPC to 12 categories with 2 IPC. Given the multiplicative function suggested earlier, these two sets of values should produce identical recall. Dallett's Ss were not, however, given the category names nor told that the list contained, in the extreme case, 12 categories. In the absence of discovery of the category structure by the Ss, the set of categories from which category recall occurs is frequently smaller than 12. In that case we would expect a decreasing function as the number of categories increases. It should be noted that Tulving and Pearlstone's Ss were given the category names during input and some of their data suggest that their Ss had the category structure available at time of noncued output.

Mathew, in a pioneering experiment on categorization and recall, also used a constant-length list with varying numbers of categories and varying IPC. In her experiment, however, Ss had category names available to them at the time of recall. With 2, 3, and 6 categories per list and 12, 8, and 4 IPC, respectively, she found increasing recall as a function of number of categories. With no problem of category recall, the large drop in the proportion of items recalled between 4 and 12 IPC would predict such a function on the basis of the values shown in Fig. 7 and the simple multiplicative function discussed earlier.

The discussion of these various studies makes it apparent that experimenter-defined categories, varying numbers of categories, and varying IPC make possible any one of several functions between the number of categories used and the resultant recall. The values obtained from Fig. 7 permit the construction of ascending or descending functions, just as these various experiments have shown.

The data from our experiments permit the evaluation of the more general relationship between numbers of categories and recall. In the first instance, the ˈcategories are subject-selected and therefore not dependent on discovery during input. We can assume that all Ss have their categories available and accessible. Second, the extensive conceptualization training overtrains Ss on these categories so that there should be no loss due to forgetting of the categories up to about seven categories, and our data have shown this to be the case. Finally, by permitting Ss to vary category size freely there is no general interaction between category size and number of categories. It is true, of course, that Ss who use a large number of categories will also tend to use fewer items per category—on the average. But with any given choice of number of categories, the size of any one category may, and does, vary widely.

K. Category Size and Organization

The discussion of the generality of the relation between mean recall and category size should not obscure or confuse some of our earlier findings. It was concluded previously that in the recall of organized lists, Ss will, depending on conditions, recall about 3–7 words per category. In the first instance, that statement was limited to those cases where Ss use seven categories or less, and use categories that are immediately available (that is, not subject to forgetting). In the light of Fig. 7 and the subsequent discussion, what is the relevance of the number 5 ± 2? Obviously Ss recall less when IPC is very small and as much as three times the implied limit when category size is large. For the lower values of IPC an obvious ceiling is operating and it has already been shown that up to an IPC value of about 4 the median value of recall is equal to the items in the category. For the larger values it seems reasonable to argue that whenever recall goes above 7–9 items, Ss are using subcategories within the categories. Some evidence on this point will be discussed later. For the time being all that needs to be said is that the number of items gained per category is, of course, an average value, made up of recall from different categories with varying values of IPC. The generality of the category–recall relation is not disturbed by the subsequent, more detailed, analysis that showed that there is a highly stable and general function between IPC and recall. Given a well-organized list of items, it may still be said that Ss will add about 5 ± 2 items per category to their recall.

It has been noted that in situations where category recall occurs under conditions similar to IPC recall, the same function applies. Up till now we have dealt only with two levels of organization, categories and items within categories. Is it reasonable to expect more extended organization, and what does such an assumption imply for the organization of human memory?

It is appropriate to consider evidence from some of the categories—necessarily large ones—where recall was well above the assumed limit of five to seven words per category. We will first examine such instances and then proceed to a more general discussion of higher level organization.

Even cursory inspection shows that whenever a S did use a very large category, the category name or label was vague and the concept used to determine category membership tended to be highly inclusive. Three Ss from Experiment F will be discussed here for illustrative purposes: S F1 used three categories to sort the 100 words and obtained a recall score of 31. His first category, labeled "senses," contained 6 items and produced a recall of 5 items; his second category, containing 9 items, was labeled "spirit, mind, character," and produced a recall of 5 items, while the third category, of interest here, contained 85 items, was labeled "everything else," and produced a recall of 21 words. Looking at the recall protocol, it is quite obvious that "everything else" was subdivided by the S and the following list of the third-category items, in the order in which they were produced in recall, makes this quite obvious. Ellipses indicate intervening recall of items from the other categories.

GRASS	END	UNCLE
PAINT	MOUTH	GENTLEMAN
. . .	. . .	QUEEN
TABLE	MUSIC	. . .
KITCHEN	CLASS	WALK
DINNER	MEMBER	SUPPORT
. . .	. . .	. . .
SKIP	FEAR	SALT
. . .	FACT	. . .
FINGER	. . .	FLOWER

The list contains such obvious categories as "kitchen items" and "people" and other clusters that have been organized by being fitted into mnemonic devices such as images, syntactic clusters, and others.

Similar sequential clustering can be found for S F2, who used four categories: "verbs," with 20 items and a recall of 5; "art," with 17 items and a recall of 11; "abstract ideas," with 10 items and a recall of 3; "ordinary words," with 53 items and a recall of 19. The last category distributed its recall in the protocol as follows.

WIND	PAPER	. . .	TASTE
. . .	. . .	HOUR	. . .
CENTURY	UNCLE	YEAR	SENSE
. . .	. . .	. . .	SILVER
OFFICE	GENTLEMAN	COAT	FARMER
BUILDING	DINNER	. . .	. . .
NEWS	FOOD	SHOULDER	HAIR

And finally, the recall by *S* F3 of a category called "objects" with 64 items and a recall of 17 words was as follows.

LIFE	GENTLEMAN	BOAT
. . .	QUEEN	TABLE
SOUND	FINGER	. . .
. . .	FARMER	COMPANY
BUILDING	. . .	CROSS
MATERIAL	CENTURY	END
. . .	DAY	. . .
OIL	PERIOD	
. . .	. . .	

Some of these clusters are obvious, others are obscure, and some "intrusions" within clusters (for example, finger) are highly idiosyncratic.

These quite typical protocols suggest that whenever very large categories are used by the *S*s, they tend to be superordinate categories that include several subordinate categories. Few categories could be more superordinate than "everything else." It should also be noted that the recall from these large categories occurs in clusters of from one to five words. While *S*s frequently recall all the words from a small category in one sequential cluster, the recall from the large clusters is broken up into smaller sequential units.

In other words, when categories with large membership are formed, they tend to be superordinate categories with recall from these categories being determined by the number of subordinate categories they contain. We can now refer back to Fig. 7 and consider the general function represented there. It seems likely that up to about 10–15 IPC we may be dealing with a single function with recall being directly determined by category size. Above these values, both theoretical consideration and the foregoing suggestive evidence support the notion that these categories produce recall as a function of the categories they themselves contain. In Fig. 7, the adjacent points of the mean recall graph that are significantly different at the .01 level have not been joined. The data suggest that the function contains several discrete recall levels. Figure 7 shows particularly distinct plateaus at 8, 10, 14, and 18 words of mean recall. Pending further investigation this suggests that categories of large sizes may contain, on the average, 2–5 subcategories with recall of about 3–5 words from each of these categories. The number of categories will depend on the size of the larger category, producing about 2 when category size is around 20 and rising to about 5 subcategories when category size is as large as 75.

The abscissa of Fig. 7 also shows the number of categories of each size. Although these values suggest that the preferred category sizes are 1–7, containing 44% of all categories, another 32% of the categories fall in the size range 8–15, with a respectable 24% in the 16–96 range.

VII. The Organization of Memory

It is now possible to suggest the general outline of the organizational system. We assume first the basic limit of the organizing system at 5 ± 2 per set of items. For any single chunk the organism can handle only that many units. Given that limitation, categories will be formed and 3–7 items assigned to them. We might note in passing that some categories will be smaller than that simply because the list may contain only one or two relevant items. Once these initial categories are filled up, new categories will be created to accommodate additional items. But in turn, there will be a limit of about 5 ± 2 categories at this first level of categorization. When all slots are taken up with first-level categories, a second level of categories will be formed, each of which may contain up to about seven first-level categories, and so forth. In this manner, a hierarchical system of categories can be built up with an increasing level of complexity and an exponential growth in the size of the system. We will return shortly to some speculations about the size of these organized systems. First, two additional items of evidence for this general scheme are relevant.

Applying these notions to multitrial experiments of free recall suggests the following mechanism to explain the increase in free recall as a function of repeated exposure to a particular list of items. We agree with Tulving (1964) and others that the free recall experiment using words is not a learning but a retention situation; that is, the S must retain the items presented on any one trial. In the sense of response learning, the items have been "learned" prior to the experiment and in terms of retention, any single word could be retained if it were presented alone. Thus, an item is "learned" at the time of presentation.

The present analysis assumes that at the time of the first trial, when S is given information as to list length and the words contained in the list, the processing system establishes the requisite number of categories, probably and preferably about five, to which the words are to be assigned. If list length is about 25 or less (that is, 5 categories with 5 items per category), this should present no particular problem. If it is longer, it is likely that superordinate categories are established in order to accommodate eventually all the words in the list. Recall after the first trial probably reflects category recall, that is, approximately one word from a large proportion of the categories. On subsequent trials these categories are then "filled up" with items up to the capacity of 5 ± 2. Given a constant number of categories, the optimal strategy might be to add one item to each category on each trial. There are serious limitations to such a process, since it is highly likely that the initial categorization might undergo changes in order to accommodate the items in the list, and it also might prove difficult to assign every word to a particular category as fewer items remain to be organized.

However, support for some such process can be found in the arguments and data presented by Tulving (1964). Tulving showed that, except for artifactual effects, intratrial retention (the number of items recalled on a trial that were not recalled on the previous trial) is constant across trials, whereas intertrial retention (items recalled on trial n that were also recalled on trial $n - 1$) increases as a function of trials. The constant intratrial effect is consistent with the reasoning presented earlier. Tulving also presents some data that suggest that the value for the intratrial retention component increases with list length. With a list length of 22 words, both initial recall on Trial 1 and the intratrial retention value for early trials were about five. With a list length of 52, the intratrial retention value is close to nine. Furthermore, the SO (subjective organization) values increase as a function of trials and covary with intertrial retention. In terms of the present model, with increasing trials, more and more words from the category are recalled in clusters.

These suggestions also offer a possible explanation why single-trial recall varies as a function of list length. The longer the list, the more initial categories will be established after a single exposure. Finally, the model predicts that multitrial free recall experiments should produce relatively inefficient learning in the sense that performance cannot reach the asymptote of 100% recall for relatively long lists. The inefficiency and subsequent rigidity of the initial category system prevents the organization of all the items and eventually prevents some items from being recalled. Contrast such a system to one that permits the S to organize the list prior to recall, as in our studies.

For example, the three Ss in Experiment G who used 8 or more categories recalled an average of 76.7 items out of 100 with an average of only 4.6 categorization trials.

The rigidity of established categorical organizations has recently been illustrated by Ozier (1965). Her Ss were given varying numbers of trials of free recall followed by instructions to recall according to alphabetic categories. The data unequivocally show a drop in recall on the trial immediately following the instructions, with the size of the decrease being a direct function of the number of previous recall trials. In other words, the organization imposed by the S becomes increasingly fixed and more difficult to exchange for a new organizational schema. Similarly, it is unlikely that the organizational schema can be changed in the late trial of a free recall experiment in order to accommodate items that do not "fit" the previously established categories.

In the experiments presented here, no attempt was made specifically to investigate the power of superordinate categories. Cohen and Bousfield (1956), however, have studied the effect of single and double level of categorization on recall. Using forty word lists, they present data for three kinds of lists: (1) four-category single-level lists with 10 IPC; (2) eight-category single-level lists with 5 IPC; and (3) eight-category dual-level lists, that is, lists with four categories, each of which had two subcategories, and with 5 IPC. In terms of the present analysis, recall should improve in ascending order for these groups. In the first group, Ss must recall 4 categories and 10 IPC; in the second, 8 categories and 5 IPC, and in the last, 4 superordinate categories times 2 subordinate categories with 5 IPC. Taking approximate values for these groups from Fig. 7, the three recall means should be 19.2, 20.1, and 24.1 for lists 1, 2, and 3, respectively. Cohen and Bousfield's data show values of 15.6, 17.6, and 18.1. Since their lists were E-constructed categories, the lower levels of recall can be expected.

Another question that our analysis raises concerns the way in which words in general may be recalled when, for example, somebody is asked to say all the words he can think of, or all the animals or countries. The prediction must be that such recall from general storage should proceed in the same way as the special categorization imposed in the laboratory. Superordinate categories must be followed by subordinate, and so forth until the search system comes to a first-level category, recalls about five words from it, proceeds to another category, and so forth. Bousfield and Sedgewick (1944) have shown that when Ss are asked, for example, to list all the birds they can think of, they will in fact produce these in clusters of subcategories with some evidence that these clusters occur in temporally discriminable sets, that is, with short pauses separating the clusters. In other words, recall from permanent vocabulary storage follows the same general organizational schema as the assignment of specific words in a memory experiment. We can also assume that the categories Ss use in the conceptualization and memory experiments are very similar to those that are represented in free emission. In that sense, the experimental situation simply utilizes the existing organization of the Ss' vocabulary. Some new organization may at times be imposed to accommodate unusual words or clusters, but generally the memory experiment is an experiment on the utilization of existing organizational schemas.

What are the limits of this kind of organization? Taking a value of five per set, we have suggested that the total content of an organizational schema rises exponentially with about five new units per level. It seems possible that the system also needs some limits on the number of levels that can be contained in a single organizational schema. One reason for this is the need to identify the level at which a particular search starts, since the level may influence a decision whether to go down the hierarchy, or up, or across. Similarly, the ease with which one can identify superordinate and subordinate concepts suggests that level identification is both useful and necessary. If levels are identified, we can assume that the limit on this task is also five, which then limits the content, in terms of final units, of an organizational schema to the value of approximately 5^5 or about 11–12 bits. Is this the limit of human memory? By no means; these speculations have only touched on a single schema. Obviously a particular unit may be contained in more than one schema, and some units or words may be in one schema and not in another. It is difficult to determine whether the number of such parallel schemas is in turn limited in light of the vast overlap of different organizations and the very specialized organizations that we construct. However, if such limits do in fact exist, they provide some interesting basis for further investigation into limits on the size of natural language vocabularies. On a highly speculative note, two suggestions might be entertained. First, the organization of any single coherent natural vocabulary may be limited to the value of 5^5 items. It is enticing to note that such divergent vocabularies as the basic sign language of the deaf, the ideographic vocabulary taught to the Japanese school child, and the basic vocabulary taught in foreign language schools all tend to fall at about 1500–2000 items, a value nicely between 5^4 and 5^5.

Second, it is possible that separate, though overlapping, organizational schemas may be organized at a still higher level of schemas of schemas.

Again assuming that the identification of schema membership is necessary for storage and retrieval, such a superorganization would contain another five levels and would produce an estimate of 5^{55} units that could be stored. Such a figure, in contrast to 5^5, is reassuringly large. It involves about 10^{17} units, certainly adequate for storing any reasonable set of human memory units.

A problem that this paper and most psychologists have avoided concerns the functional unit of memory. At the verbal level, a psychologist is tempted to say that the unit of behavior is the word, even though groups of words may, of course, make up larger units. The recent rapprochement between linguistics and psychology, on the other hand, has tempted some to speculate that verbal units may be phonemes or morphemes.

At the theoretical level it is necessary to speak of units as constructs. Such units have the main characteristics of being activated in an all-or-none manner and of being emitted in the same fashion; that is, it is not possible either to activate or emit part of a unit. If such partial activation or emission is possible, this would be prima facie evidence that the unit has constituents. None of these suggestions solve the problem of the psychological unit; they postpone the important issues. Eventually we must come to terms with the theoretical unit, which may be an image, an idea, a word, or a category (cf. Morton and Broadbent, 1964).

For the present we have confined ourselves to nouns, though the organization of other verbal units, such as adjectives or verbs, should follow similar laws. The restriction to nouns has also avoided the problem of the role of syntax in verbal memory, though grammatical considerations obviously play an important role in the organization of memory (cf. Cofer, 1965).

Within these rather restricting limitations, this chapter has talked about the organization of memory. But as we have seen previously, memory—the sheer recovery of a set of units—is just one outcome of organization. Given an organized set of units, we can recall some or all of these units according to rather simple rules. Given knowledge of the organization, we can predict with a fair degree of accuracy the amount of recall that is possible when the system is instructed to emit the constituents of the organized set. In our speculation about the organization of the available vocabulary, we have suggested that any memory experiment with words (that is, with units that are in the vocabulary), is just one way of tapping already existing organizations. In that sense, then, this chapter was not really about organization *and* memory, it was about the organization of parts of the human verbal repertory and it used memory as a way of evaluating what that organization might be. Granted that the conditions of presentation or input present certain limiting conditions for what can or will be recalled, it seems quite certain that the major limit on the memory for words is the organization of verbal units. Such organization is fully developed in adult *S*s and probably changes little over time. If we are to investigate how organization develops, we must go to the developmental study of language, semantics, and verbal behavior. That is probably the only source that will tell us about the development of organizational schemas.

ACKNOWLEDGMENTS

I am extremely grateful to Dr. Donald E. Broadbent of the Applied Psychology Research Unit, Cambridge, England, for making available the congenial facilities of his laboratory, where this chapter was written in July, 1965.

Mrs. Shirley Osler contributed faithful and hard work, imaginative suggestions, and endless patience to the execution and analysis of Experiments B–G. Miss Leslie Waghorn collected the data for the experiment on organizing and recall instructions. I am greatly indebted to William Kessen, George A. Miller, Endel Tulving, and Jean M. Mandler for critical comments on a previous draft of this paper. None of them can be blamed for any errors or misinterpretations that it still contains.

REFERENCES

Bousfield, W. A. The occurrence of clustering in the recall of randomly arranged associates. *J. gen. Psychol.,* 1953, **49,** 229–240.

Bousfield, W. A., Cohen, B. H., & Whitmarsh, G. A. Associative clustering in the recall of words of different taxonomic frequencies of occurrence. *Psychol. Rep.,* 1958, **4,** 39–44.

Bousfield, W. A., Puff, C. R., & Cowan, T. M. The development of constancies in sequential organization during repeated free recall. *J. verb. Learn. verb. Behav.,* 1964, **3,** 489–495.

Bousfield, W. A., & Sedgewick, C. H. W. An analysis of sequences of restricted associative responses. *J. gen. Psychol.,* 1944, **30,** 149–165.

Cofer, C. N. On some factors in the organizational characteristics of free recall. *Amer. Psychologist,* 1965, **20,** 261–272.

Cohen, B. H. Recall of categorized word lists. *J. exp. Psychol.,* 1963, **66,** 227–234.

Cohen, B. H. Some-or-none characteristics of coding behavior. *J. verb. Learn. verb. Behav.,* 1966, 182–187.

Cohen, B. H., and Bousfield, W. A. The effects of a dual-level stimulus-word list on the occurrence of clustering in recall. *J. gen. Psychol.,* 1956, **55,** 51–58.

Cohen, B. H., Sakoda, J. M., & Bousfield, W. A., The statistical analysis of the incidence of clustering in the recall of randomly arranged associates. Tech. Rep. No. 10, ONR Contract Nonr-631(00), Univer. of Connecticut, 1954.

Dallett, K. M. Number of categories and category information in free recall. *J. exp. Psychol.,* 1964, **68,** 1–12.

Garner, W. R. *Uncertainty and structure as psychological concepts.* New York: Wiley, 1962.

Imai, S., & Garner, W. R. Discriminability and preference for attributes in free and constrained classification. *J. exp. Psychol.*, 1965, **69**, 596–608.

Katona, G. *Organizing and memorizing.* New York: Columbia Univer. Press, 1940.

Mandler, G. Verbal learning. In *New Directions in Psychology III.* New York: Holt, 1967.

Mandler, G., & Pearlstone, Zena. Free and constrained concept learning and subsequent recall. *J. verb Learn. verb Behav.*, 1966, **5**, 126–131.

Marshall, G. R., & Cofer, C. N. Associative, category and set factors in clustering among word pairs and triads. Tech. Rep. No. 4, Contract Nonr 285 (47), Office of Naval Research, New York Univer., 1961.

Mathews, Ravenna. Recall as a function of number of classificatory categories. *J. exp. Psychol.*, 1954, **47**, 241–247.

McGeoch, J. A., & Irion, A. L. *The psychology of human learning.* New York: Longmans, Green, 1952.

Melton, A. W. Implications of short-term memory for a general theory of memory. *J. verb. Learn. verb. Behav.*, 1963, **2**, 1–21.

Miller, G. A. The magical number seven, plus or minus two: Some limits on our capacity for processing information. *Psychol. Rev.*, 1956, **63**, 81–97. (a)

Miller, G. A. Human memory and the storage of information. *IRE, Trans. Inf. Theor.*, 1956, **2**, 129–137. (b)

Miller, G. A. *Psychology: The science of mental life.* New York: Harper, 1962.

Miller, G. A., Galanter, E., & Pribram. K. H. *Plans and the structure of behavior.* New York: Holt, 1960.

Morton, J., & Broadbent, D. E. Passive vs. active recognition models or Is your homunculus really necessary. Paper read at the AFCRL Sympos. on models for the perception of speech and visual forms, Boston, November, 1964.

Ozier, Marcia. Alphabetic organization in memory. Unpublished doctoral dissertation, Univer. of Toronto, 1965.

Seibel, R. An experimental paradigm for studying the organization and strategies utilized by individual Ss in human learning and an experimental evaluation of it. Paper presented at meetings of The Psychonomic Soc., Niagara Falls, Ontario, October, 1964.

Tulving, E. Subjective organization in free recall of "unrelated" words. *Psychol., Rev.*, 1962, **69**, 344–354.

Tulving, E. Intratrial and intertrial retention: Notes towards a theory of free recall verbal learning. *Psychol. Rev.*, 1964, **71**, 219–237.

Tulving, E., & Patkau, Jeannette E. Concurrent effects of contextual constraint and word frequency on immediate recall and learning of verbal material. *Canad. J. Psychol.*, 1962, **16**, 83–95.

Tulving, E., & Pearlstone, Zena. Availability versus accessibility of information in memory for words. *J. verb. Learn. verb. Behav.*, 1966, **5**, 381–391.

Underwood, B. J. The representativeness of rote verbal learning. In A. W. Melton (Ed.), *Categories of human learning.* New York: Academic Press, 1964. Pp. 47–78.

Waugh, Nancy C. Free versus serial recall. *J. exp. Psychol.*, 1961, **62**, 496–502.

Waugh, Nancy C., & Norman, D. A. Primary memory. *Psychol. Rev.*, 1965, **72**, 89–104.

Wertheimer, M. Untersuchungen zur Lehre von der Gestalt. I. *Psychol. Forsch.*, 1921, **1**, 47–58.

AUTHOR INDEX

Numbers in italic indicate the pages on which the complete references are listed.

SUBJECT INDEX